WHITEOUT

COMPENDIUM

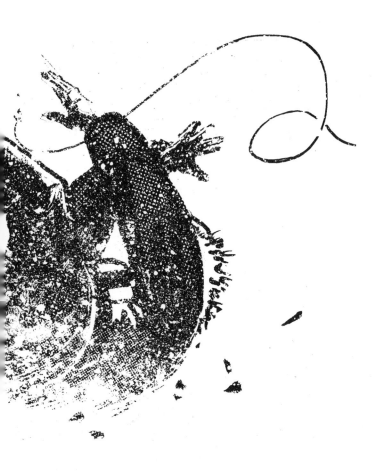

COMPENDIUM

WRITTEN BY
GREG RUCKA

ILLUSTRATED & LETTERED BY
STEVE LIEBER

COMPENDIUM COVER COLORS BY
RON CHAN

ORIGINALLY EDITED BY
BOB SCHRECK & JAMIE S. RICH

COLLECTION EDITION EDITED BY
JAMES LUCAS JONES

LOGO DESIGNED BY
STEVEN BIRCH @ SERVO

BOOK DESIGNED BY
HILARY THOMPSON

AN ONI PRESS PUBLICATION

PUBLISHED BY ONI PRESS, INC.

JOE NOZEMACK, PUBLISHER

JAMES LUCAS JONES, EDITOR IN CHIEF

BRAD ROOKS, DIRECTOR OF OPERATIONS

DAVID DISSANAYAKE, DIRECTOR OF SALES

RACHEL REED, PUBLICITY MANAGER

MELISSA MESZAROS MACFADYEN, MARKETING ASSISTANT

TROY LOOK, DIRECTOR OF DESIGN & PRODUCTION

HILARY THOMPSON, GRAPHIC DESIGNER

KATE Z. STONE, JUNIOR GRAPHIC DESIGNER

ANGIE KNOWLES, DIGITAL PREPRESS TECHNICIAN

ARI YARWOOD, MANAGING EDITOR

CHARLIE CHU, SENIOR EDITOR

ROBIN HERRERA, EDITOR

DESIREE WILSON, ASSOCIATE EDITOR

ALISSA SALLAH, ADMINISTRATIVE ASSISTANT

JUNG LEE, LOGISTICS ASSOCIATE

ONIPRESS.COM
FACEBOOK.COM/ONIPRESS
TWITTER.COM/ONIPRESS
ONIPRESS.TUMBLR.COM
INSTAGRAM.COM/ONIPRESS

FIRST EDITION: DECEMBER 2017

ISBN 978-1-62010-448-4
EISBN 978-1-62010-449-1

PRINTED IN CHINA

LIBRARY OF CONGRESS CONTROL NUMBER: 2017941852

2 3 4 5 6 7 8 9 10

CHAPTER ONE

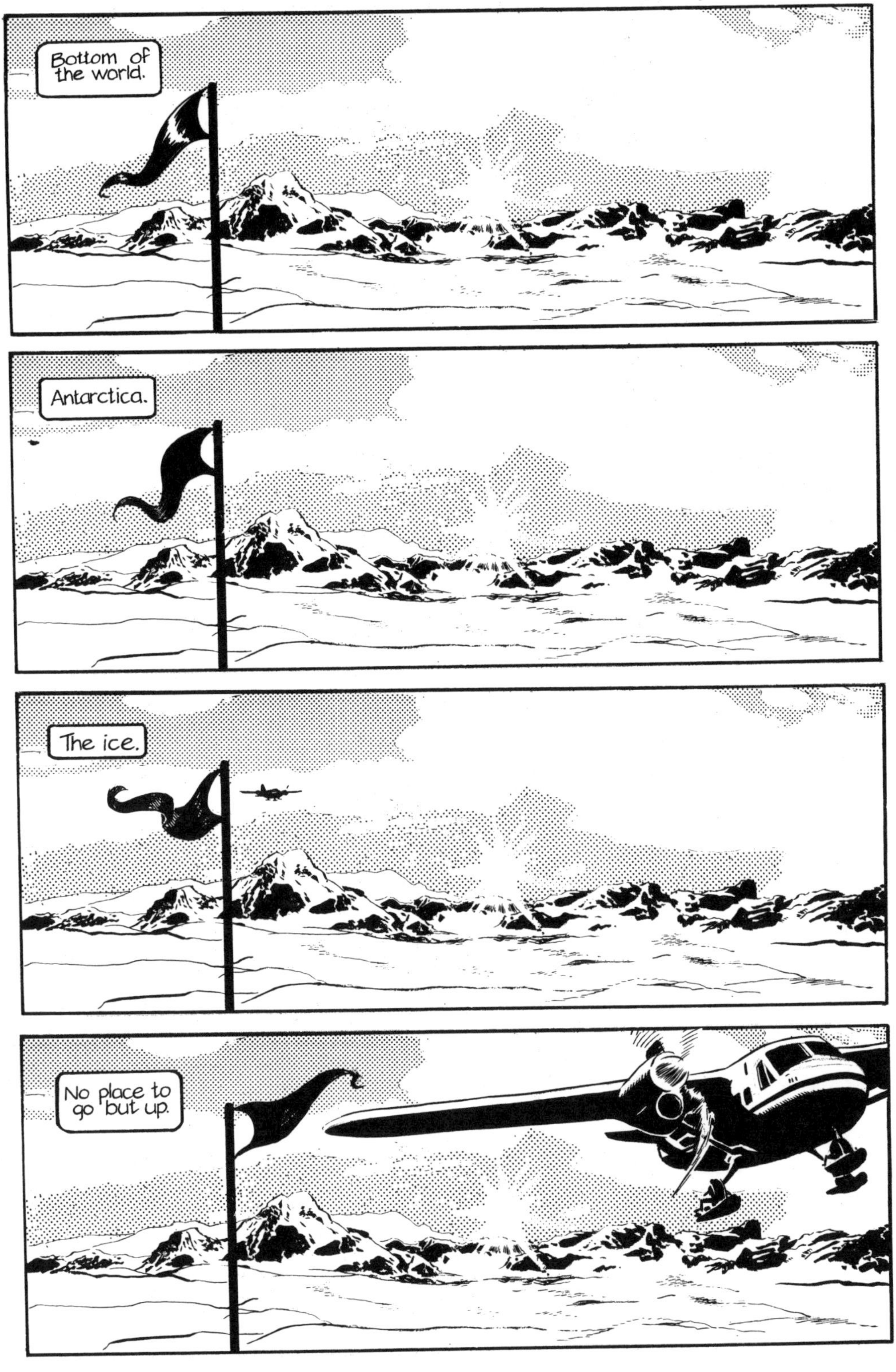
Bottom of the world.
Antarctica.
The ice.
No place to go but up.

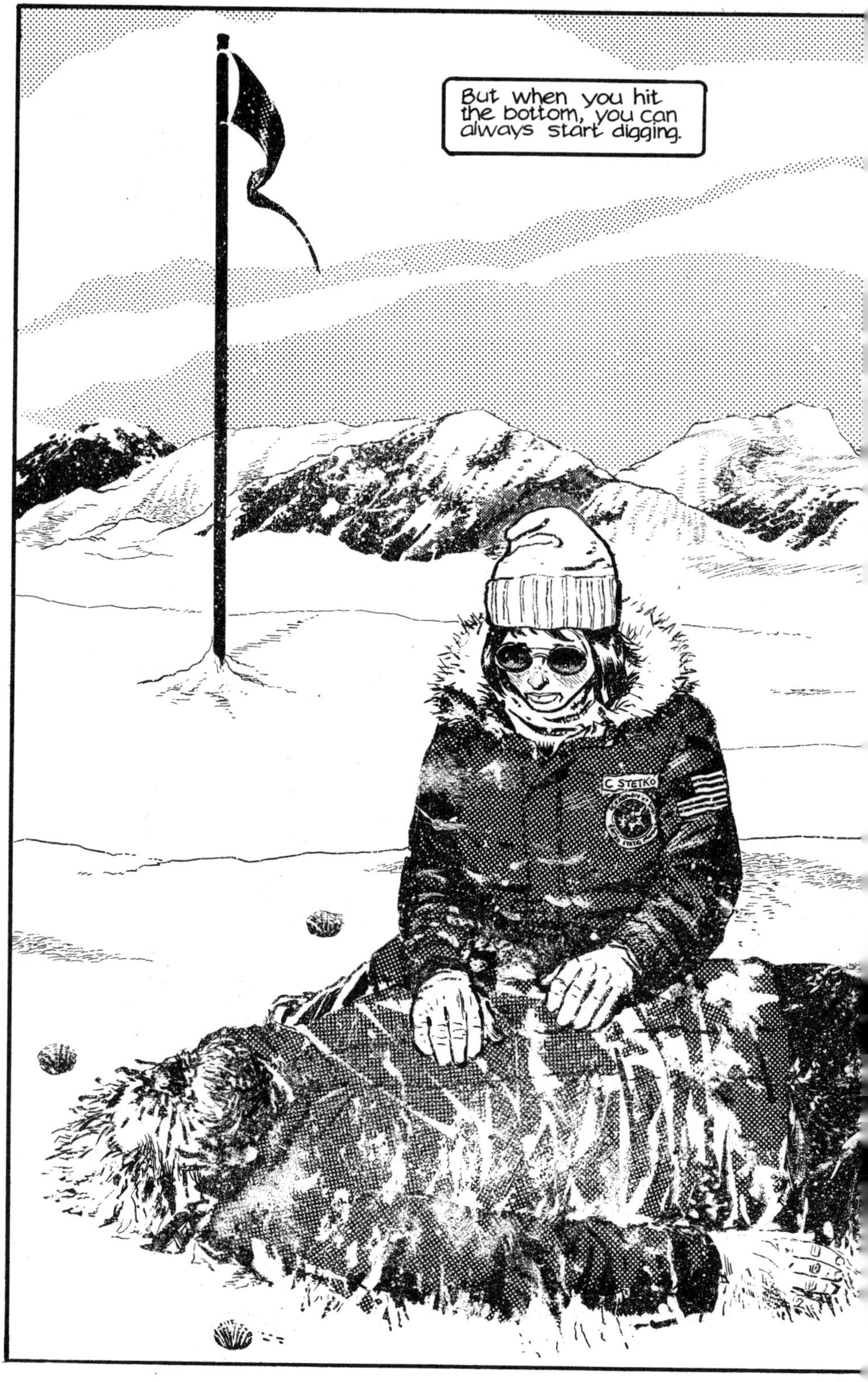
But when you hit the bottom, you can always start digging.
C STETKO

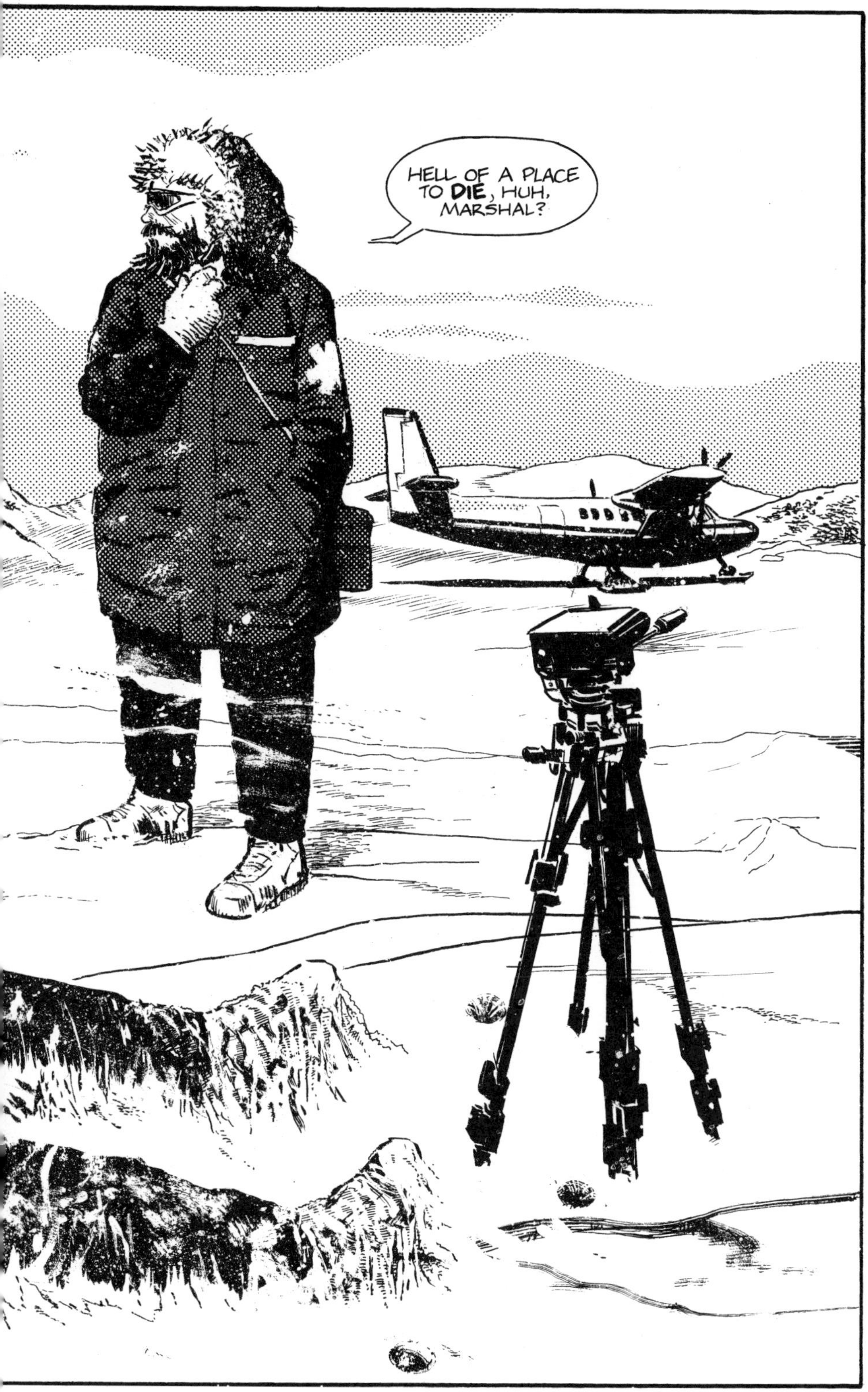
HELL OF A PLACE TO **DIE**, HUH, MARSHAL?

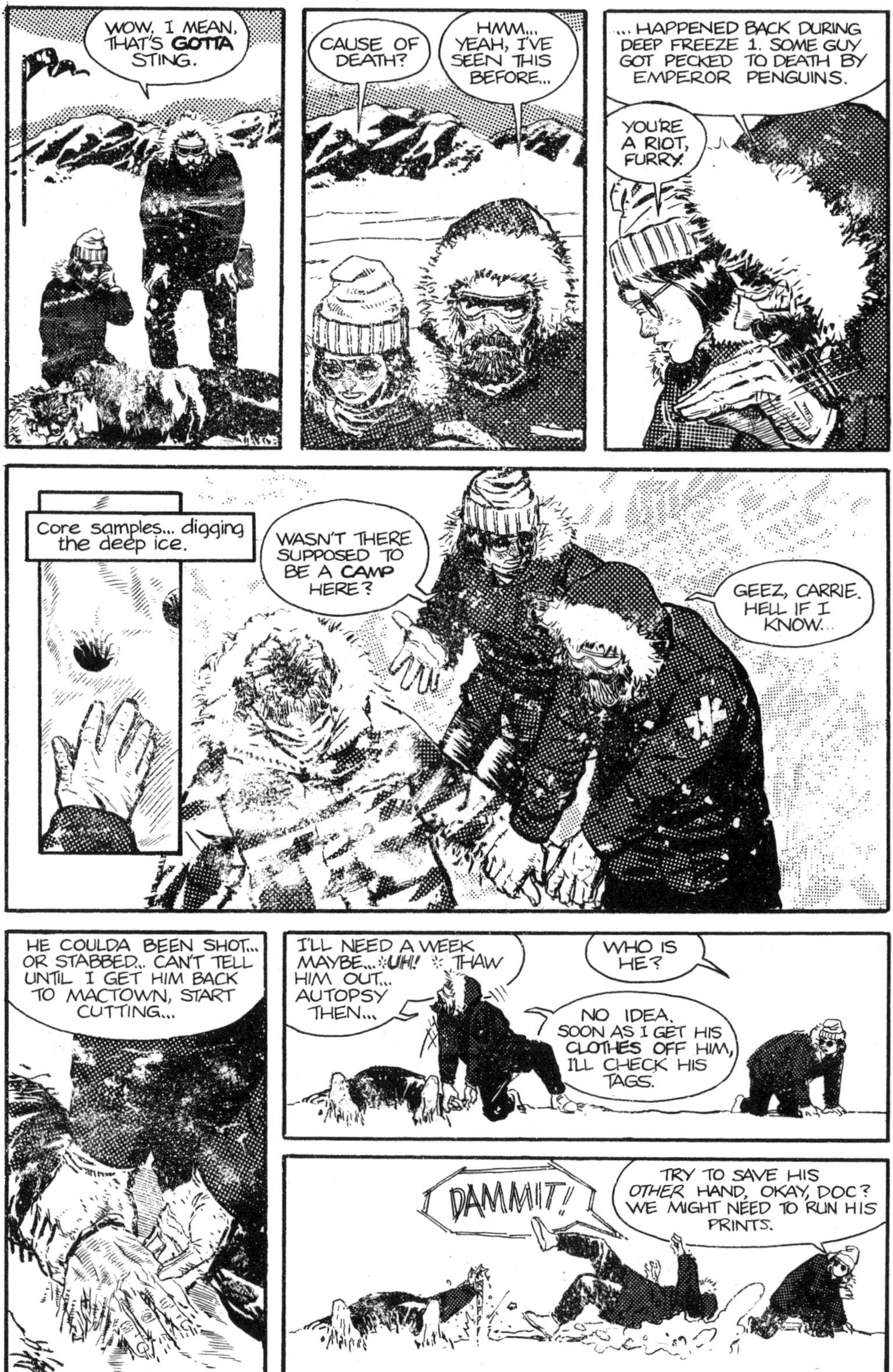
WOW, I MEAN, THAT'S **GOTTA** STING.
CAUSE OF DEATH?
HMM... YEAH, I'VE SEEN THIS BEFORE...
... HAPPENED BACK DURING DEEP FREEZE 1. SOME GUY GOT PECKED TO DEATH BY EMPEROR PENGUINS.
YOU'RE A RIOT, FURRY.
Core samples... digging the deep ice.
WASN'T THERE SUPPOSED TO BE A **CAMP** HERE?
GEEZ, CARRIE. HELL IF I KNOW...
HE COULDA BEEN SHOT... OR STABBED.. CAN'T TELL UNTIL I GET HIM BACK TO MACTOWN, START CUTTING...
I'LL NEED A WEEK MAYBE... *UH!* THAW HIM OUT... AUTOPSY THEN...
WHO IS HE?
NO IDEA. SOON AS I GET HIS **CLOTHES OFF** HIM, I'LL CHECK HIS TAGS.
DAMMIT!
TRY TO SAVE HIS *OTHER* HAND, OKAY, DOC? WE MIGHT NEED TO RUN HIS PRINTS.

DEFINITELY MURDERED?

FURRY CAN'T DO AN AUTOPSY YET, BUT THAT'S HOW IT LOOKS.

ONE OF OURS?

WE DON'T KNOW.

U.S. Marshal Brett McEwan—safe and warm in Hawaii—knows dick about The Ice.

But The Ice and I, we're kindred spirits, now.

We don't care.

DID YOU CHECK HIS TAGS, **DEPUTY** STETKO?

HE WASN'T WEARING TAGS, **MARSHAL** McEWAN. BUT HE HAD THE FLAG ON HIS PARKA.

SOMEONE **TOOK** HIS TAGS?

I DON'T KNOW.

RESEARCH CAMPS JUST DON'T UP AND DISAPPEAR. WHERE ARE THE OTHERS?

I DON'T KNOW.

YOU'RE FUCKING USELESS.

THERE WERE **FIVE MEN** ON THAT TEAM, FOR GOD'S SAKE.

COULD BE ANYWHERE. COULD STILL BE OUT THERE.

ALL THE BASES ARE GOING TO WINTER STAFF IN THE NEXT TWO WEEKS. NINETY PERCENT OF ALL PERSONNEL ON THE ICE ARE SHIPPING BACK HOME. YOU'VE GOT UNTIL THEN, DEPUTY...

...OR ELSE I'LL HAVE YOUR BADGE.

I WANT YOUR JOHN DOE IDENTIFIED. I WANT THIS DAMN THING SOLVED. FIND THE MEN. FIND THE CAMP. MAKE AN ARREST.

UNDERSTOOD?

YES.

...KICKING THE ICE QUEEN'S ASS! THESE GUYS JUST **DISAPPEARED** OUT THERE, AND IF SHE DOESN'T PUT OUT, HE'S PULLING HER PLUG! AND THE MARSHAL JUST TOOK IT, DIDN'T KICK BACK OR ANYTHING.

SHE'S BEEN DOWN HERE TOO LONG, SHE'S GONE COLD.

FRIGID.

FROZEN.

YOU KNOW IT! TALK ABOUT N.S.F.A.—

TIGH

NO SEX FOR AWHILE.

ING

NO SEX FU EVER...

DOESN'T OW WHA E'S MIS

WHOOPS.

CRASH.

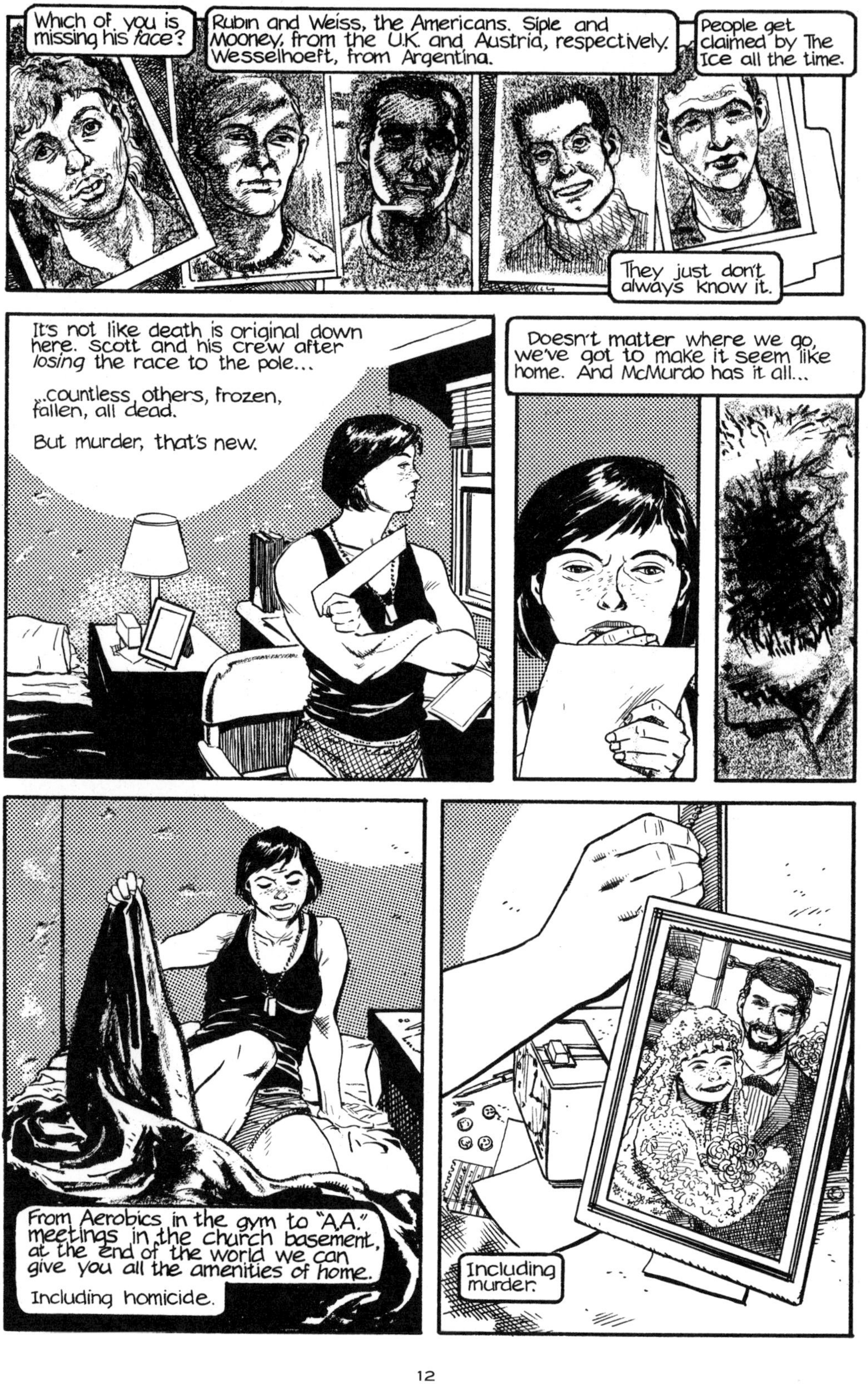
Which of you is missing his *face*?
Rubin and Weiss, the Americans. Siple and Mooney, from the U.K. and Austria, respectively. Wesselhoeft, from Argentina.
People get claimed by The Ice all the time.
They just don't always know it.
It's not like death is original down here. Scott and his crew after *losing* the race to the pole...
...countless others, frozen, fallen, all dead.
But murder, that's new.
Doesn't matter where we go, we've got to make it seem like home. And McMurdo has it all...
From Aerobics in the gym to "A.A." meetings in the church basement, at the end of the world we can give you all the amenities of home.
Including homicide.
Including murder.

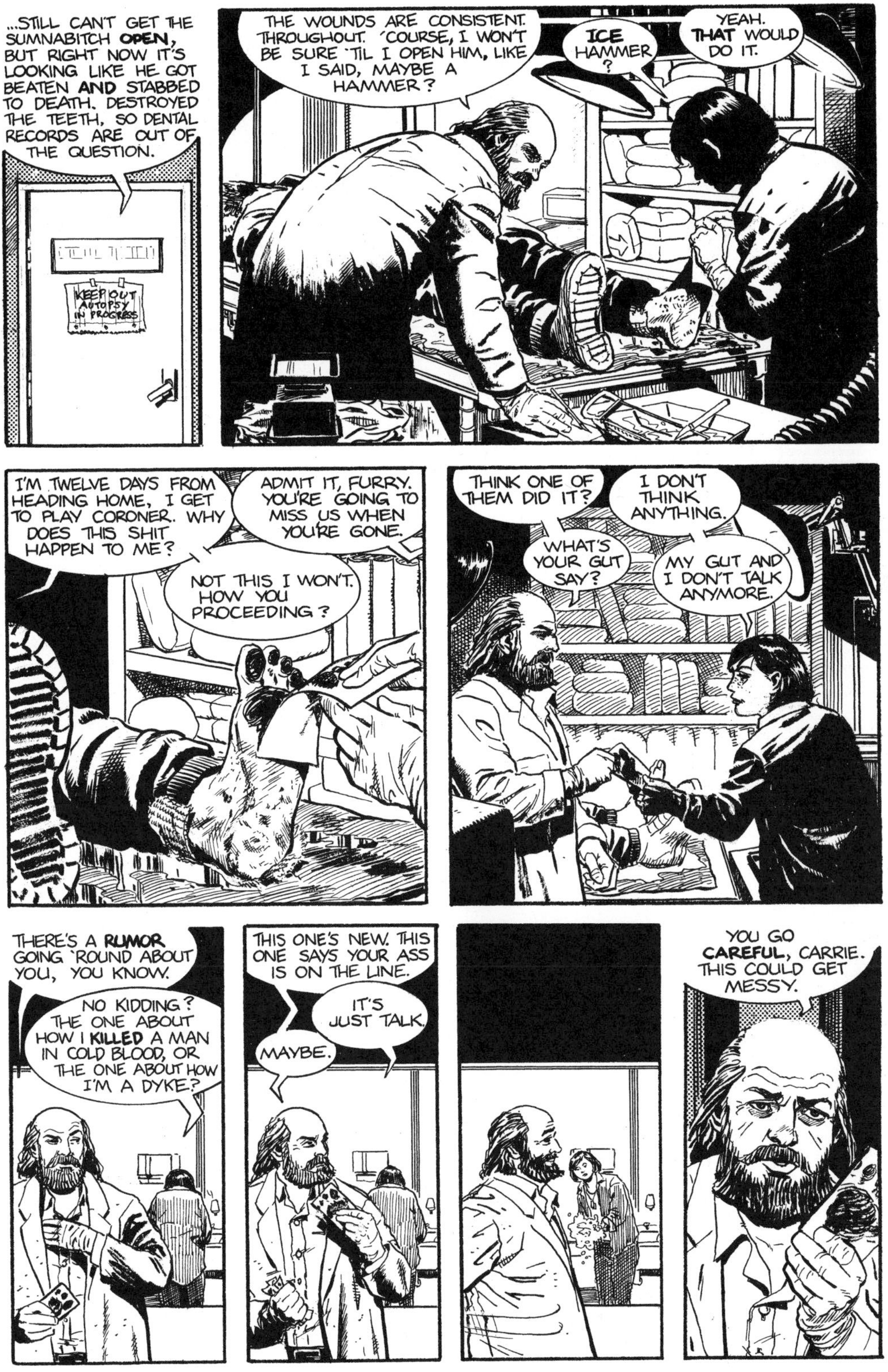
...STILL CAN'T GET THE SUMNABITCH **OPEN**, BUT RIGHT NOW IT'S LOOKING LIKE HE GOT BEATEN **AND** STABBED TO DEATH. DESTROYED THE TEETH, SO DENTAL RECORDS ARE OUT OF THE QUESTION.
KEEP OUT AUTOPSY IN PROGRESS
THE WOUNDS ARE CONSISTENT. THROUGHOUT. 'COURSE, I WON'T BE SURE 'TIL I OPEN HIM, LIKE I SAID, MAYBE A HAMMER?
ICE HAMMER?
YEAH. **THAT** WOULD DO IT.
I'M TWELVE DAYS FROM HEADING HOME, I GET TO PLAY CORONER. WHY DOES THIS SHIT HAPPEN TO ME?
ADMIT IT, FURRY. YOU'RE GOING TO MISS US WHEN YOU'RE GONE.
NOT THIS I WON'T. HOW YOU PROCEEDING?
THINK ONE OF THEM DID IT?
I DON'T THINK ANYTHING.
WHAT'S YOUR GUT SAY?
MY GUT AND I DON'T TALK ANYMORE.
THERE'S A **RUMOR** GOING 'ROUND ABOUT YOU, YOU KNOW.
NO KIDDING? THE ONE ABOUT HOW I **KILLED** A MAN IN COLD BLOOD, OR THE ONE ABOUT HOW I'M A DYKE?
THIS ONE'S NEW. THIS ONE SAYS YOUR ASS IS ON THE LINE.
IT'S JUST TALK.
MAYBE.
YOU GO **CAREFUL**, CARRIE. THIS COULD GET MESSY.

It'll take McEwan and his crew three hours to run the prints.

I kill the time hoping.

I don't want to know.

But of course...

...it's exactly what I **didn't** want.

ALEXANDER KELLER
age 28 UNIVERSITY of CHICAGO
Dept of Geology + Geophysical S/b

United States Marshals Service
Eduardo Gonzalez— Director

Office of the U. S. Marshal
District of Hawaii
US Courthouse
300 Moana Blvd. Room c-103
Honolulu, HI 96850

Stetko:

He's one of ours. Get to fucking work.

McEwan

P.S.- You DIDN'T...

ALEXANDER KELLI
age 28 UNIVERSITY of CHI
Dept of Geology + Geophys

...use
...a Blvd. Room
..., HI 96850

...etko;

...he's one of ours. Get to fucking work.

McEwan

P.S.- YOU DIDN'T KILL HIM, TOO, DID YOU?

Bastard.

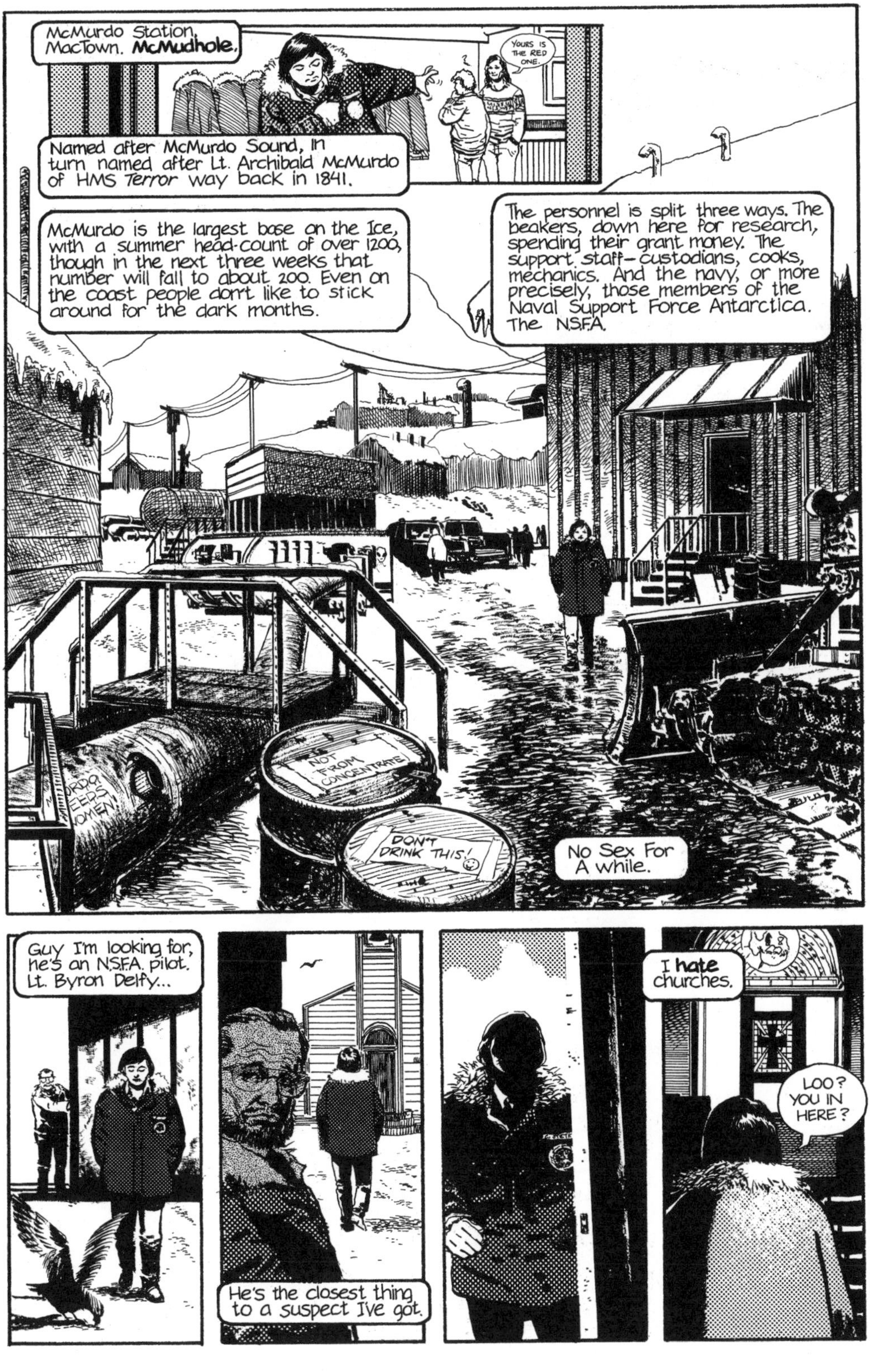
McMurdo Station.
MacTown. **McMudhole.**
YOURS IS THE RED ONE.
Named after McMurdo Sound, In turn named after Lt. Archibald McMurdo of HMS *Terror* way back in 1841.
McMurdo is the largest base on the Ice, with a summer head-count of over 1200, though in the next three weeks that number will fall to about 200. Even on the coast people don't like to stick around for the dark months.
The personnel is split three ways. The beakers, down here for research, spending their grant money. The support staff—custodians, cooks, mechanics. And the navy, or more precisely, those members of the Naval Support Force Antarctica. The N.S.F.A.
NOT FROM CONCENTRATE
DON'T DRINK THIS!
No Sex For A while.
Guy I'm looking for, he's an N.S.F.A. pilot. Lt. Byron Delfy...
He's the closest thing to a suspect I've got.
I **hate** churches.
LOO? YOU IN HERE?

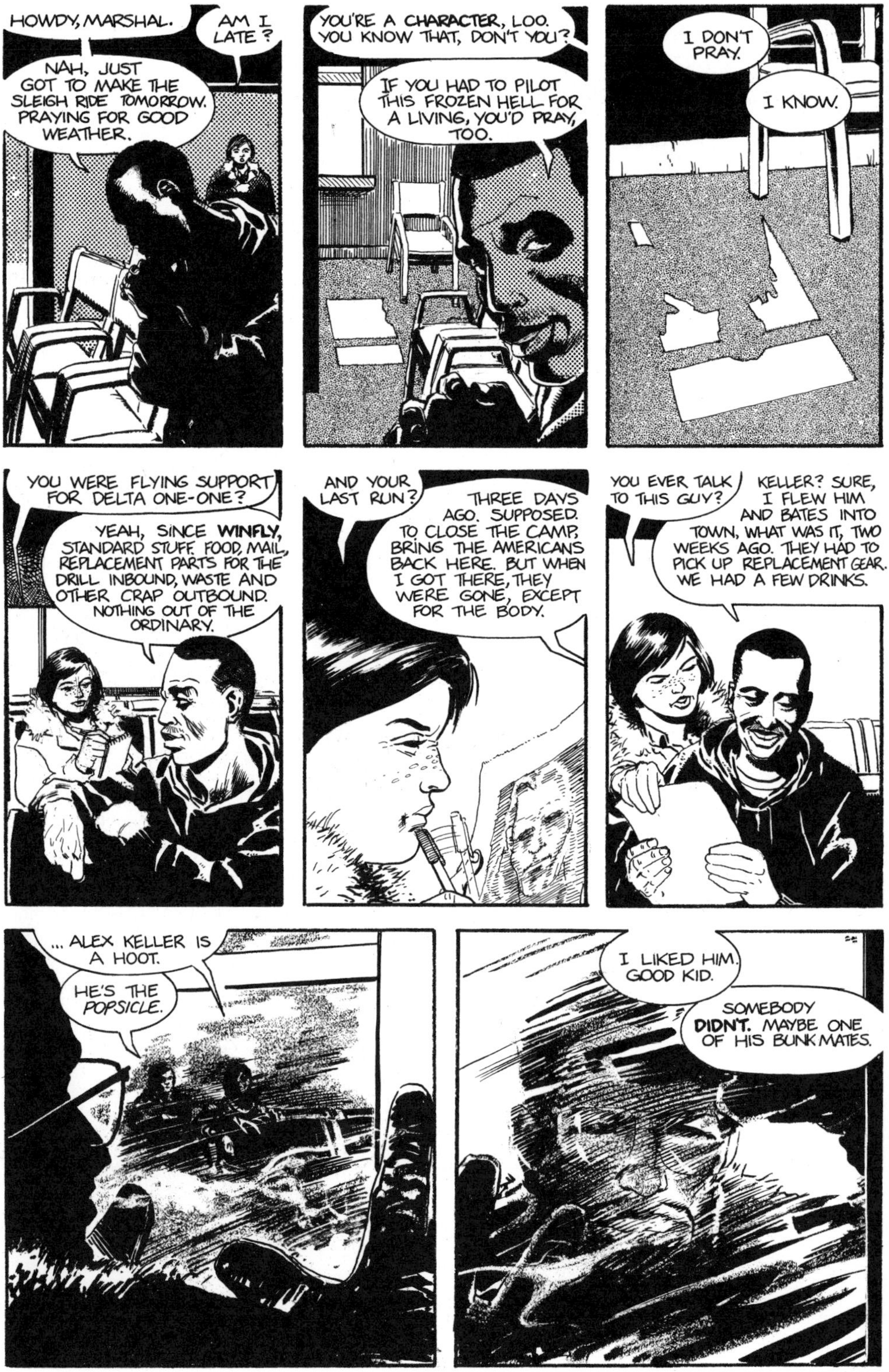

HOWDY, MARSHAL.
AM I LATE?
NAH, JUST GOT TO MAKE THE SLEIGH RIDE TOMORROW. PRAYING FOR GOOD WEATHER.
YOU'RE A **CHARACTER**, LOO. YOU KNOW THAT, DON'T YOU?
IF YOU HAD TO PILOT THIS FROZEN HELL FOR A LIVING, YOU'D PRAY, TOO.
I DON'T PRAY.
I KNOW.
YOU WERE FLYING SUPPORT FOR DELTA ONE-ONE?
YEAH, SINCE **WINFLY**, STANDARD STUFF. FOOD, MAIL, REPLACEMENT PARTS FOR THE DRILL INBOUND, WASTE AND OTHER CRAP OUTBOUND. NOTHING OUT OF THE ORDINARY.
AND YOUR LAST RUN?
THREE DAYS AGO. SUPPOSED TO CLOSE THE CAMP, BRING THE AMERICANS BACK HERE. BUT WHEN I GOT THERE, THEY WERE GONE, EXCEPT FOR THE BODY.
YOU EVER TALK TO THIS GUY?
KELLER? SURE, I FLEW HIM AND BATES INTO TOWN, WHAT WAS IT, TWO WEEKS AGO. THEY HAD TO PICK UP REPLACEMENT GEAR. WE HAD A FEW DRINKS.
... ALEX KELLER IS A HOOT.
HE'S THE *POPSICLE*.
I LIKED HIM. GOOD KID.
SOMEBODY **DIDN'T.** MAYBE ONE OF HIS BUNK MATES.

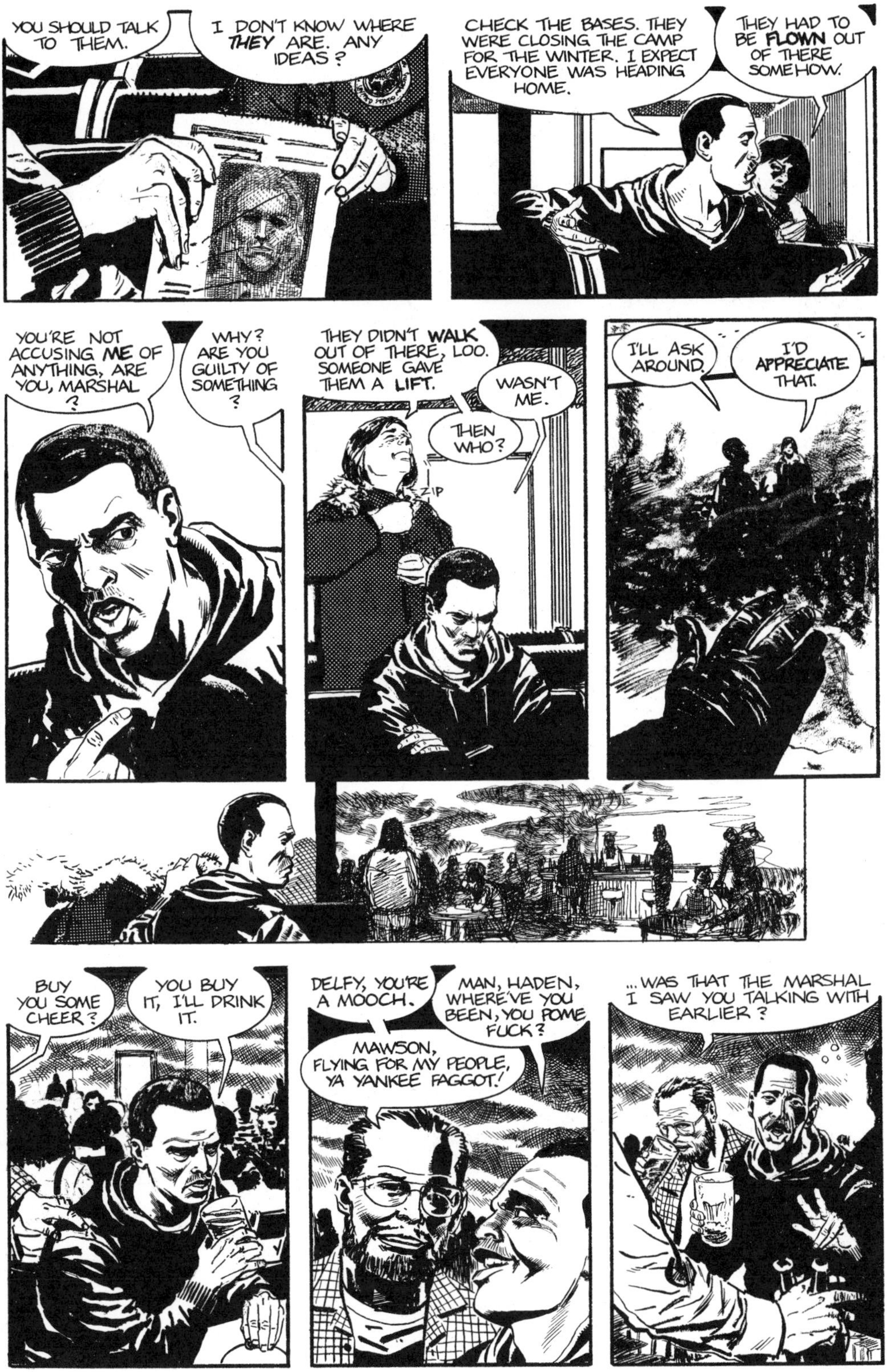
YOU SHOULD TALK TO THEM.
I DON'T KNOW WHERE THEY ARE. ANY IDEAS?
CHECK THE BASES. THEY WERE CLOSING THE CAMP FOR THE WINTER. I EXPECT EVERYONE WAS HEADING HOME.
THEY HAD TO BE FLOWN OUT OF THERE SOMEHOW.
YOU'RE NOT ACCUSING ME OF ANYTHING, ARE YOU, MARSHAL?
WHY? ARE YOU GUILTY OF SOMETHING?
THEY DIDN'T WALK OUT OF THERE, LOO. SOMEONE GAVE THEM A LIFT.
WASN'T ME.
THEN WHO?
ZIP
I'LL ASK AROUND.
I'D APPRECIATE THAT.
BUY YOU SOME CHEER?
YOU BUY IT, I'LL DRINK IT.
DELFY, YOU'RE A MOOCH.
MAN, HADEN, WHERE'VE YOU BEEN, YOU POME FUCK?
MAWSON, FLYING FOR MY PEOPLE, YA YANKEE FAGGOT!
...WAS THAT THE MARSHAL I SAW YOU TALKING WITH EARLIER?

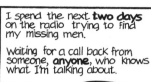

I spend the next **two days** on the radio trying to find my missing men.

Waiting for a call back from someone, **anyone**, who knows what I'm talking about.

I get fucking nowhere.

I dream of a memory four years old...

I don't like how it makes me **feel**...

18

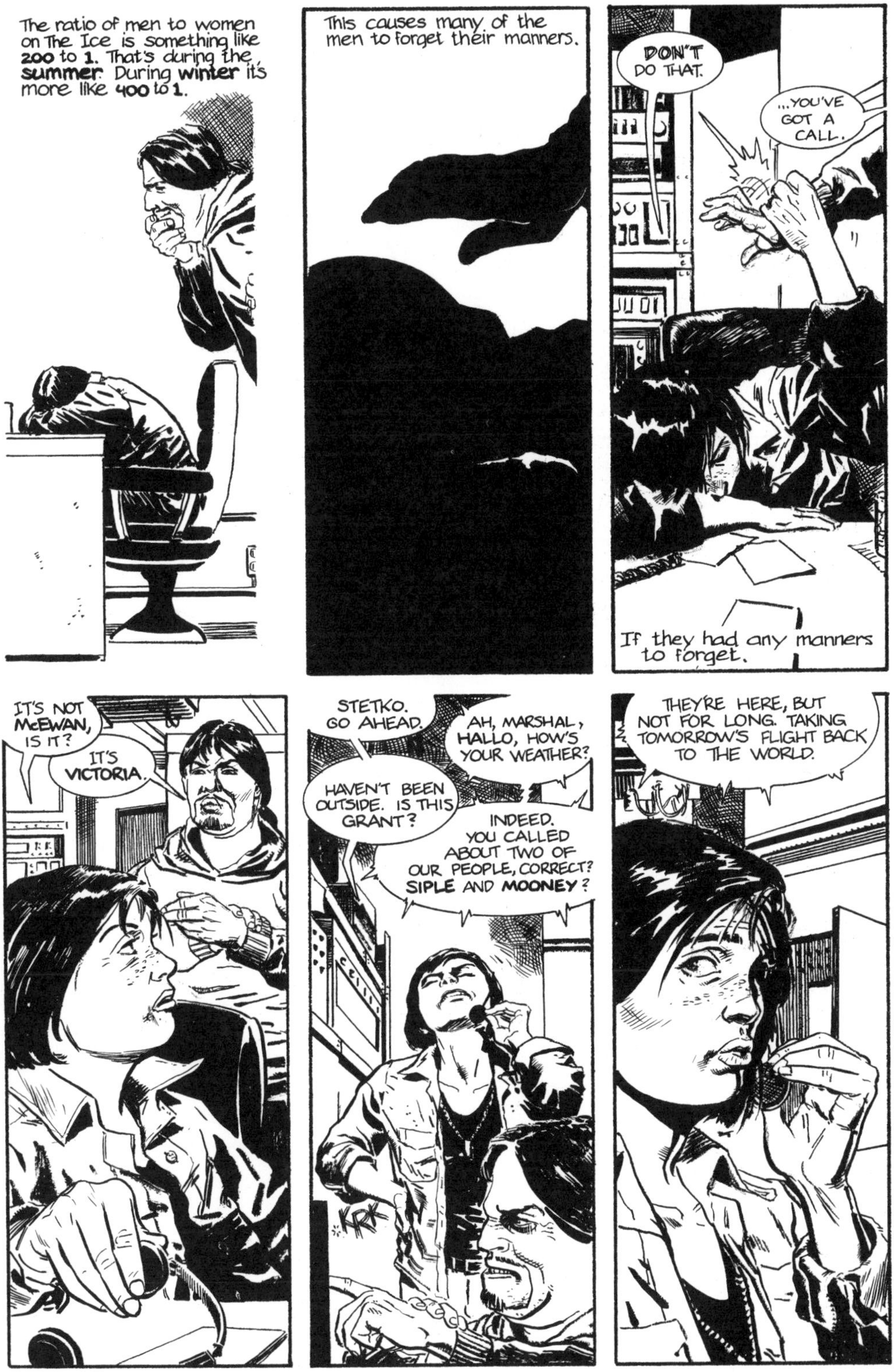
The ratio of men to women on The Ice is something like 200 to 1. That's during the summer. During winter it's more like 400 to 1.
This causes many of the men to forget their manners.
DON'T DO THAT.
...YOU'VE GOT A CALL.
If they had any manners to forget.
IT'S NOT McEWAN, IS IT?
IT'S VICTORIA.
STETKO. GO AHEAD.
AH, MARSHAL, HALLO, HOW'S YOUR WEATHER?
HAVEN'T BEEN OUTSIDE. IS THIS GRANT?
INDEED. YOU CALLED ABOUT TWO OF OUR PEOPLE, CORRECT? SIPLE AND MOONEY?
KRK
THEY'RE HERE, BUT NOT FOR LONG. TAKING TOMORROW'S FLIGHT BACK TO THE WORLD.

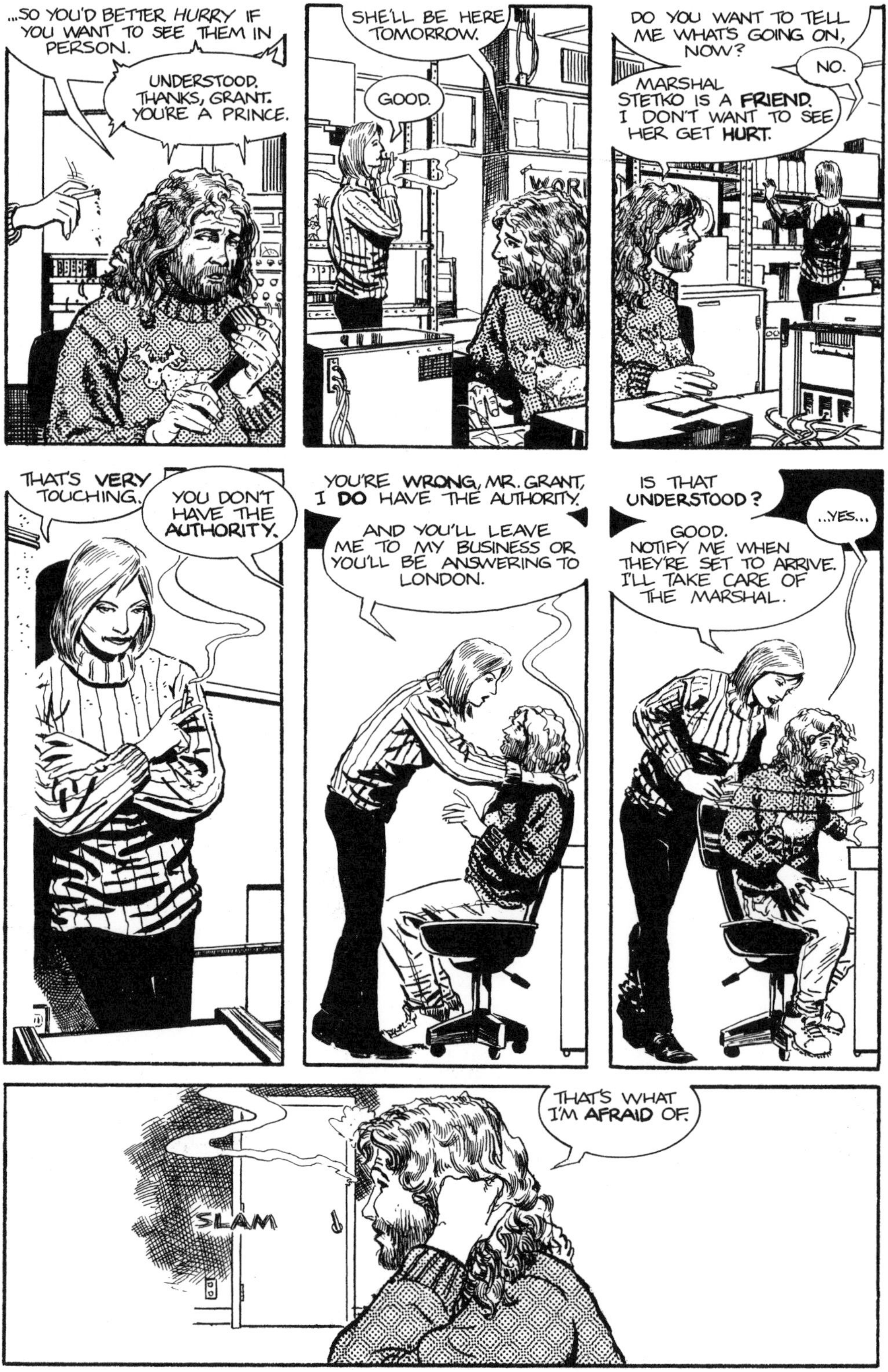
...SO YOU'D BETTER HURRY IF YOU WANT TO SEE THEM IN PERSON.
UNDERSTOOD. THANKS, GRANT. YOU'RE A PRINCE.
SHE'LL BE HERE TOMORROW.
GOOD.
WORL
DO YOU WANT TO TELL ME WHAT'S GOING ON, NOW?
NO.
MARSHAL STETKO IS A FRIEND. I DON'T WANT TO SEE HER GET HURT.
THAT'S VERY TOUCHING.
YOU DON'T HAVE THE AUTHORITY.
YOU'RE WRONG, MR. GRANT, I DO HAVE THE AUTHORITY.
AND YOU'LL LEAVE ME TO MY BUSINESS OR YOU'LL BE ANSWERING TO LONDON.
IS THAT UNDERSTOOD?
...YES...
GOOD. NOTIFY ME WHEN THEY'RE SET TO ARRIVE. I'LL TAKE CARE OF THE MARSHAL.
SLAM
THAT'S WHAT I'M AFRAID OF.

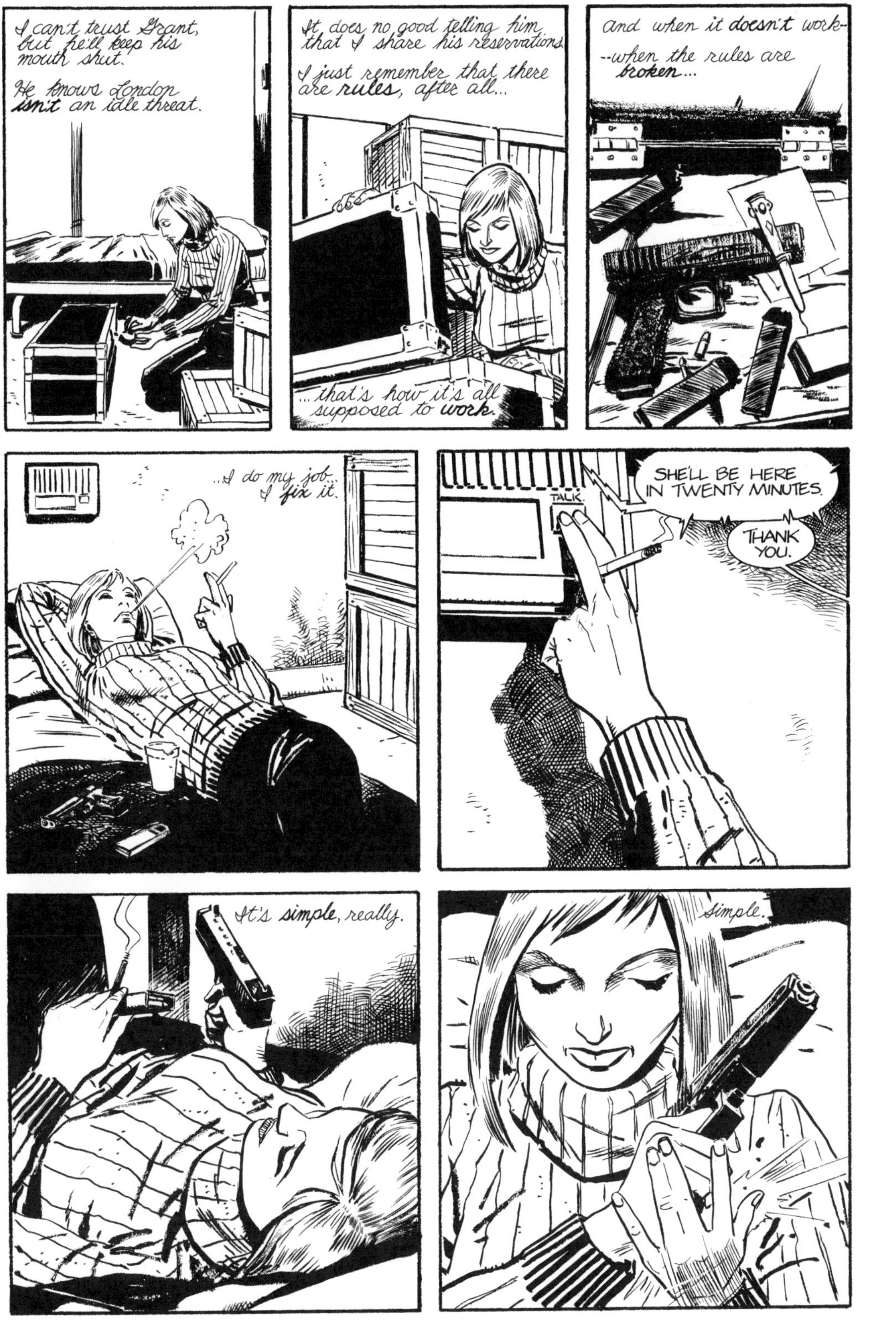
I can't trust Grant, but he'll keep his mouth shut.
He knows London isn't an idle threat.
It does no good telling him that I share his reservations.
I just remember that there are rules, after all...
...that's how it's all supposed to work.
And when it doesn't work--
--when the rules are broken...
...I do my job. I fix it.
TALK
SHE'LL BE HERE IN TWENTY MINUTES.
THANK YOU.
It's simple, really.
Simple.

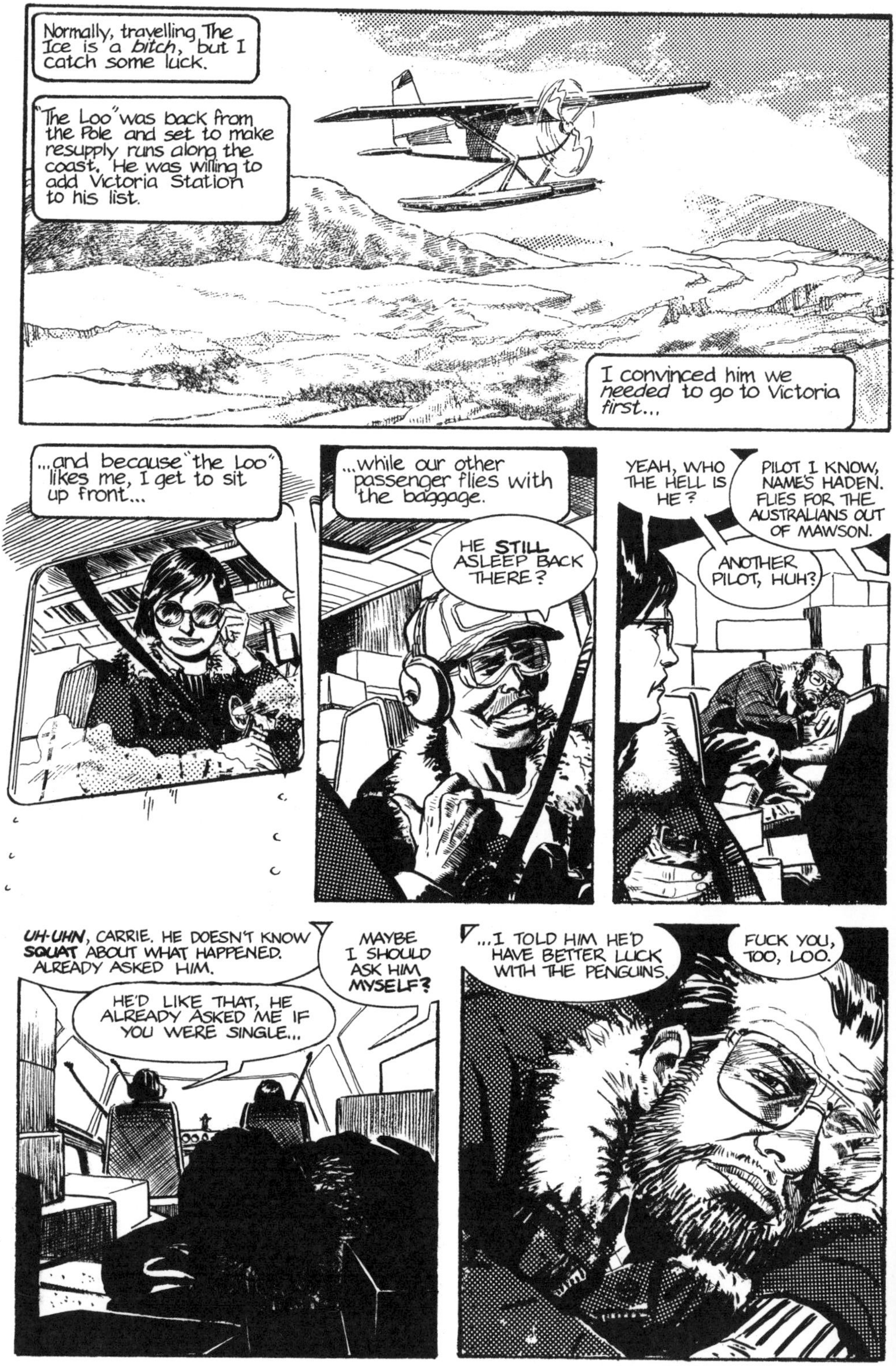

Normally, travelling The Ice is a *bitch*, but I catch some luck.
"The Loo" was back from the Pole and set to make resupply runs along the coast. He was willing to add Victoria Station to his list.
I convinced him we *needed* to go to Victoria *first*...
...and because "the Loo" likes me, I get to sit up front...
...while our other passenger flies with the baggage.
HE **STILL** ASLEEP BACK THERE?
YEAH, WHO THE HELL IS HE?
PILOT I KNOW, NAME'S HADEN. FLIES FOR THE AUSTRALIANS OUT OF MAWSON.
ANOTHER PILOT, HUH?
UH-UHN, CARRIE. HE DOESN'T KNOW **SQUAT** ABOUT WHAT HAPPENED. ALREADY ASKED HIM.
MAYBE I SHOULD ASK HIM **MYSELF?**
HE'D LIKE THAT, HE ALREADY ASKED ME IF YOU WERE SINGLE...
...I TOLD HIM HE'D HAVE BETTER LUCK WITH THE PENGUINS.
FUCK YOU, TOO, LOO.

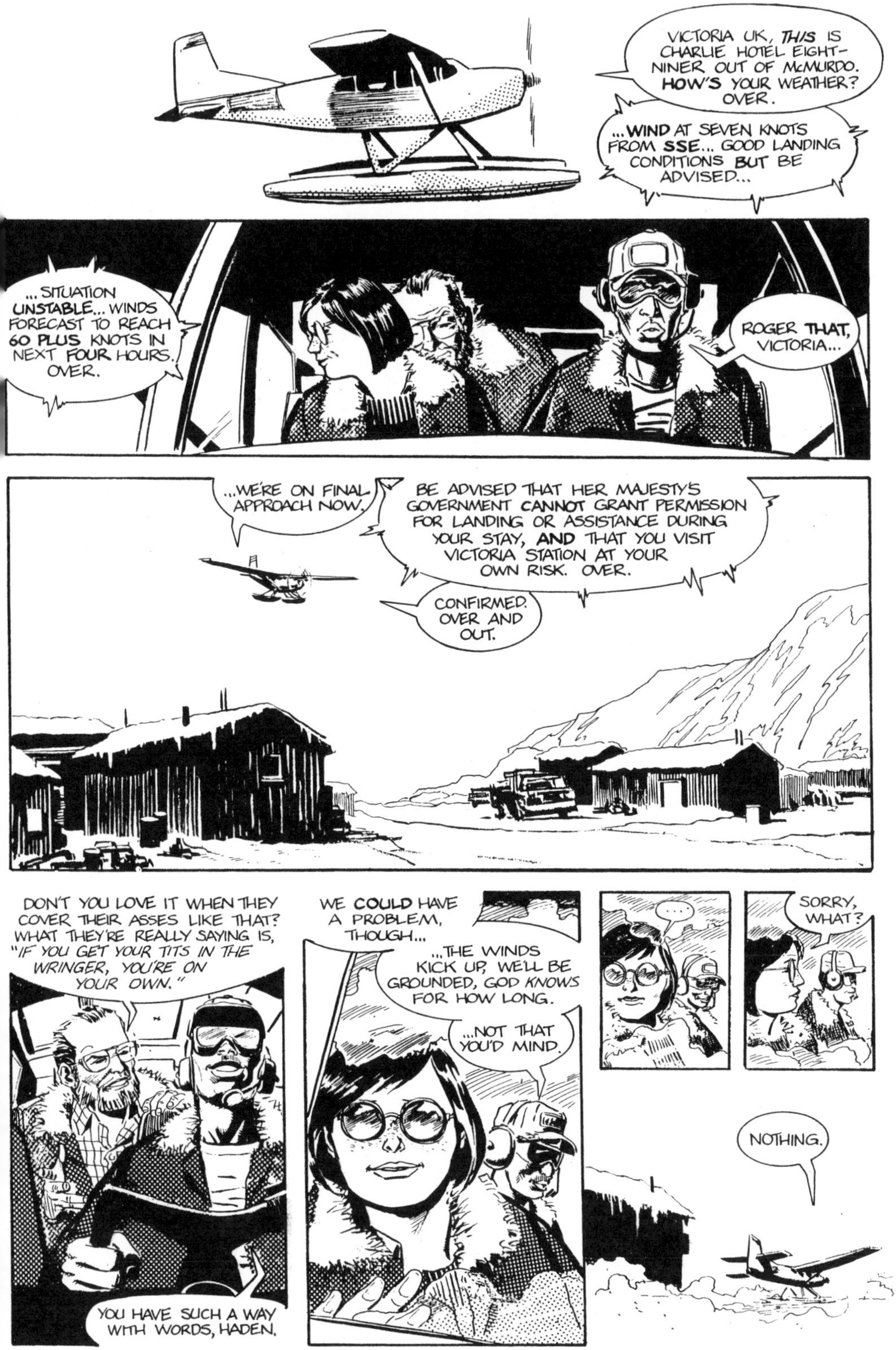
VICTORIA UK, THIS IS CHARLIE HOTEL EIGHT-NINER OUT OF McMURDO. HOW'S YOUR WEATHER? OVER.
...WIND AT SEVEN KNOTS FROM SSE... GOOD LANDING CONDITIONS BUT BE ADVISED...
...SITUATION UNSTABLE... WINDS FORECAST TO REACH 60 PLUS KNOTS IN NEXT FOUR HOURS. OVER.
ROGER THAT, VICTORIA...
...WE'RE ON FINAL APPROACH NOW.
BE ADVISED THAT HER MAJESTY'S GOVERNMENT CANNOT GRANT PERMISSION FOR LANDING OR ASSISTANCE DURING YOUR STAY, AND THAT YOU VISIT VICTORIA STATION AT YOUR OWN RISK. OVER.
CONFIRMED. OVER AND OUT.
DON'T YOU LOVE IT WHEN THEY COVER THEIR ASSES LIKE THAT? WHAT THEY'RE REALLY SAYING IS, "IF YOU GET YOUR TITS IN THE WRINGER, YOU'RE ON YOUR OWN."
YOU HAVE SUCH A WAY WITH WORDS, HADEN.
WE COULD HAVE A PROBLEM, THOUGH...
...THE WINDS KICK UP, WE'LL BE GROUNDED, GOD KNOWS FOR HOW LONG.
...NOT THAT YOU'D MIND.
...
SORRY, WHAT?
NOTHING.

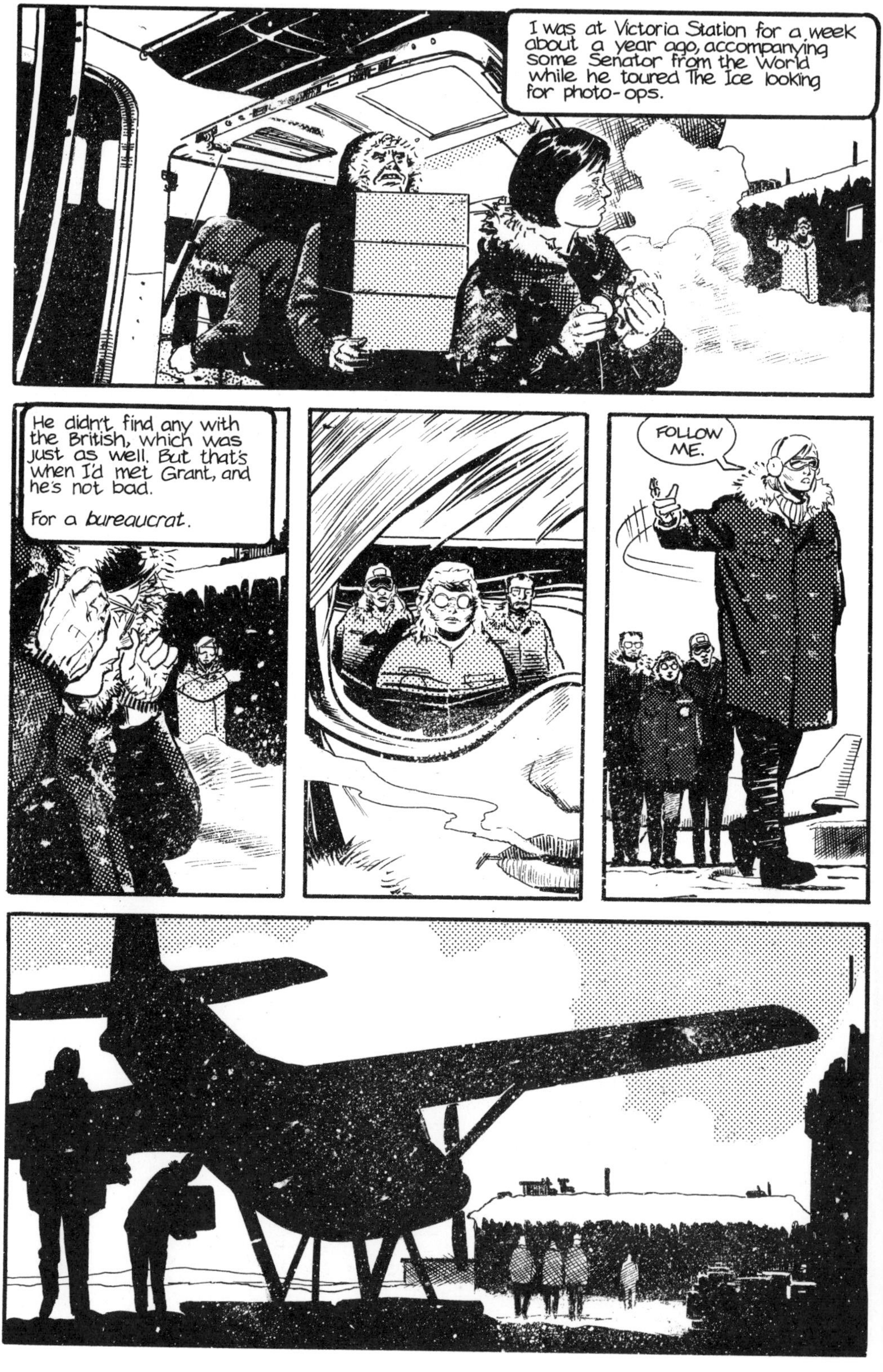
I was at Victoria Station for a week about a year ago, accompanying some Senator from the World while he toured The Ice looking for photo-ops.
He didn't find any with the British, which was just as well. But that's when I'd met Grant, and he's not bad.
For a *bureaucrat*.
FOLLOW ME.

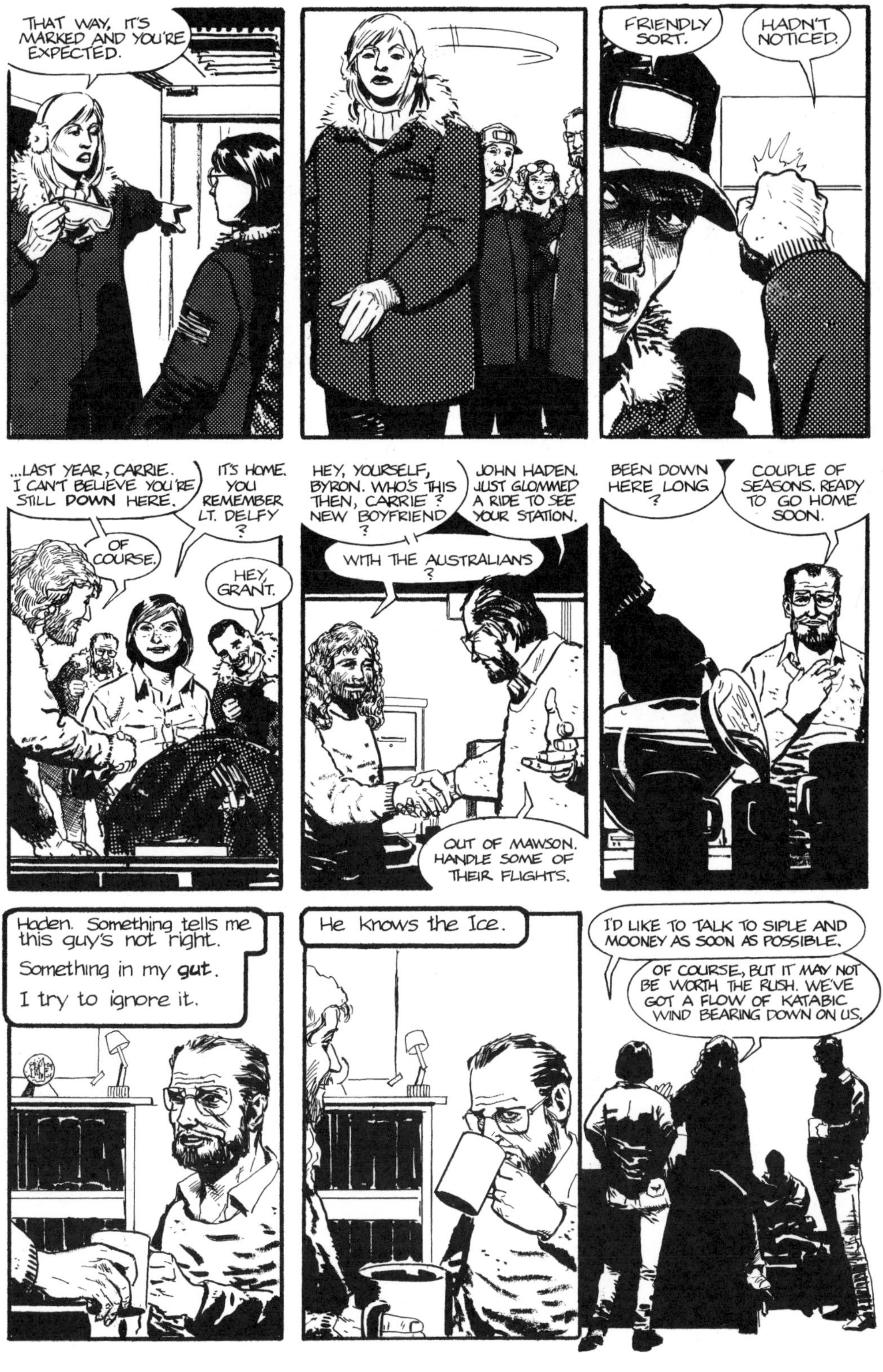
THAT WAY. IT'S MARKED AND YOU'RE EXPECTED.
FRIENDLY SORT.
HADN'T NOTICED.
...LAST YEAR, CARRIE. I CAN'T BELIEVE YOU'RE STILL DOWN HERE.
OF COURSE.
IT'S HOME. YOU REMEMBER LT. DELFY?
HEY, GRANT.
HEY, YOURSELF, BYRON. WHO'S THIS THEN, CARRIE? NEW BOYFRIEND?
JOHN HADEN. JUST GLOMMED A RIDE TO SEE YOUR STATION.
WITH THE AUSTRALIANS?
OUT OF MAWSON. HANDLE SOME OF THEIR FLIGHTS.
BEEN DOWN HERE LONG?
COUPLE OF SEASONS. READY TO GO HOME SOON.
Haden. Something tells me this guy's not right.
Something in my gut.
I try to ignore it.
He knows the Ice.
I'D LIKE TO TALK TO SIPLE AND MOONEY AS SOON AS POSSIBLE.
OF COURSE, BUT IT MAY NOT BE WORTH THE RUSH. WE'VE GOT A FLOW OF KATABIC WIND BEARING DOWN ON US.

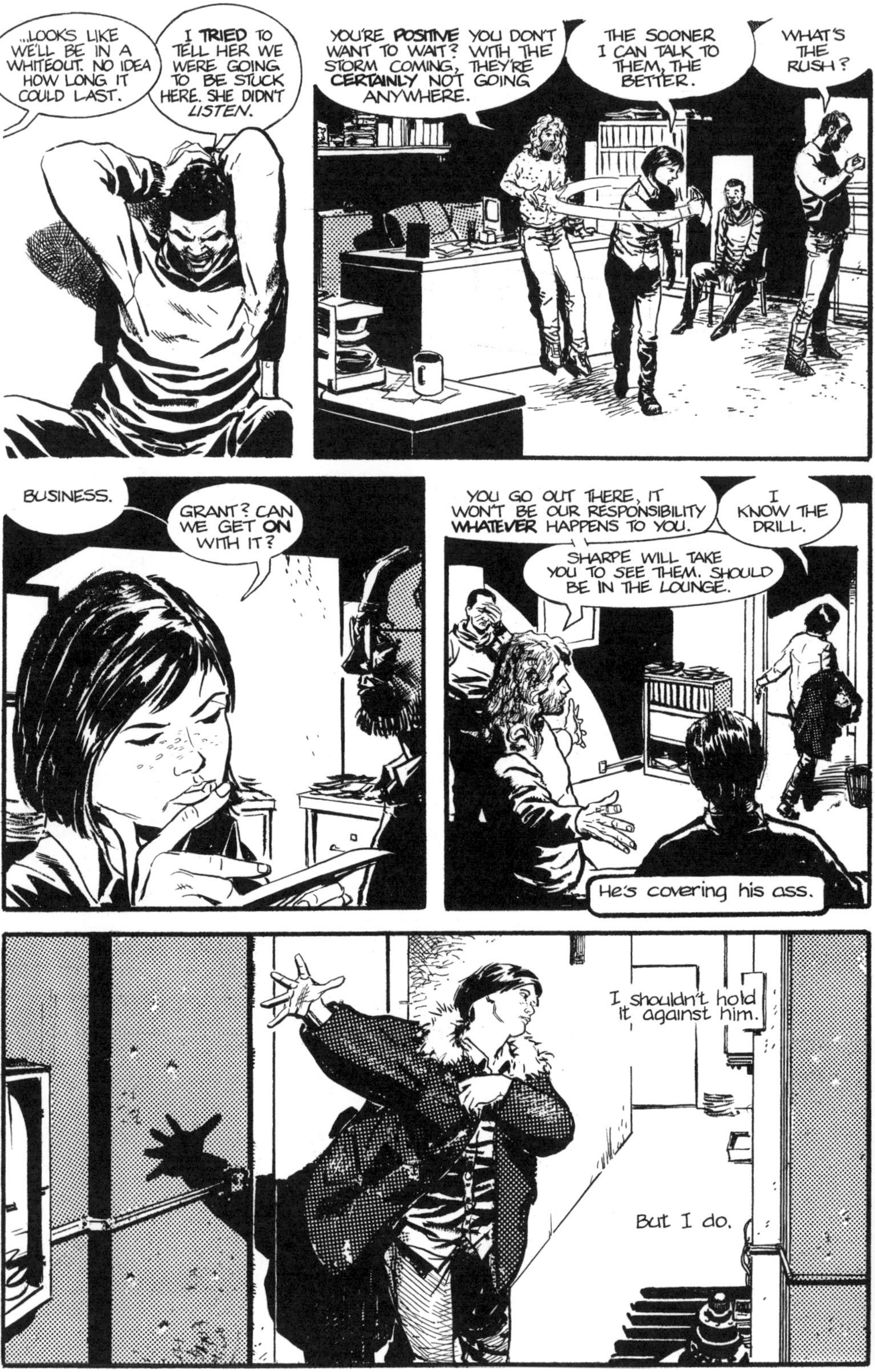
...LOOKS LIKE WE'LL BE IN A WHITEOUT. NO IDEA HOW LONG IT COULD LAST.
I TRIED TO TELL HER WE WERE GOING TO BE STUCK HERE. SHE DIDN'T LISTEN.
YOU'RE POSITIVE YOU DON'T WANT TO WAIT? WITH THE STORM COMING, THEY'RE CERTAINLY NOT GOING ANYWHERE.
THE SOONER I CAN TALK TO THEM, THE BETTER.
WHAT'S THE RUSH?
BUSINESS.
GRANT? CAN WE GET ON WITH IT?
YOU GO OUT THERE, IT WON'T BE OUR RESPONSIBILITY WHATEVER HAPPENS TO YOU.
I KNOW THE DRILL.
SHARPE WILL TAKE YOU TO SEE THEM. SHOULD BE IN THE LOUNGE.
He's covering his ass.
I shouldn't hold it against him.
But I do.

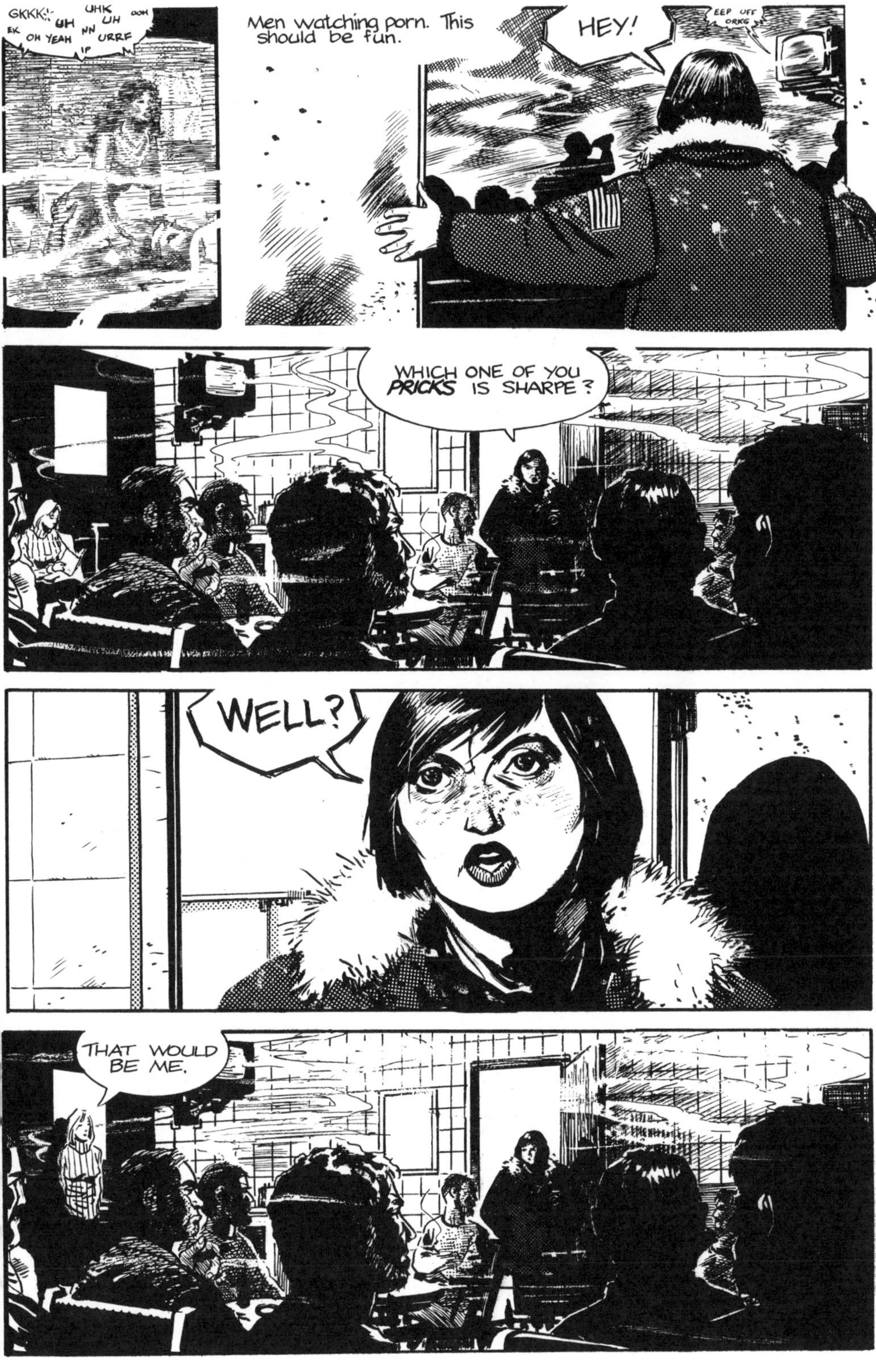
GKKK!
UHK
OOH
UH
UH
EK
NN
OH YEAH
URRF
IP
Men watching porn. This should be fun.
HEY!
EEP UFF ORKG
WHICH ONE OF YOU *PRICKS* IS SHARPE?
WELL?
THAT WOULD BE ME.

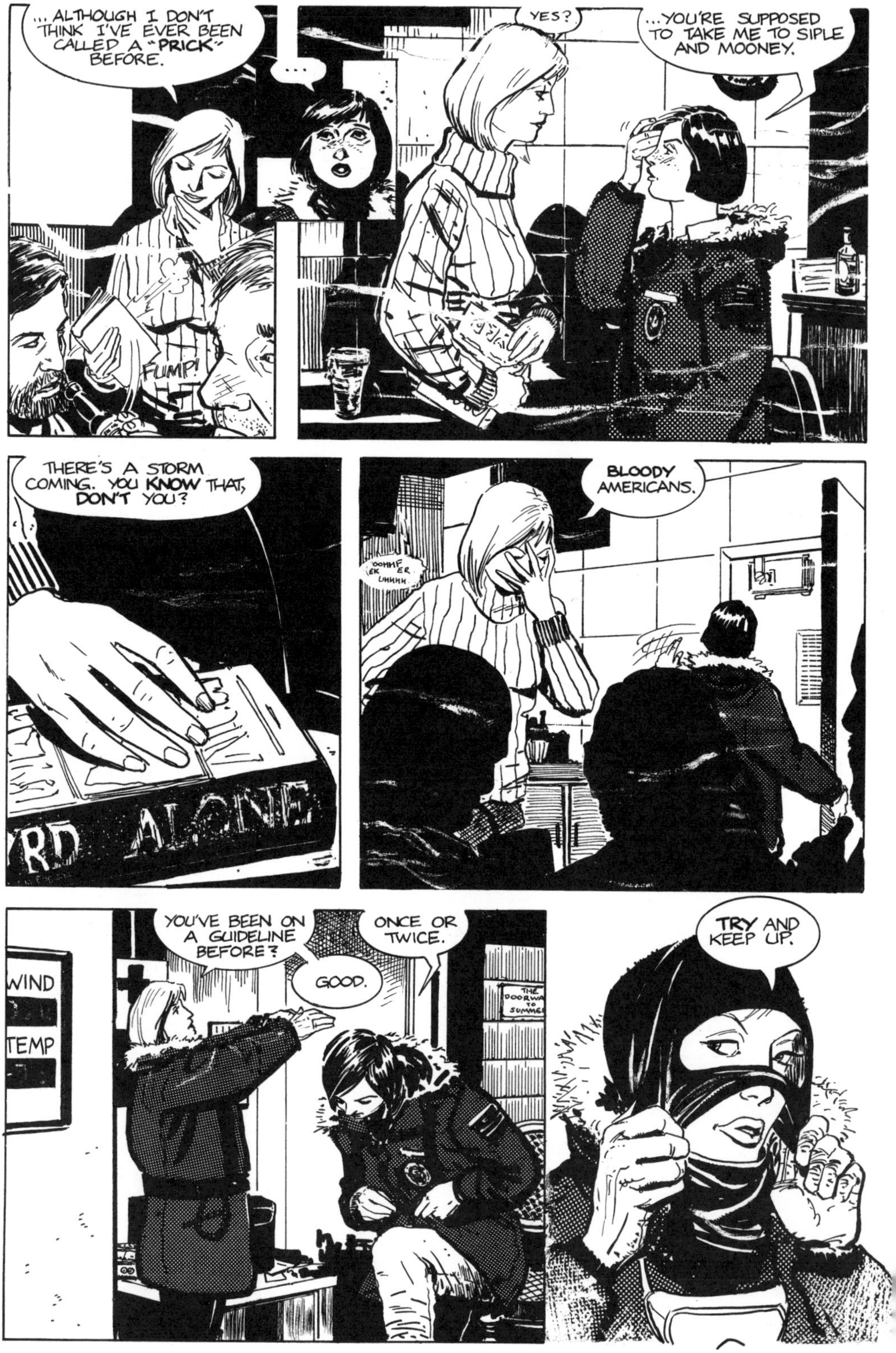

...ALTHOUGH I DON'T THINK I'VE EVER BEEN CALLED A "PRICK" BEFORE.
FUMP!
...
YES?
...YOU'RE SUPPOSED TO TAKE ME TO SIPLE AND MOONEY.
THERE'S A STORM COMING. YOU KNOW THAT, DON'T YOU?
BLOODY AMERICANS.
WIND
TEMP
YOU'VE BEEN ON A GUIDELINE BEFORE?
ONCE OR TWICE.
GOOD.
TRY AND KEEP UP.

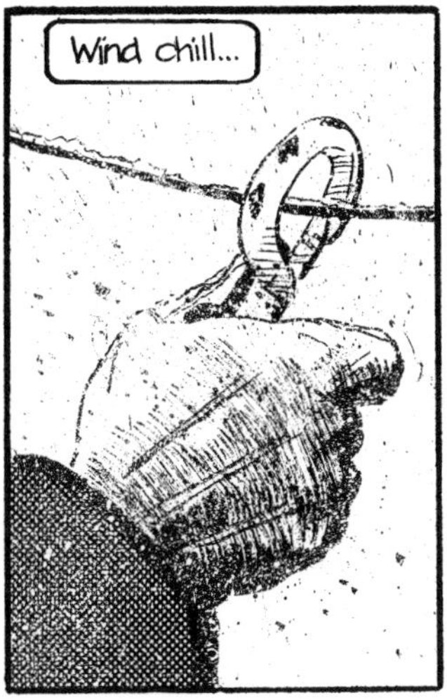
Wind chill...

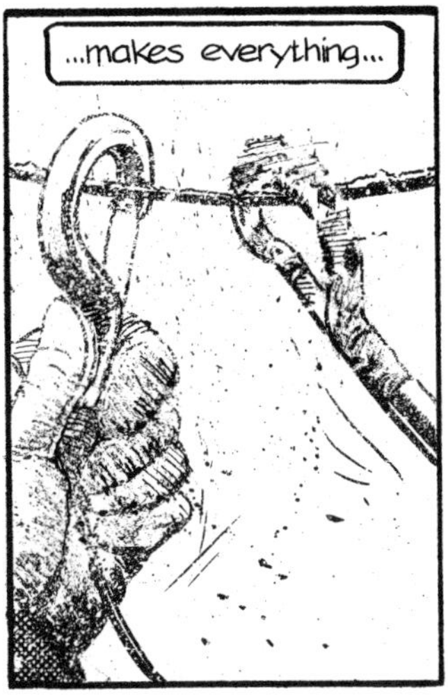
...makes everything...

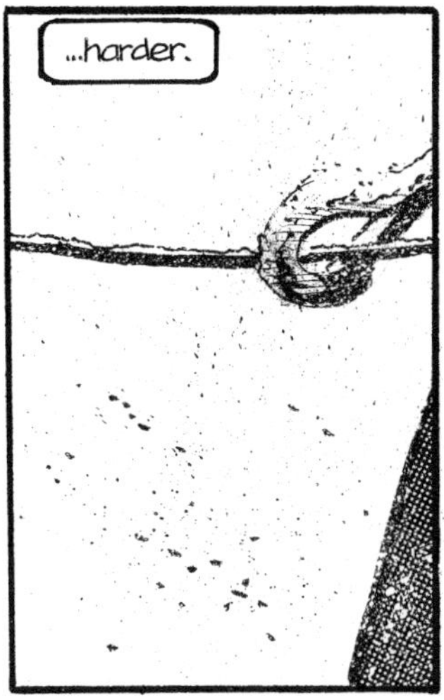
...harder.

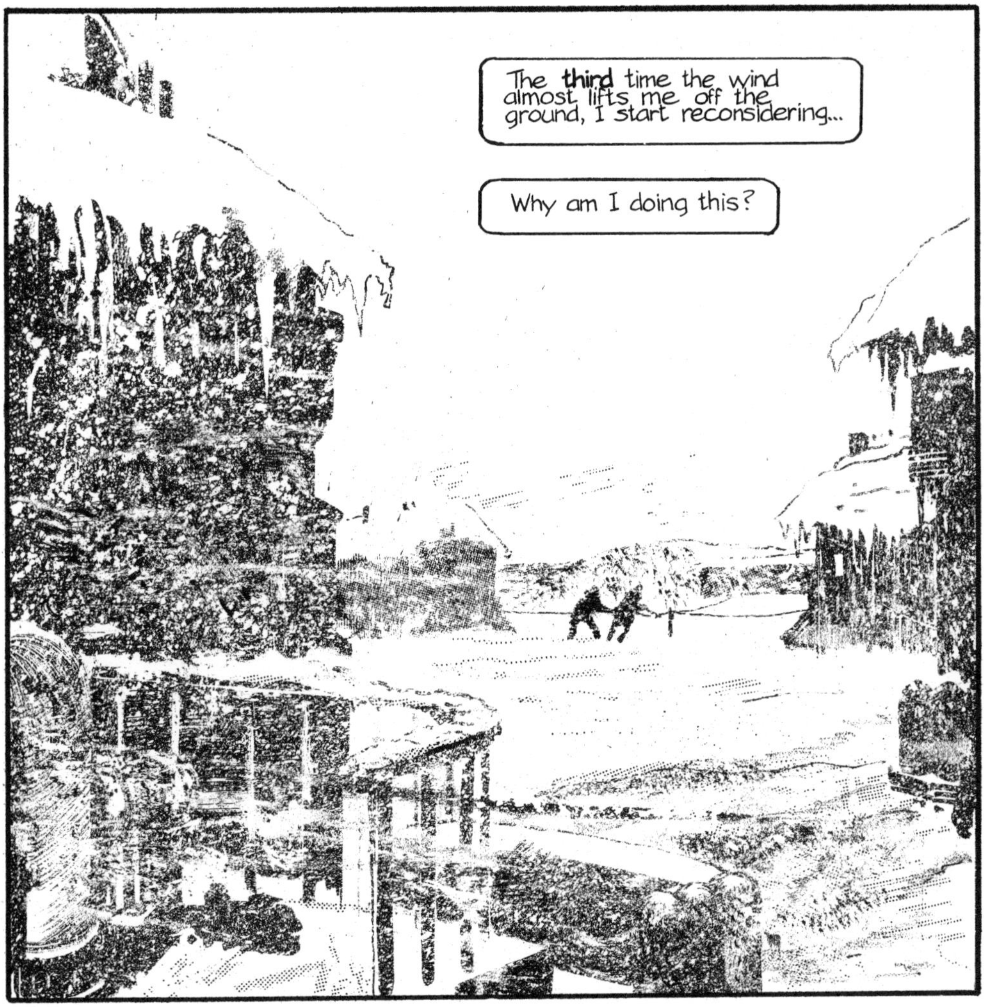
The **third** time the wind almost lifts me off the ground, I start reconsidering...
Why am I doing this?

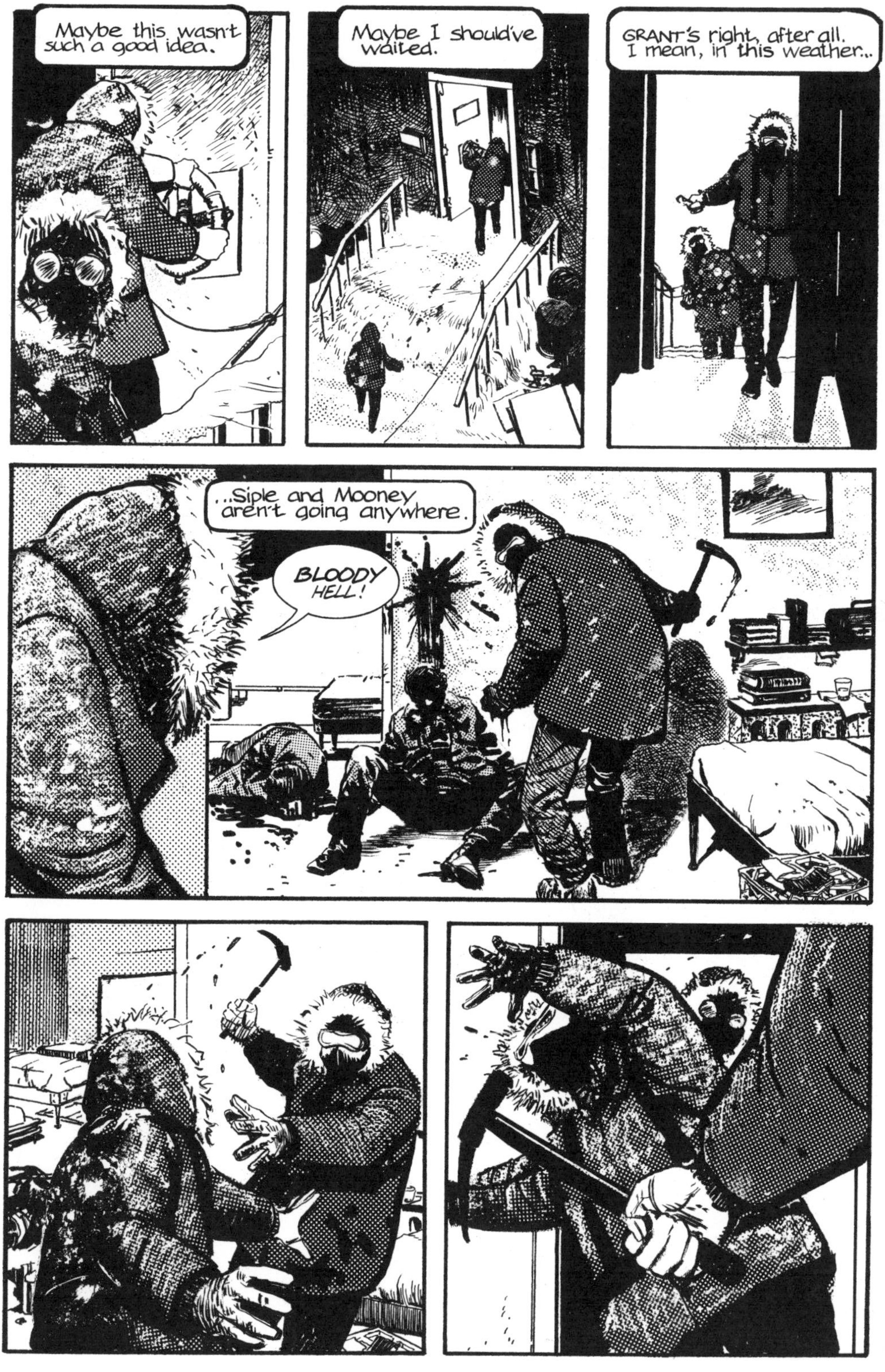
Maybe this wasn't such a good idea.
Maybe I should've waited.
GRANT's right, after all. I mean, in this weather...
...Siple and Mooney aren't going anywhere.
BLOODY HELL!

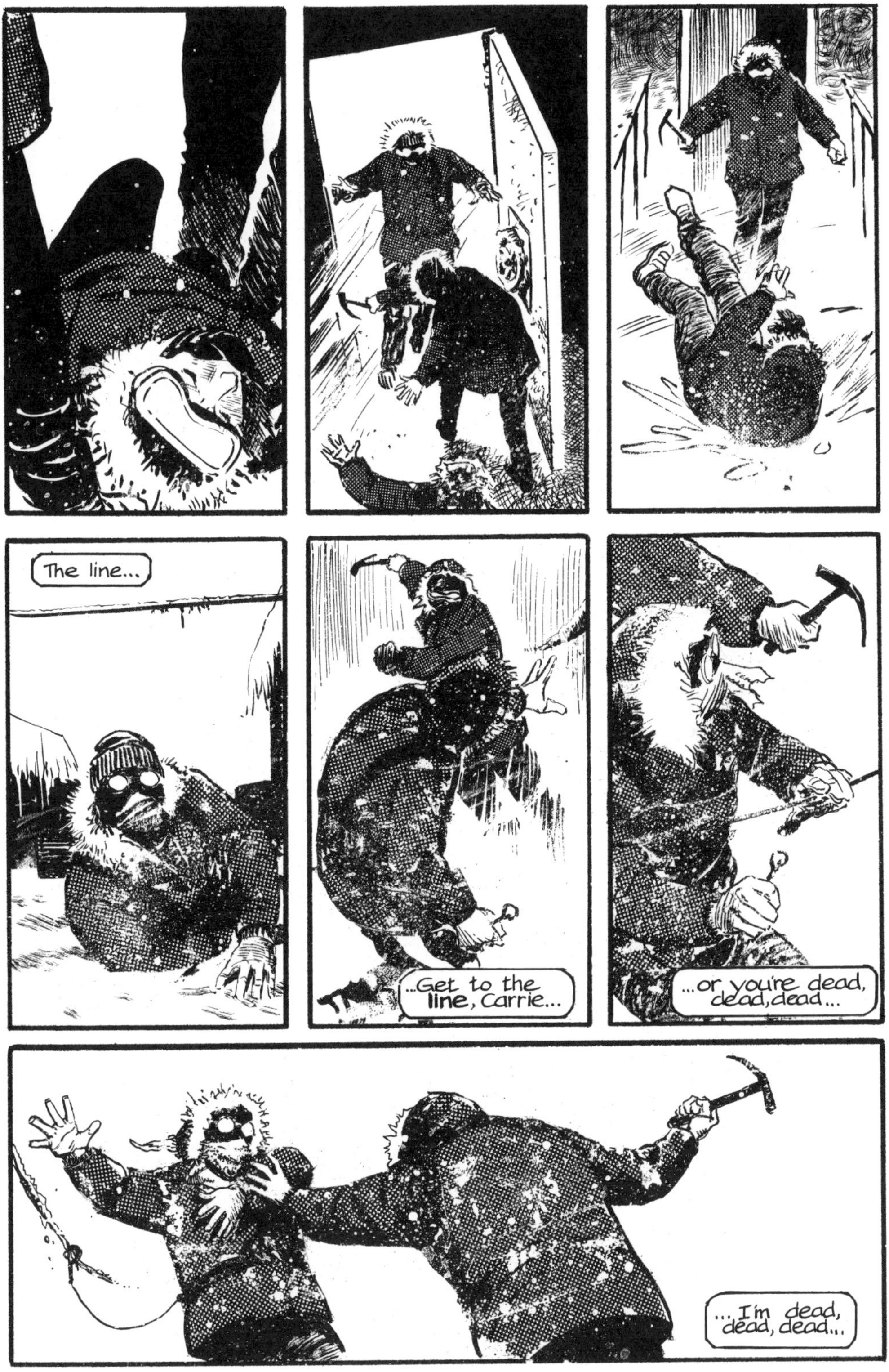
The line...
...Get to the line, Carrie...
...or you're dead, dead, dead...
...I'm dead, dead, dead...

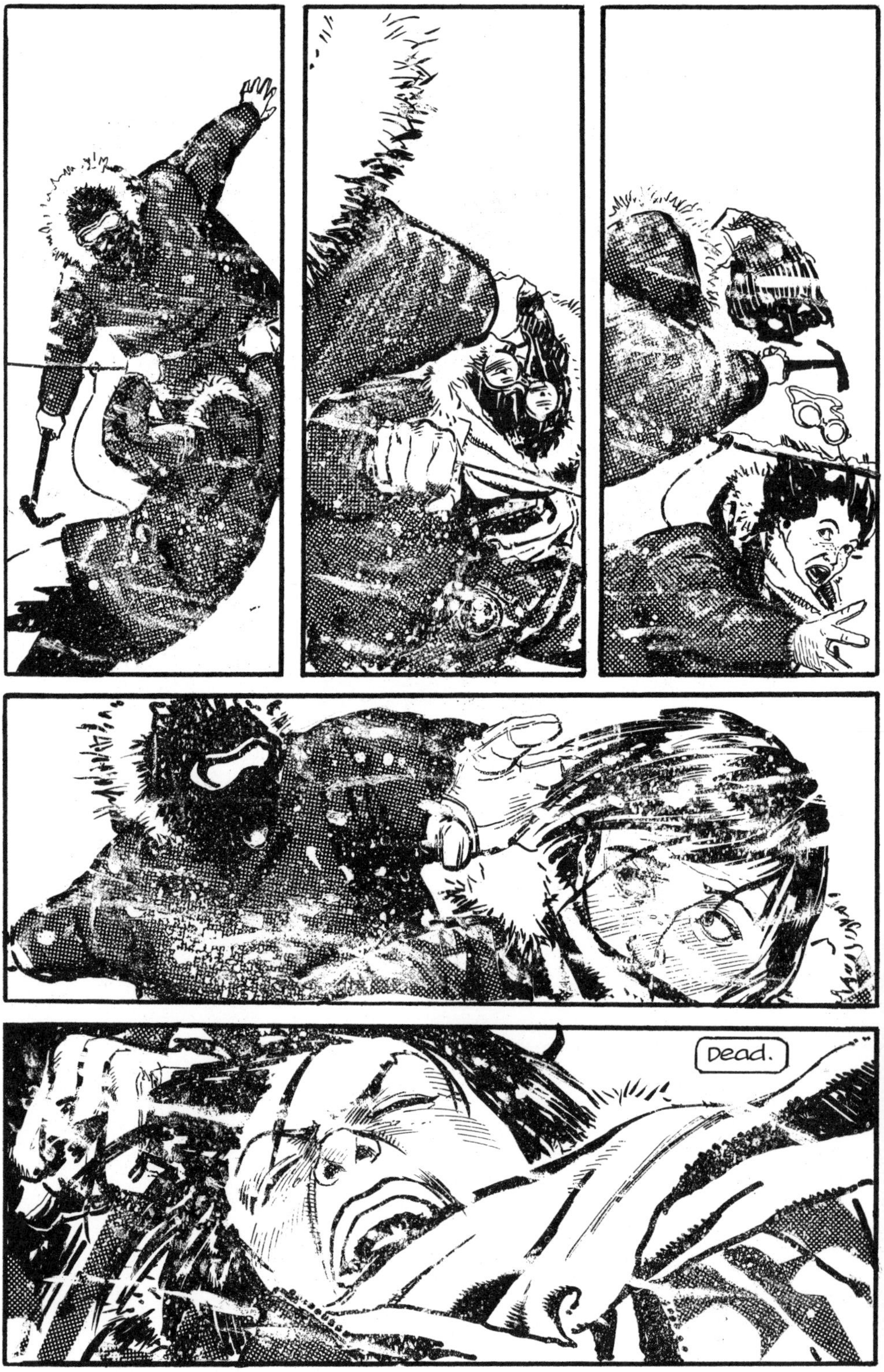
Dead.

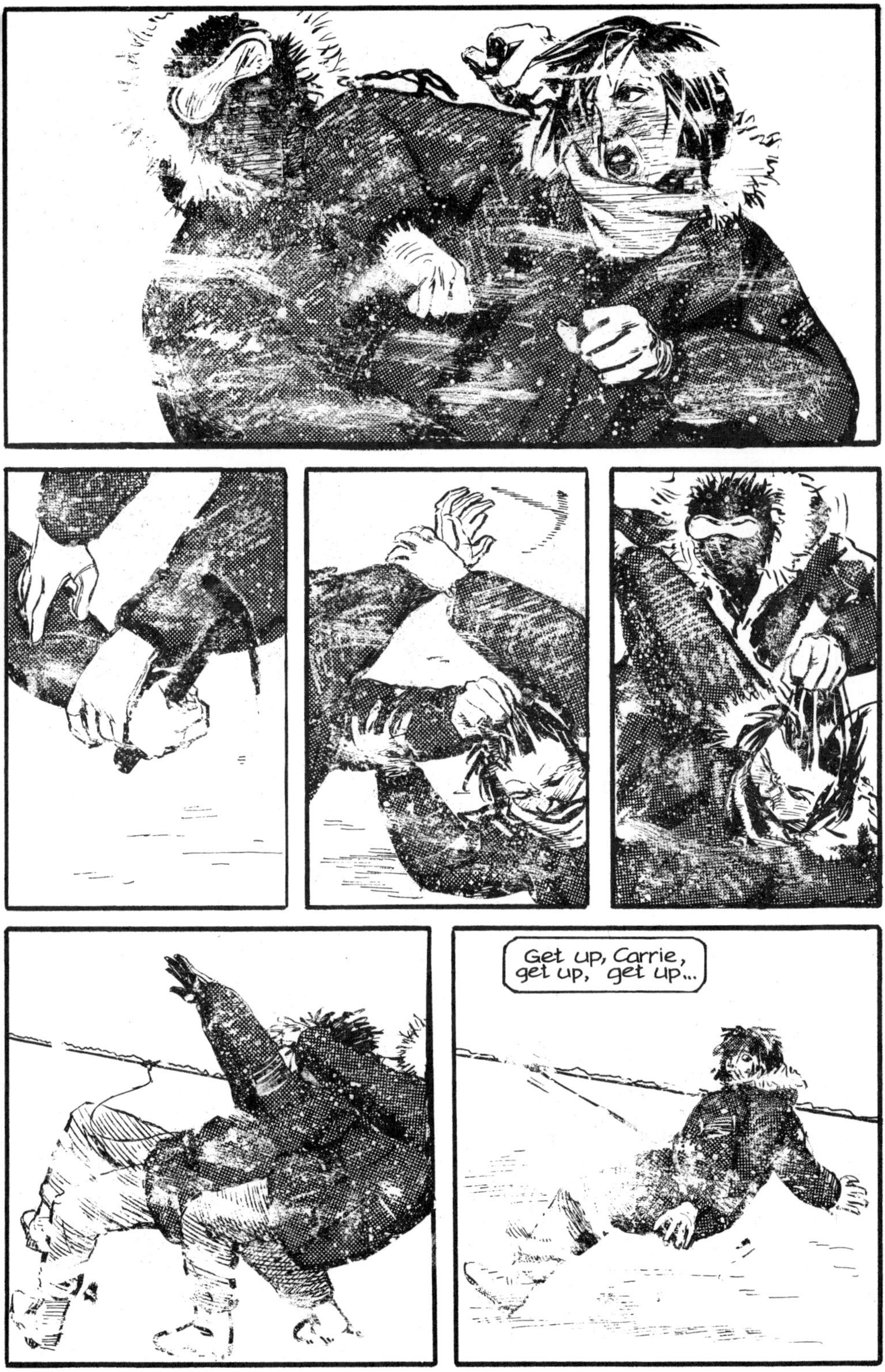
Get up, Carrie, get up, get up...

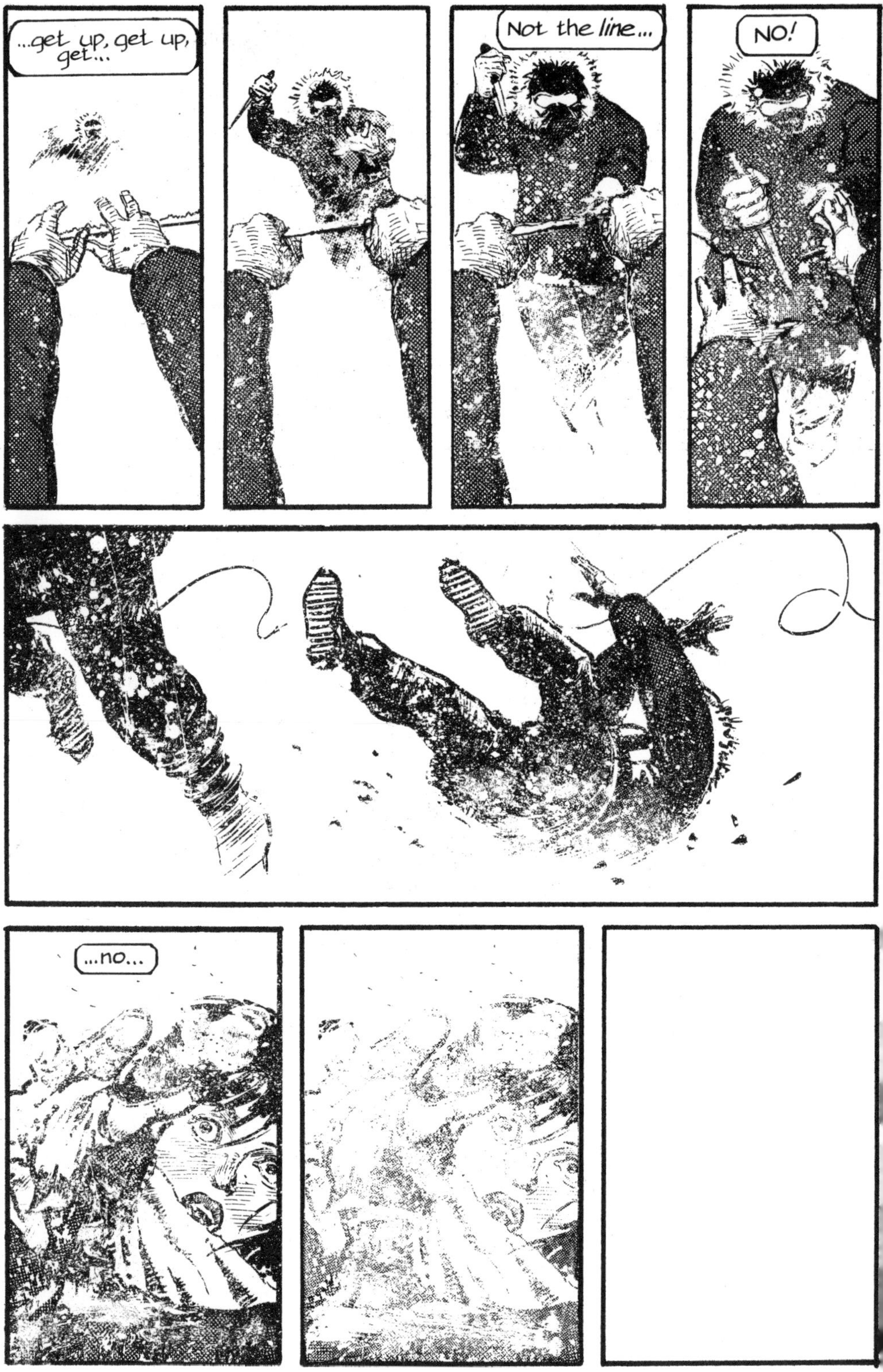
...get up, get up, get...
Not the line...
NO!
...no...

CHAPTER TWO

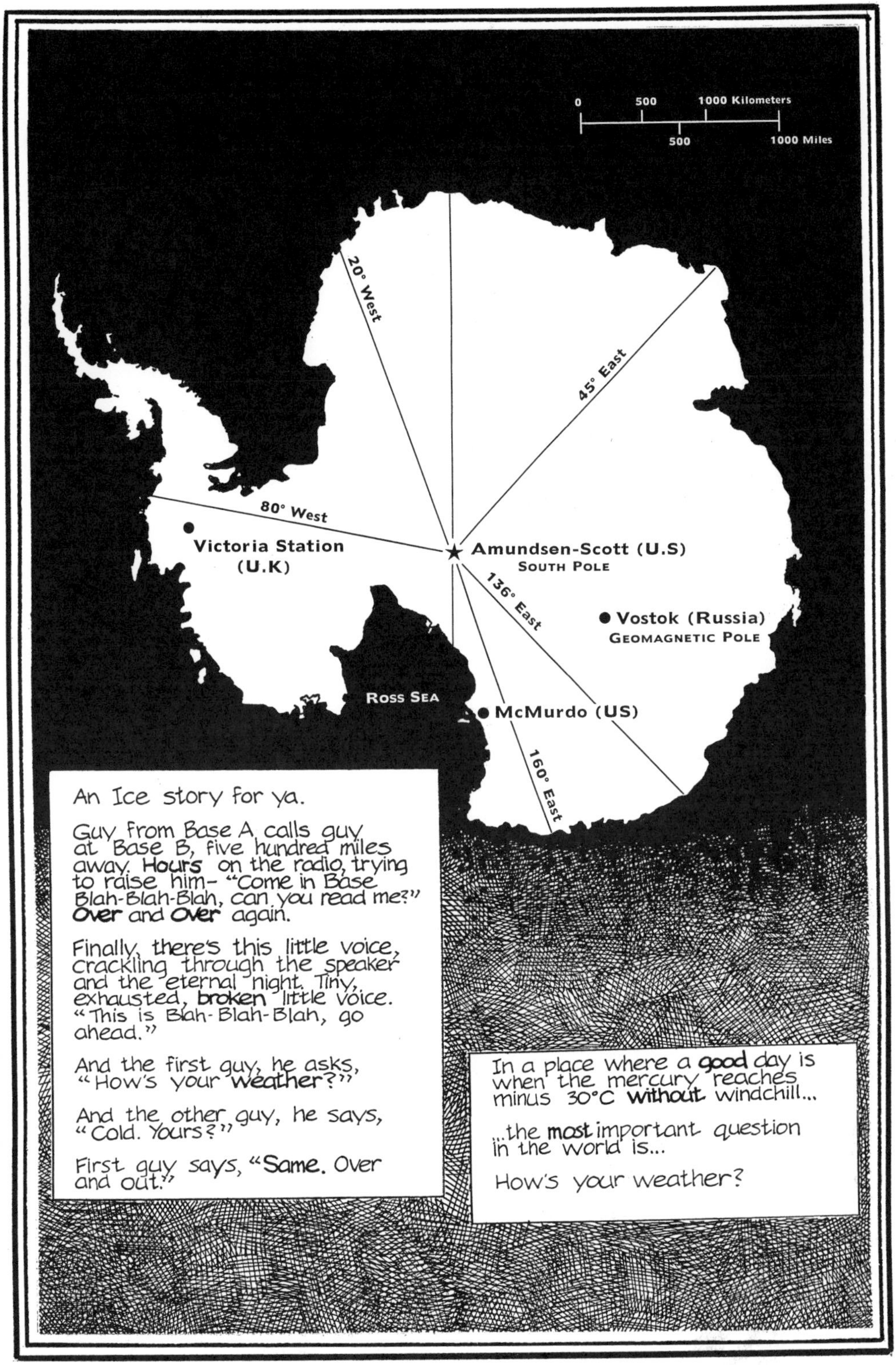
0 500 1000 Kilometers
500 1000 Miles
20° West
45° East
80° West
Victoria Station (U.K)
Amundsen-Scott (U.S) SOUTH POLE
136° East
Vostok (Russia) GEOMAGNETIC POLE
ROSS SEA
McMurdo (US)
160° East
An Ice story for ya.
Guy from Base A calls guy at Base B, five hundred miles away. Hours on the radio, trying to raise him– "Come in Base Blah-Blah-Blah, can you read me?" Over and Over again.
Finally, there's this little voice, crackling through the speaker and the eternal night. Tiny, exhausted, broken little voice. "This is Blah-Blah-Blah, go ahead."
And the first guy, he asks, "How's your weather?"
And the other guy, he says, "Cold. Yours?"
First guy says, "Same. Over and out."
In a place where a good day is when the mercury reaches minus 30°C without windchill...
...the most important question in the world is...
How's your weather?

My weather sucks.

Tru Fax. Antarctica is about 14.2 million square kilometers, not counting the tail or the islands...

Rock covered with 30 million cubic kilometers of ice. It's the **highest** continent, average elevation 2320 meters above sea level. That's 7380 feet, for those of you who never learned metric...

Think about how cold it has to be to keep 30 million cubic kilometers frozen.

Pretty fucking cold.

On the coast, at McMurdo, it's a balmy minus 5°C...

Survivable. Life exists to prove the point. Penguins, seals, insects, other birds, some particularly masochistic fish...

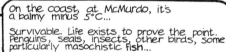

In the interior though, temperatures are **much** lower. Minus 70°C during the winter. Not counting windchill...

It's so fucking cold that **nothing** survives on it's own. No seals. No birds. No bugs. Not even bacteria...

Piece of trivia.— coldest temperature ever recorded on Earth was by the Russians at Vostok Station. Get this— minus 89.6°C, recorded July 21, 1983.

Cold like that kills. Water vapor in your lungs freezes instantly, bursts cells...

Kind of like exploding from within...

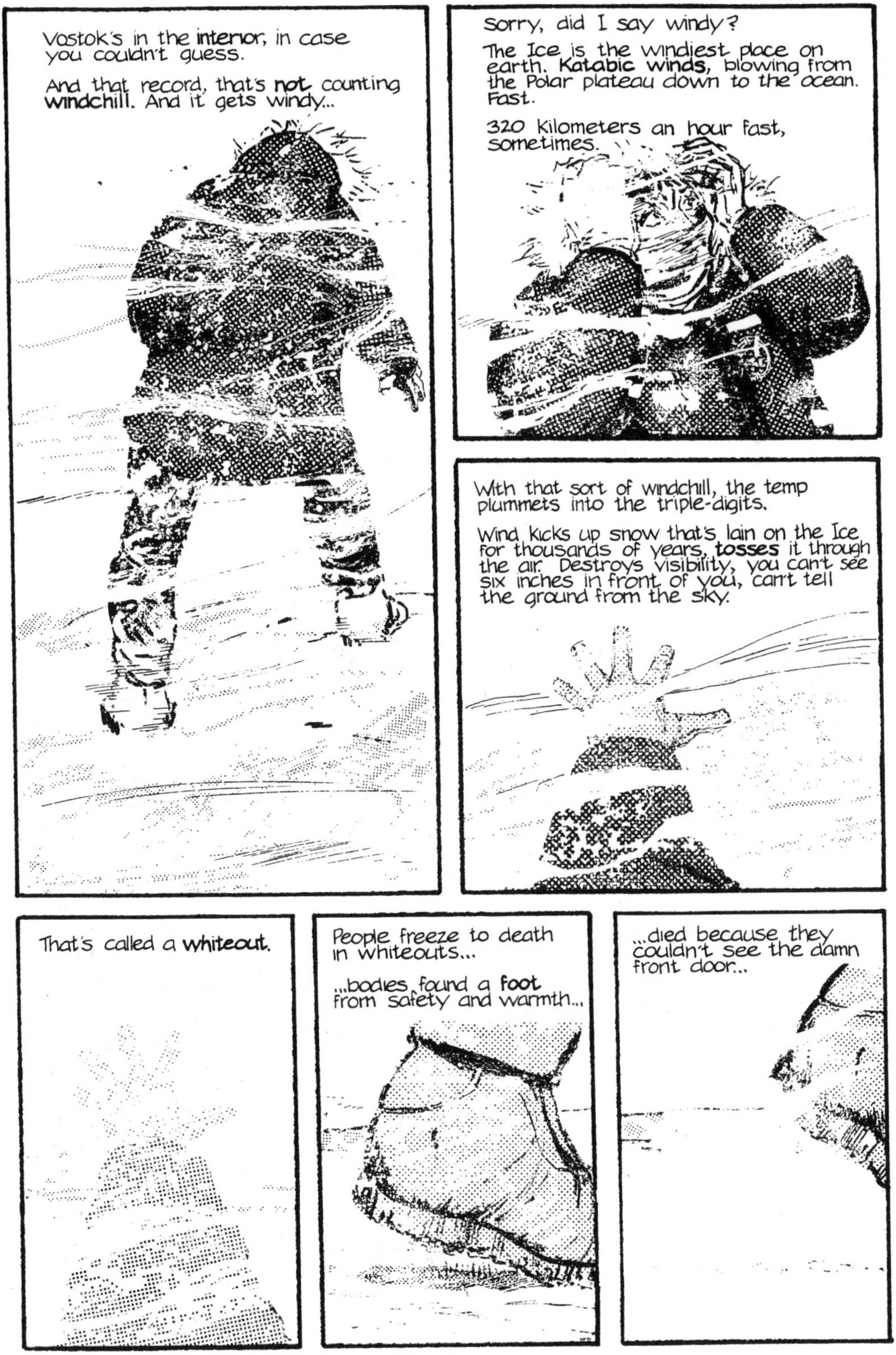
Vostok's in the interior, in case you couldn't guess.
And that record, that's not counting windchill. And it gets windy...
Sorry, did I say windy?
The Ice is the windiest place on earth. Katabic winds, blowing from the Polar plateau down to the ocean. Fast.
320 Kilometers an hour fast, sometimes.
With that sort of windchill, the temp plummets into the triple-digits.
Wind kicks up snow that's lain on the Ice for thousands of years, tosses it through the air. Destroys visibility, you can't see six inches in front of you, can't tell the ground from the sky.
That's called a whiteout.
People freeze to death in whiteouts...
...bodies found a foot from safety and warmth...
...died because they couldn't see the damn front door...

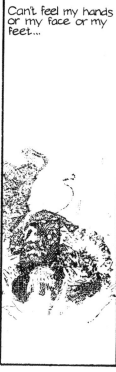

Can't feel my hands or my face or my feet...

...know I'm hypothermic...

...numb hands can't feel...

...no choice...

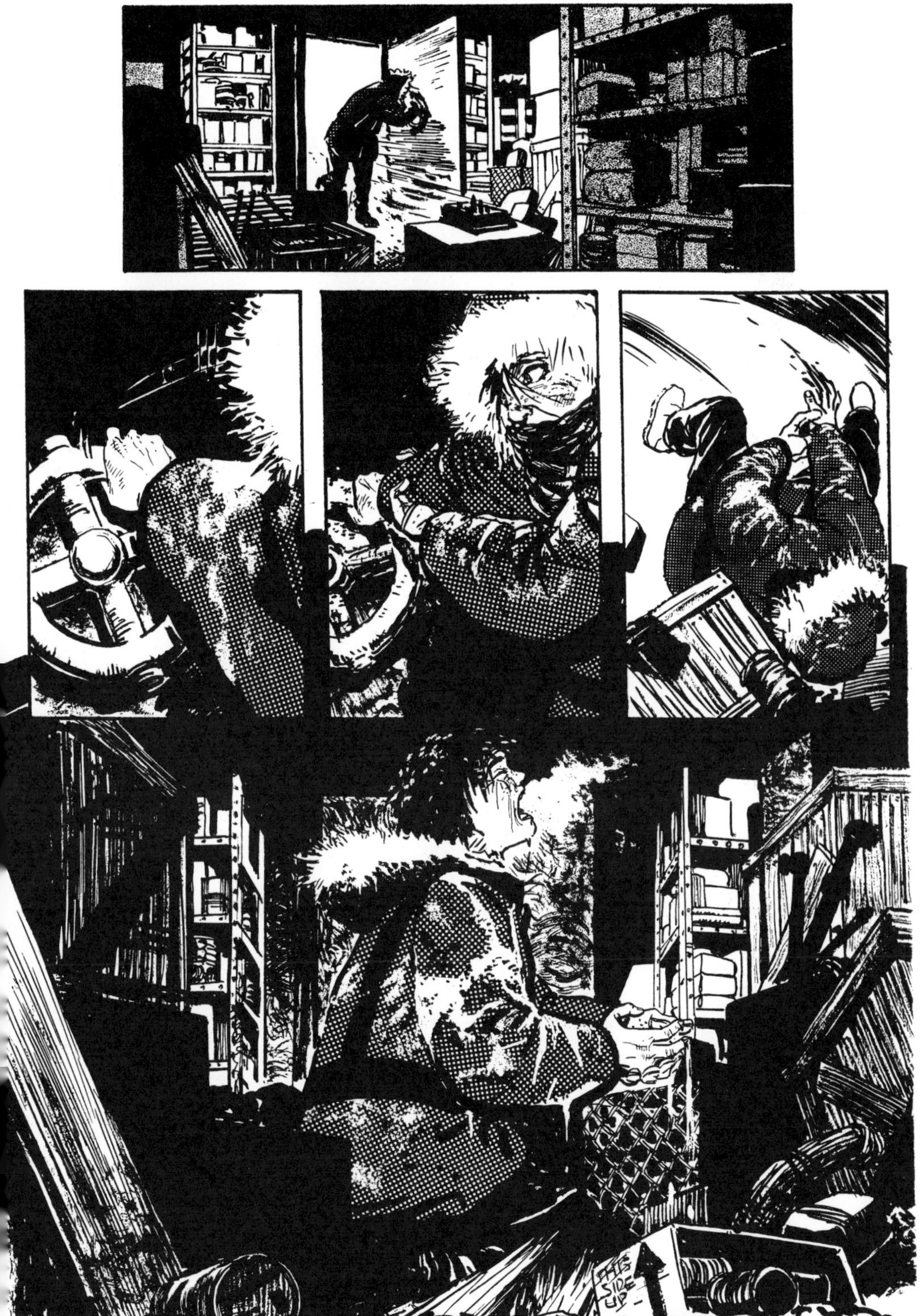
THIS SIDE UP

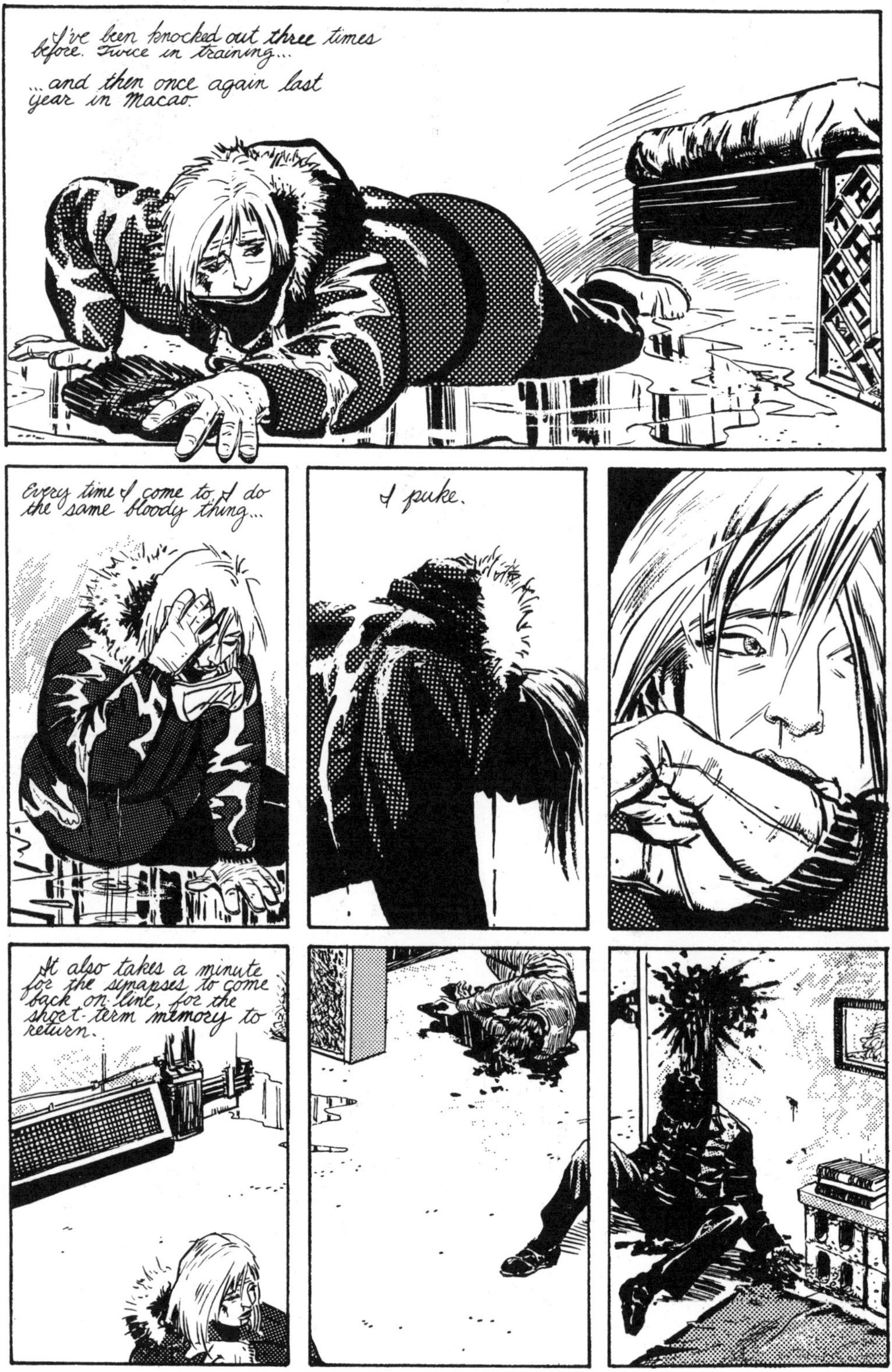
I've been knocked out three times before. Twice in training...
...and then once again last year in Macao.
Every time I come to, I do the same bloody thing...
I puke.
It also takes a minute for the synapses to come back on-line, for the short-term memory to return.

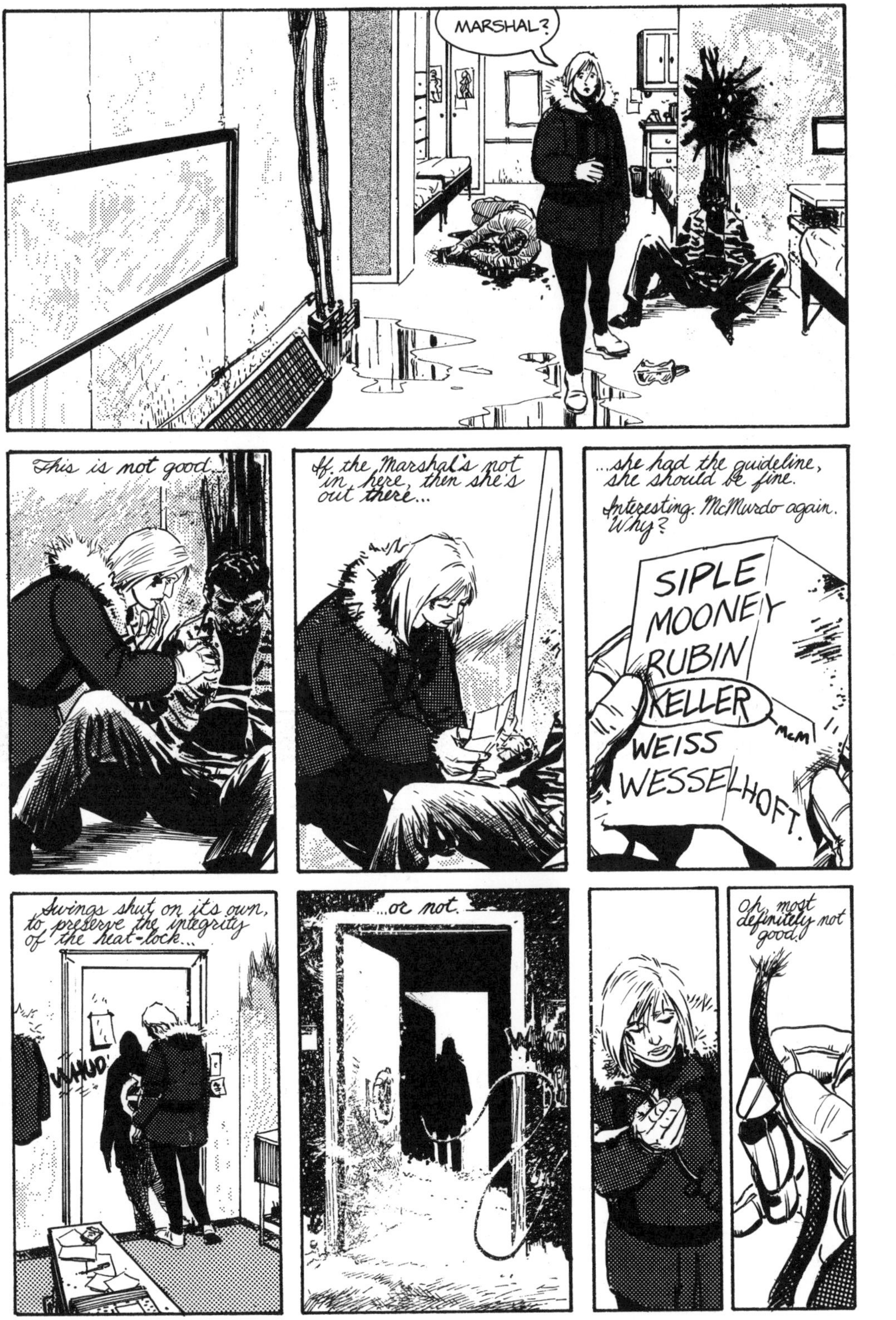

MARSHAL?
This is not good...
If the Marshal's not in here, then she's out there...
...she had the guideline, she should be fine.
Interesting. McMurdo again. Why?
SIPLE
MOONEY
RUBIN
KELLER
McM
WEISS
WESSELHOFT.
Swings shut on its own, to preserve the integrity of the heat-lock...
WHUD
...or not.
Oh, most definitely not good.

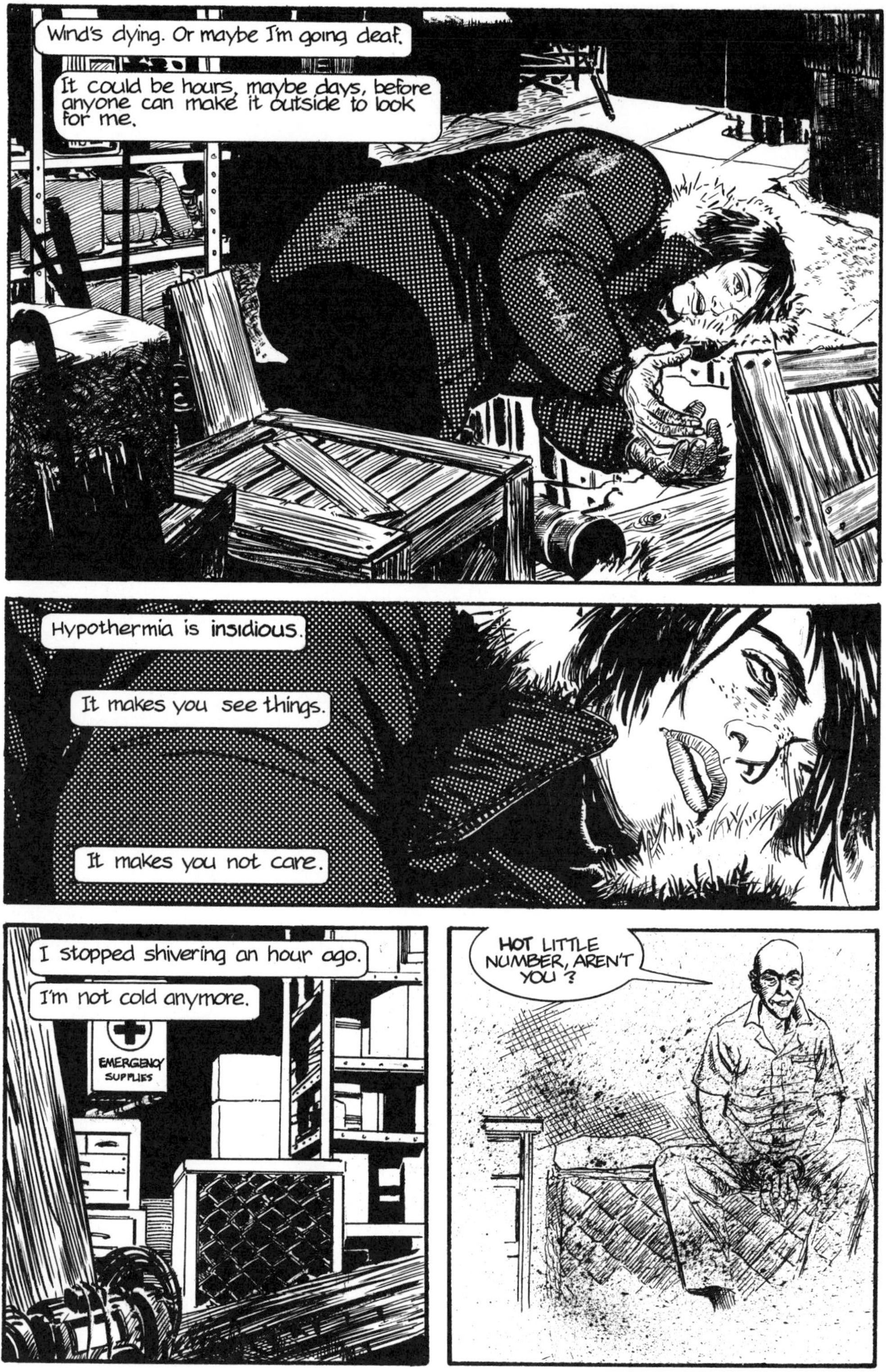
Wind's dying. Or maybe I'm going deaf.
It could be hours, maybe days, before anyone can make it outside to look for me.
Hypothermia is insidious.
It makes you see things.
It makes you not care.
I stopped shivering an hour ago.
I'm not cold anymore.
EMERGENCY SUPPLIES
HOT LITTLE NUMBER, AREN'T YOU ?

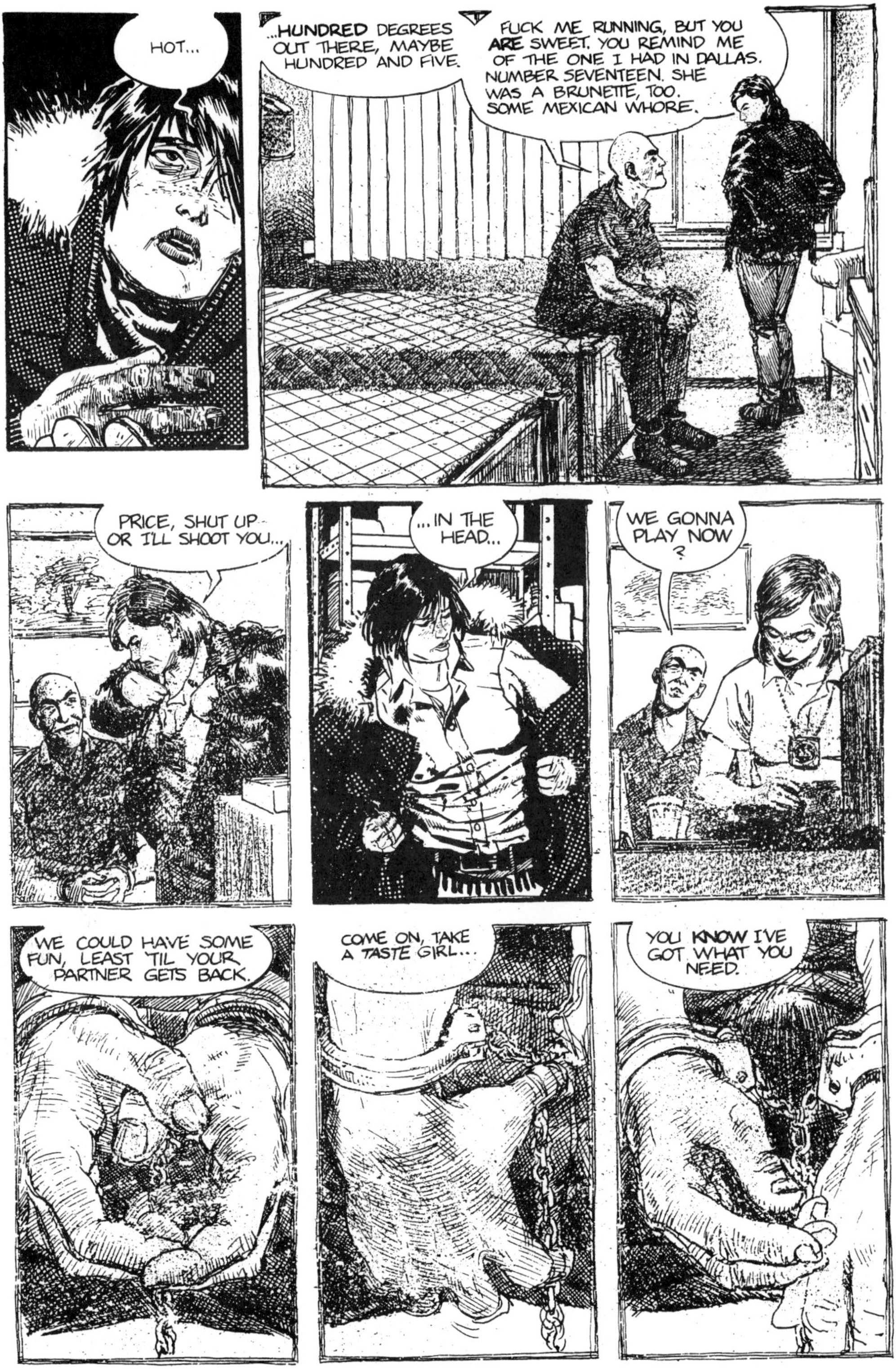
HOT...
...HUNDRED DEGREES OUT THERE, MAYBE HUNDRED AND FIVE.
FUCK ME RUNNING, BUT YOU ARE SWEET. YOU REMIND ME OF THE ONE I HAD IN DALLAS. NUMBER SEVENTEEN. SHE WAS A BRUNETTE, TOO. SOME MEXICAN WHORE.
PRICE, SHUT UP OR I'LL SHOOT YOU...
...IN THE HEAD...
WE GONNA PLAY NOW ?
WE COULD HAVE SOME FUN, LEAST 'TIL YOUR PARTNER GETS BACK.
COME ON, TAKE A TASTE GIRL...
YOU KNOW I'VE GOT WHAT YOU NEED.

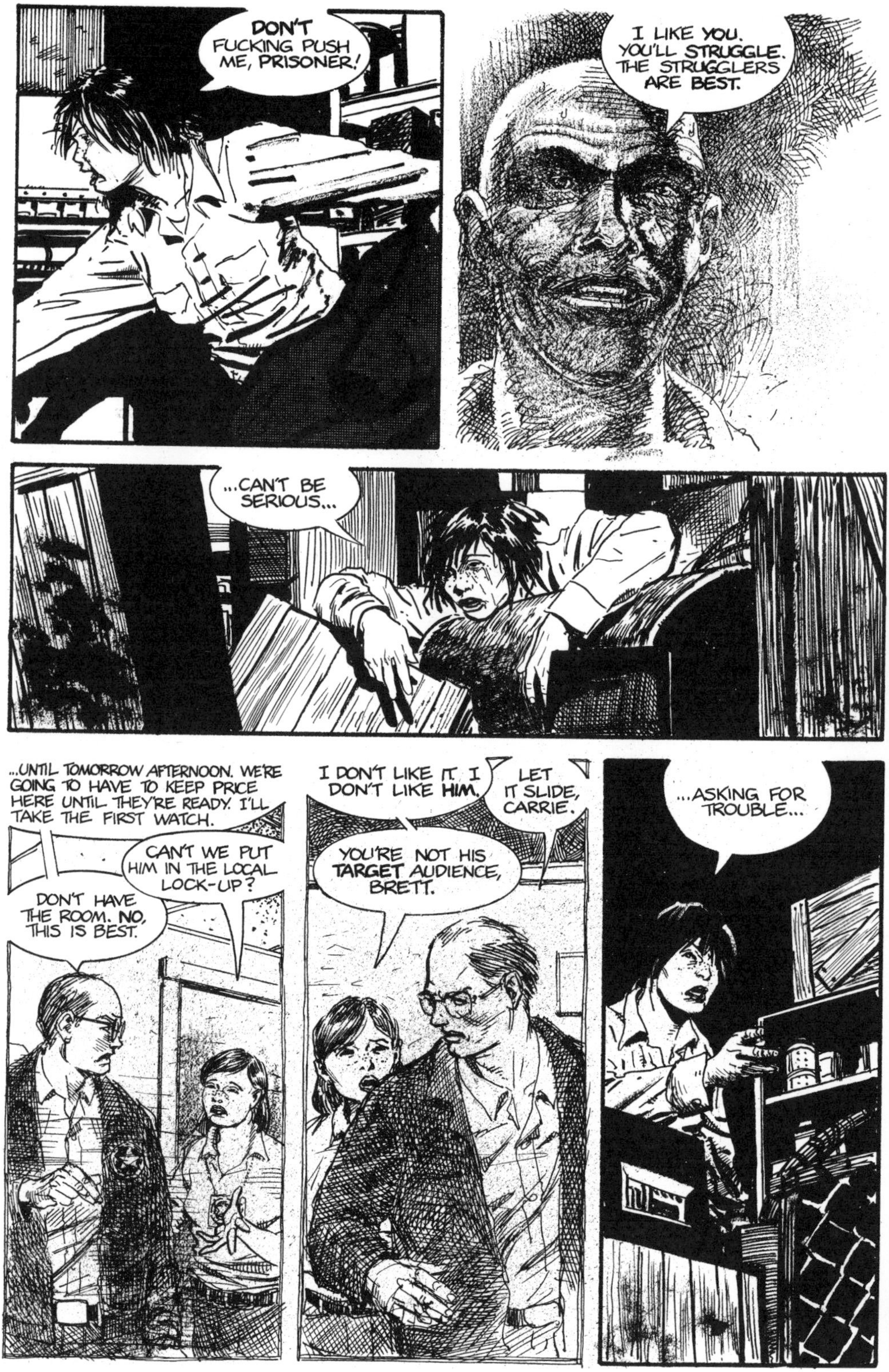

DON'T FUCKING PUSH ME, PRISONER!
I LIKE YOU. YOU'LL STRUGGLE. THE STRUGGLERS ARE BEST.
...CAN'T BE SERIOUS...
...UNTIL TOMORROW AFTERNOON. WE'RE GOING TO HAVE TO KEEP PRICE HERE UNTIL THEY'RE READY. I'LL TAKE THE FIRST WATCH.
CAN'T WE PUT HIM IN THE LOCAL LOCK-UP?
DON'T HAVE THE ROOM. NO, THIS IS BEST.
I DON'T LIKE IT. I DON'T LIKE HIM.
LET IT SLIDE, CARRIE.
YOU'RE NOT HIS TARGET AUDIENCE, BRETT.
...ASKING FOR TROUBLE...

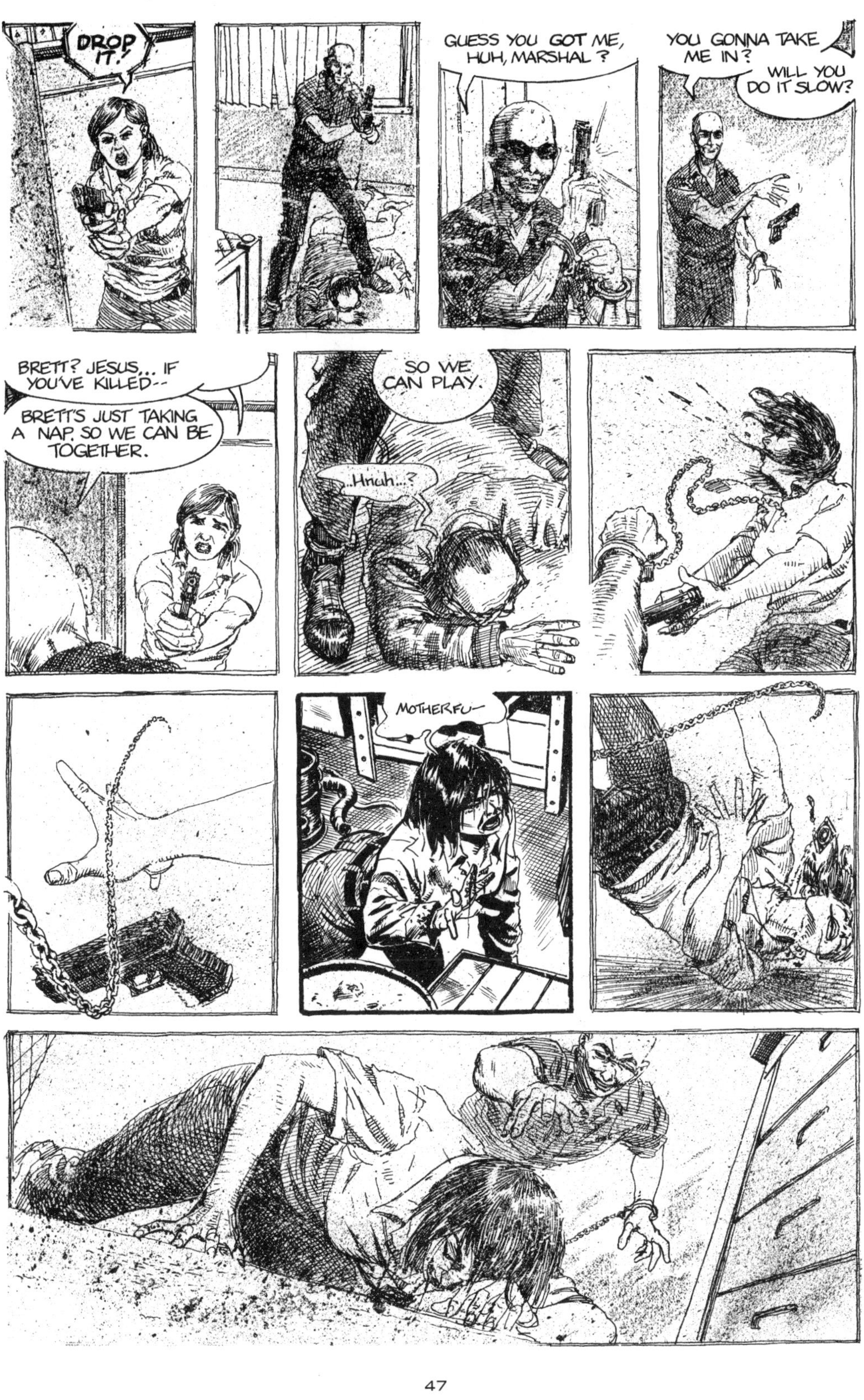
DROP IT.'
GUESS YOU GOT ME, HUH, MARSHAL ?
YOU GONNA TAKE ME IN?
WILL YOU DO IT SLOW?
BRETT? JESUS... IF YOU'VE KILLED--
BRETT'S JUST TAKING A NAP, SO WE CAN BE TOGETHER.
SO WE CAN PLAY.
..Hnuh...?
MOTHERFU—

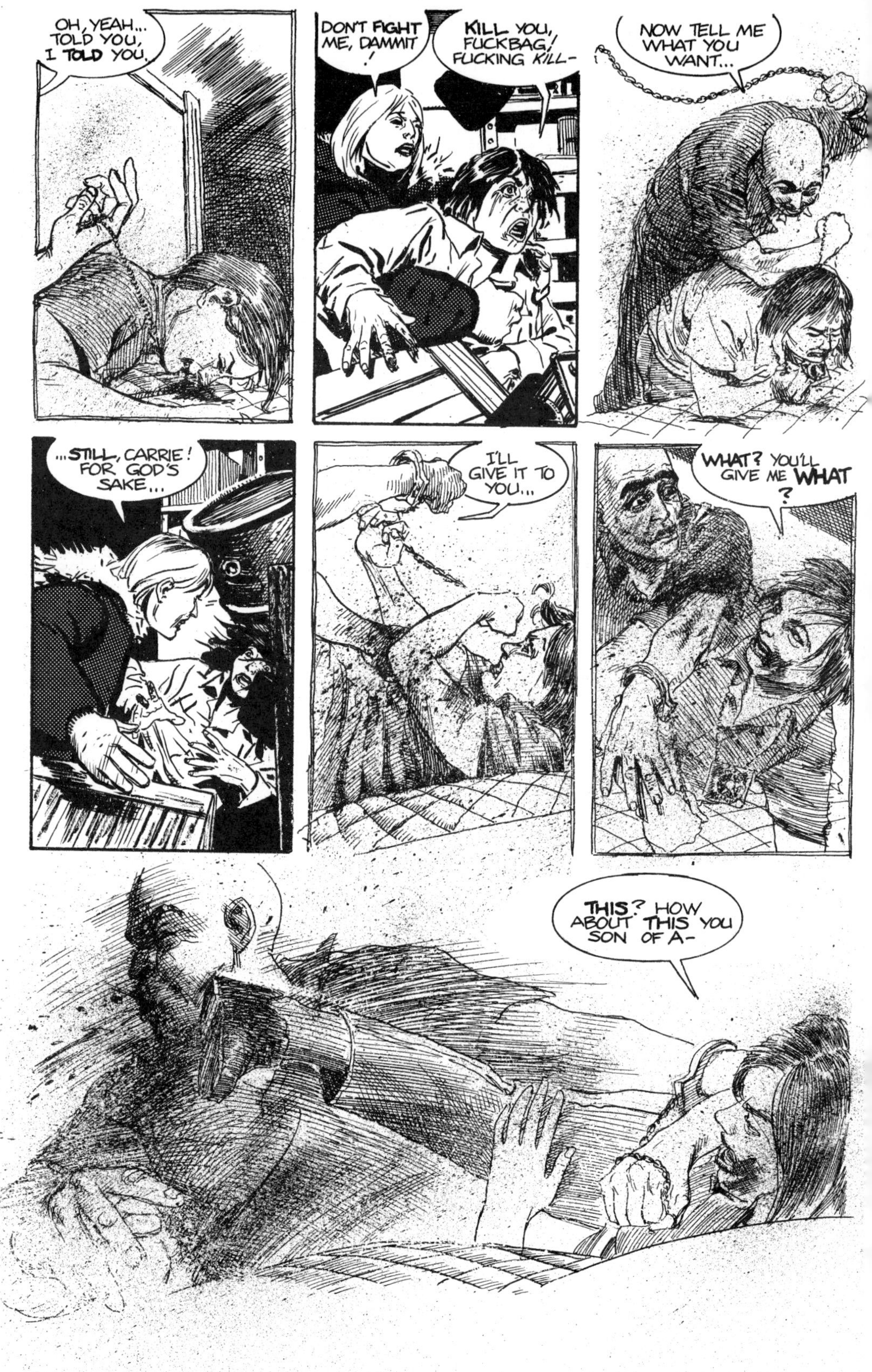

OH, YEAH... TOLD YOU, I TOLD YOU.
DON'T FIGHT ME, DAMMIT!
KILL YOU, FUCKBAG! FUCKING KILL-
NOW TELL ME WHAT YOU WANT...
...STILL, CARRIE! FOR GOD'S SAKE...
I'LL GIVE IT TO YOU...
WHAT? YOU'LL GIVE ME WHAT?
THIS? HOW ABOUT THIS YOU SON OF A-

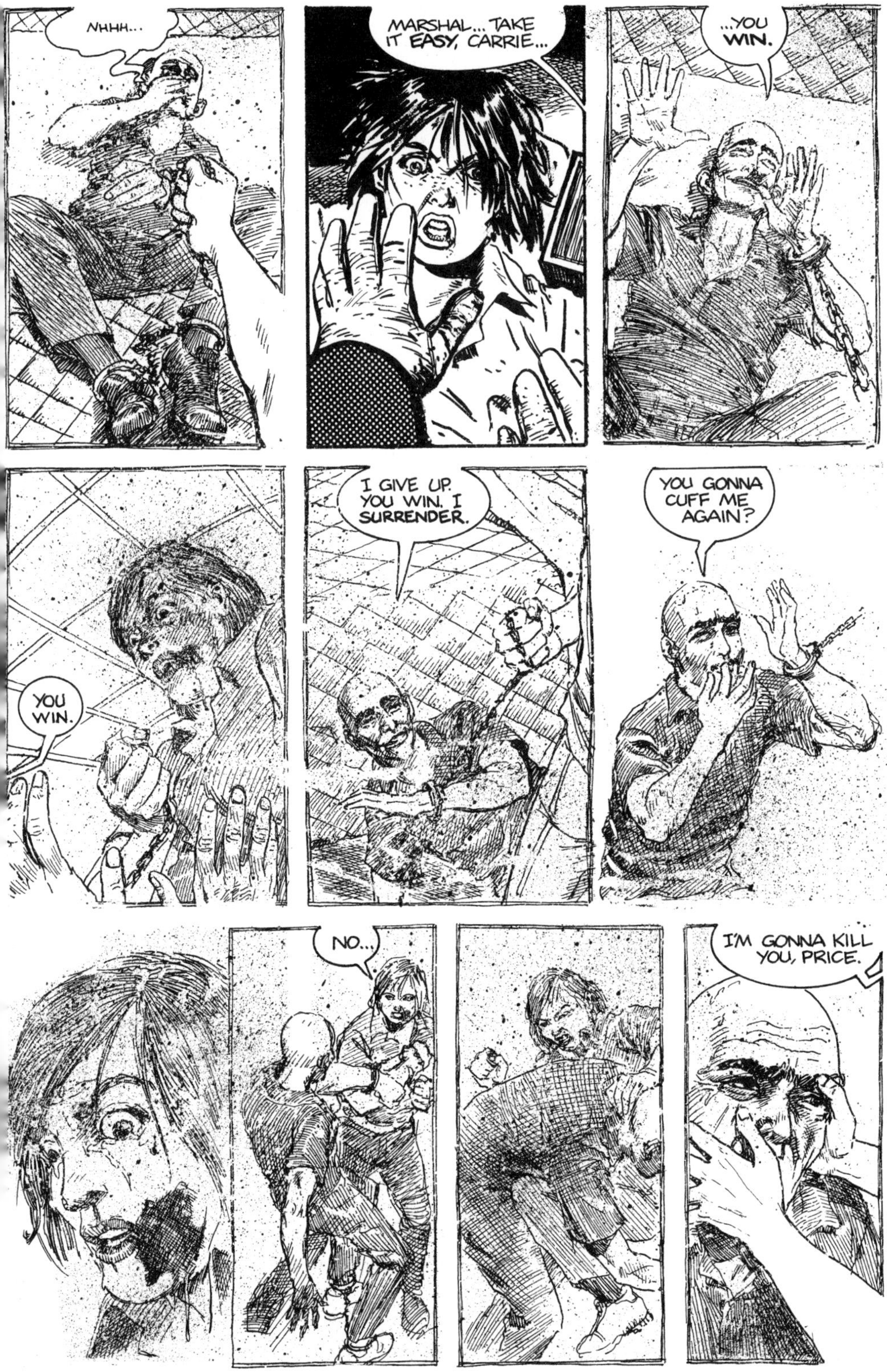
NHHH...
MARSHAL... TAKE IT EASY, CARRIE...
...YOU WIN.
YOU WIN.
I GIVE UP. YOU WIN. I SURRENDER.
YOU GONNA CUFF ME AGAIN?
NO...
I'M GONNA KILL YOU, PRICE.

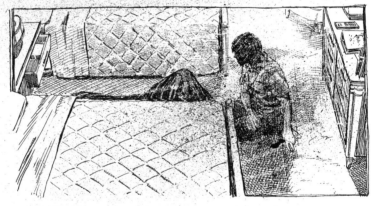

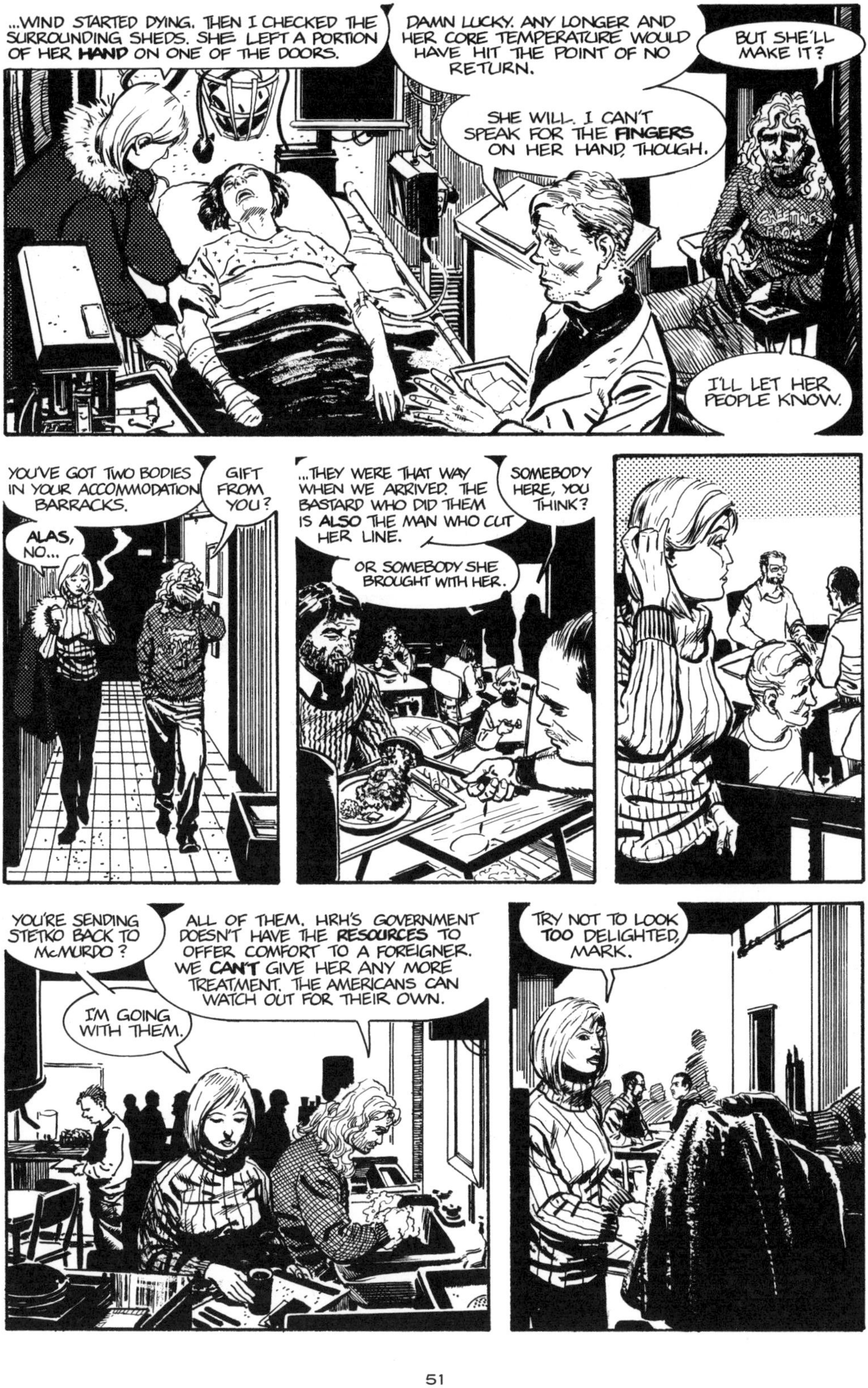
...WIND STARTED DYING. THEN I CHECKED THE SURROUNDING SHEDS. SHE LEFT A PORTION OF HER HAND ON ONE OF THE DOORS.
DAMN LUCKY. ANY LONGER AND HER CORE TEMPERATURE WOULD HAVE HIT THE POINT OF NO RETURN.
BUT SHE'LL MAKE IT?
SHE WILL. I CAN'T SPEAK FOR THE FINGERS ON HER HAND, THOUGH.
I'LL LET HER PEOPLE KNOW.
YOU'VE GOT TWO BODIES IN YOUR ACCOMMODATION BARRACKS.
GIFT FROM YOU?
ALAS, NO...
...THEY WERE THAT WAY WHEN WE ARRIVED. THE BASTARD WHO DID THEM IS ALSO THE MAN WHO CUT HER LINE.
SOMEBODY HERE, YOU THINK?
OR SOMEBODY SHE BROUGHT WITH HER.
YOU'RE SENDING STETKO BACK TO McMURDO?
ALL OF THEM. HRH'S GOVERNMENT DOESN'T HAVE THE RESOURCES TO OFFER COMFORT TO A FOREIGNER. WE CAN'T GIVE HER ANY MORE TREATMENT. THE AMERICANS CAN WATCH OUT FOR THEIR OWN.
I'M GOING WITH THEM.
TRY NOT TO LOOK TOO DELIGHTED, MARK.

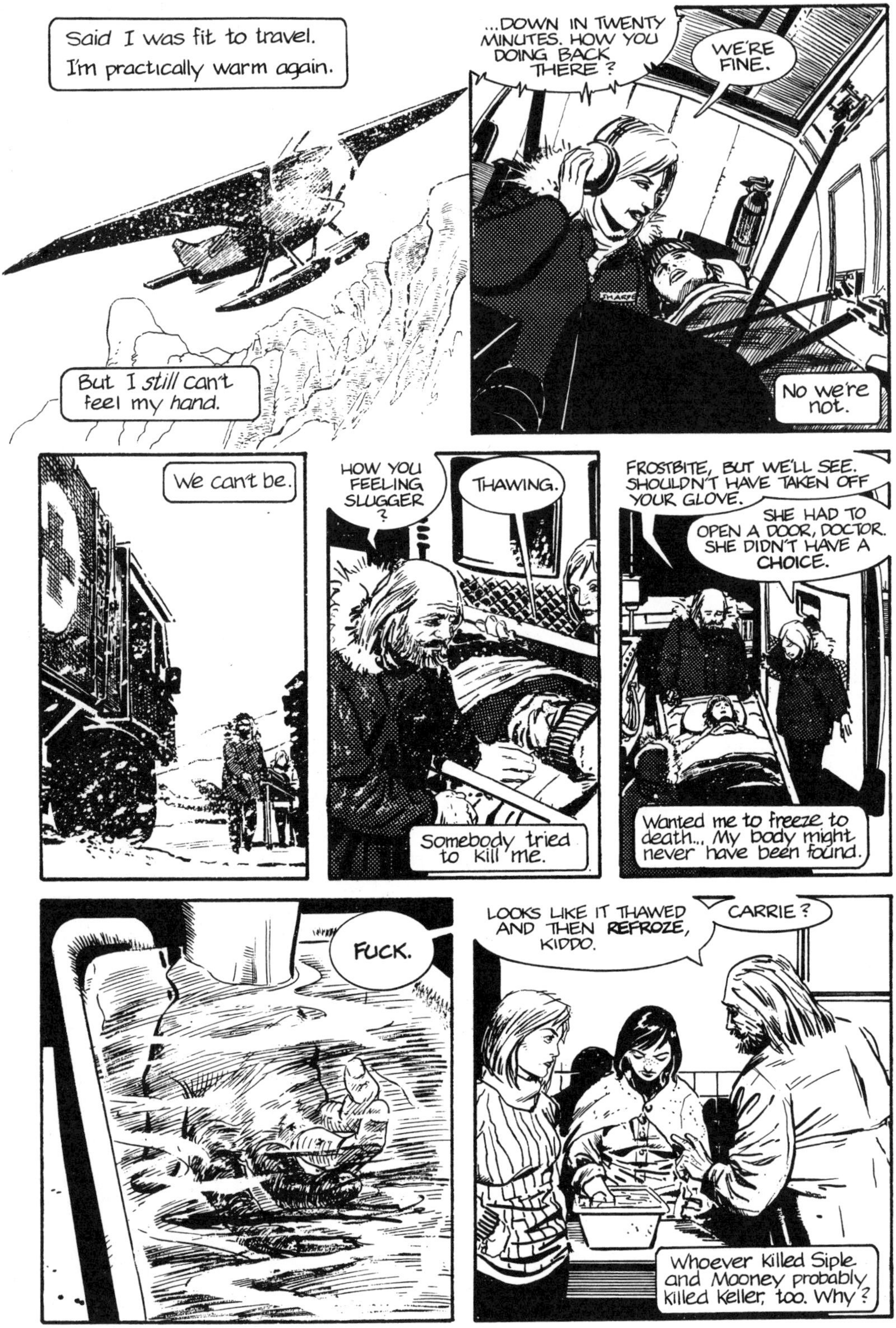

Said I was fit to travel. I'm practically warm again.
...DOWN IN TWENTY MINUTES. HOW YOU DOING BACK THERE ?
WE'RE FINE.
SHARPE
But I still can't feel my hand.
No we're not.
We can't be.
HOW YOU FEELING SLUGGER ?
THAWING.
Somebody tried to kill me.
FROSTBITE, BUT WE'LL SEE. SHOULDN'T HAVE TAKEN OFF YOUR GLOVE.
SHE HAD TO OPEN A DOOR, DOCTOR. SHE DIDN'T HAVE A CHOICE.
Wanted me to freeze to death... My body might never have been found.
FUCK.
LOOKS LIKE IT THAWED AND THEN REFROZE, KIDDO.
CARRIE ?
Whoever killed Siple and Mooney probably killed Keller, too. Why ?

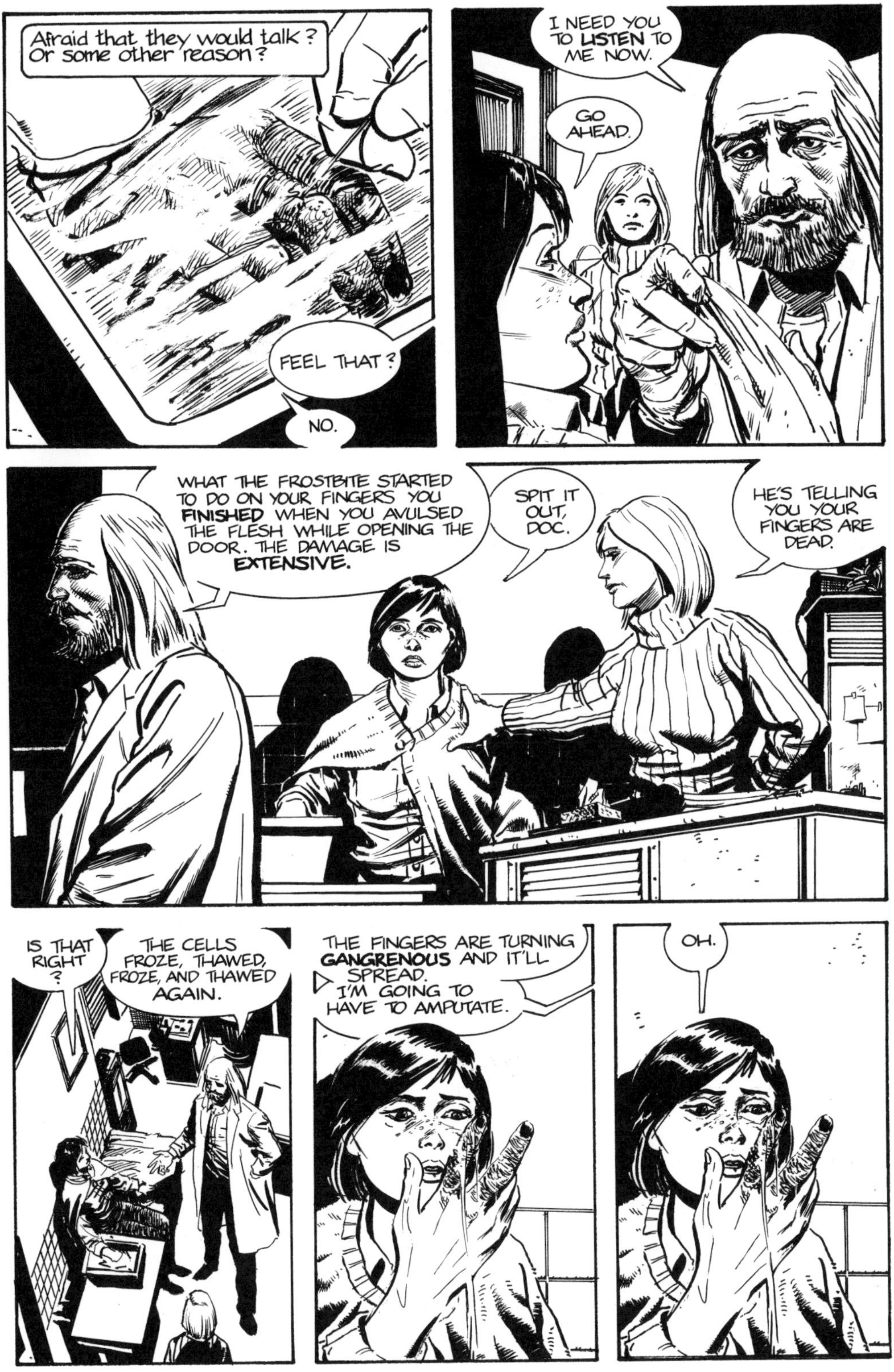
Afraid that they would talk? Or some other reason?
FEEL THAT?
NO.
I NEED YOU TO LISTEN TO ME NOW.
GO AHEAD.
WHAT THE FROSTBITE STARTED TO DO ON YOUR FINGERS YOU FINISHED WHEN YOU AVULSED THE FLESH WHILE OPENING THE DOOR. THE DAMAGE IS EXTENSIVE.
SPIT IT OUT, DOC.
HE'S TELLING YOU YOUR FINGERS ARE DEAD.
IS THAT RIGHT?
THE CELLS FROZE, THAWED, FROZE, AND THAWED AGAIN.
THE FINGERS ARE TURNING GANGRENOUS AND IT'LL SPREAD.
I'M GOING TO HAVE TO AMPUTATE.
OH.

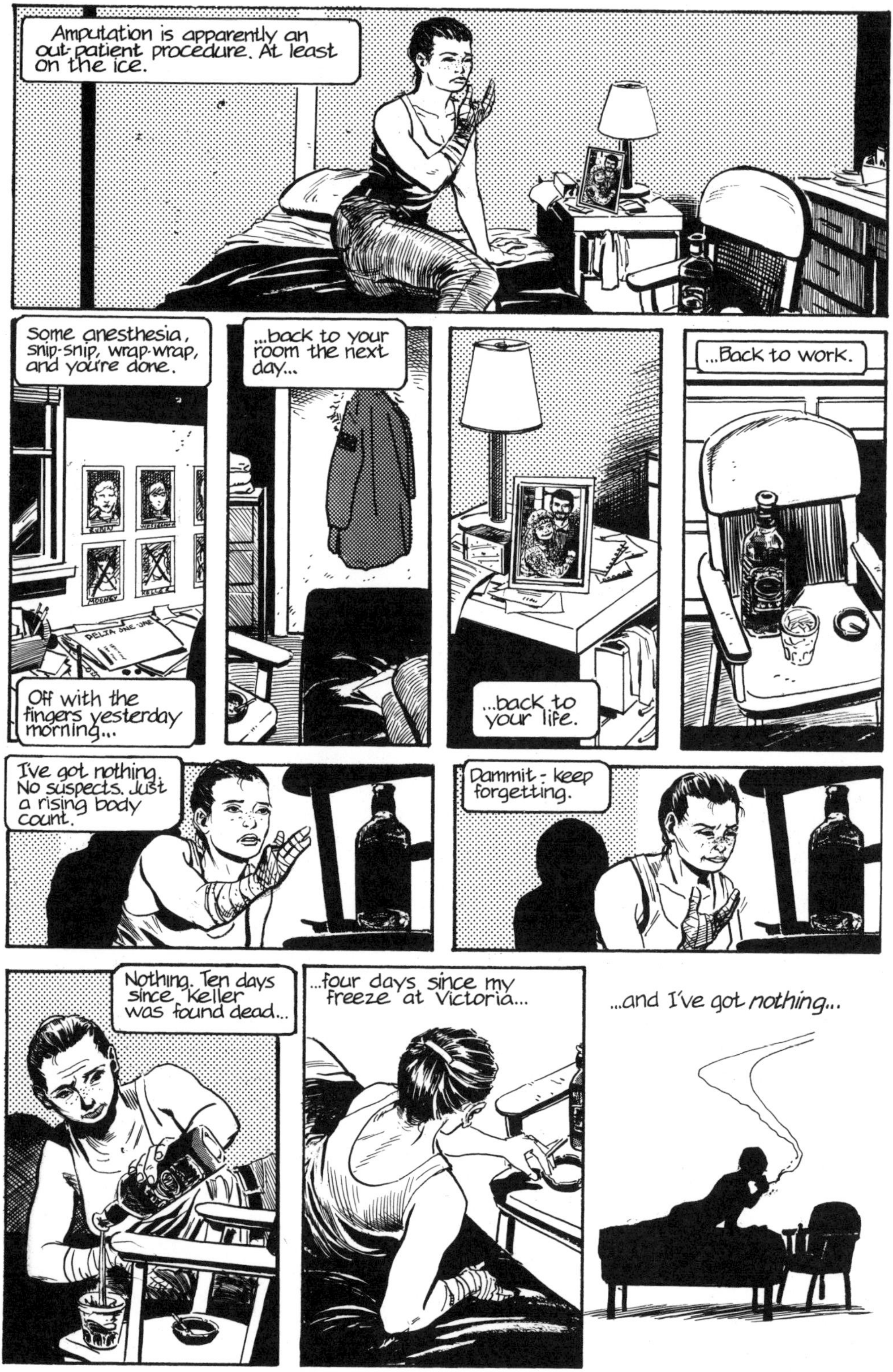
Amputation is apparently an out-patient procedure. At least on the ice.
Some anesthesia, snip-snip, wrap-wrap, and you're done.
Off with the fingers yesterday morning...
...back to your room the next day...
...back to your life.
...Back to work.
I've got nothing. No suspects. Just a rising body count.
Dammit - keep forgetting.
Nothing. Ten days since Keller was found dead...
...four days since my freeze at Victoria...
...and I've got *nothing*...

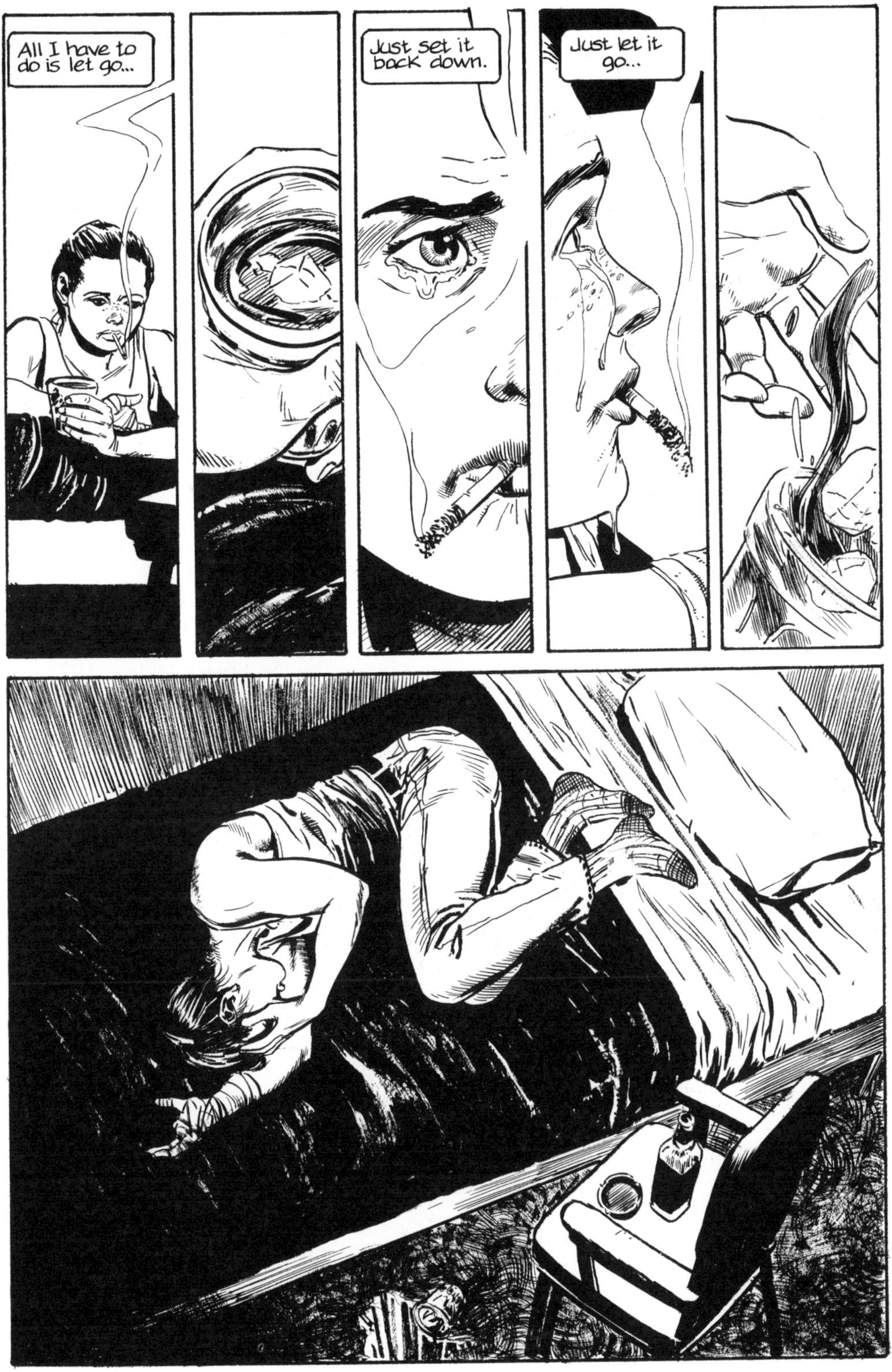

All I have to do is let go...
Just set it back down.
Just let it go...

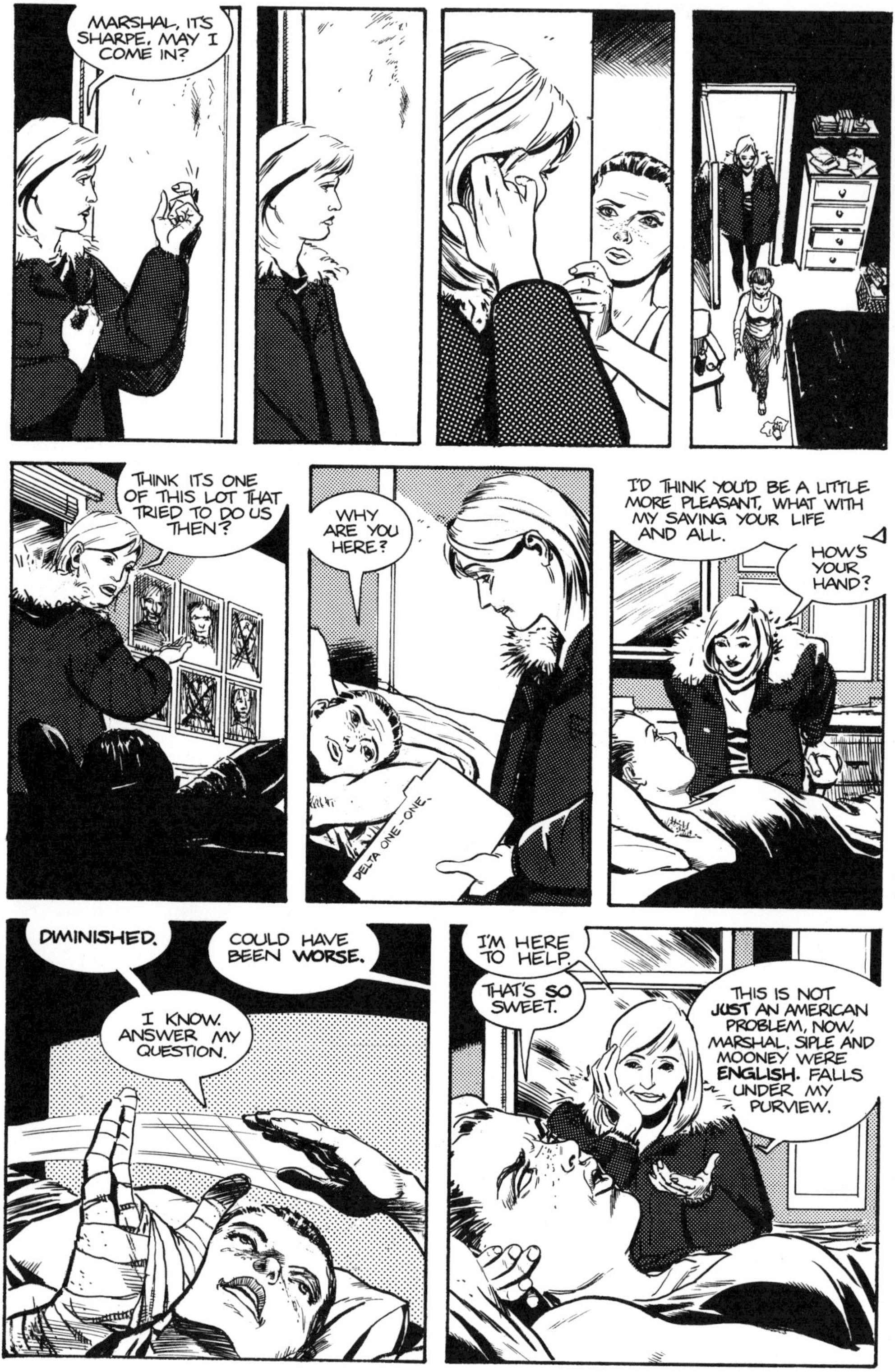
MARSHAL, IT'S SHARPE, MAY I COME IN?
THINK ITS ONE OF THIS LOT THAT TRIED TO DO US THEN?
WHY ARE YOU HERE?
DELTA ONE-ONE
I'D THINK YOU'D BE A LITTLE MORE PLEASANT, WHAT WITH MY SAVING YOUR LIFE AND ALL.
HOW'S YOUR HAND?
DIMINISHED.
COULD HAVE BEEN WORSE.
I KNOW. ANSWER MY QUESTION.
I'M HERE TO HELP.
THAT'S SO SWEET.
THIS IS NOT JUST AN AMERICAN PROBLEM, NOW, MARSHAL. SIPLE AND MOONEY WERE ENGLISH. FALLS UNDER MY PURVIEW.

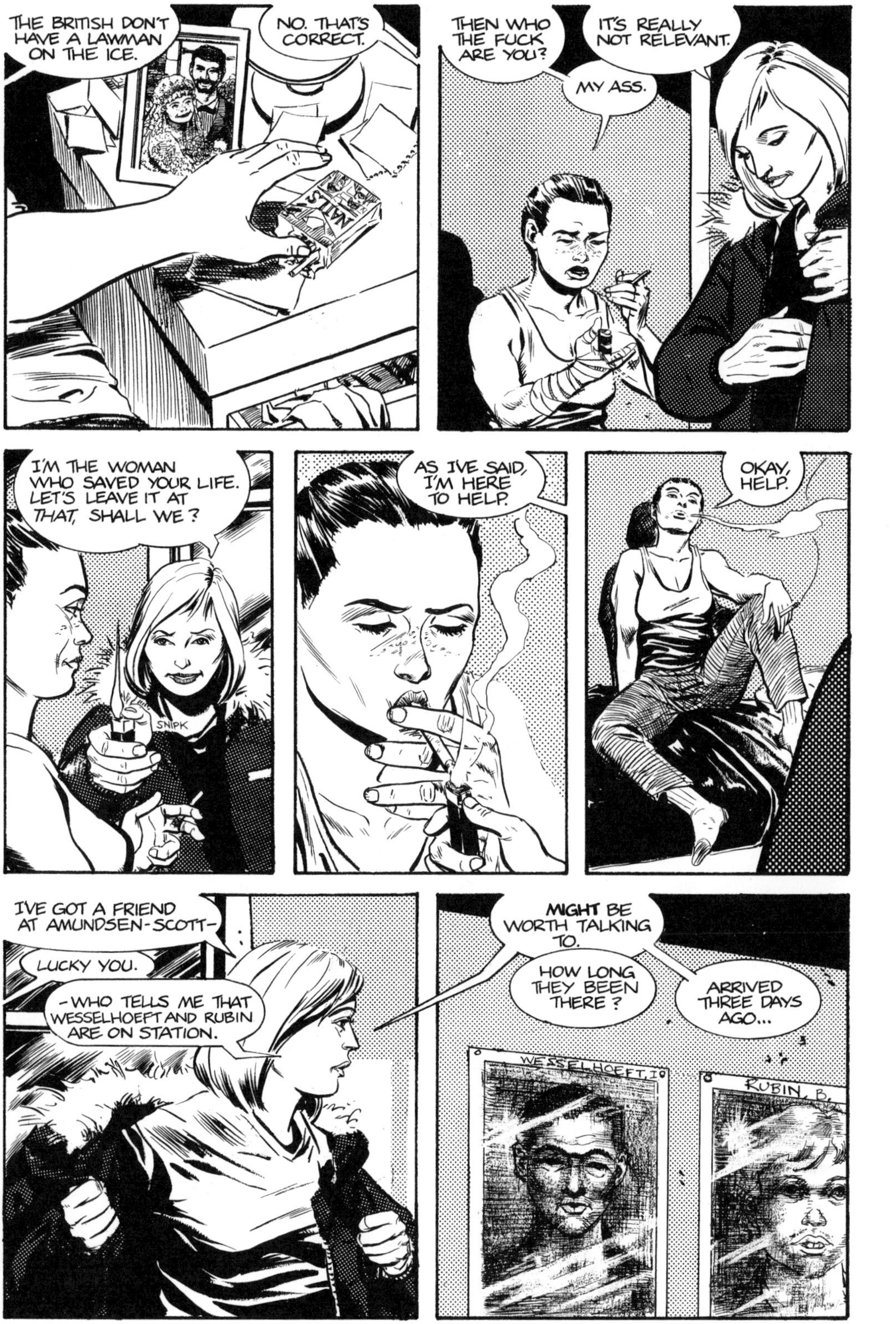

THE BRITISH DON'T HAVE A LAWMAN ON THE ICE.
NO. THAT'S CORRECT.
THEN WHO THE FUCK ARE YOU?
IT'S REALLY NOT RELEVANT.
MY ASS.
I'M THE WOMAN WHO SAVED YOUR LIFE. LET'S LEAVE IT AT *THAT*, SHALL WE ?
SNIPK
AS I'VE SAID, I'M HERE TO HELP.
OKAY, HELP.
I'VE GOT A FRIEND AT AMUNDSEN-SCOTT-
LUCKY YOU.
-WHO TELLS ME THAT WESSELHOEFT AND RUBIN ARE ON STATION.
MIGHT BE WORTH TALKING TO.
HOW LONG THEY BEEN THERE ?
ARRIVED THREE DAYS AGO...
WESSELHOEFT, I.
RUBIN, B.

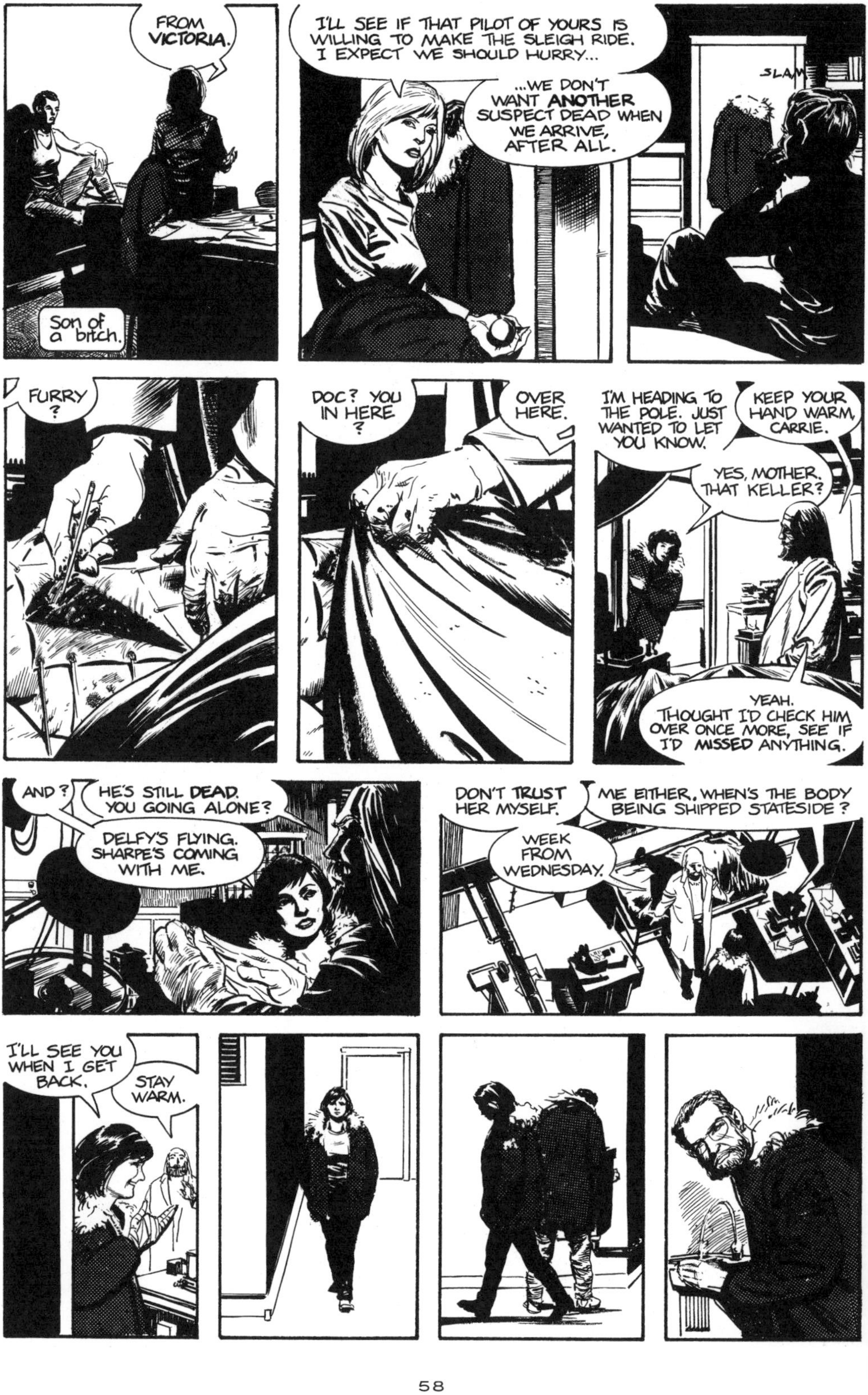
FROM VICTORIA.
Son of a bitch.
I'LL SEE IF THAT PILOT OF YOURS IS WILLING TO MAKE THE SLEIGH RIDE. I EXPECT WE SHOULD HURRY...
...WE DON'T WANT ANOTHER SUSPECT DEAD WHEN WE ARRIVE, AFTER ALL.
SLAM
FURRY?
DOC? YOU IN HERE?
OVER HERE.
I'M HEADING TO THE POLE. JUST WANTED TO LET YOU KNOW.
KEEP YOUR HAND WARM, CARRIE.
YES, MOTHER. THAT KELLER?
YEAH. THOUGHT I'D CHECK HIM OVER ONCE MORE, SEE IF I'D MISSED ANYTHING.
AND?
HE'S STILL DEAD. YOU GOING ALONE?
DELFY'S FLYING. SHARPE'S COMING WITH ME.
DON'T TRUST HER MYSELF.
ME EITHER. WHEN'S THE BODY BEING SHIPPED STATESIDE?
WEEK FROM WEDNESDAY.
I'LL SEE YOU WHEN I GET BACK.
STAY WARM.

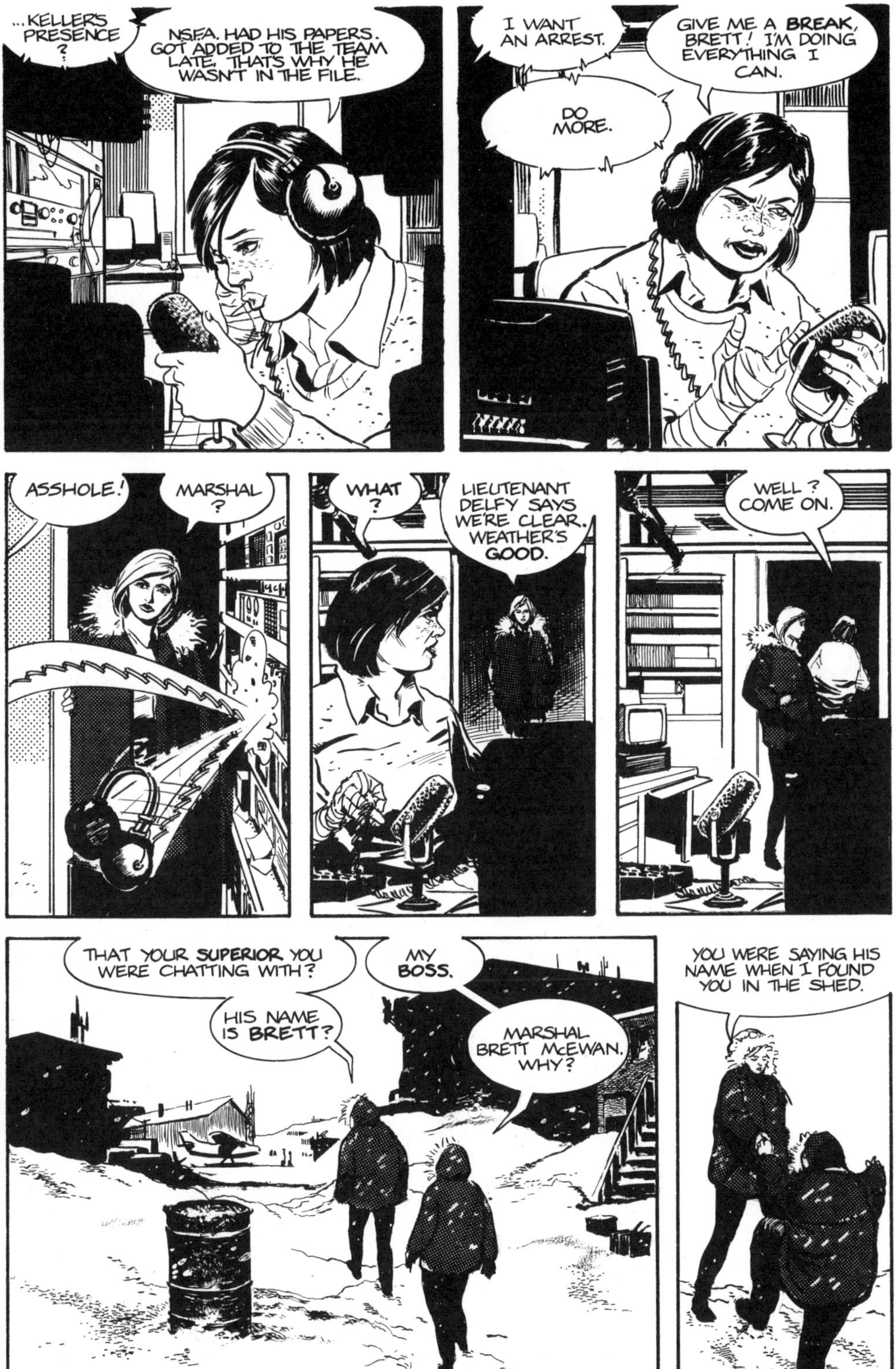
...KELLER'S PRESENCE ?
N.S.F.A. HAD HIS PAPERS. GOT ADDED TO THE TEAM LATE, THAT'S WHY HE WASN'T IN THE FILE.
I WANT AN ARREST.
DO MORE.
GIVE ME A BREAK, BRETT! I'M DOING EVERYTHING I CAN.
ASSHOLE!
MARSHAL ?
WHAT ?
LIEUTENANT DELFY SAYS WE'RE CLEAR. WEATHER'S GOOD.
WELL ? COME ON.
THAT YOUR SUPERIOR YOU WERE CHATTING WITH?
MY BOSS.
HIS NAME IS BRETT?
MARSHAL BRETT McEWAN. WHY?
YOU WERE SAYING HIS NAME WHEN I FOUND YOU IN THE SHED.

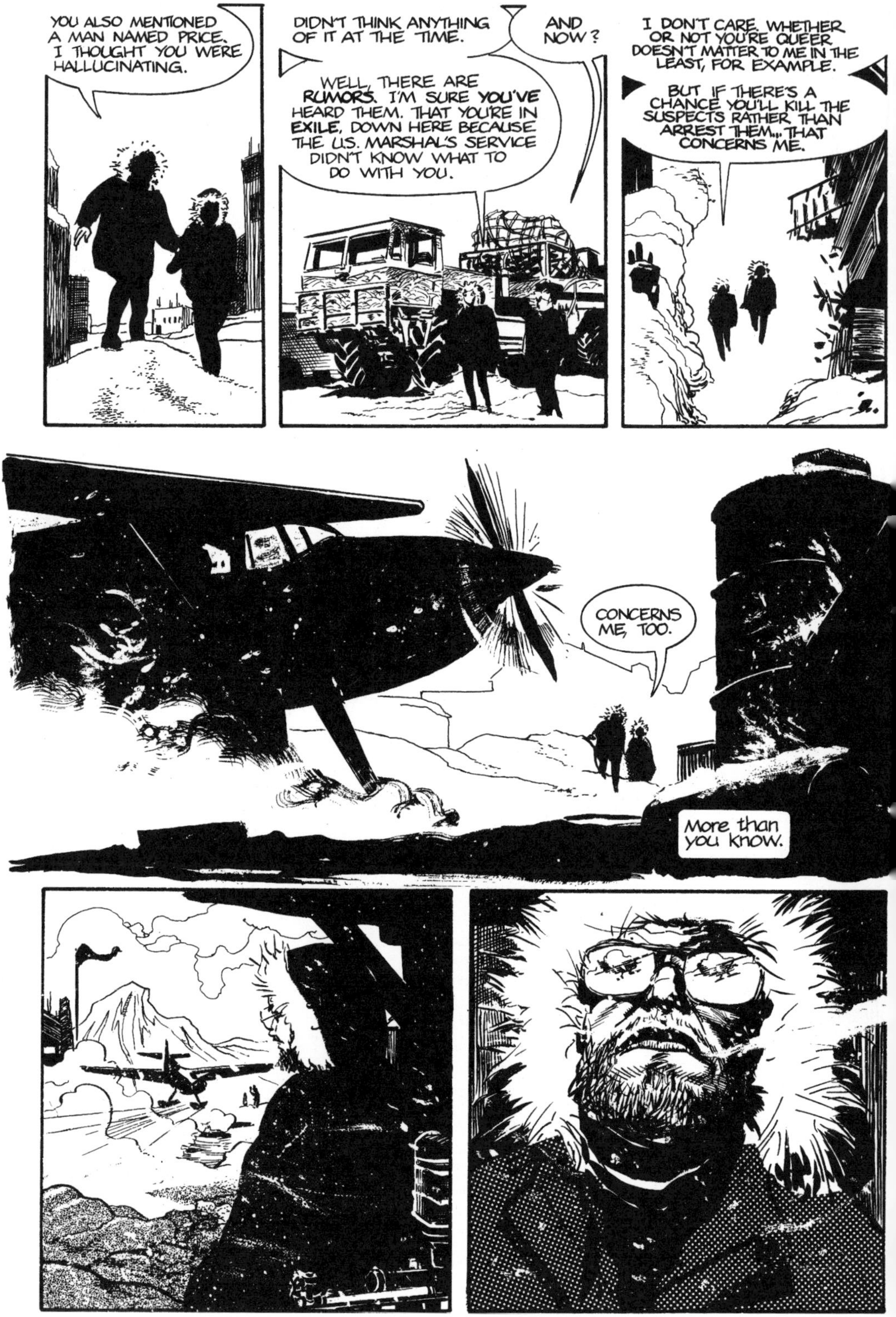
YOU ALSO MENTIONED A MAN NAMED PRICE. I THOUGHT YOU WERE HALLUCINATING.
DIDN'T THINK ANYTHING OF IT AT THE TIME.
AND NOW?
WELL, THERE ARE RUMORS. I'M SURE YOU'VE HEARD THEM. THAT YOU'RE IN EXILE, DOWN HERE BECAUSE THE U.S. MARSHAL'S SERVICE DIDN'T KNOW WHAT TO DO WITH YOU.
I DON'T CARE. WHETHER OR NOT YOU'RE QUEER DOESN'T MATTER TO ME IN THE LEAST, FOR EXAMPLE.
BUT IF THERE'S A CHANCE YOU'LL KILL THE SUSPECTS RATHER THAN ARREST THEM... THAT CONCERNS ME.
CONCERNS ME, TOO.
More than you know.

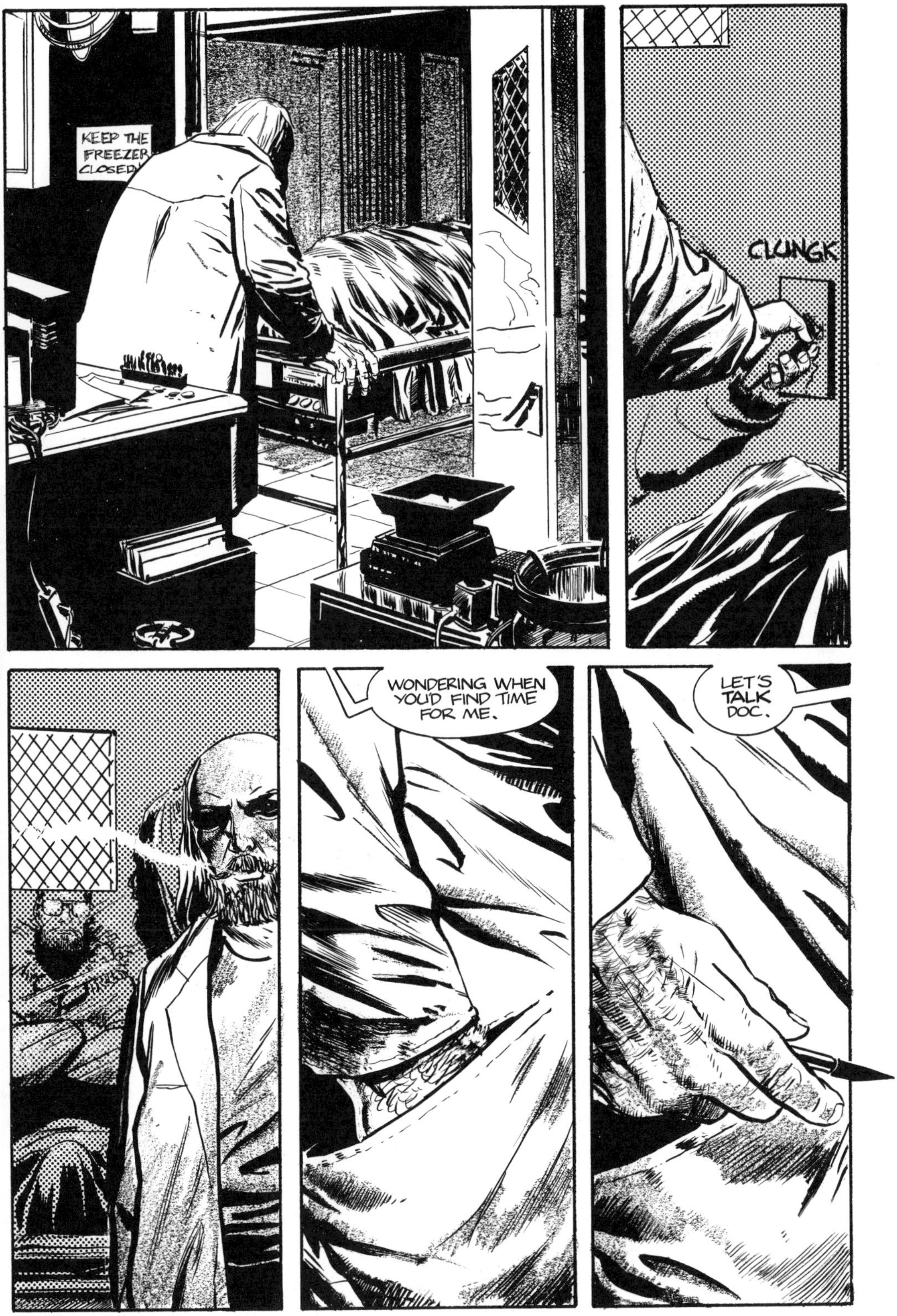
KEEP THE FREEZER CLOSED
CLUNGK
WONDERING WHEN YOU'D FIND TIME FOR ME.
LET'S TALK DOC.

Welcome to 90° South. From here you can walk around the world in under a minute.

That's not the real Pole, of course. That's the "Ceremonial Pole" used for publicity shots to be shown to taxpayers back in the world.

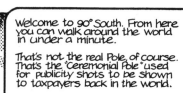

The "real" pole is simply a stick.

I prefer the stick.

Twilight here, at least for another couple weeks. Then it goes **dark**, and the sun won't shine for another three months.

Temperature's about minus 40° F, and that's only **one** of the polar worries.

See, at the Pole, you're at 9,300 feet above sea level. But because of the atmosphere's thinness and the cold, it feels like 10,500 feet.

So, you have the added bonus of altitude sickness.

I'LL MEET YOU IN THE MESS HALL, MARSHAL. I WANT TO TALK TO MY CONTACT FIRST.

I'LL COME WITH YOU.

AMUNDSEN-SCOTT

NO.

SO, WHO IS SHE?

NOT A SCIENTIST?

SHE'S A SPOOK.

NOPE. MAYBE MILITARY INTELLIGENCE.

REMINDS ME OF YOU, KIND OF.

YOU'RE BOTH BITCHY.

YOU CAN'T TELL, BUT I'M GIVING YOU THE FINGER.

GETTING A REFILL. WANT ONE?

SURE.

ALEXANDER KELLER
UNIVERSITY of CHICAGO
Dept. of Geology, Geophysical Sci.

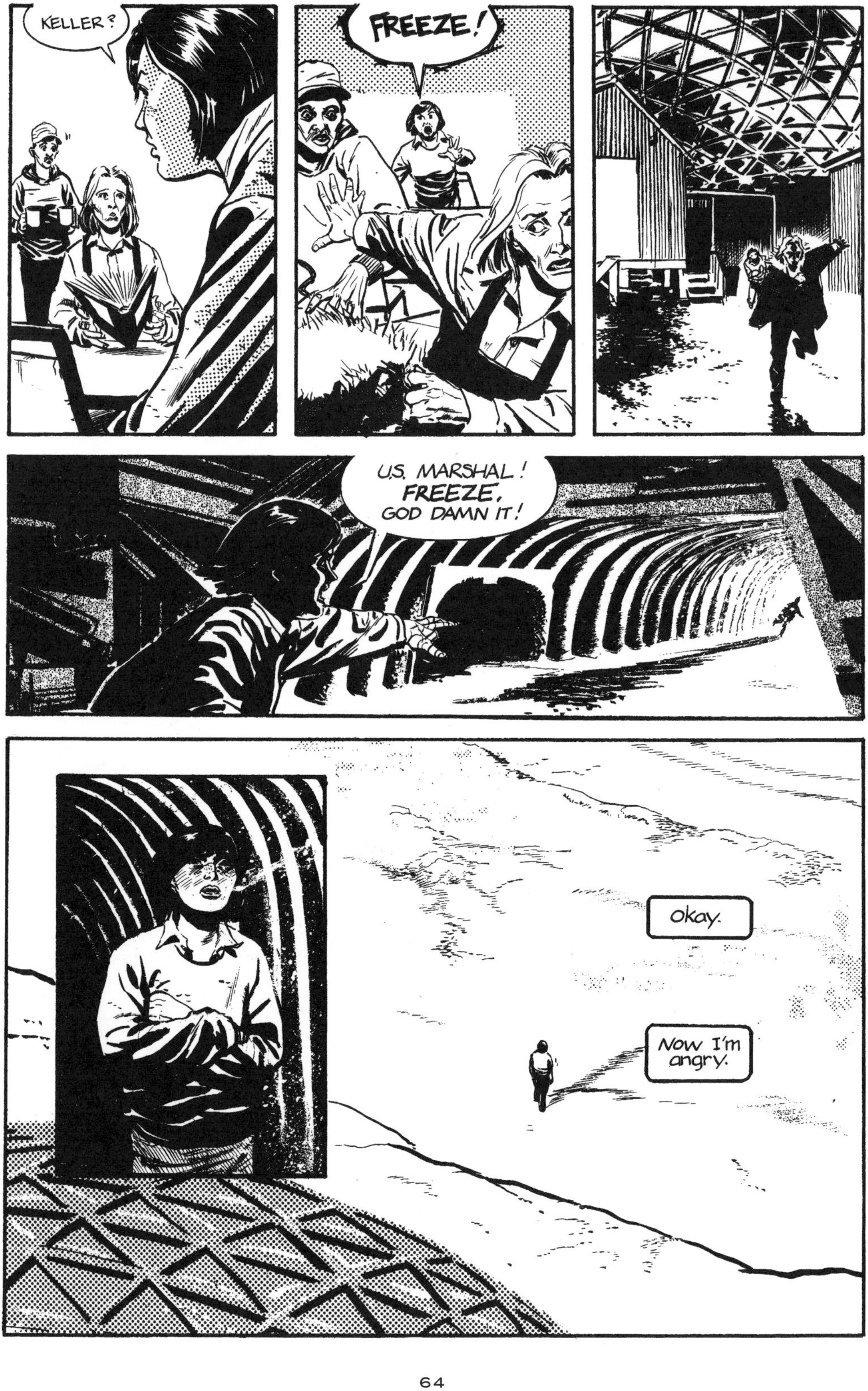
KELLER?
FREEZE!
U.S. MARSHAL! FREEZE, GOD DAMN IT!
Okay.
Now I'm angry.

CHAPTER THREE

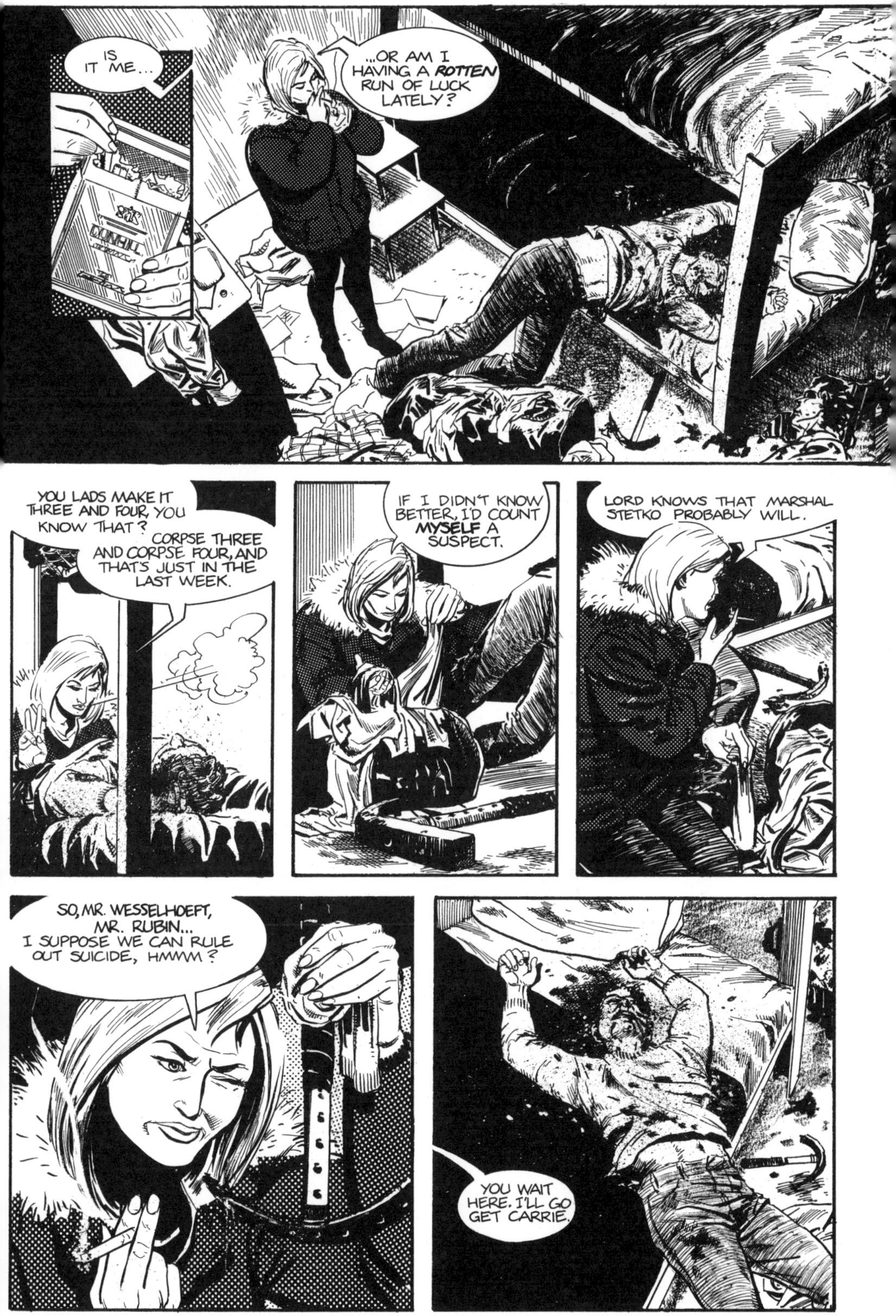

IS IT ME...
DUNHILL
...OR AM I HAVING A ROTTEN RUN OF LUCK LATELY?
YOU LADS MAKE IT THREE AND FOUR, YOU KNOW THAT?
CORPSE THREE AND CORPSE FOUR, AND THAT'S JUST IN THE LAST WEEK.
IF I DIDN'T KNOW BETTER, I'D COUNT MYSELF A SUSPECT.
LORD KNOWS THAT MARSHAL STETKO PROBABLY WILL.
SO, MR. WESSELHOEFT, MR. RUBIN... I SUPPOSE WE CAN RULE OUT SUICIDE, HMMM?
YOU WAIT HERE. I'LL GO GET CARRIE.

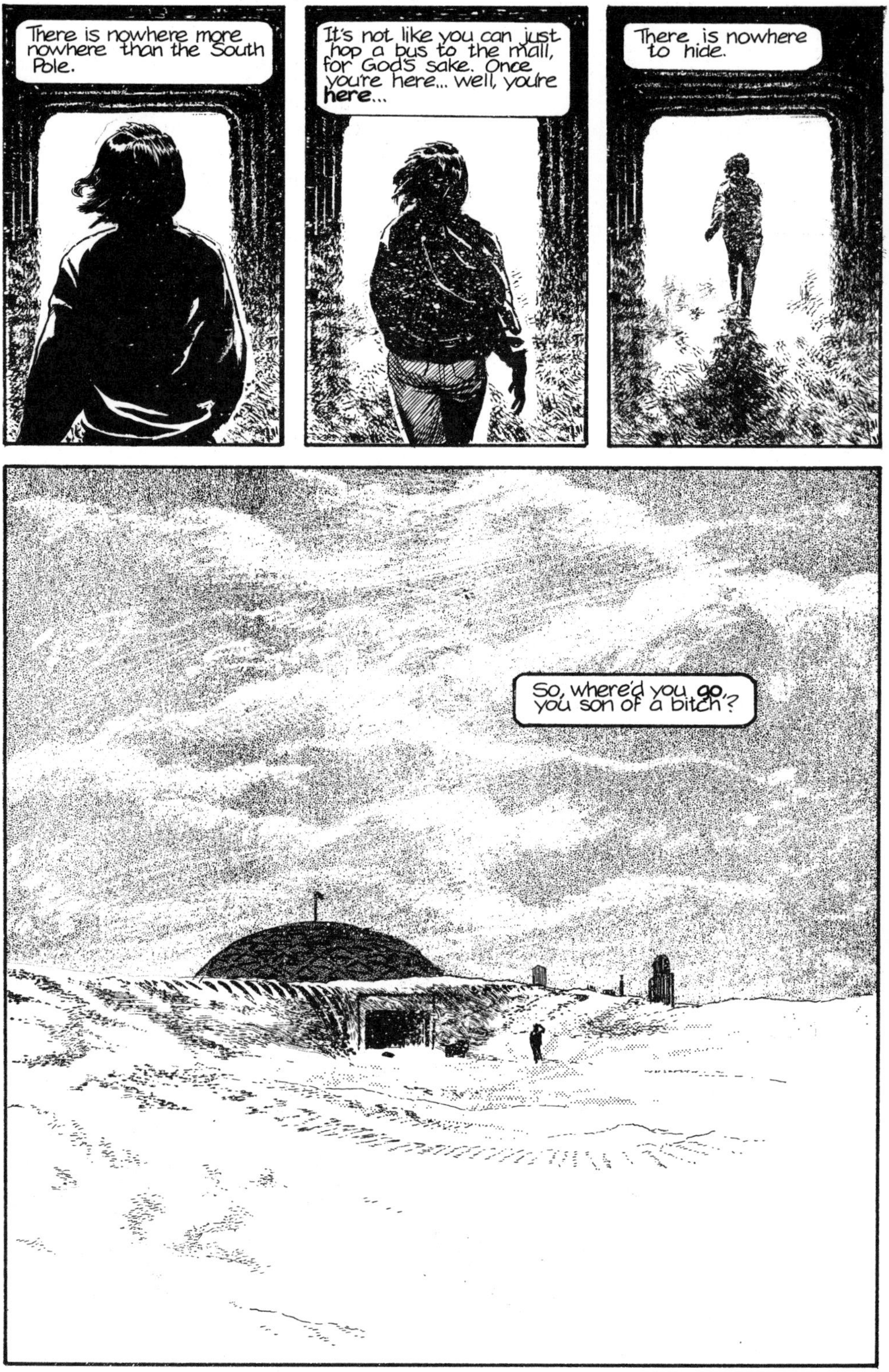
There is nowhere more nowhere than the South Pole.
It's not like you can just hop a bus to the mall, for God's sake. Once you're here... well, you're **here**...
There is nowhere to hide.
So, where'd you **go**, you son of a bitch?

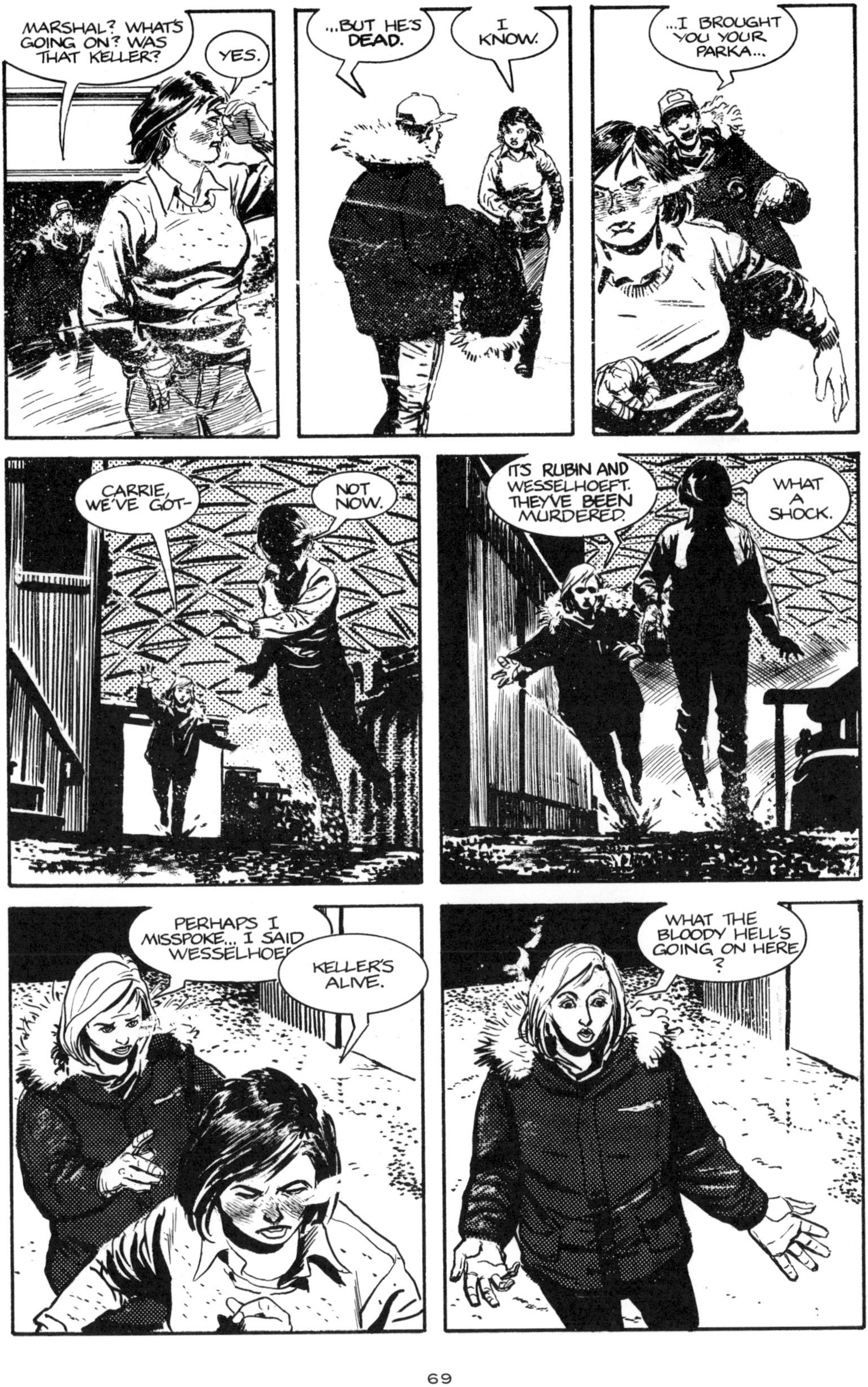
MARSHAL? WHAT'S GOING ON? WAS THAT KELLER?
YES.
...BUT HE'S DEAD.
I KNOW.
...I BROUGHT YOU YOUR PARKA...
CARRIE, WE'VE GOT-
NOT NOW.
IT'S RUBIN AND WESSELHOEFT. THEY'VE BEEN MURDERED.
WHAT A SHOCK.
PERHAPS I MISSPOKE... I SAID WESSELHOE
KELLER'S ALIVE.
WHAT THE BLOODY HELL'S GOING ON HERE ?

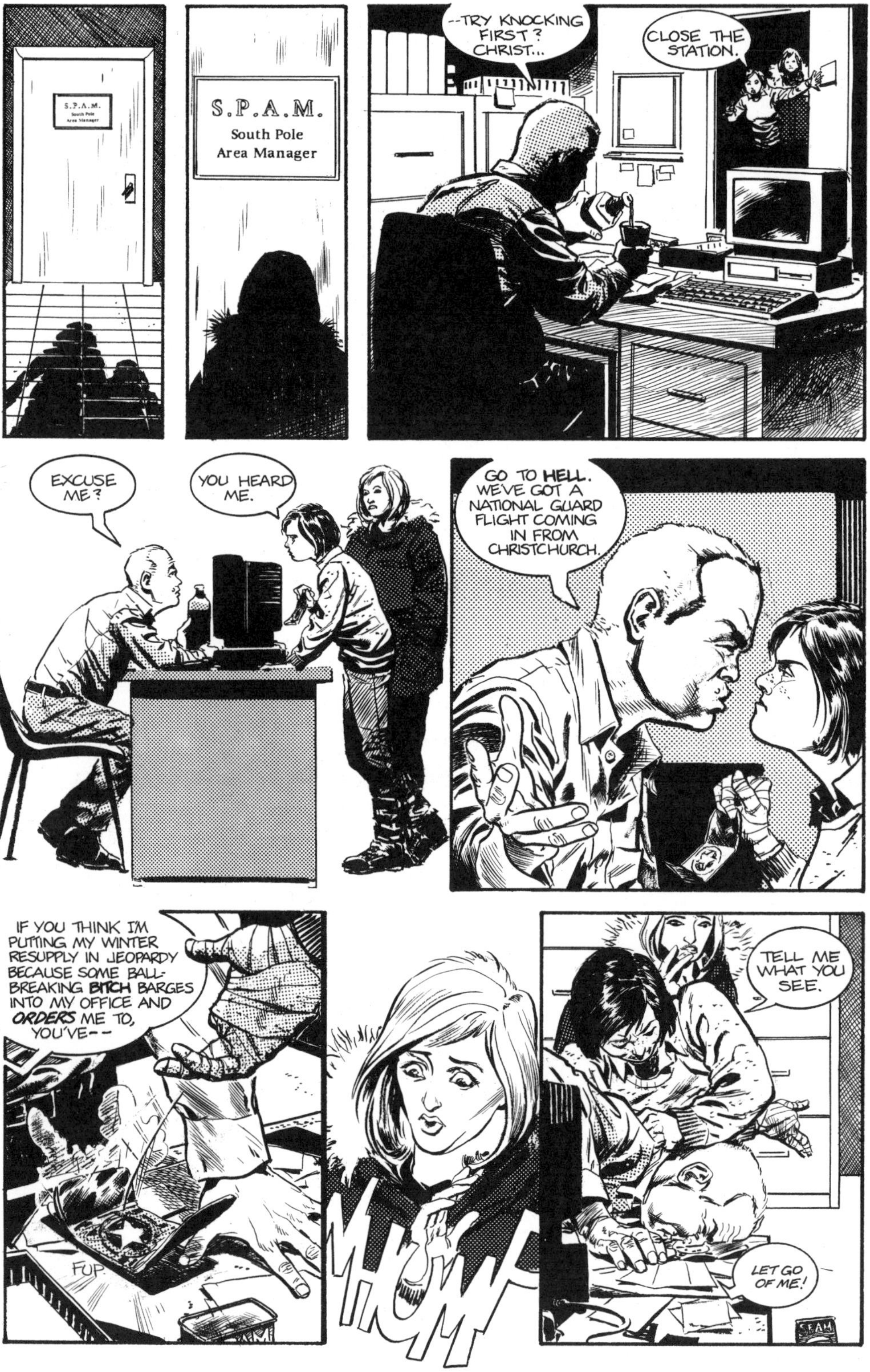
S.P.A.M.
South Pole
Area Manager
S.P.A.M.
South Pole
Area Manager
--TRY KNOCKING FIRST? CHRIST...
CLOSE THE STATION.
EXCUSE ME?
YOU HEARD ME.
GO TO HELL. WE'VE GOT A NATIONAL GUARD FLIGHT COMING IN FROM CHRISTCHURCH.
IF YOU THINK I'M PUTTING MY WINTER RESUPPLY IN JEOPARDY BECAUSE SOME BALL-BREAKING BITCH BARGES INTO MY OFFICE AND ORDERS ME TO, YOU'VE--
FUP
WHUMP
TELL ME WHAT YOU SEE.
LET GO OF ME!
S.P.A.M.

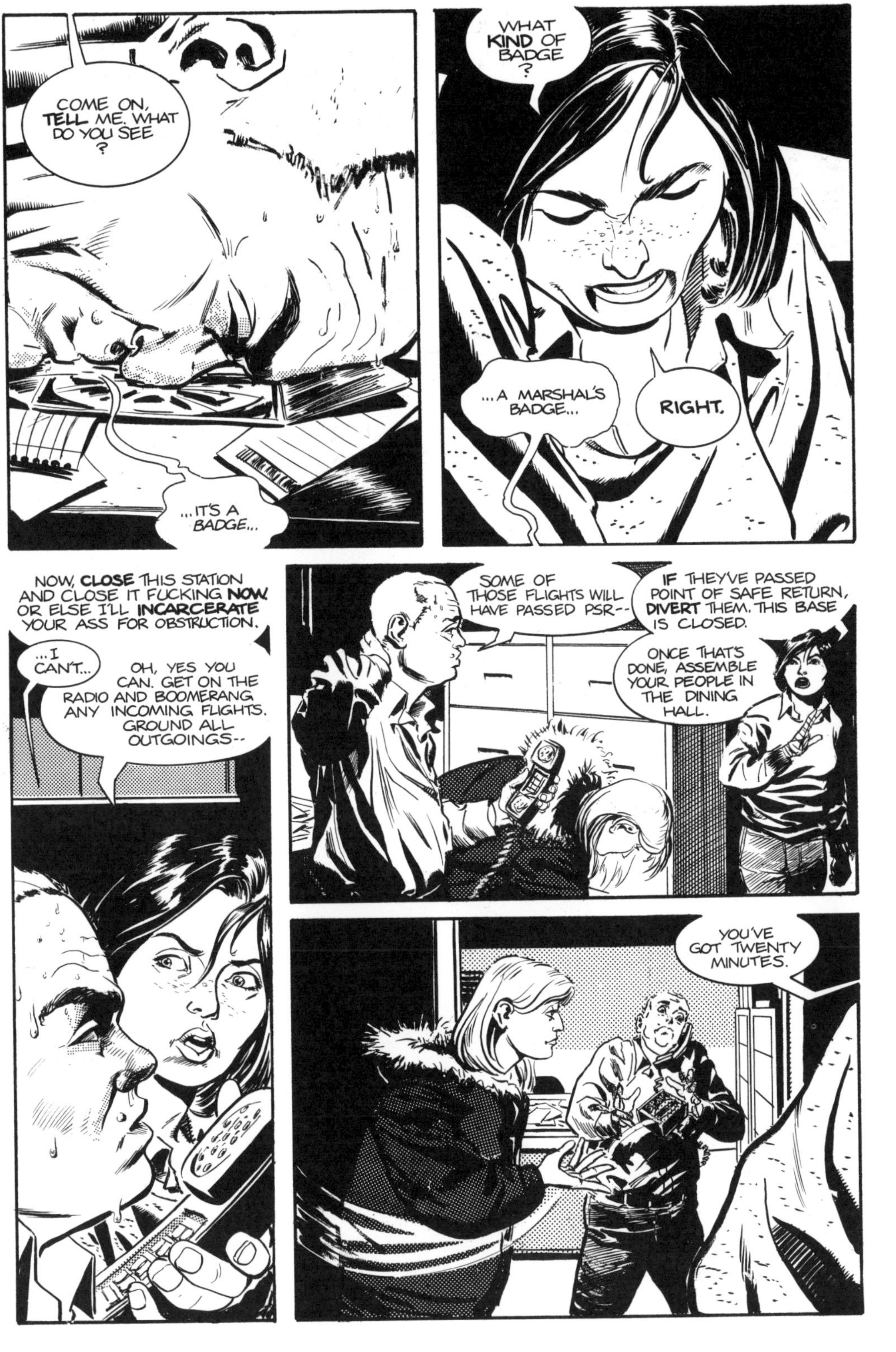
COME ON, TELL ME. WHAT DO YOU SEE?
...IT'S A BADGE...
WHAT KIND OF BADGE?
...A MARSHAL'S BADGE...
RIGHT.
NOW, CLOSE THIS STATION AND CLOSE IT FUCKING NOW. OR ELSE I'LL INCARCERATE YOUR ASS FOR OBSTRUCTION.
...I CAN'T...
OH, YES YOU CAN. GET ON THE RADIO AND BOOMERANG ANY INCOMING FLIGHTS. GROUND ALL OUTGOINGS--
SOME OF THOSE FLIGHTS WILL HAVE PASSED PSR--
IF THEY'VE PASSED POINT OF SAFE RETURN, DIVERT THEM. THIS BASE IS CLOSED.
ONCE THAT'S DONE, ASSEMBLE YOUR PEOPLE IN THE DINING HALL.
YOU'VE GOT TWENTY MINUTES.

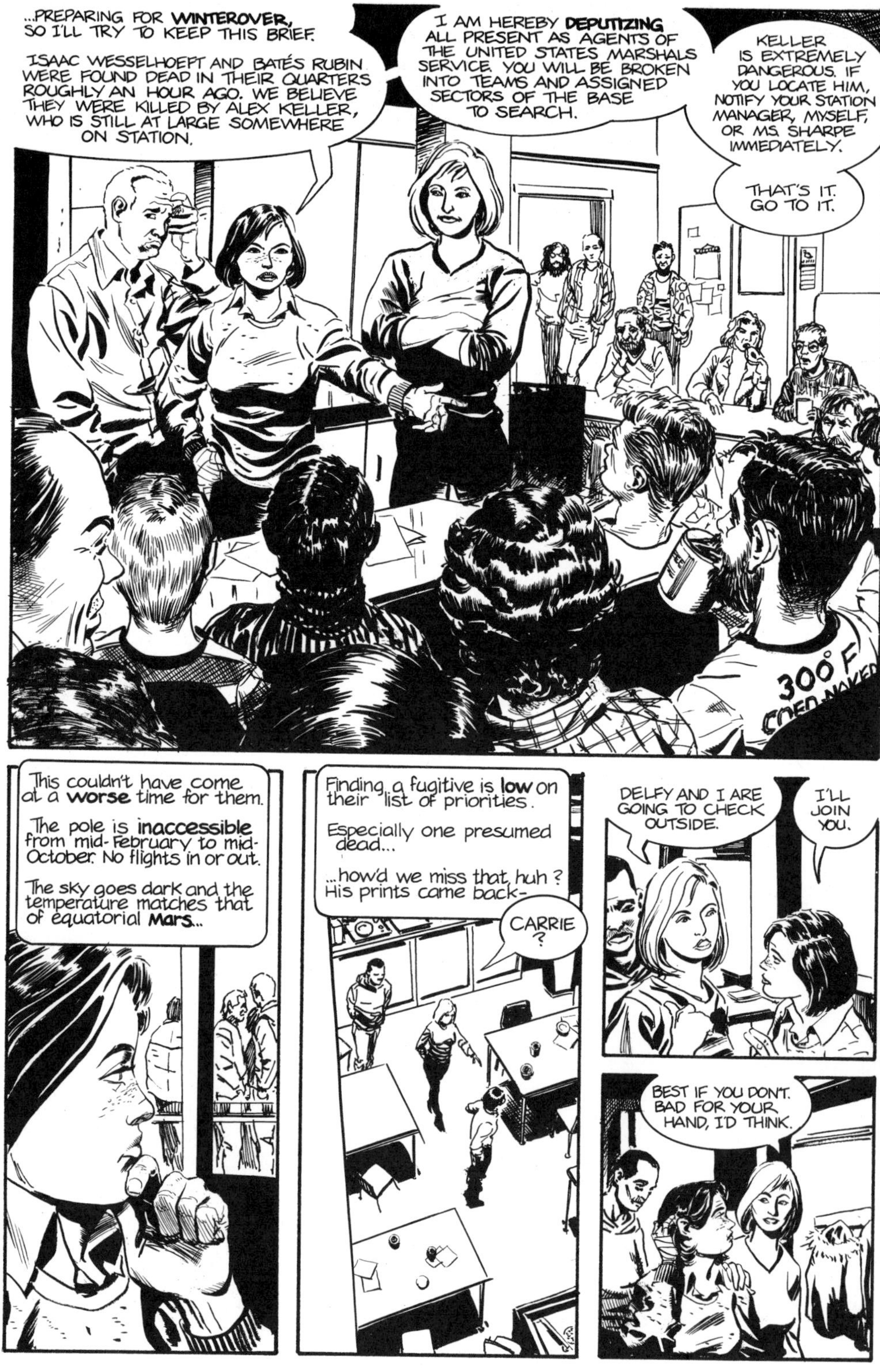
...PREPARING FOR WINTEROVER, SO I'LL TRY TO KEEP THIS BRIEF.
ISAAC WESSELHOEFT AND BATÉS RUBIN WERE FOUND DEAD IN THEIR QUARTERS ROUGHLY AN HOUR AGO. WE BELIEVE THEY WERE KILLED BY ALEX KELLER, WHO IS STILL AT LARGE SOMEWHERE ON STATION.
I AM HEREBY DEPUTIZING ALL PRESENT AS AGENTS OF THE UNITED STATES MARSHALS SERVICE. YOU WILL BE BROKEN INTO TEAMS AND ASSIGNED SECTORS OF THE BASE TO SEARCH.
KELLER IS EXTREMELY DANGEROUS. IF YOU LOCATE HIM, NOTIFY YOUR STATION MANAGER, MYSELF, OR MS. SHARPE IMMEDIATELY.
THAT'S IT. GO TO IT.
300° F
This couldn't have come at a worse time for them.
The pole is inaccessible from mid-February to mid-October. No flights in or out.
The sky goes dark and the temperature matches that of equatorial Mars...
Finding a fugitive is low on their list of priorities.
Especially one presumed dead...
...how'd we miss that, huh? His prints came back-
CARRIE?
DELFY AND I ARE GOING TO CHECK OUTSIDE.
I'LL JOIN YOU.
BEST IF YOU DON'T. BAD FOR YOUR HAND, I'D THINK.

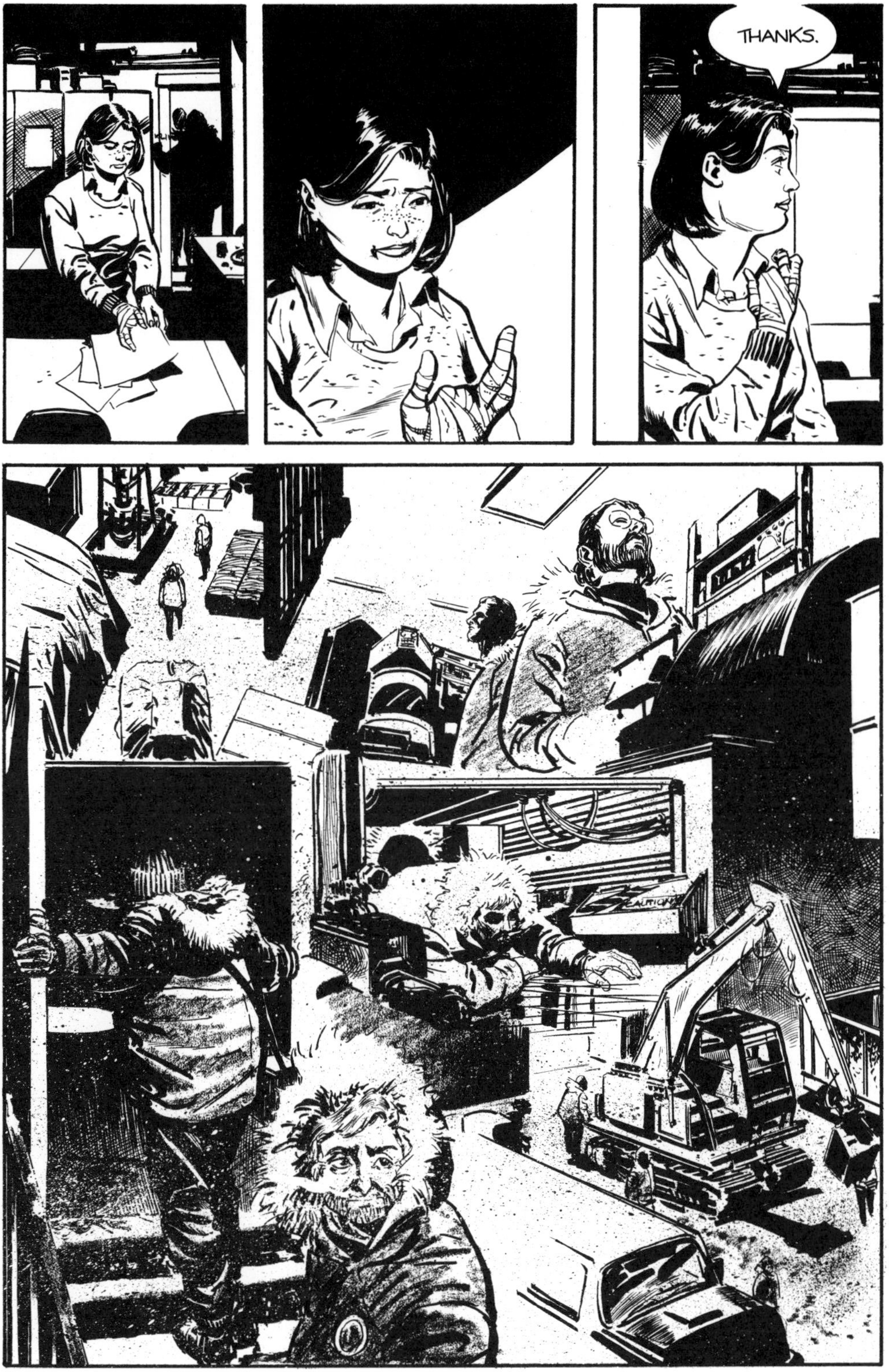
THANKS.
CAUTION

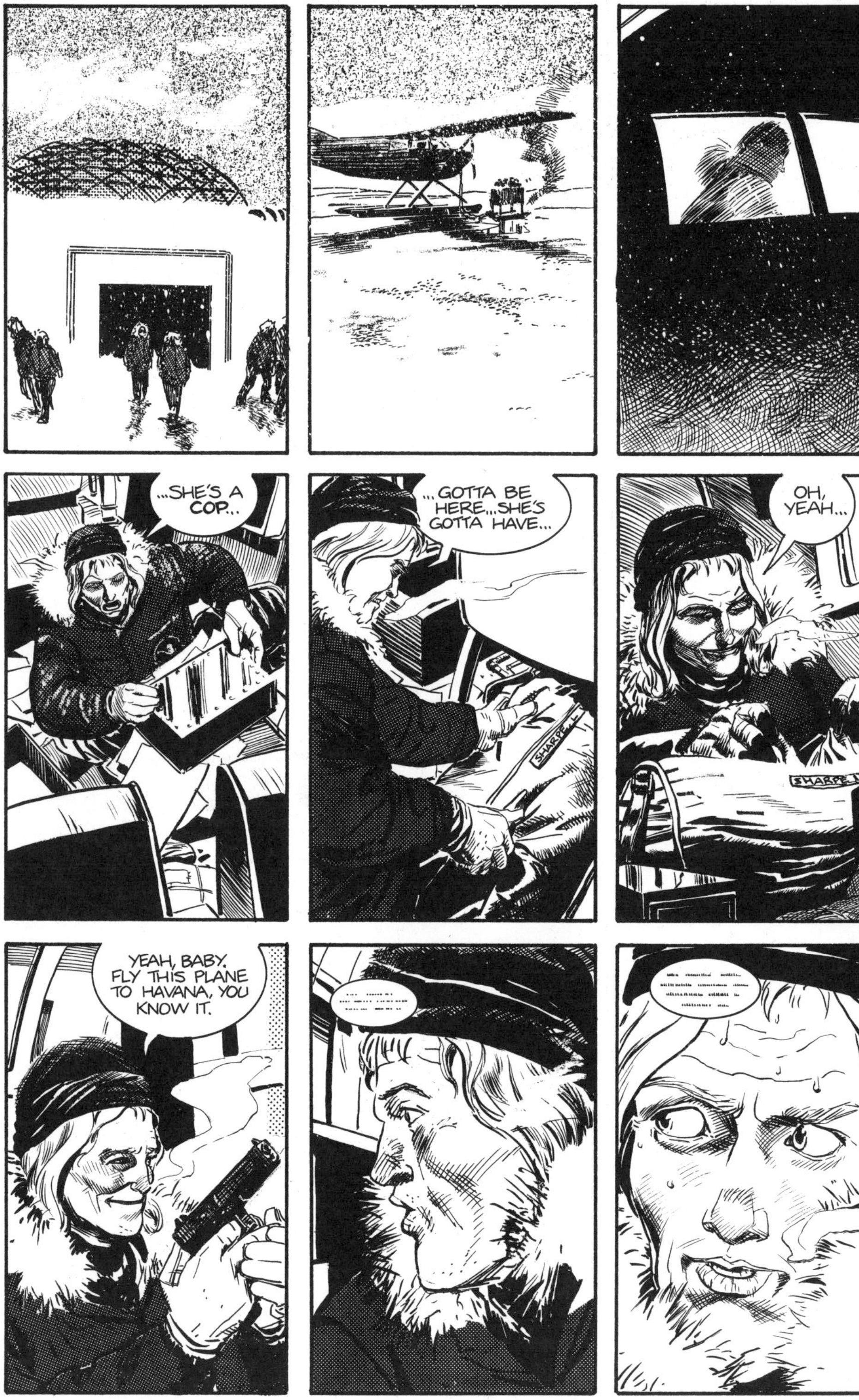
...SHE'S A COP...
...GOTTA BE HERE...SHE'S GOTTA HAVE...
SHARPE, L.
OH, YEAH...
SHARPE, L.
YEAH, BABY. FLY THIS PLANE TO HAVANA, YOU KNOW IT.

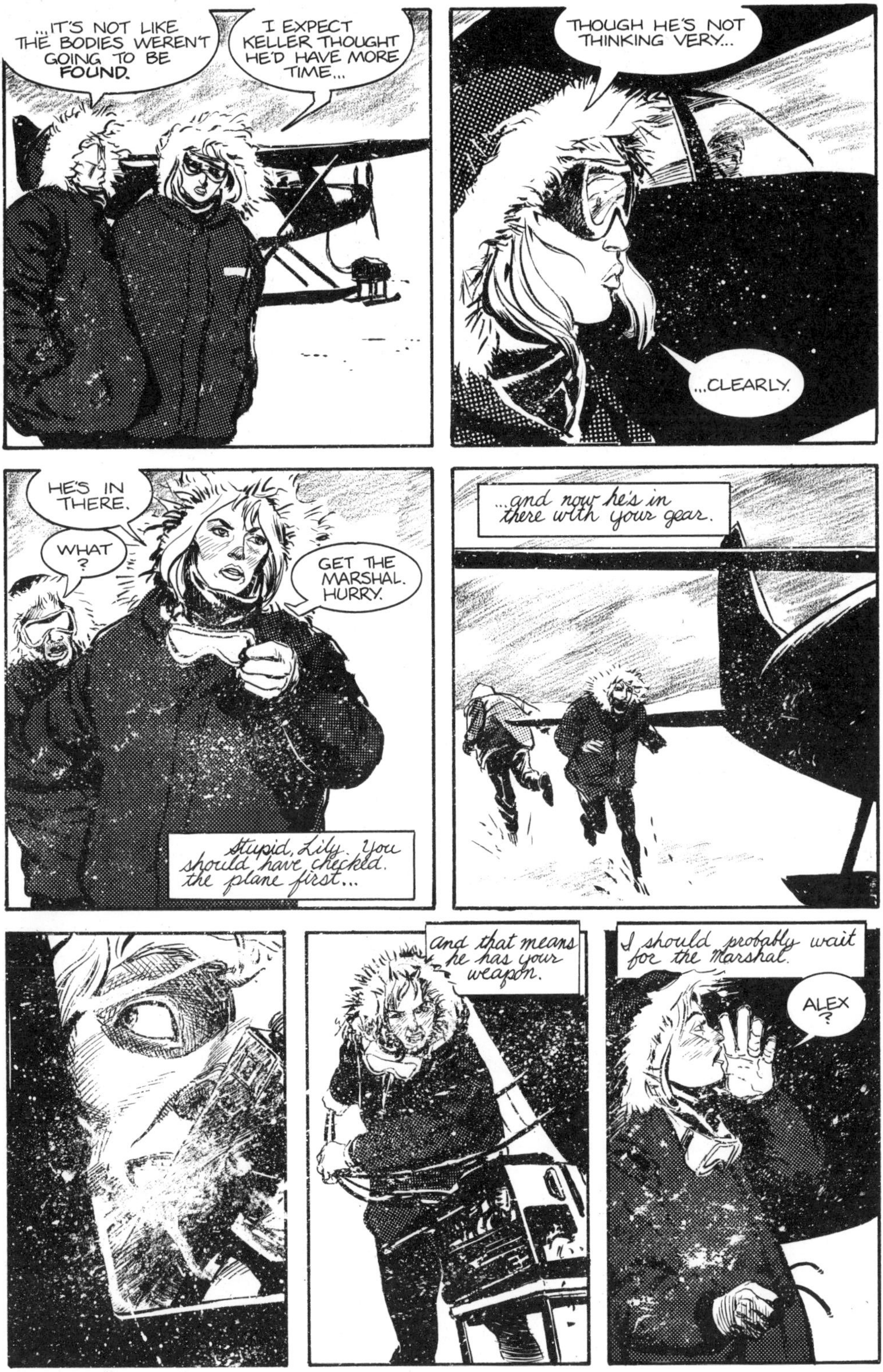
...IT'S NOT LIKE THE BODIES WEREN'T GOING TO BE FOUND.
I EXPECT KELLER THOUGHT HE'D HAVE MORE TIME...
THOUGH HE'S NOT THINKING VERY...
...CLEARLY.
HE'S IN THERE.
WHAT?
GET THE MARSHAL. HURRY.
Stupid, Lily. You should have checked the plane first...
...and now he's in there with your gear.
And that means he has your weapon.
I should probably wait for the Marshal.
ALEX?

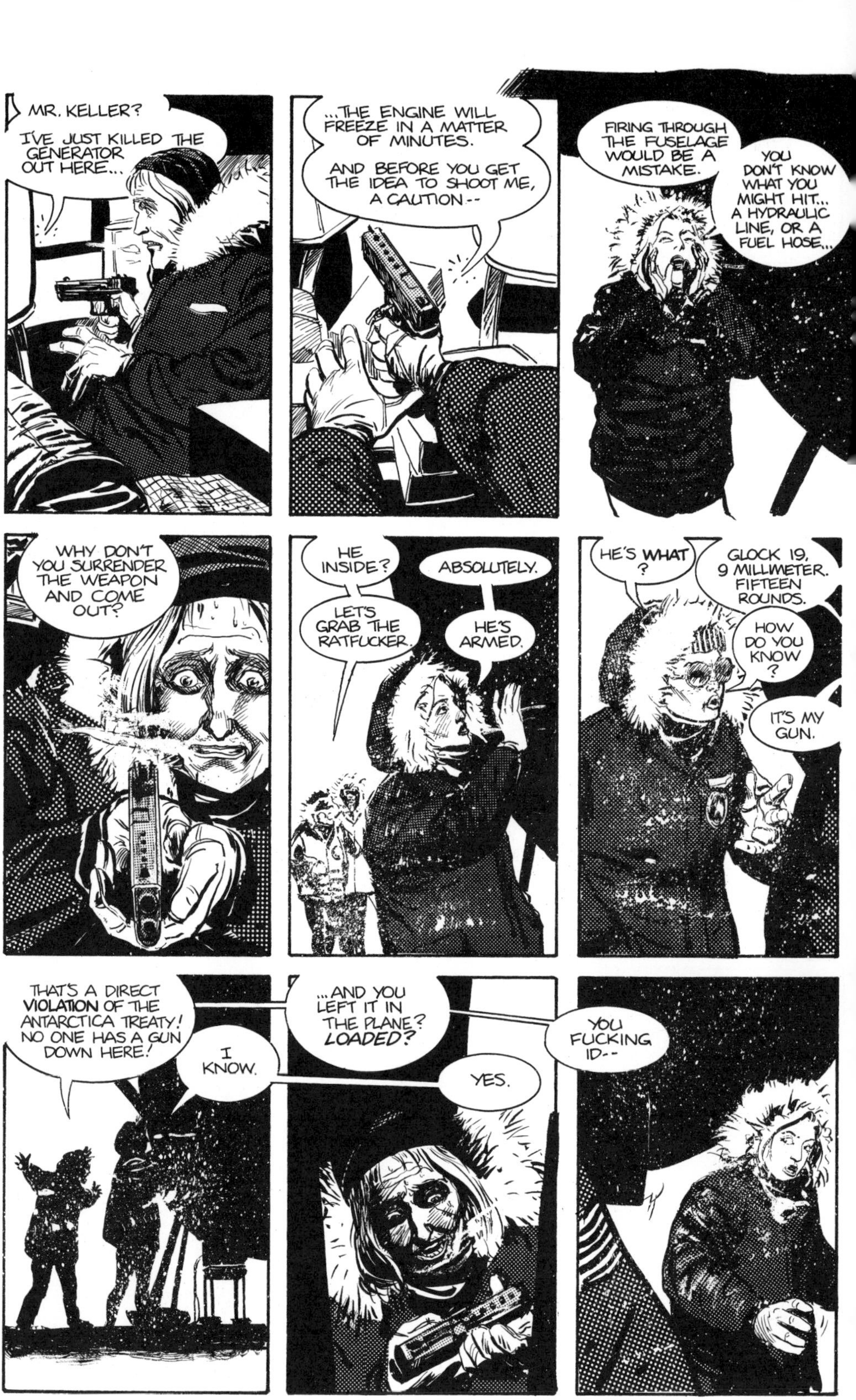
MR. KELLER?
I'VE JUST KILLED THE GENERATOR OUT HERE...
...THE ENGINE WILL FREEZE IN A MATTER OF MINUTES.
AND BEFORE YOU GET THE IDEA TO SHOOT ME, A CAUTION--
FIRING THROUGH THE FUSELAGE WOULD BE A MISTAKE.
YOU DON'T KNOW WHAT YOU MIGHT HIT... A HYDRAULIC LINE, OR A FUEL HOSE...
WHY DON'T YOU SURRENDER THE WEAPON AND COME OUT?
HE INSIDE?
ABSOLUTELY.
LET'S GRAB THE RATFUCKER.
HE'S ARMED.
HE'S WHAT?
GLOCK 19, 9 MILLIMETER. FIFTEEN ROUNDS.
HOW DO YOU KNOW?
IT'S MY GUN.
THAT'S A DIRECT VIOLATION OF THE ANTARCTICA TREATY! NO ONE HAS A GUN DOWN HERE!
I KNOW.
...AND YOU LEFT IT IN THE PLANE? LOADED?
YES.
YOU FUCKING ID--

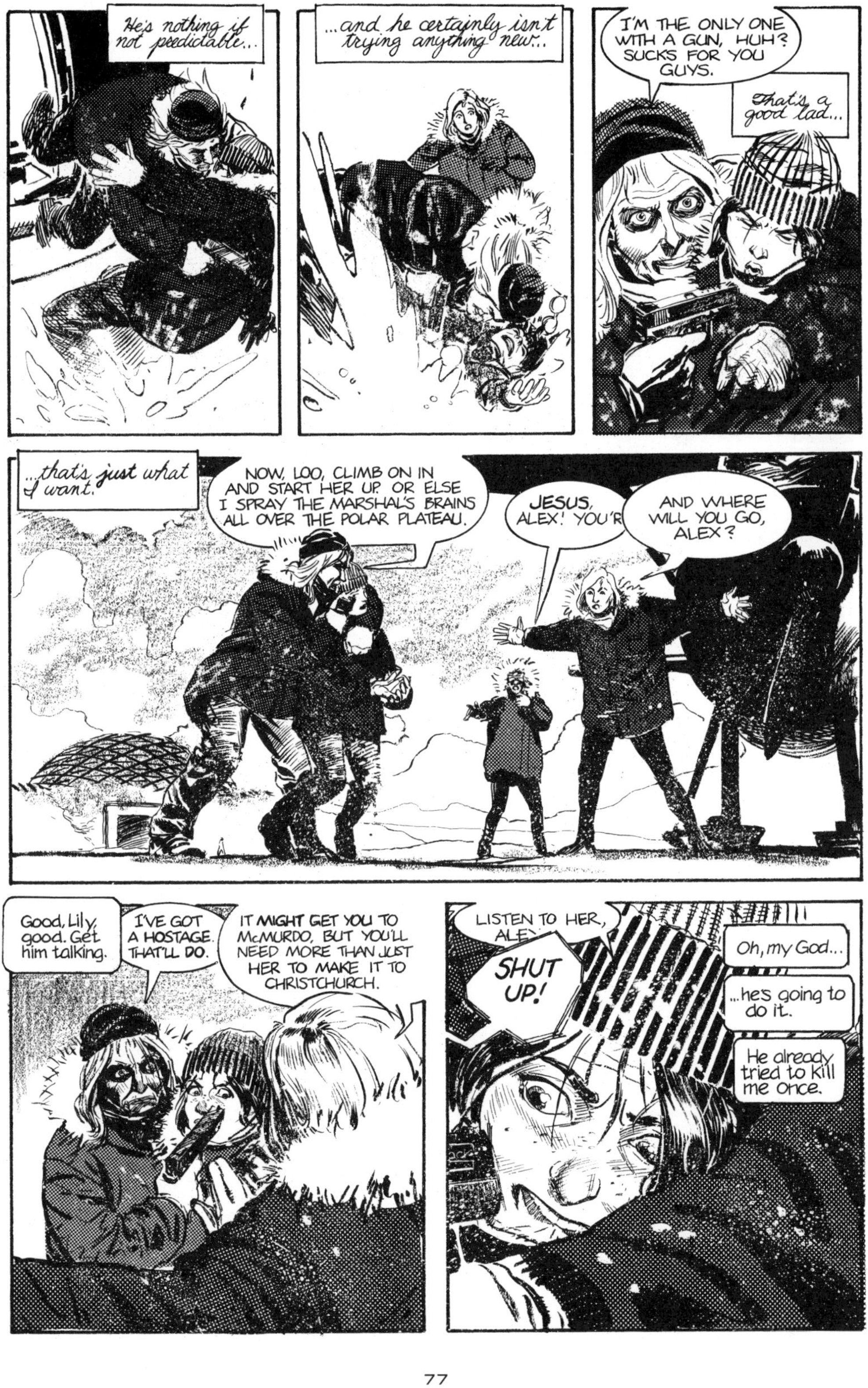
He's nothing if not predictable...
...and he certainly isn't trying anything new...
I'M THE ONLY ONE WITH A GUN, HUH? SUCKS FOR YOU GUYS.
That's a good lad...
...that's just what I want.
NOW, LOO, CLIMB ON IN AND START HER UP. OR ELSE I SPRAY THE MARSHAL'S BRAINS ALL OVER THE POLAR PLATEAU.
JESUS, ALEX! YOU'R
AND WHERE WILL YOU GO, ALEX?
Good, Lily, good. Get him talking.
I'VE GOT A HOSTAGE. THAT'LL DO.
IT MIGHT GET YOU TO McMURDO, BUT YOU'LL NEED MORE THAN JUST HER TO MAKE IT TO CHRISTCHURCH.
LISTEN TO HER, ALE
SHUT UP!
Oh, my God...
...he's going to do it.
He already tried to kill me once.

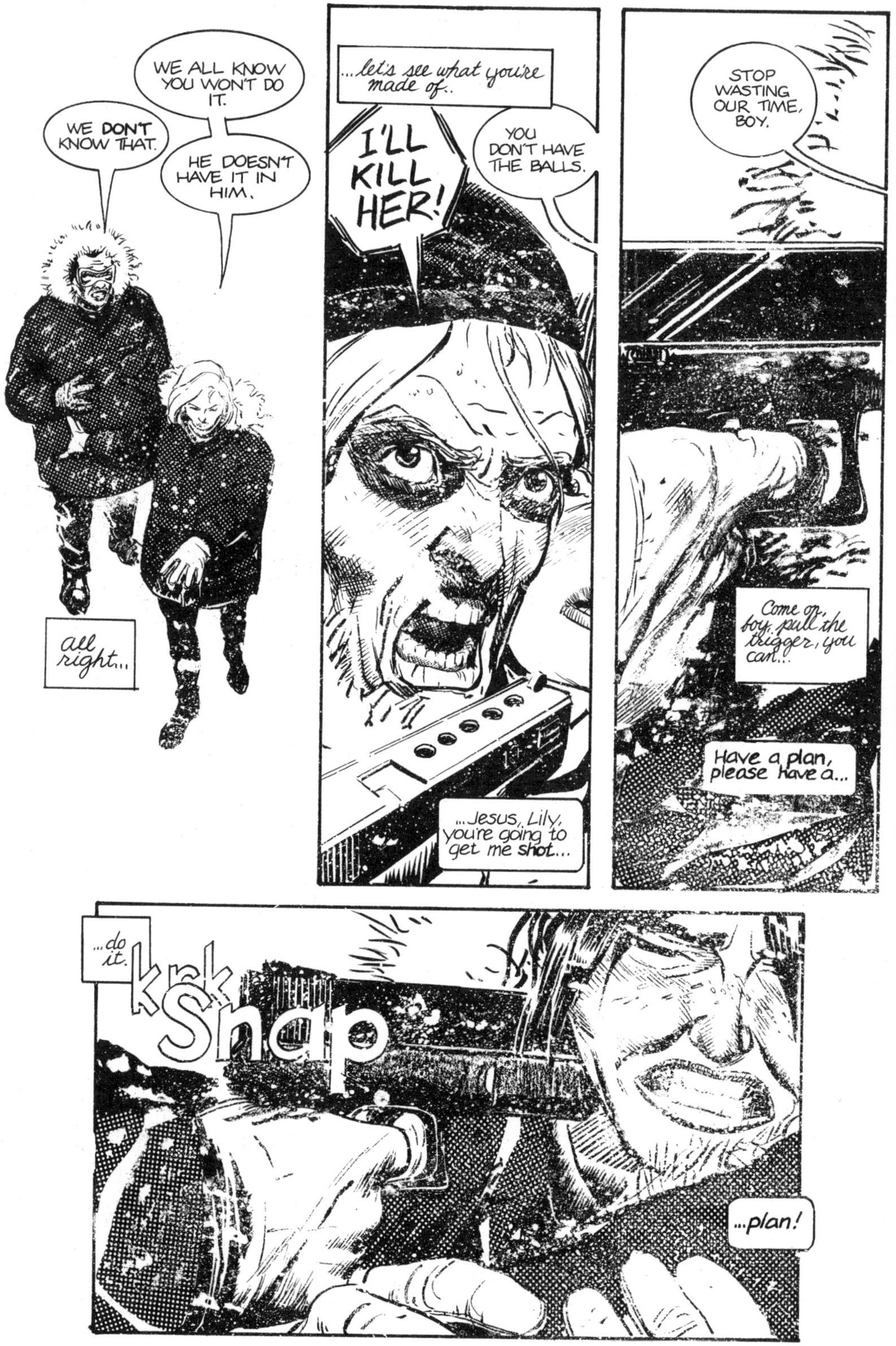
WE ALL KNOW YOU WON'T DO IT.
WE DON'T KNOW THAT.
HE DOESN'T HAVE IT IN HIM.
all right...
...let's see what you're made of..
I'LL KILL HER!
YOU DON'T HAVE THE BALLS.
...Jesus, Lily, you're going to get me shot...
STOP WASTING OUR TIME, BOY.
Come on, boy, pull the trigger, you can...
Have a plan, please have a...
...do it.
krk
Snap
...plan!

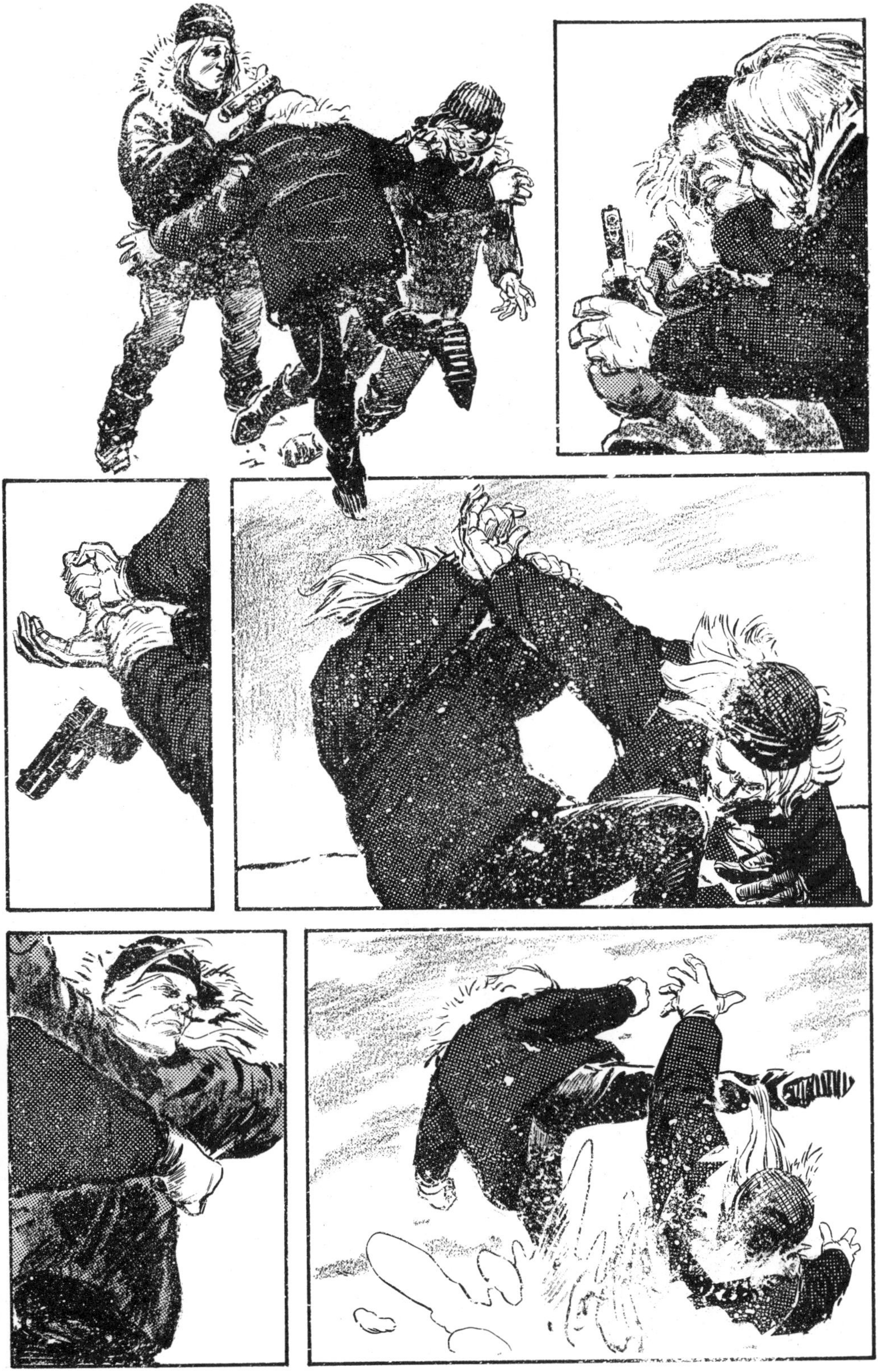

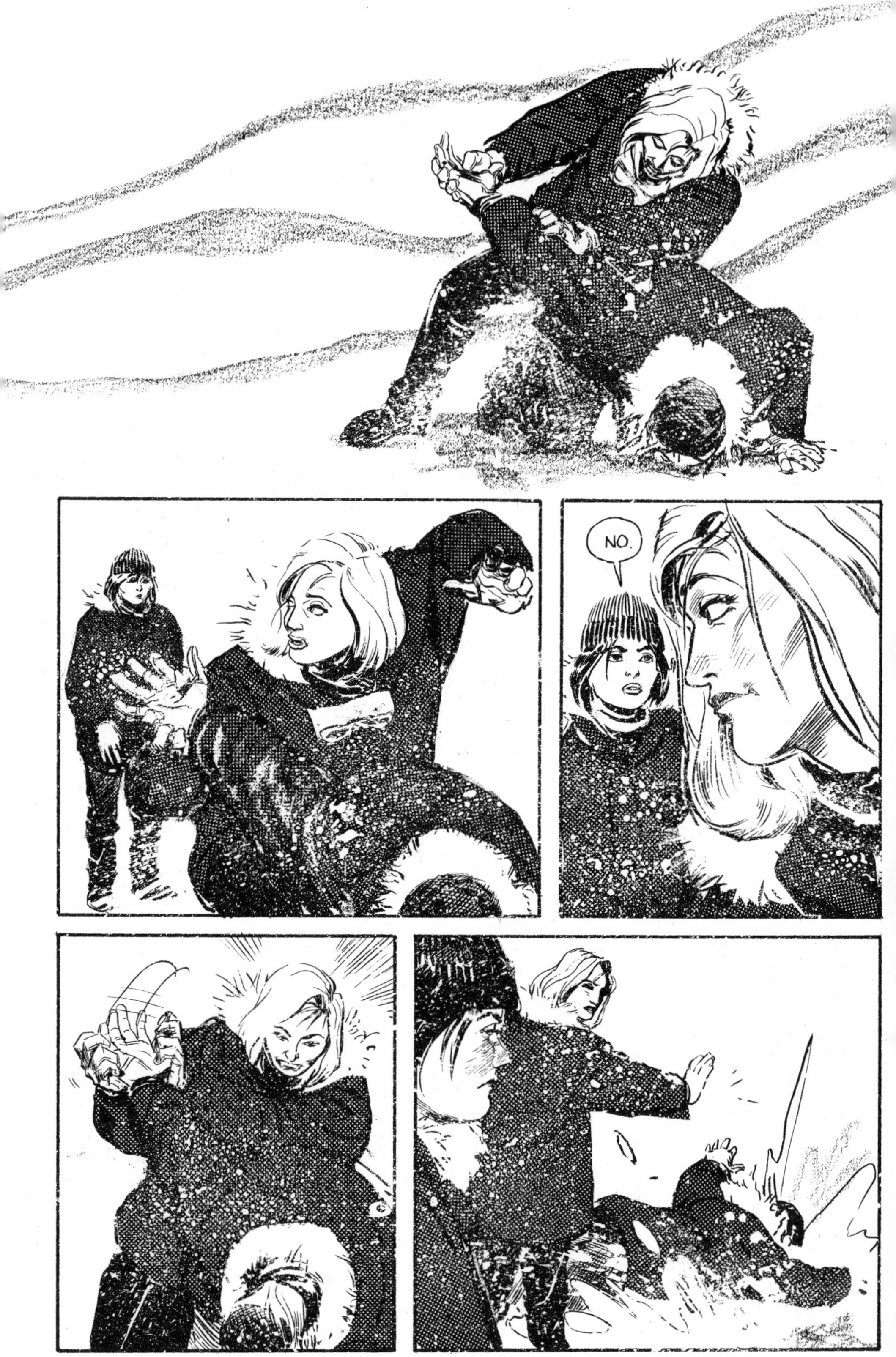
NO.

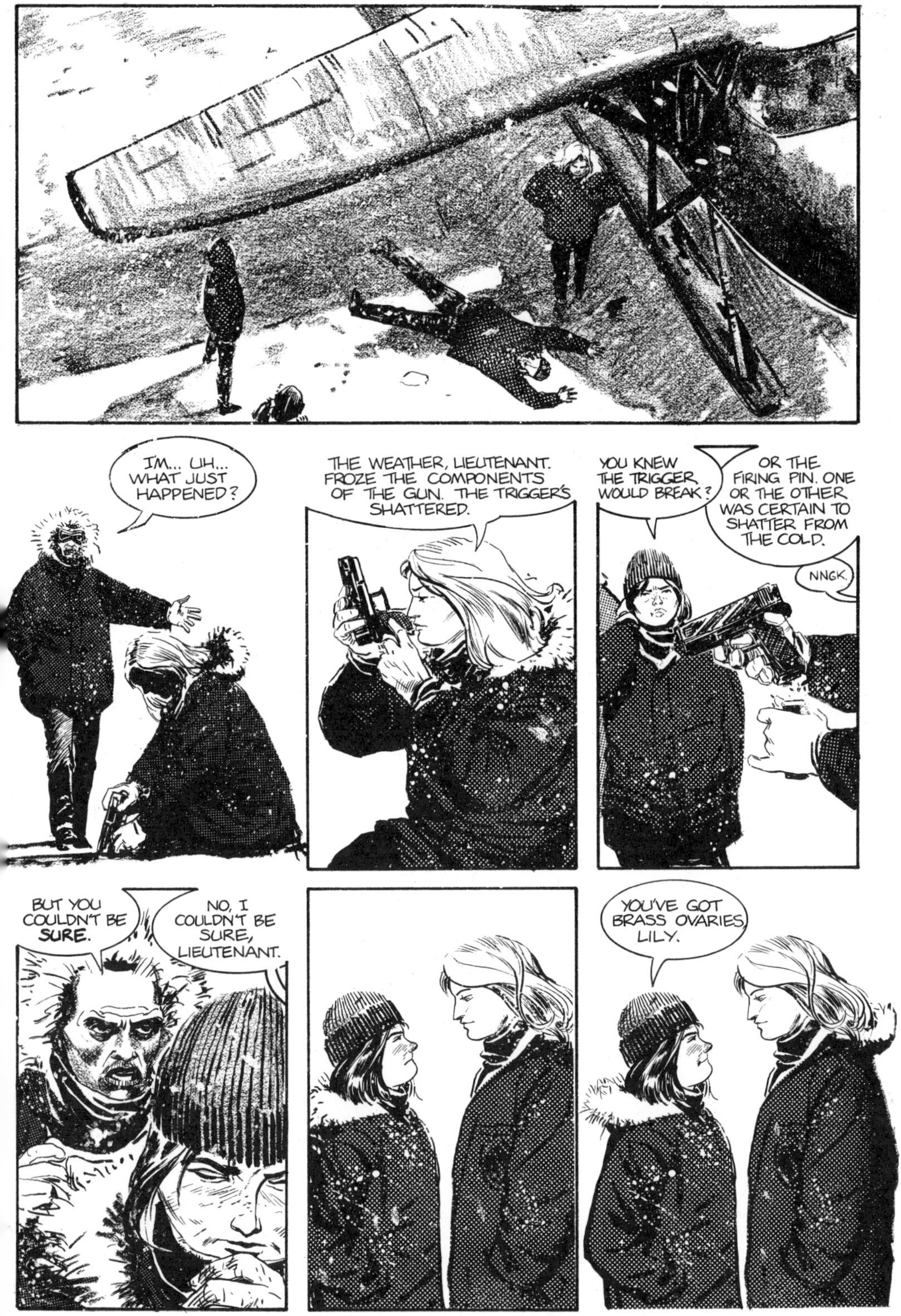

I'M... UH... WHAT JUST HAPPENED?
THE WEATHER, LIEUTENANT. FROZE THE COMPONENTS OF THE GUN. THE TRIGGER'S SHATTERED.
YOU KNEW THE TRIGGER WOULD BREAK?
OR THE FIRING PIN. ONE OR THE OTHER WAS CERTAIN TO SHATTER FROM THE COLD.
NNGK.
BUT YOU COULDN'T BE **SURE**.
NO, I COULDN'T BE SURE, LIEUTENANT.
YOU'VE GOT BRASS OVARIES, LILY.

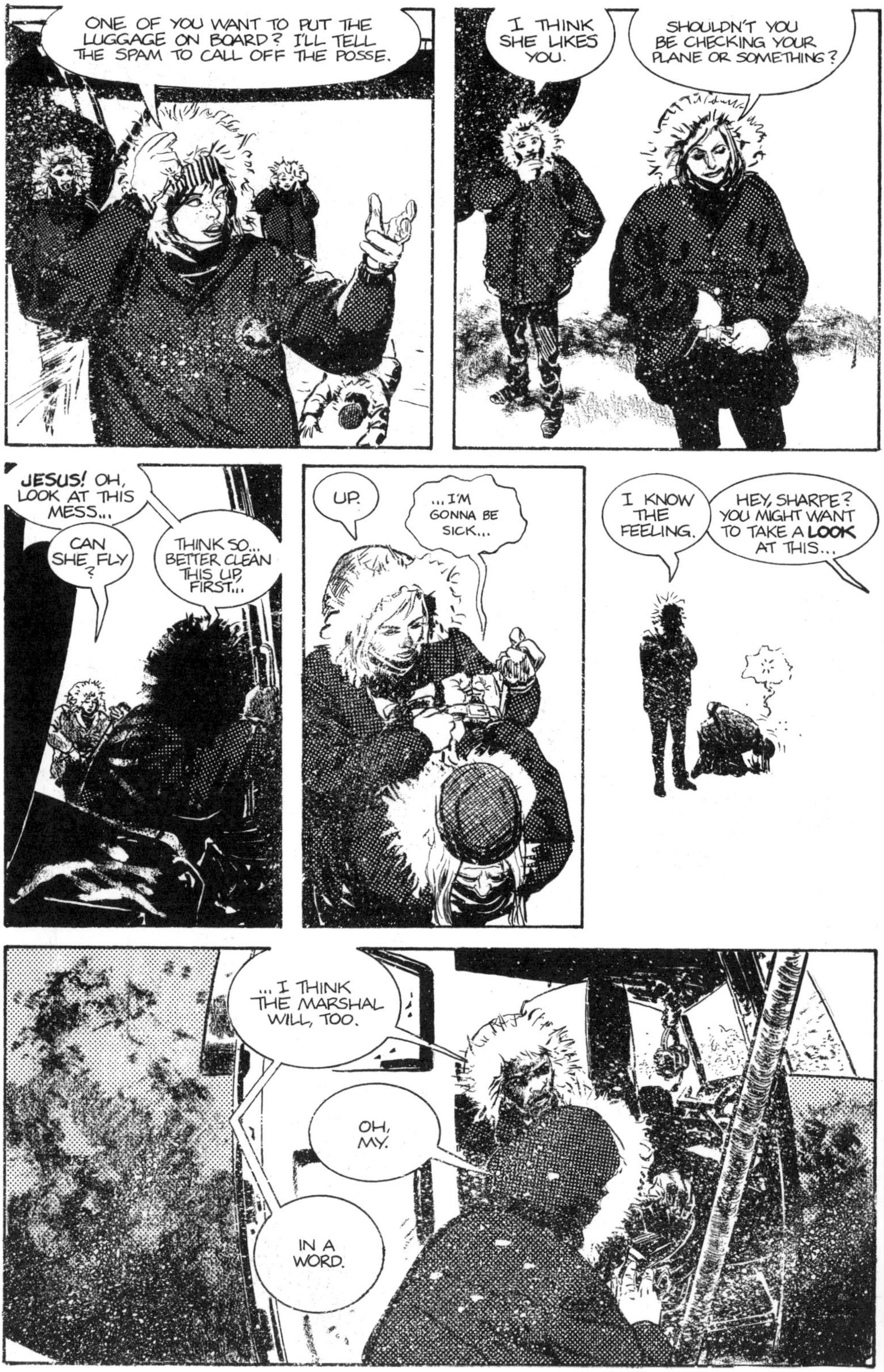
ONE OF YOU WANT TO PUT THE LUGGAGE ON BOARD? I'LL TELL THE SPAM TO CALL OFF THE POSSE.
I THINK SHE LIKES YOU.
SHOULDN'T YOU BE CHECKING YOUR PLANE OR SOMETHING?
JESUS! OH, LOOK AT THIS MESS...
CAN SHE FLY?
THINK SO... BETTER CLEAN THIS UP FIRST...
UP.
...I'M GONNA BE SICK...
I KNOW THE FEELING.
HEY, SHARPE? YOU MIGHT WANT TO TAKE A LOOK AT THIS...
...I THINK THE MARSHAL WILL, TOO.
OH, MY.
IN A WORD.

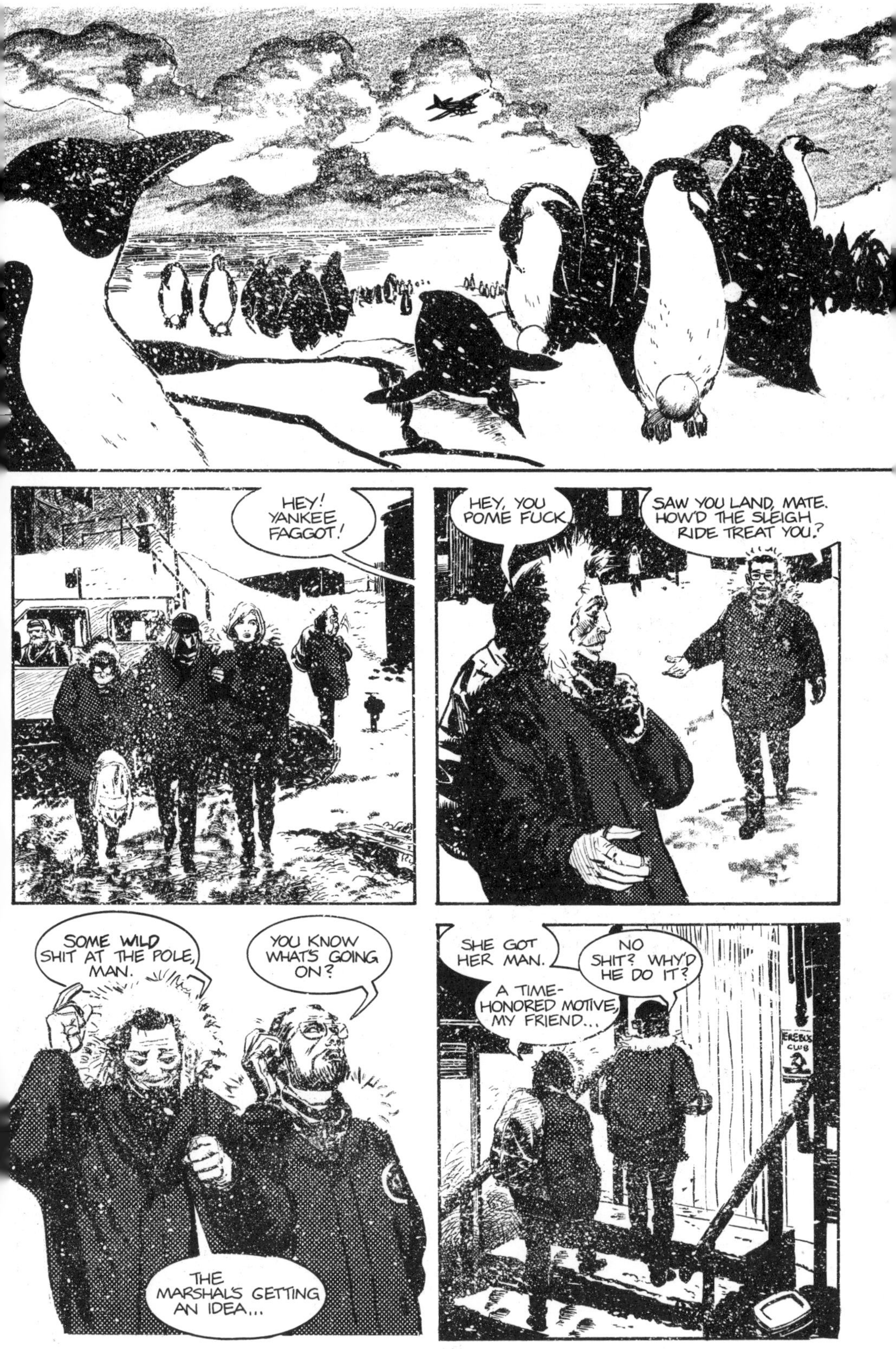
HEY! YANKEE FAGGOT!
HEY, YOU POME FUCK
SAW YOU LAND, MATE. HOW'D THE SLEIGH RIDE TREAT YOU?
SOME WILD SHIT AT THE POLE, MAN.
YOU KNOW WHAT'S GOING ON?
THE MARSHAL'S GETTING AN IDEA...
SHE GOT HER MAN.
NO SHIT? WHY'D HE DO IT?
A TIME-HONORED MOTIVE, MY FRIEND...
EREBUS CLUB

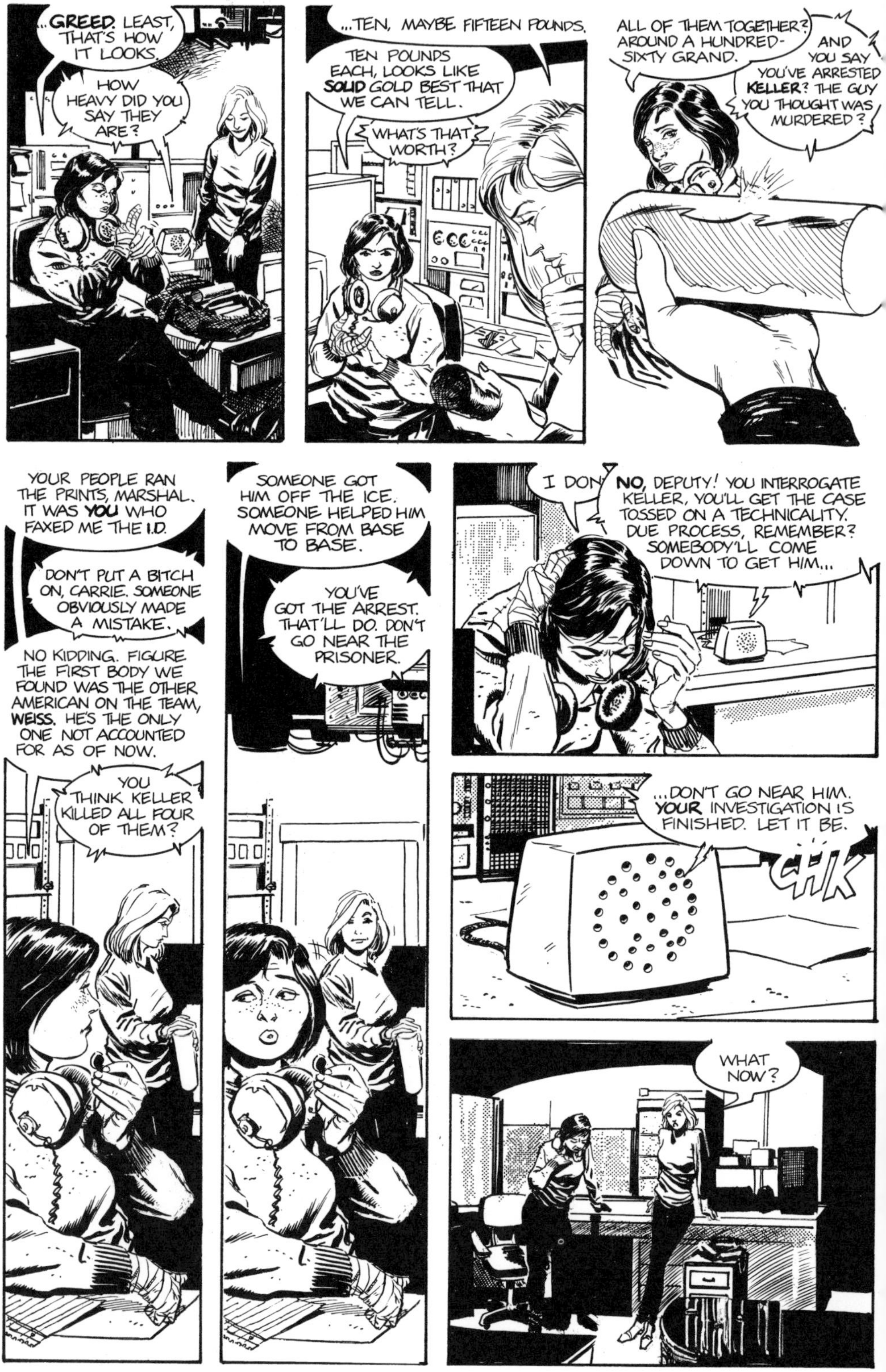
...GREED. LEAST, THAT'S HOW IT LOOKS.
HOW HEAVY DID YOU SAY THEY ARE?
...TEN, MAYBE FIFTEEN POUNDS.
TEN POUNDS EACH, LOOKS LIKE SOLID GOLD BEST THAT WE CAN TELL.
WHAT'S THAT WORTH?
ALL OF THEM TOGETHER? AROUND A HUNDRED-SIXTY GRAND.
AND YOU SAY YOU'VE ARRESTED KELLER? THE GUY YOU THOUGHT WAS MURDERED?
YOUR PEOPLE RAN THE PRINTS, MARSHAL. IT WAS YOU WHO FAXED ME THE I.D.
DON'T PUT A BITCH ON, CARRIE. SOMEONE OBVIOUSLY MADE A MISTAKE.
NO KIDDING. FIGURE THE FIRST BODY WE FOUND WAS THE OTHER AMERICAN ON THE TEAM, WEISS. HE'S THE ONLY ONE NOT ACCOUNTED FOR AS OF NOW.
YOU THINK KELLER KILLED ALL FOUR OF THEM?
SOMEONE GOT HIM OFF THE ICE. SOMEONE HELPED HIM MOVE FROM BASE TO BASE.
YOU'VE GOT THE ARREST. THAT'LL DO. DON'T GO NEAR THE PRISONER.
I DON
NO, DEPUTY! YOU INTERROGATE KELLER, YOU'LL GET THE CASE TOSSED ON A TECHNICALITY. DUE PROCESS, REMEMBER? SOMEBODY'LL COME DOWN TO GET HIM...
...DON'T GO NEAR HIM. YOUR INVESTIGATION IS FINISHED. LET IT BE.
CHK
WHAT NOW?

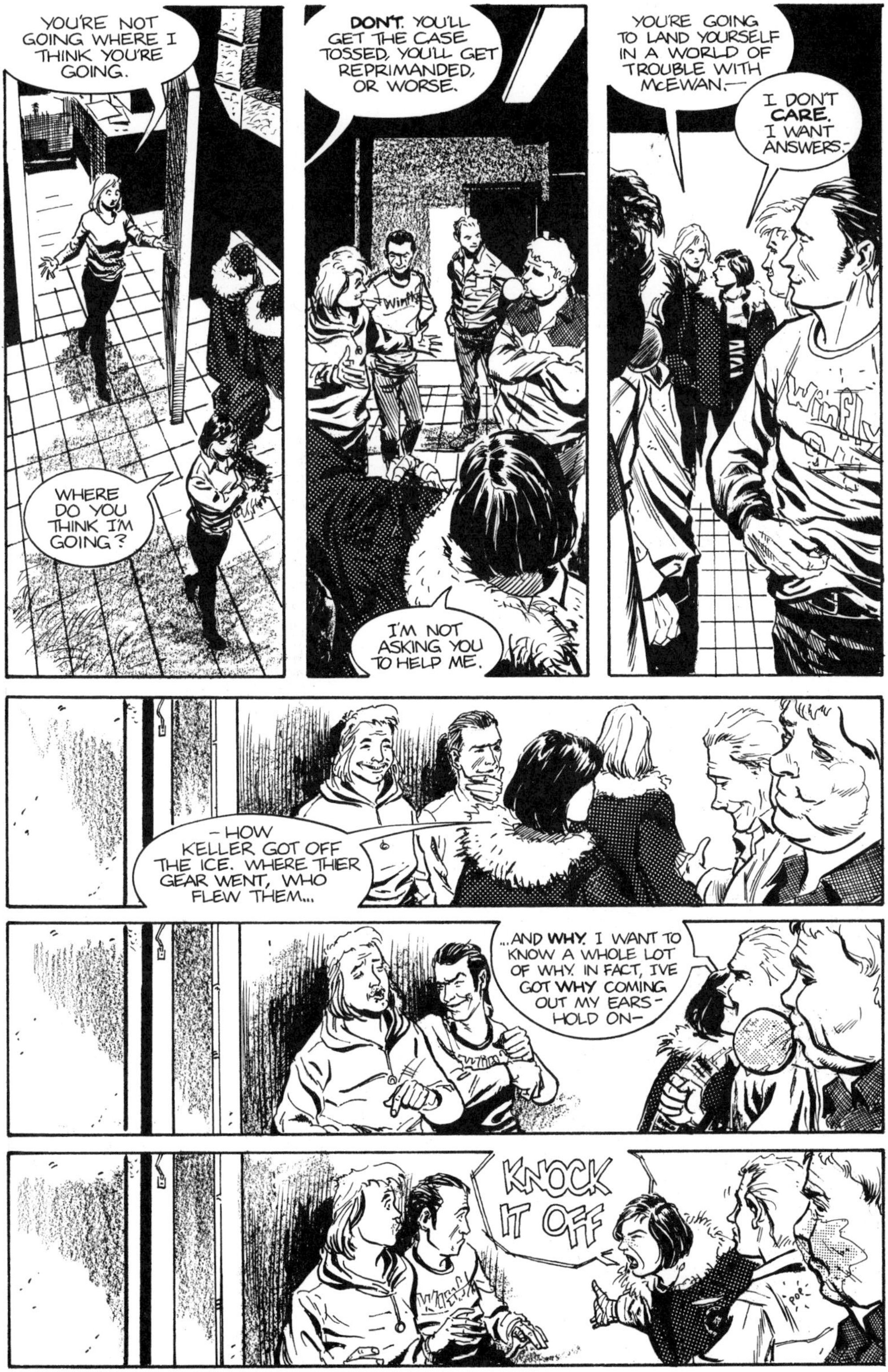
YOU'RE NOT GOING WHERE I THINK YOU'RE GOING.
WHERE DO YOU THINK I'M GOING?
DON'T. YOU'LL GET THE CASE TOSSED, YOU'LL GET REPRIMANDED, OR WORSE.
I'M NOT ASKING YOU TO HELP ME.
YOU'RE GOING TO LAND YOURSELF IN A WORLD OF TROUBLE WITH McEWAN.—
I DON'T CARE. I WANT ANSWERS-
-HOW KELLER GOT OFF THE ICE. WHERE THIER GEAR WENT, WHO FLEW THEM...
...AND WHY. I WANT TO KNOW A WHOLE LOT OF WHY. IN FACT, I'VE GOT WHY COMING OUT MY EARS- HOLD ON—
KNOCK IT OFF
POP

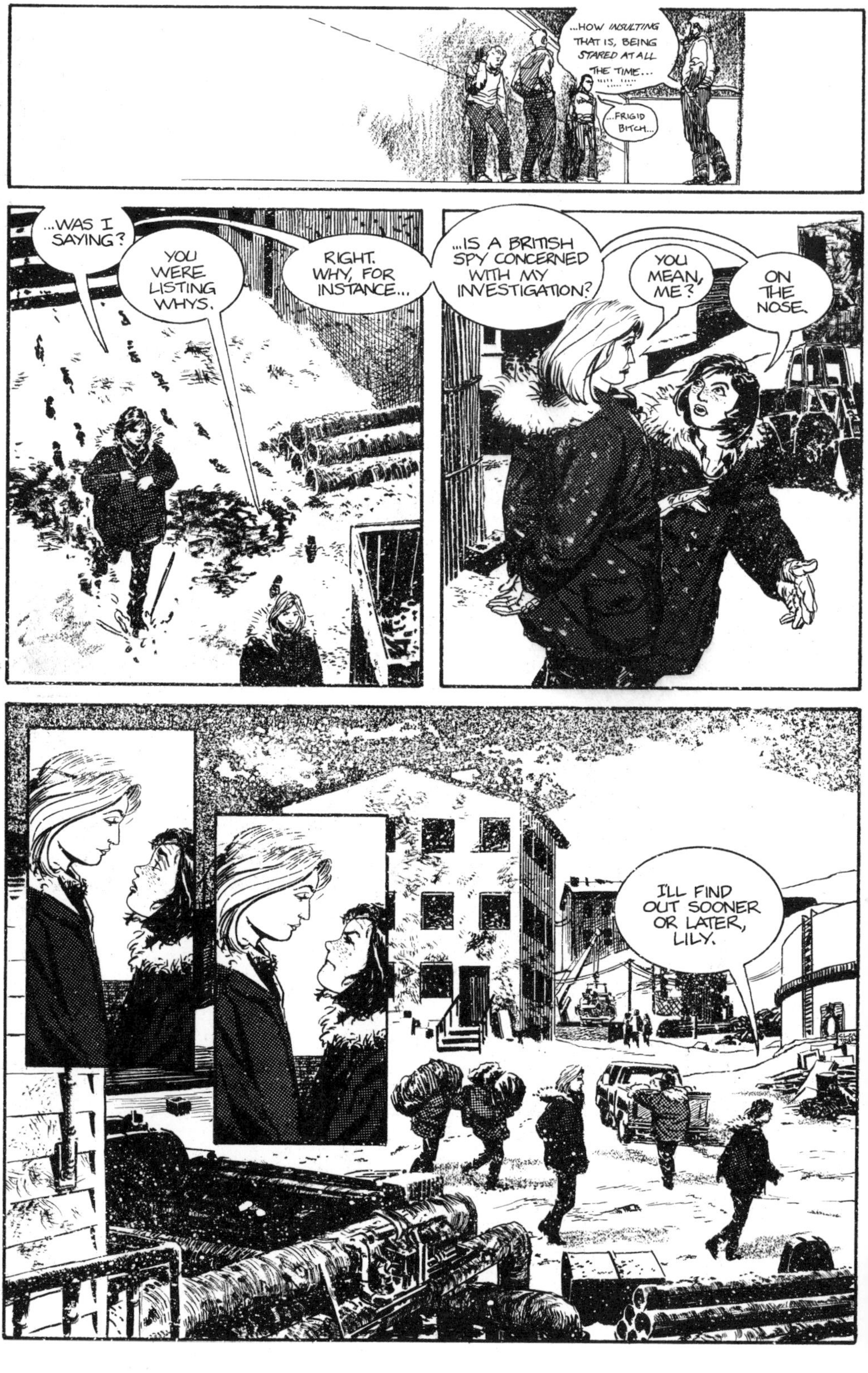

...HOW INSULTING THAT IS, BEING STARED AT ALL THE TIME...
...FRIGID BITCH...
...WAS I SAYING?
YOU WERE LISTING WHYS.
RIGHT. WHY, FOR INSTANCE...
...IS A BRITISH SPY CONCERNED WITH MY INVESTIGATION?
YOU MEAN, ME?
ON THE NOSE.
I'LL FIND OUT SOONER OR LATER, LILY.

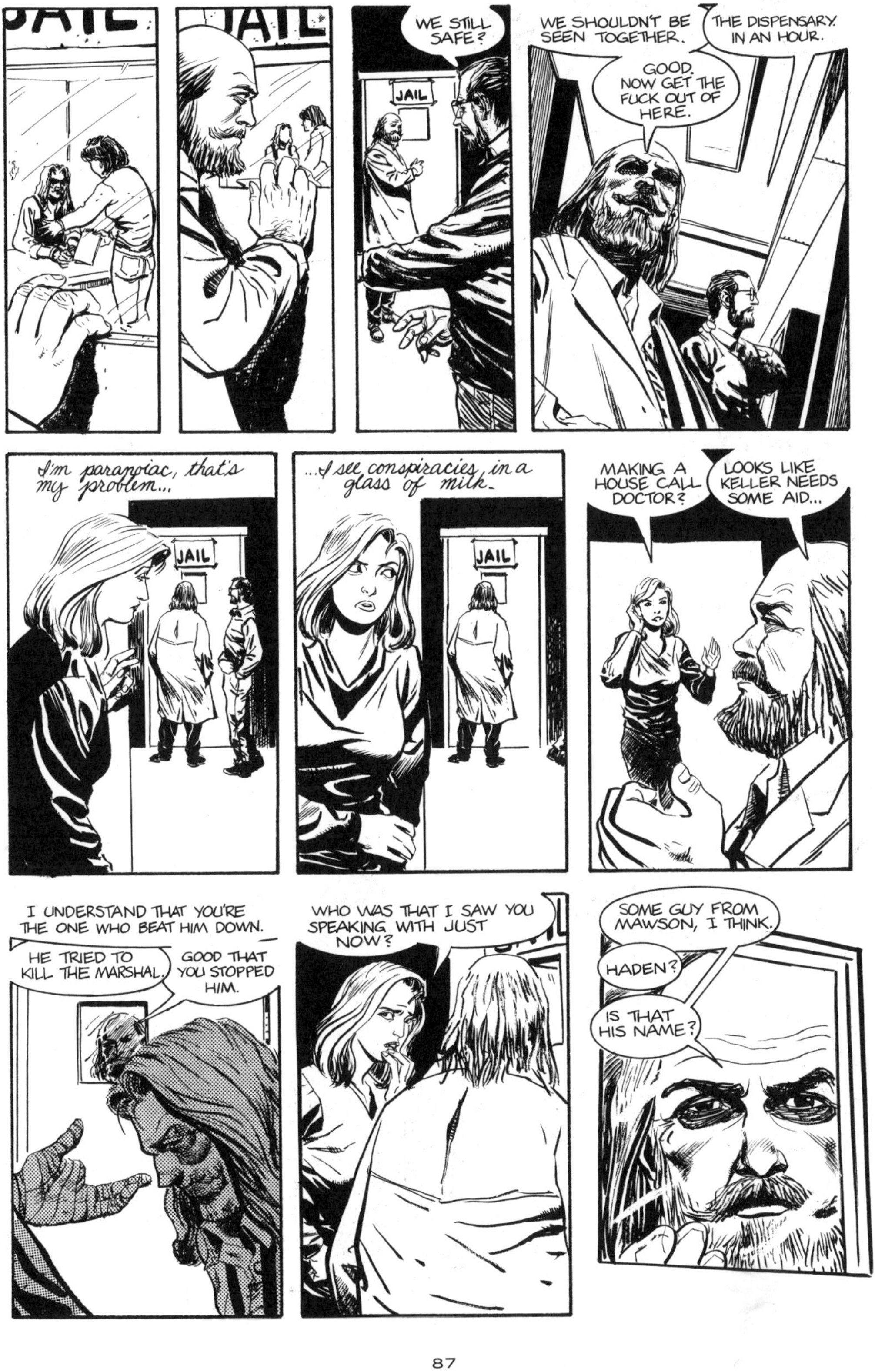
JAIL
JAIL
WE STILL SAFE?
JAIL
WE SHOULDN'T BE SEEN TOGETHER.
THE DISPENSARY. IN AN HOUR.
GOOD. NOW GET THE FUCK OUT OF HERE.
I'm paranoiac, that's my problem...
JAIL
...I see conspiracies in a glass of milk.
JAIL
MAKING A HOUSE CALL DOCTOR?
LOOKS LIKE KELLER NEEDS SOME AID...
I UNDERSTAND THAT YOU'RE THE ONE WHO BEAT HIM DOWN.
HE TRIED TO KILL THE MARSHAL.
GOOD THAT YOU STOPPED HIM.
WHO WAS THAT I SAW YOU SPEAKING WITH JUST NOW?
SOME GUY FROM MAWSON, I THINK.
HADEN?
IS THAT HIS NAME?

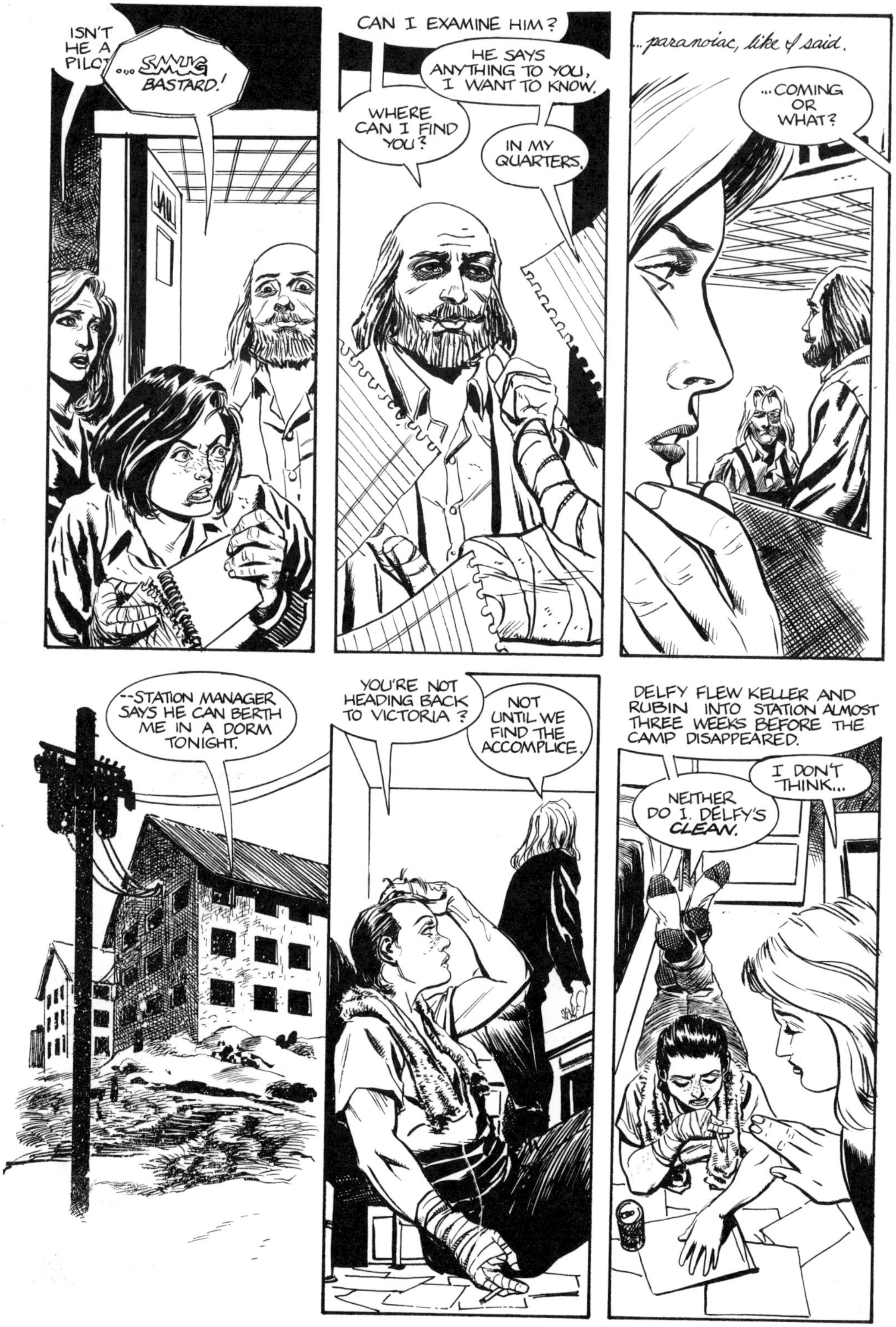
ISN'T HE A PILOT
...SMUG SMUG BASTARD!
CAN I EXAMINE HIM?
WHERE CAN I FIND YOU?
HE SAYS ANYTHING TO YOU, I WANT TO KNOW.
IN MY QUARTERS.
...paranoiac, like I said.
...COMING OR WHAT?
--STATION MANAGER SAYS HE CAN BERTH ME IN A DORM TONIGHT.
YOU'RE NOT HEADING BACK TO VICTORIA?
NOT UNTIL WE FIND THE ACCOMPLICE.
DELFY FLEW KELLER AND RUBIN INTO STATION ALMOST THREE WEEKS BEFORE THE CAMP DISAPPEARED.
I DON'T THINK...
NEITHER DO I. DELFY'S CLEAN.

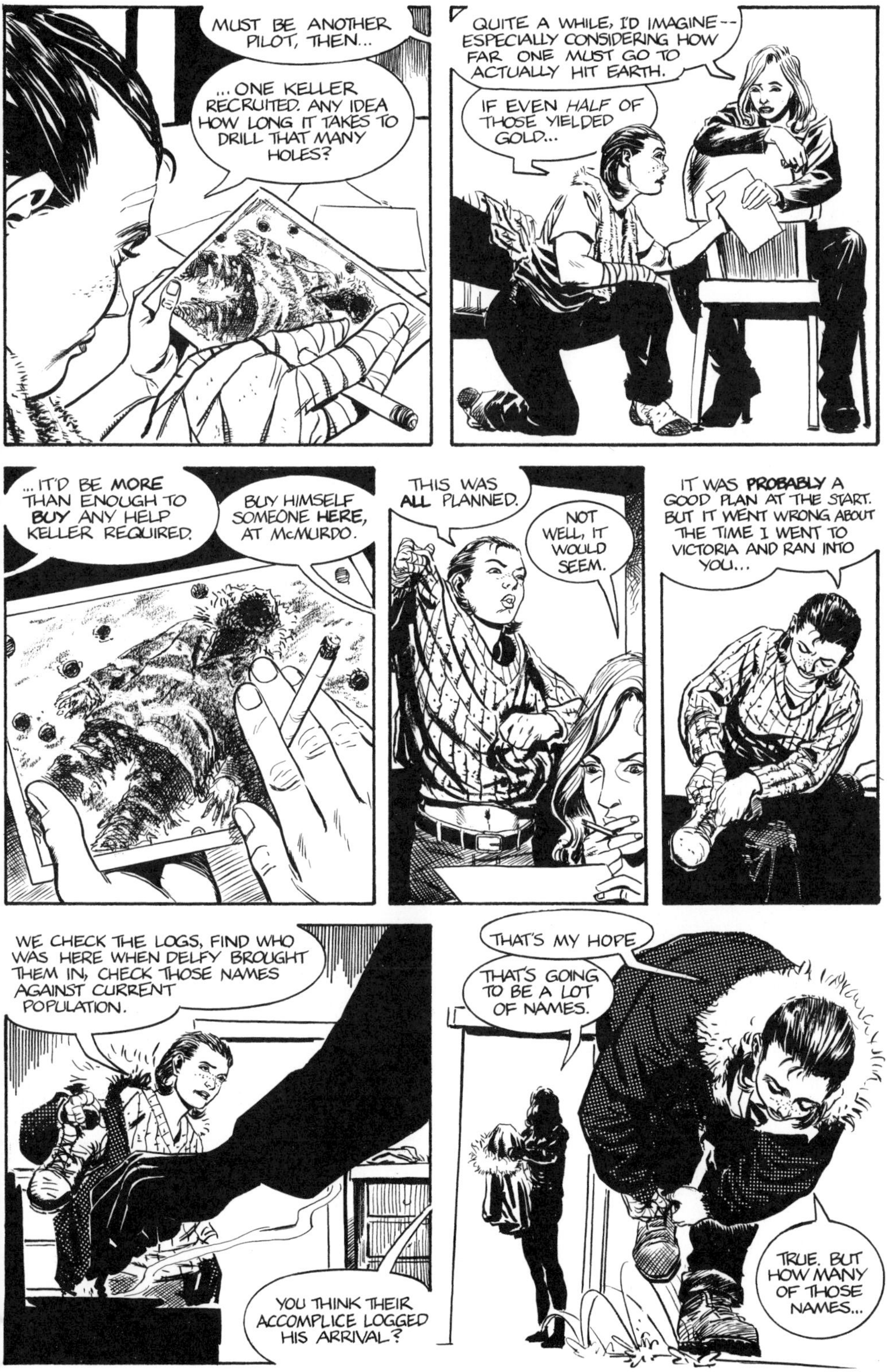
MUST BE ANOTHER PILOT, THEN...
...ONE KELLER RECRUITED. ANY IDEA HOW LONG IT TAKES TO DRILL THAT MANY HOLES?
QUITE A WHILE, I'D IMAGINE-- ESPECIALLY CONSIDERING HOW FAR ONE MUST GO TO ACTUALLY HIT EARTH.
IF EVEN *HALF* OF THOSE YIELDED GOLD...
...IT'D BE **MORE** THAN ENOUGH TO **BUY** ANY HELP KELLER REQUIRED.
BUY HIMSELF SOMEONE **HERE**, AT McMURDO.
THIS WAS **ALL** PLANNED.
NOT WELL, IT WOULD SEEM.
IT WAS **PROBABLY** A GOOD PLAN AT THE START. BUT IT WENT WRONG ABOUT THE TIME I WENT TO VICTORIA AND RAN INTO YOU...
WE CHECK THE LOGS, FIND WHO WAS HERE WHEN DELFY BROUGHT THEM IN, CHECK THOSE NAMES AGAINST CURRENT POPULATION.
YOU THINK THEIR ACCOMPLICE LOGGED HIS ARRIVAL?
THAT'S MY HOPE.
THAT'S GOING TO BE A LOT OF NAMES.
TRUE, BUT HOW MANY OF THOSE NAMES...

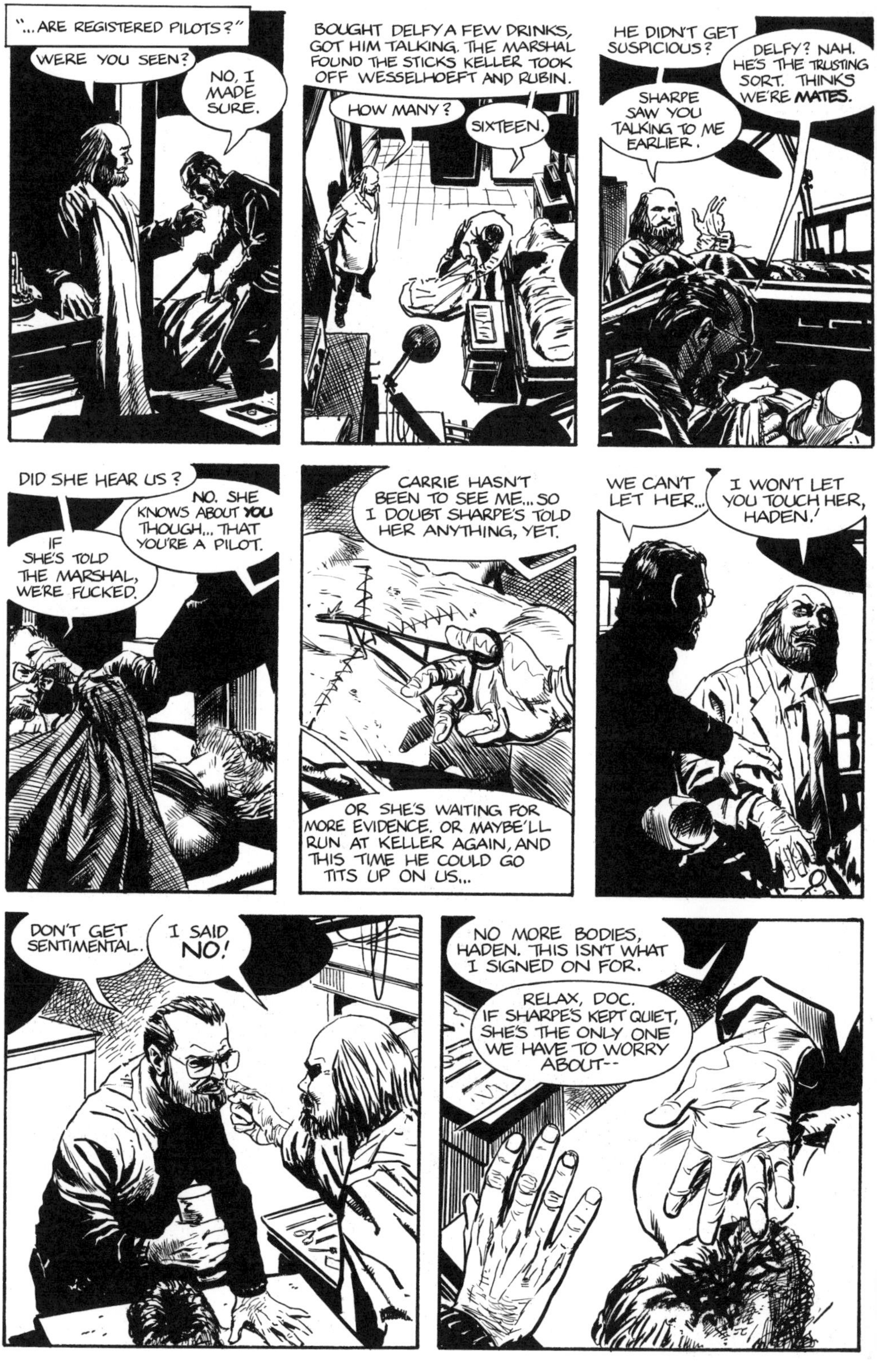
"...ARE REGISTERED PILOTS?"
WERE YOU SEEN?
NO, I MADE SURE.
BOUGHT DELFY A FEW DRINKS, GOT HIM TALKING. THE MARSHAL FOUND THE STICKS KELLER TOOK OFF WESSELHOEFT AND RUBIN.
HOW MANY?
SIXTEEN.
HE DIDN'T GET SUSPICIOUS?
DELFY? NAH. HE'S THE TRUSTING SORT. THINKS WE'RE MATES.
SHARPE SAW YOU TALKING TO ME EARLIER.
DID SHE HEAR US?
NO. SHE KNOWS ABOUT YOU THOUGH... THAT YOU'RE A PILOT.
IF SHE'S TOLD THE MARSHAL, WE'RE FUCKED.
CARRIE HASN'T BEEN TO SEE ME... SO I DOUBT SHARPE'S TOLD HER ANYTHING, YET.
OR SHE'S WAITING FOR MORE EVIDENCE. OR MAYBE'LL RUN AT KELLER AGAIN, AND THIS TIME HE COULD GO TITS UP ON US...
WE CAN'T LET HER...
I WON'T LET YOU TOUCH HER, HADEN.!
DON'T GET SENTIMENTAL.
I SAID NO!
NO MORE BODIES, HADEN. THIS ISN'T WHAT I SIGNED ON FOR.
RELAX, DOC. IF SHARPE'S KEPT QUIET, SHE'S THE ONLY ONE WE HAVE TO WORRY ABOUT--

"—YOU **FIND** OUT. I'LL DO THE REST."

FURRY! SOCIAL OR BUSINESS?

BIT OF BOTH.

...DIDN'T MEAN TO INTERRUPT.

NAH, WE'RE JUST TRYING TO FILL IN SOME BLANKS.

DOCTOR.

IS THAT BOTTLE FOR SHOW OR ARE YOU GOING TO POUR?

...REMEMBER THE GUY WITH THE CLAW HAMMER?

OH, MY GOD!

THIS WOULD'VE BEEN THREE, FOUR YEARS AGO— SOME MECHO IN THE MOTOR POOL STARTED CHASING EVERYONE IN THE GARAGE WITH A CLAW HAMMER.

HOLD STILL—

PUT TWO PEOPLE IN THE DISPENSARY.

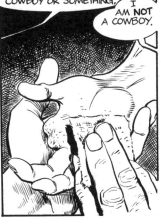

THE MARSHAL HERE, SHE **WALTZES** INTO THE V.M.F. LIKE SHE'S SOME COWBOY OR SOMETHING.

I AM **NOT** A COWBOY.

AND SHE **ORDERS** THIS GUY TO DROP THE HAMMER.

AND?

AND OF COURSE HE SAYS "NO."

ACTUALLY, HE SAID "EAT ME, BITCH."

—STOMACH, I WAS AIMING FOR HIS STOMACH—

SO CARRIE SHRUGS, STEPS FORWARD, AND KICKS HIM IN THE GNADS.

GUY DOUBLES OVER, LOSES THE HAMMER...

...AND **THAT'S** HOW CARRIE INTRODUCED HERSELF TO McMURDO STATION.

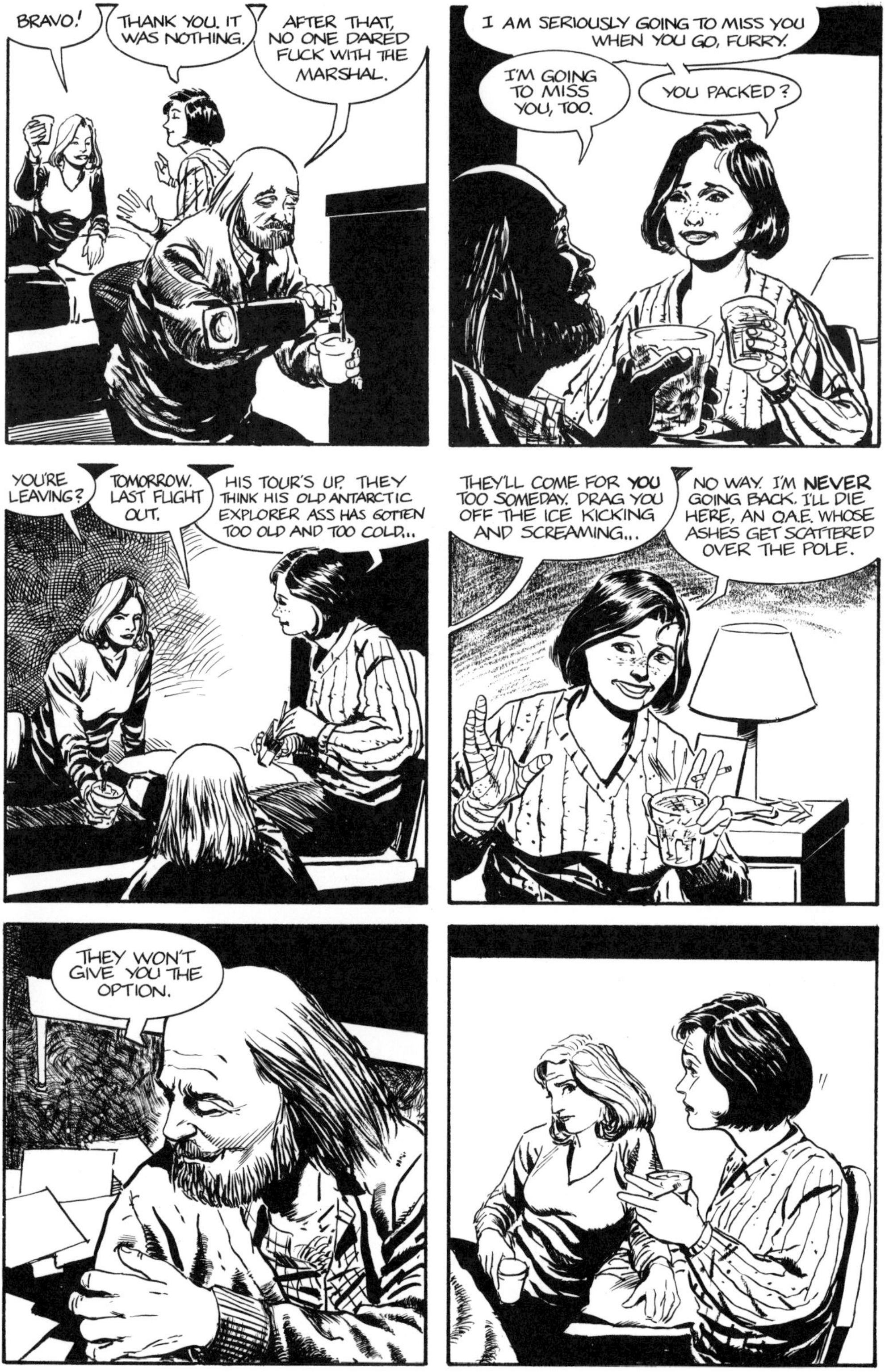
BRAVO!
THANK YOU. IT WAS NOTHING.
AFTER THAT, NO ONE DARED FUCK WITH THE MARSHAL.
I AM SERIOUSLY GOING TO MISS YOU WHEN YOU GO, FURRY.
I'M GOING TO MISS YOU, TOO.
YOU PACKED?
YOU'RE LEAVING?
TOMORROW. LAST FLIGHT OUT.
HIS TOUR'S UP. THEY THINK HIS OLD ANTARCTIC EXPLORER ASS HAS GOTTEN TOO OLD AND TOO COLD...
THEY'LL COME FOR YOU TOO SOMEDAY. DRAG YOU OFF THE ICE KICKING AND SCREAMING...
NO WAY. I'M NEVER GOING BACK. I'LL DIE HERE, AN O.A.E. WHOSE ASHES GET SCATTERED OVER THE POLE.
THEY WON'T GIVE YOU THE OPTION.

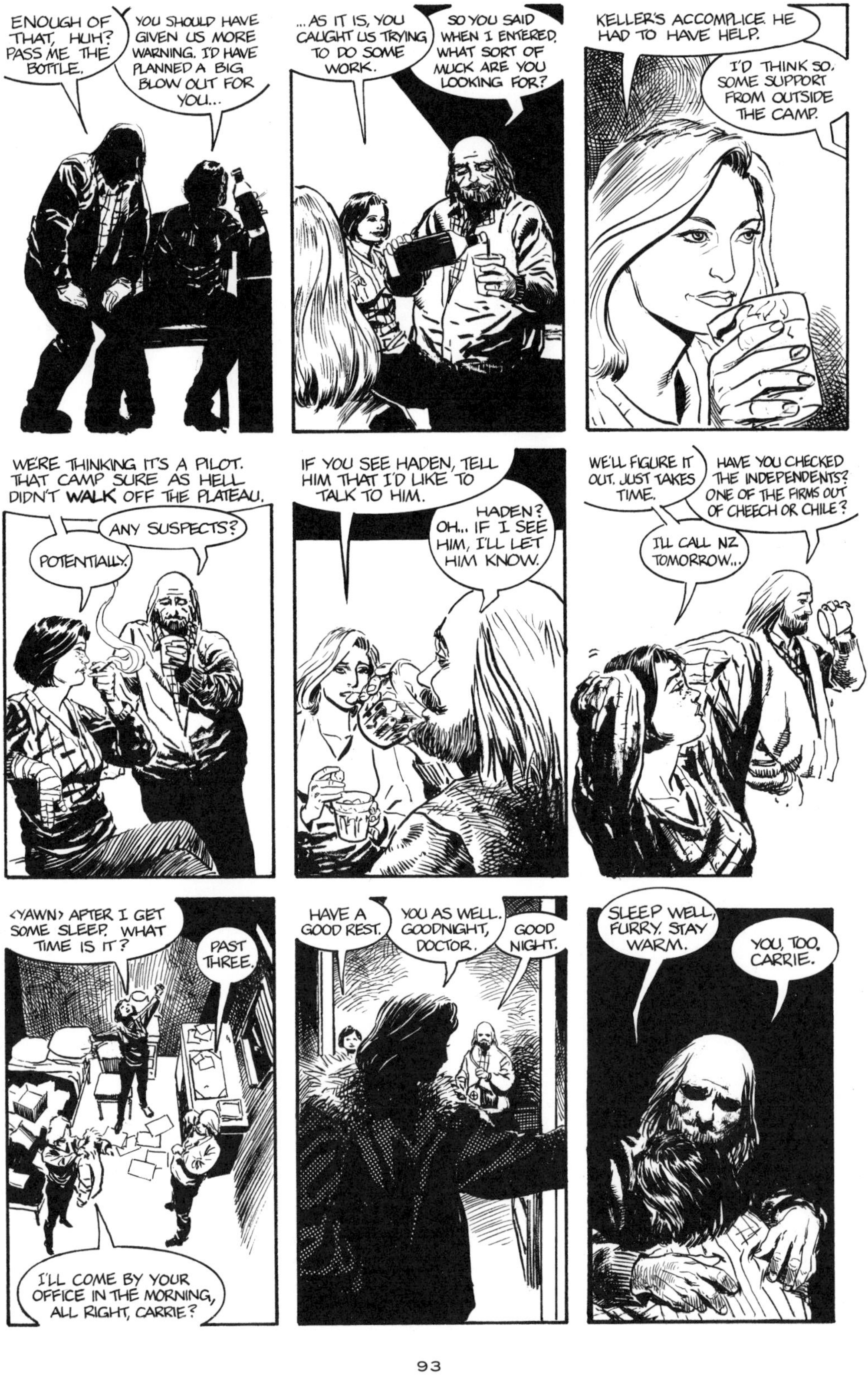
ENOUGH OF THAT, HUH? PASS ME THE BOTTLE.
YOU SHOULD HAVE GIVEN US MORE WARNING. I'D HAVE PLANNED A BIG BLOW OUT FOR YOU...
...AS IT IS, YOU CAUGHT US TRYING TO DO SOME WORK.
SO YOU SAID WHEN I ENTERED. WHAT SORT OF MUCK ARE YOU LOOKING FOR?
KELLER'S ACCOMPLICE. HE HAD TO HAVE HELP.
I'D THINK SO. SOME SUPPORT FROM OUTSIDE THE CAMP.
WE'RE THINKING IT'S A PILOT. THAT CAMP SURE AS HELL DIDN'T WALK OFF THE PLATEAU.
ANY SUSPECTS?
POTENTIALLY.
IF YOU SEE HADEN, TELL HIM THAT I'D LIKE TO TALK TO HIM.
HADEN? OH... IF I SEE HIM, I'LL LET HIM KNOW.
WE'LL FIGURE IT OUT. JUST TAKES TIME.
HAVE YOU CHECKED THE INDEPENDENTS? ONE OF THE FIRMS OUT OF CHEECH OR CHILE?
I'LL CALL NZ TOMORROW...
<YAWN> AFTER I GET SOME SLEEP. WHAT TIME IS IT?
PAST THREE.
I'LL COME BY YOUR OFFICE IN THE MORNING, ALL RIGHT, CARRIE?
HAVE A GOOD REST.
YOU AS WELL. GOODNIGHT, DOCTOR.
GOOD NIGHT.
SLEEP WELL, FURRY. STAY WARM.
YOU, TOO. CARRIE.

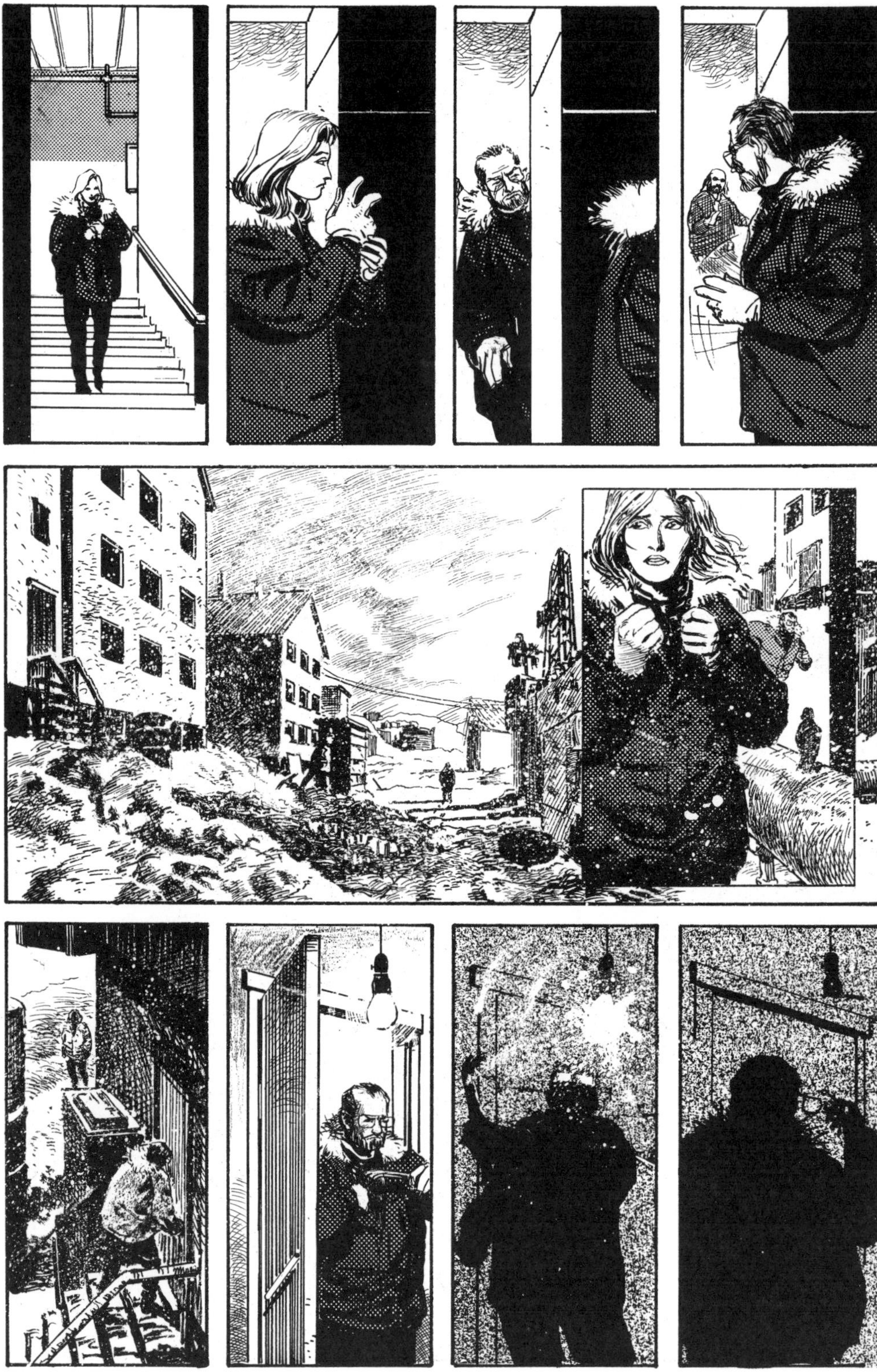

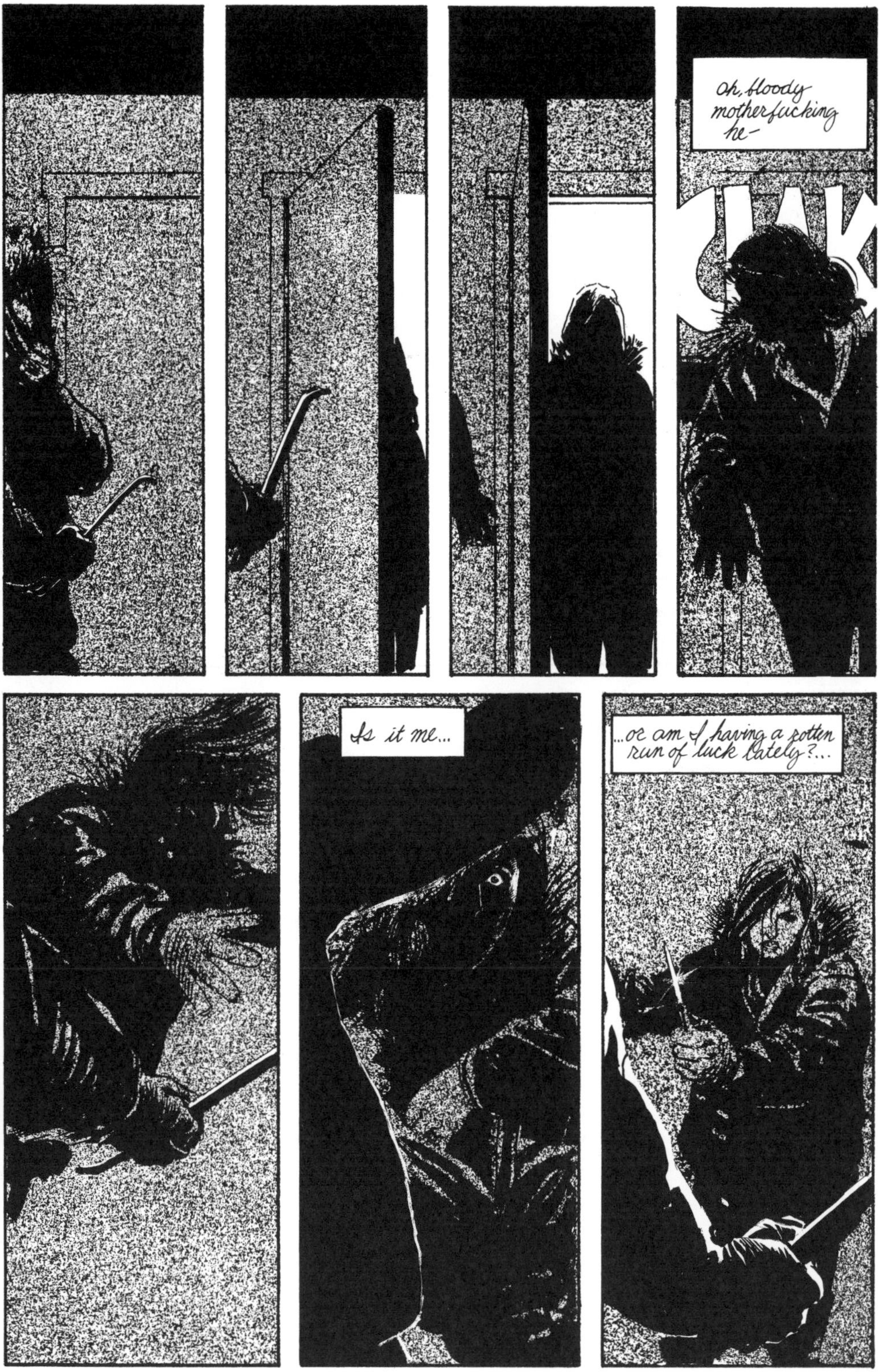
Oh, bloody motherfucking he-
Is it me...
...or am I having a rotten run of luck lately?...

CHAPTER FOUR

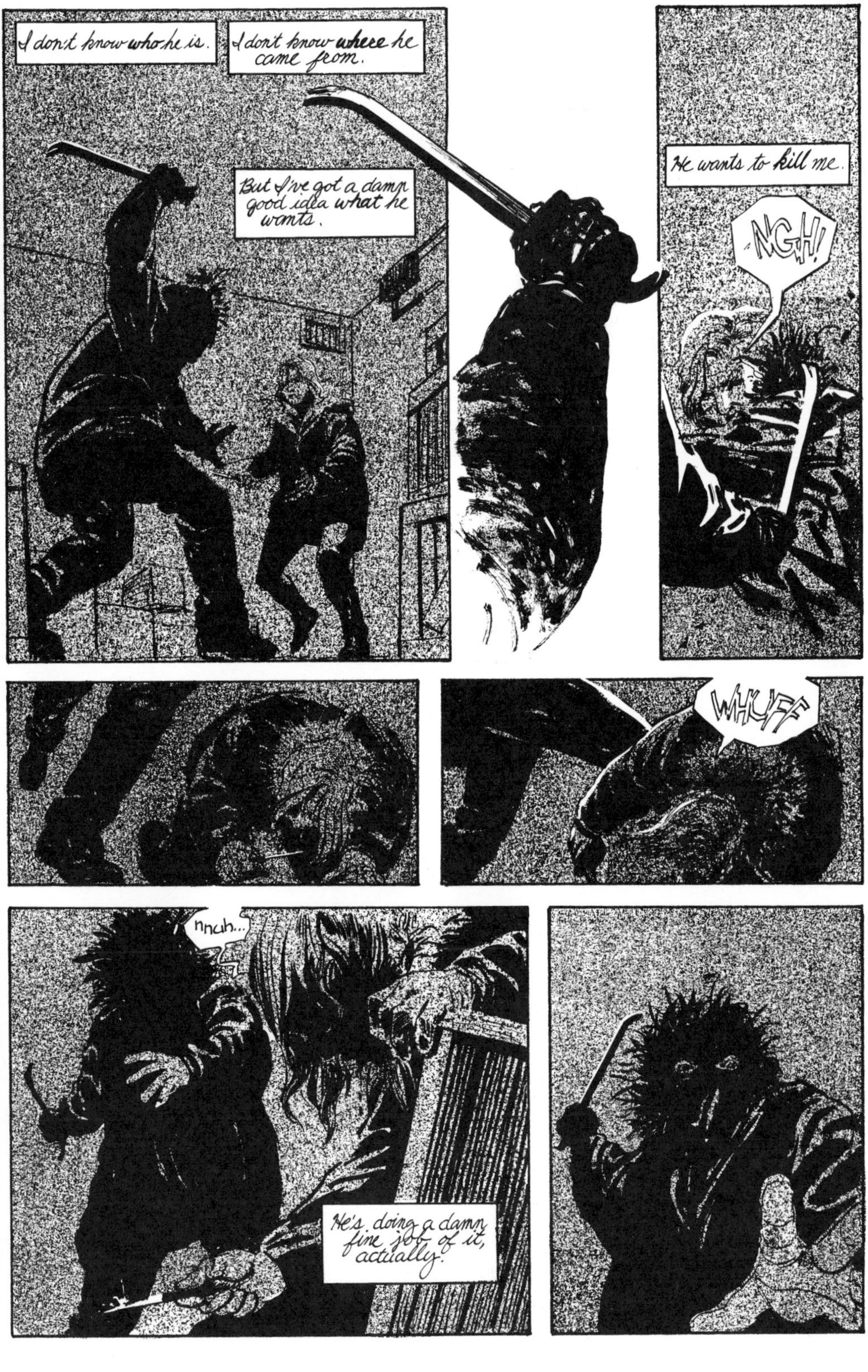
I don't know who he is.
I don't know where he came from.
But I've got a damn good idea what he wants.
He wants to kill me.
NGH!
WHUFF
nnuh...
He's doing a damn fine job of it, actually.

The knife's made by Carl Emerson...

...gift from an S.A.S. bloke I went with once.

David, his name was.

David's dead now...

...*knife* still works.

DAMN BITCH!

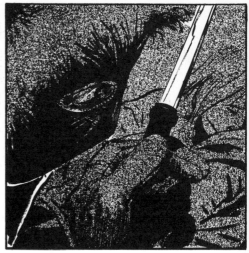

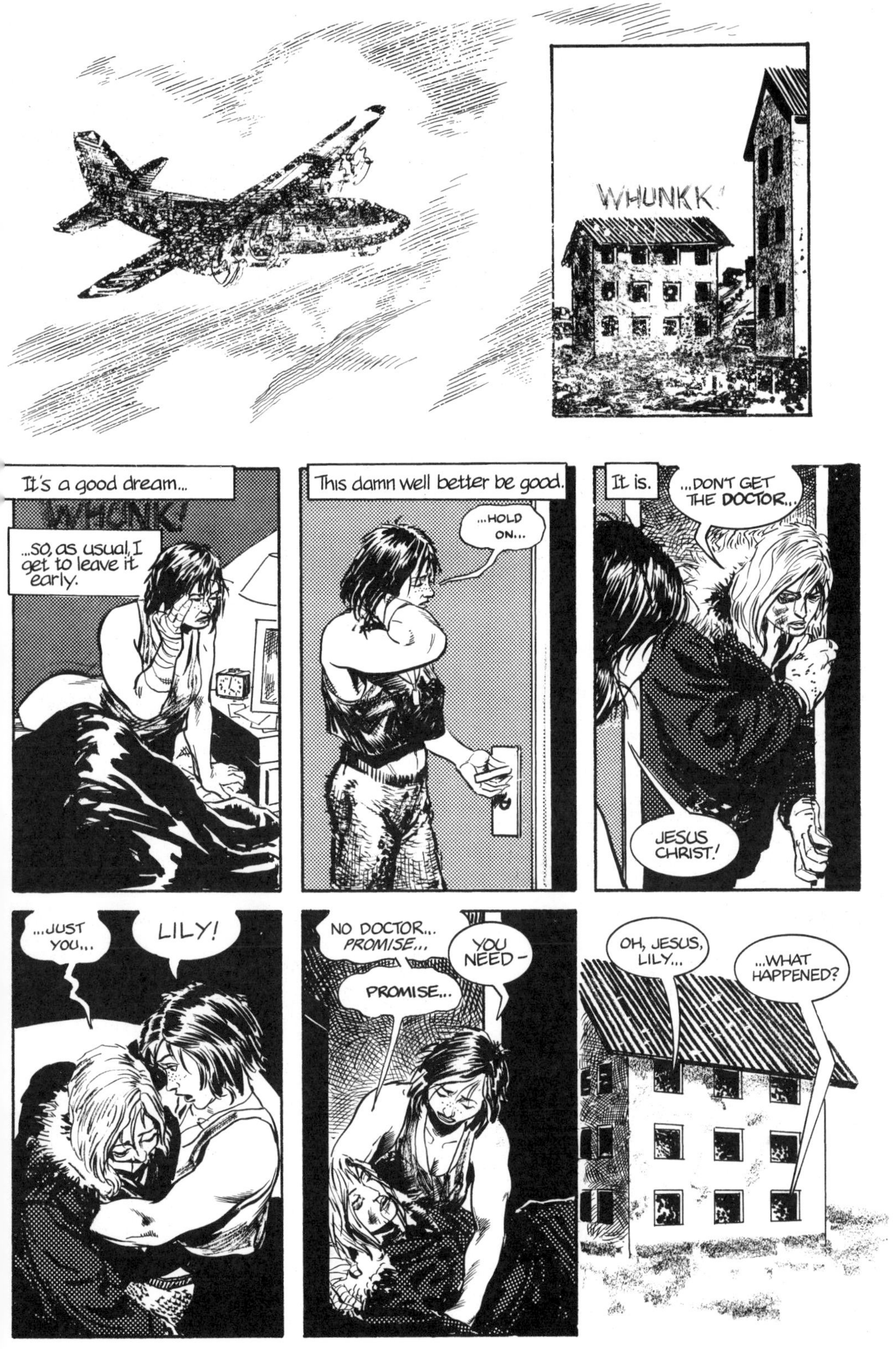
WHUNKK!
It's a good dream...
WHUNK!
...SO, as usual, I get to leave it early.
This damn well better be good.
...HOLD ON...
It is.
...DON'T GET THE DOCTOR...
JESUS CHRIST!
...JUST YOU...
LILY!
NO DOCTOR... PROMISE...
PROMISE...
YOU NEED-
OH, JESUS, LILY...
...WHAT HAPPENED?

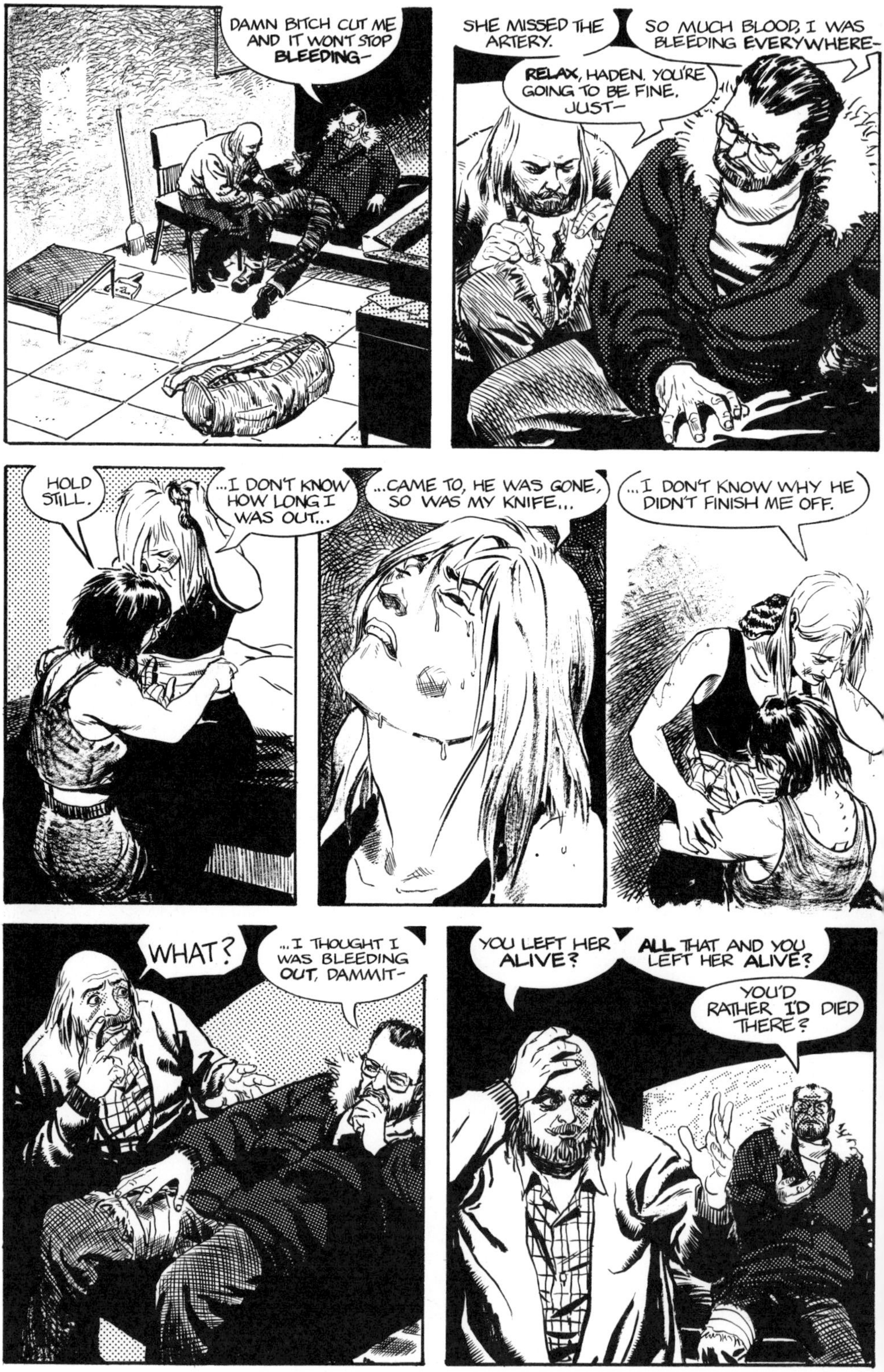
DAMN BITCH CUT ME AND IT WON'T STOP BLEEDING-
SHE MISSED THE ARTERY.
SO MUCH BLOOD, I WAS BLEEDING EVERYWHERE-
RELAX, HADEN. YOU'RE GOING TO BE FINE. JUST-
HOLD STILL.
...I DON'T KNOW HOW LONG I WAS OUT...
...CAME TO, HE WAS GONE, SO WAS MY KNIFE...
...I DON'T KNOW WHY HE DIDN'T FINISH ME OFF.
WHAT?
...I THOUGHT I WAS BLEEDING OUT, DAMMIT-
YOU LEFT HER ALIVE?
ALL THAT AND YOU LEFT HER ALIVE?
YOU'D RATHER I'D DIED THERE?

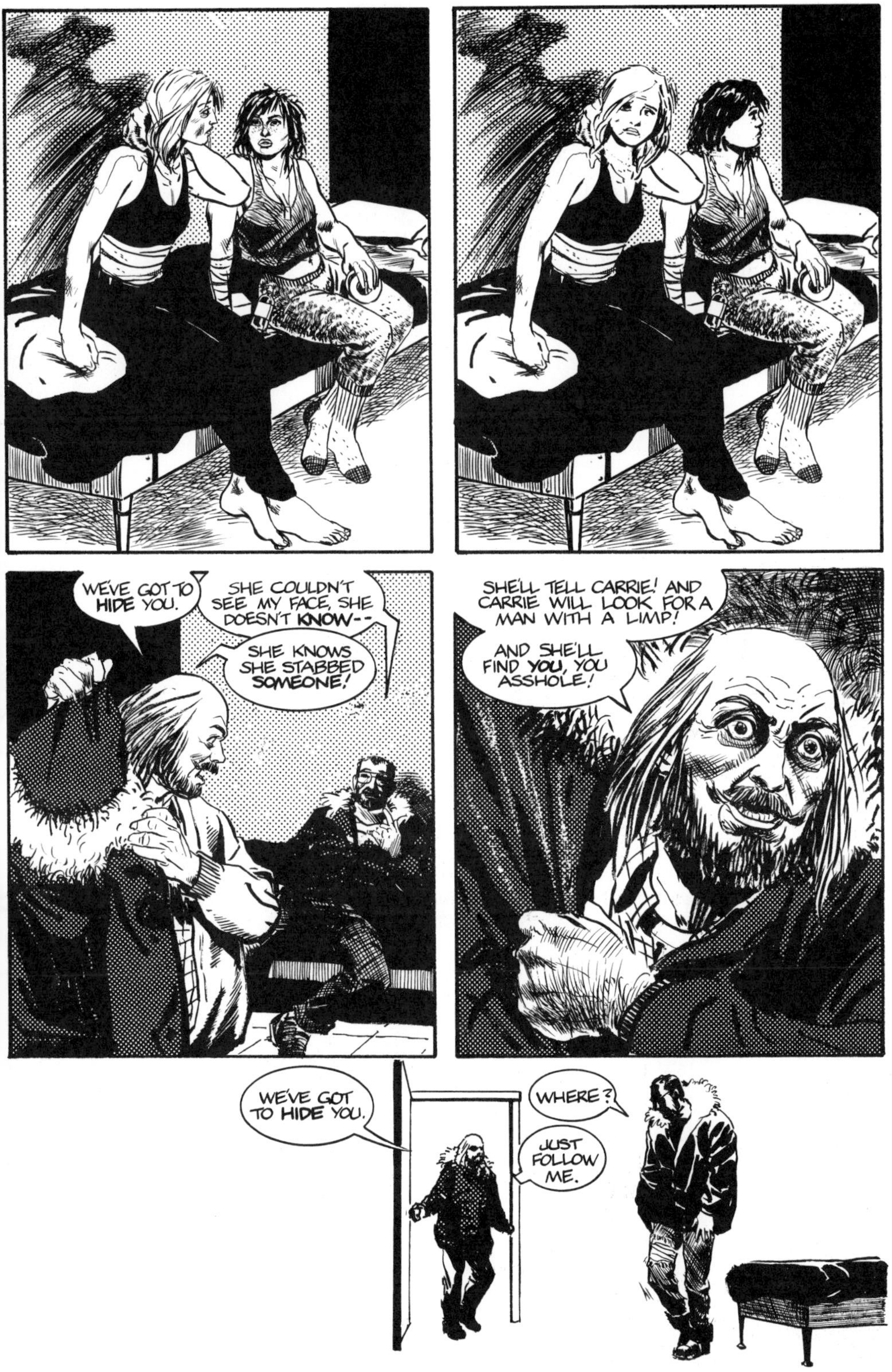
WE'VE GOT TO **HIDE** YOU.
SHE COULDN'T SEE MY FACE, SHE DOESN'T **KNOW**--
SHE KNOWS SHE STABBED **SOMEONE**!
SHE'LL TELL CARRIE! AND CARRIE WILL LOOK FOR A MAN WITH A LIMP!
AND SHE'LL FIND **YOU**, YOU ASSHOLE!
WE'VE GOT TO **HIDE** YOU.
WHERE?
JUST FOLLOW ME.

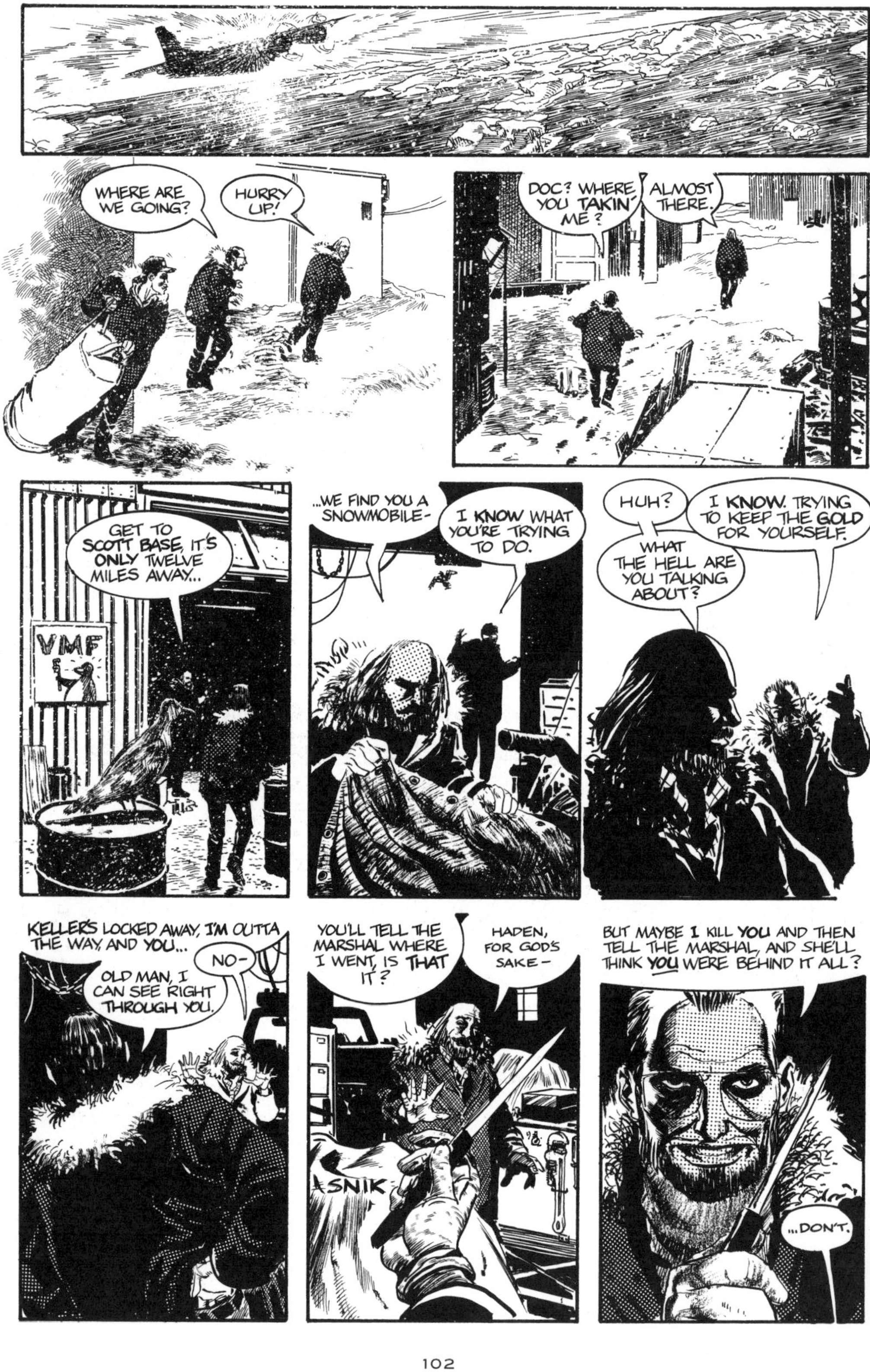
WHERE ARE WE GOING?
HURRY UP!
DOC? WHERE YOU TAKIN' ME?
ALMOST THERE.
GET TO SCOTT BASE, IT'S ONLY TWELVE MILES AWAY...
VMF
...WE FIND YOU A SNOWMOBILE-
I KNOW WHAT YOU'RE TRYING TO DO.
HUH?
I KNOW. TRYING TO KEEP THE GOLD FOR YOURSELF.
WHAT THE HELL ARE YOU TALKING ABOUT?
KELLER'S LOCKED AWAY, I'M OUTTA THE WAY, AND YOU...
NO-
OLD MAN, I CAN SEE RIGHT THROUGH YOU.
YOU'LL TELL THE MARSHAL WHERE I WENT, IS THAT IT?
HADEN, FOR GOD'S SAKE-
SNIK
BUT MAYBE I KILL YOU AND THEN TELL THE MARSHAL, AND SHE'LL THINK YOU WERE BEHIND IT ALL?
...DON'T.

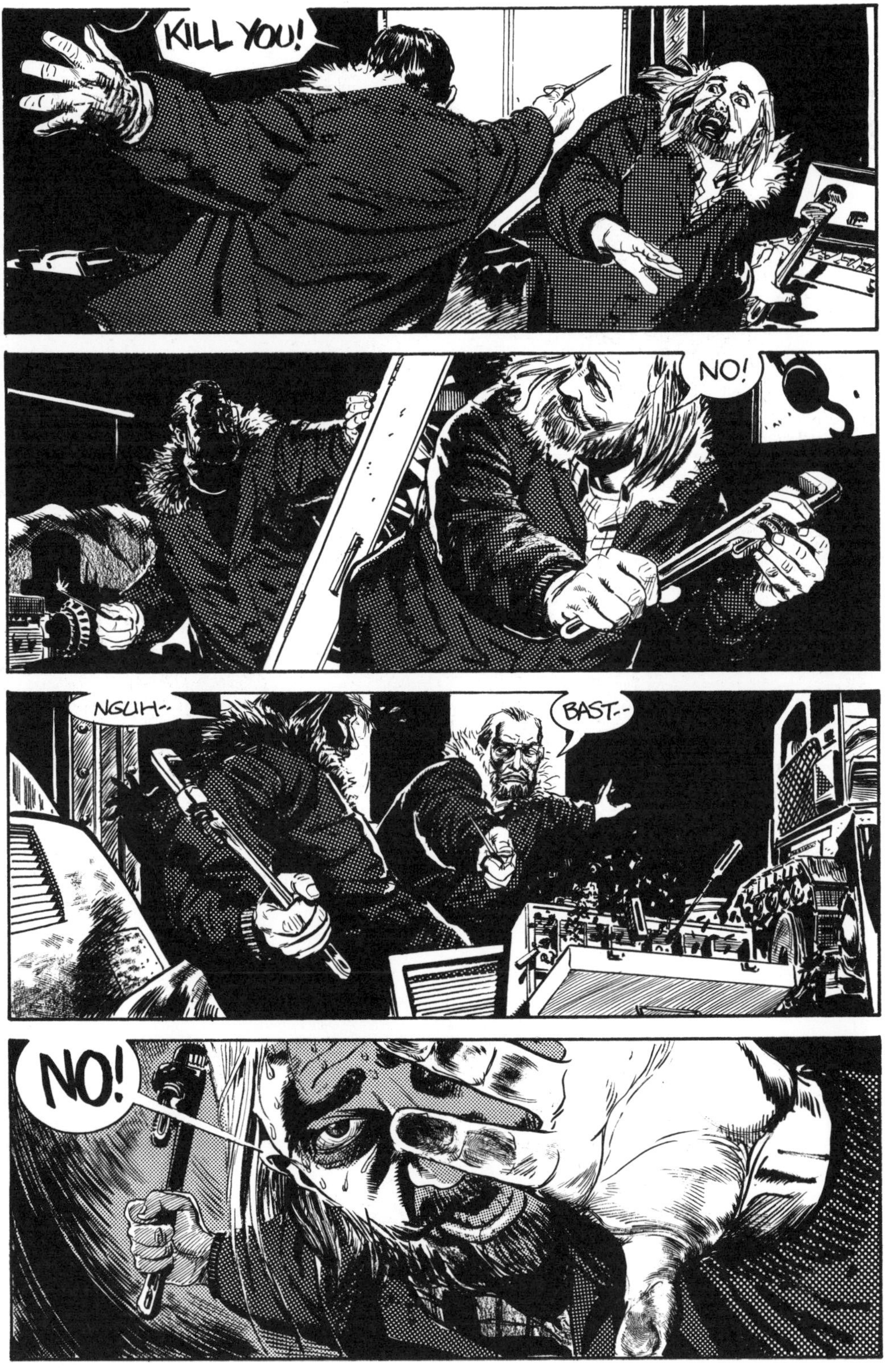
KILL YOU!
NO!
NGUH--
BAST--
NO!

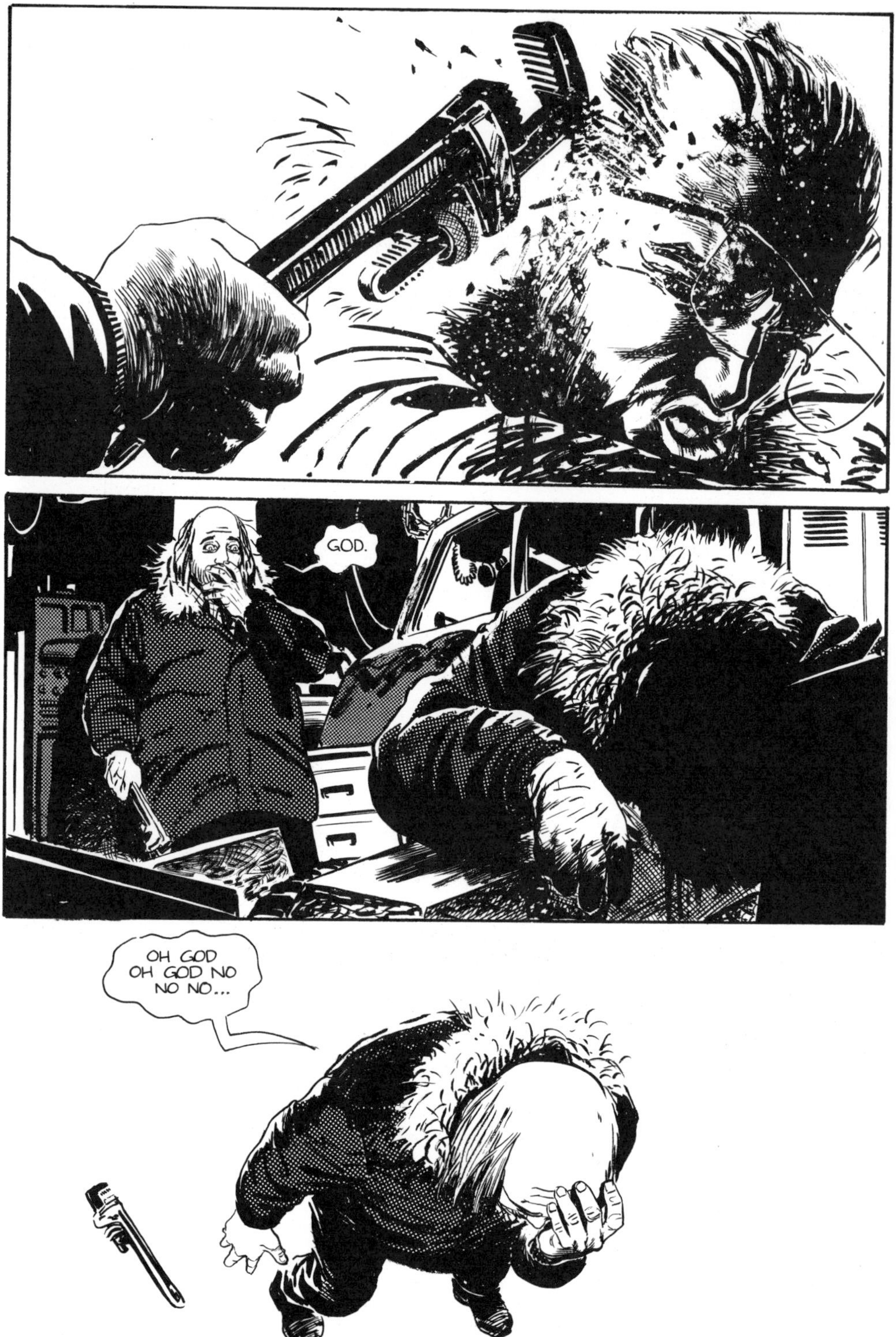
GOD.
OH GOD
OH GOD NO
NO NO...

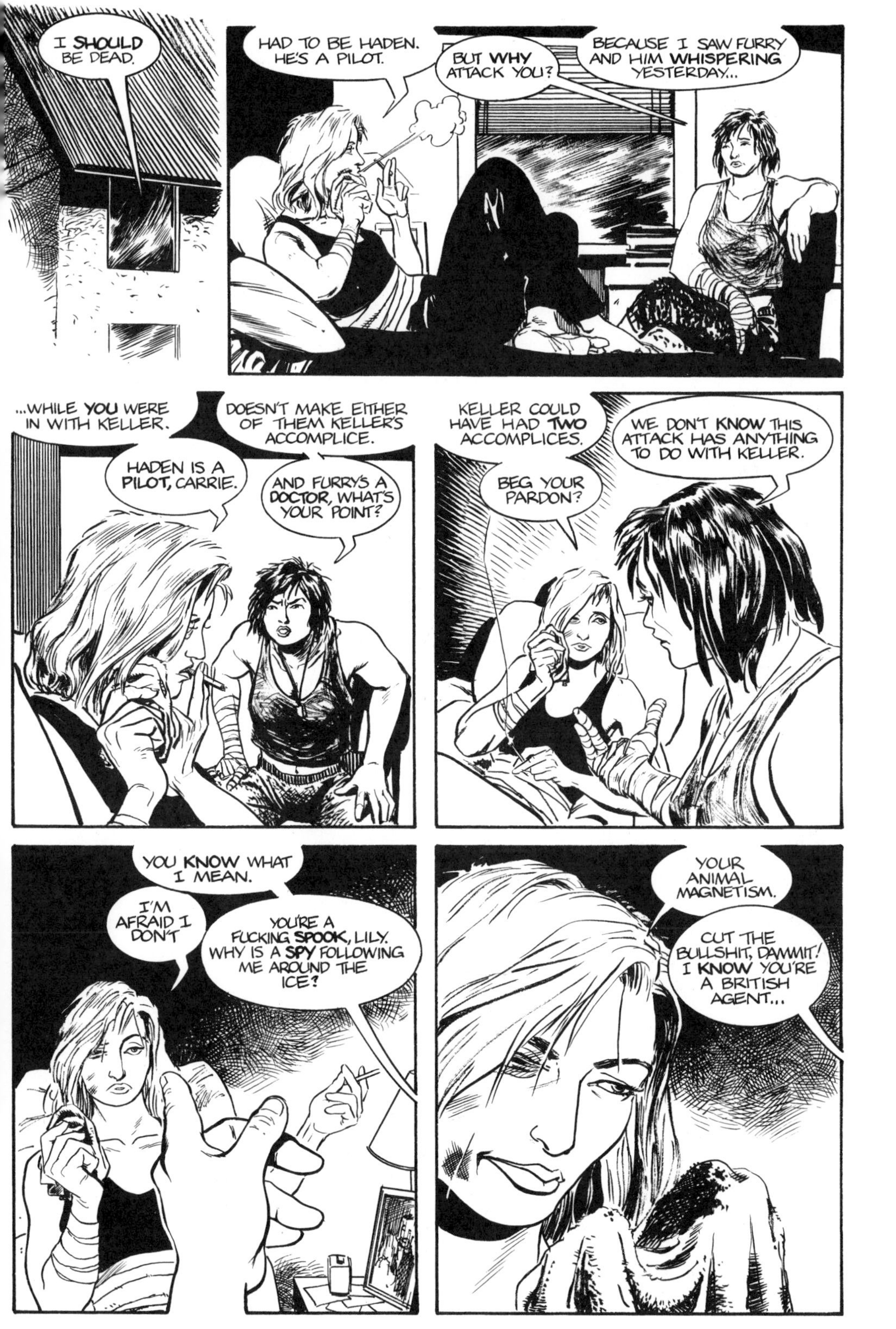
I SHOULD BE DEAD.
HAD TO BE HADEN. HE'S A PILOT.
BUT WHY ATTACK YOU?
BECAUSE I SAW FURRY AND HIM WHISPERING YESTERDAY...
...WHILE YOU WERE IN WITH KELLER.
DOESN'T MAKE EITHER OF THEM KELLER'S ACCOMPLICE.
HADEN IS A PILOT, CARRIE.
AND FURRY'S A DOCTOR, WHAT'S YOUR POINT?
KELLER COULD HAVE HAD TWO ACCOMPLICES.
BEG YOUR PARDON?
WE DON'T KNOW THIS ATTACK HAS ANYTHING TO DO WITH KELLER.
YOU KNOW WHAT I MEAN.
I'M AFRAID I DON'T
YOU'RE A FUCKING SPOOK, LILY. WHY IS A SPY FOLLOWING ME AROUND THE ICE?
YOUR ANIMAL MAGNETISM.
CUT THE BULLSHIT, DAMMIT! I KNOW YOU'RE A BRITISH AGENT...

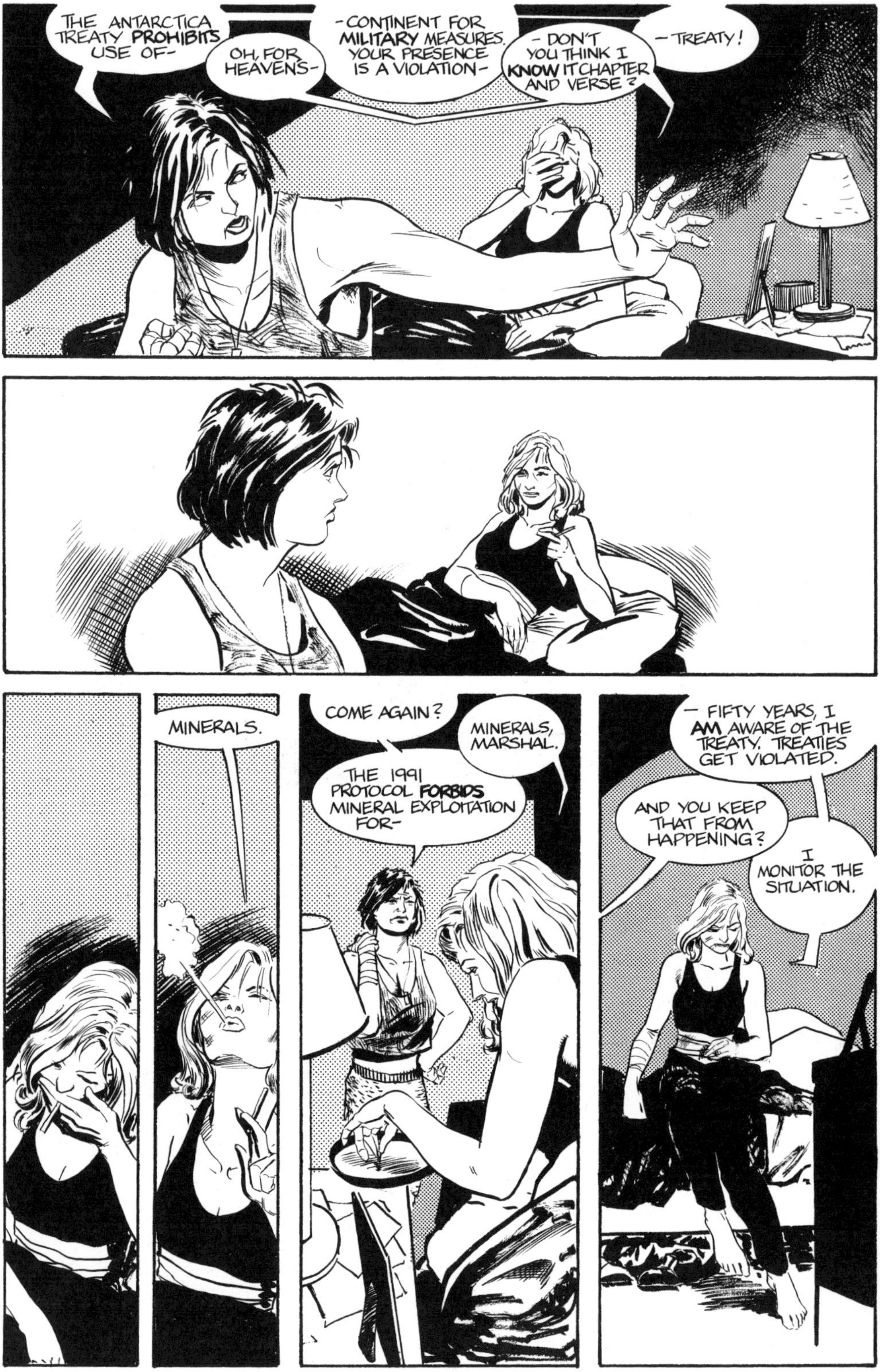
THE ANTARCTICA TREATY PROHIBITS USE OF-
OH, FOR HEAVENS-
-CONTINENT FOR MILITARY MEASURES. YOUR PRESENCE IS A VIOLATION-
-DON'T YOU THINK I KNOW IT CHAPTER AND VERSE?
-TREATY!
MINERALS.
COME AGAIN?
MINERALS, MARSHAL.
THE 1991 PROTOCOL FORBIDS MINERAL EXPLOITATION FOR-
-FIFTY YEARS, I AM AWARE OF THE TREATY. TREATIES GET VIOLATED.
AND YOU KEEP THAT FROM HAPPENING?
I MONITOR THE SITUATION.

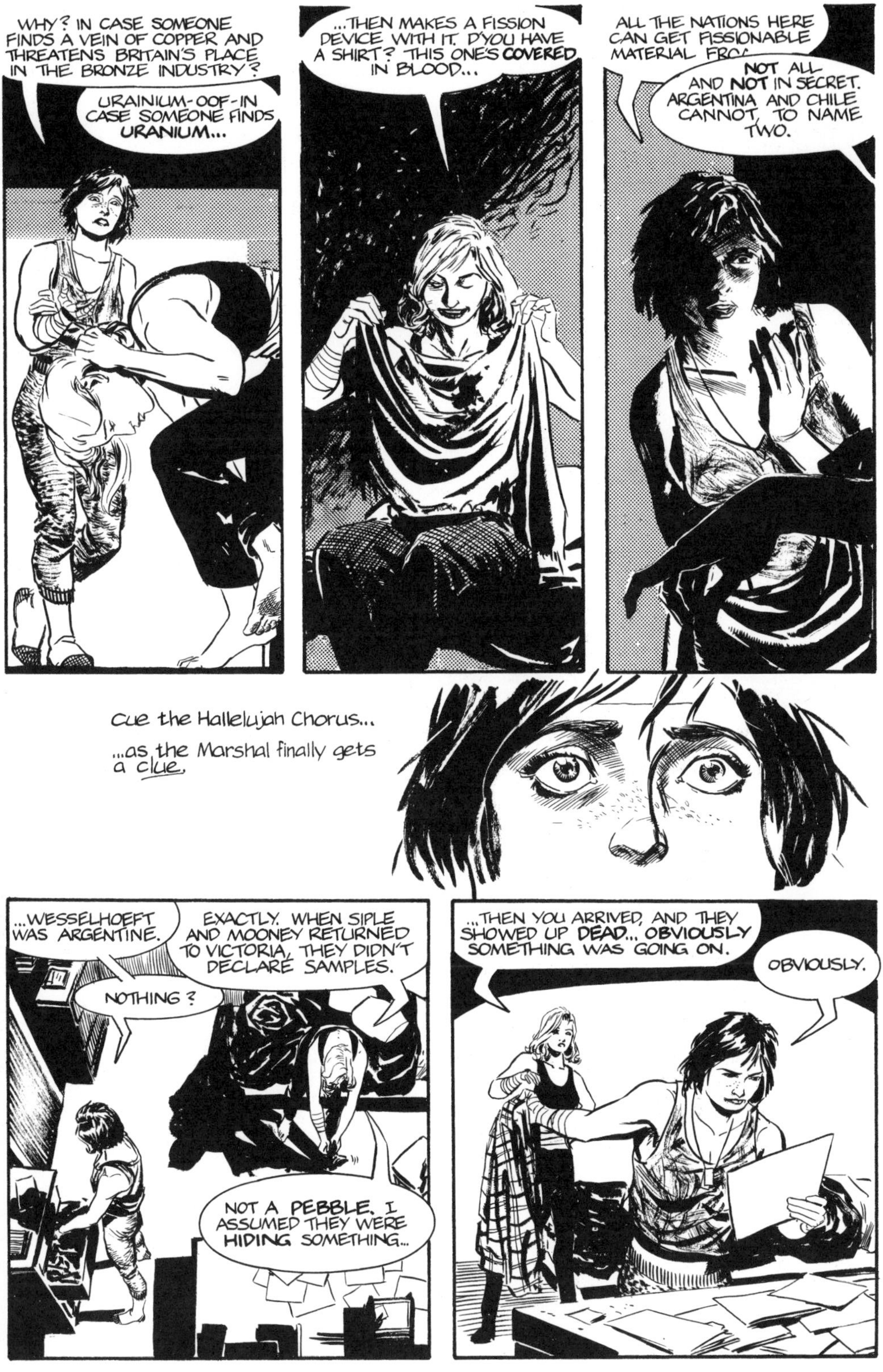
WHY? IN CASE SOMEONE FINDS A VEIN OF COPPER AND THREATENS BRITAIN'S PLACE IN THE BRONZE INDUSTRY?
URAINIUM-OOF-IN CASE SOMEONE FINDS URANIUM...
...THEN MAKES A FISSION DEVICE WITH IT. D'YOU HAVE A SHIRT? THIS ONE'S COVERED IN BLOOD...
ALL THE NATIONS HERE CAN GET FISSIONABLE MATERIAL FRO—
NOT ALL AND NOT IN SECRET. ARGENTINA AND CHILE CANNOT, TO NAME TWO.
Cue the Hallelujah Chorus...
...as the Marshal finally gets a clue.
...WESSELHOEFT WAS ARGENTINE.
EXACTLY. WHEN SIPLE AND MOONEY RETURNED TO VICTORIA, THEY DIDN'T DECLARE SAMPLES.
NOTHING?
NOT A PEBBLE. I ASSUMED THEY WERE HIDING SOMETHING...
...THEN YOU ARRIVED, AND THEY SHOWED UP DEAD... OBVIOUSLY SOMETHING WAS GOING ON.
OBVIOUSLY.

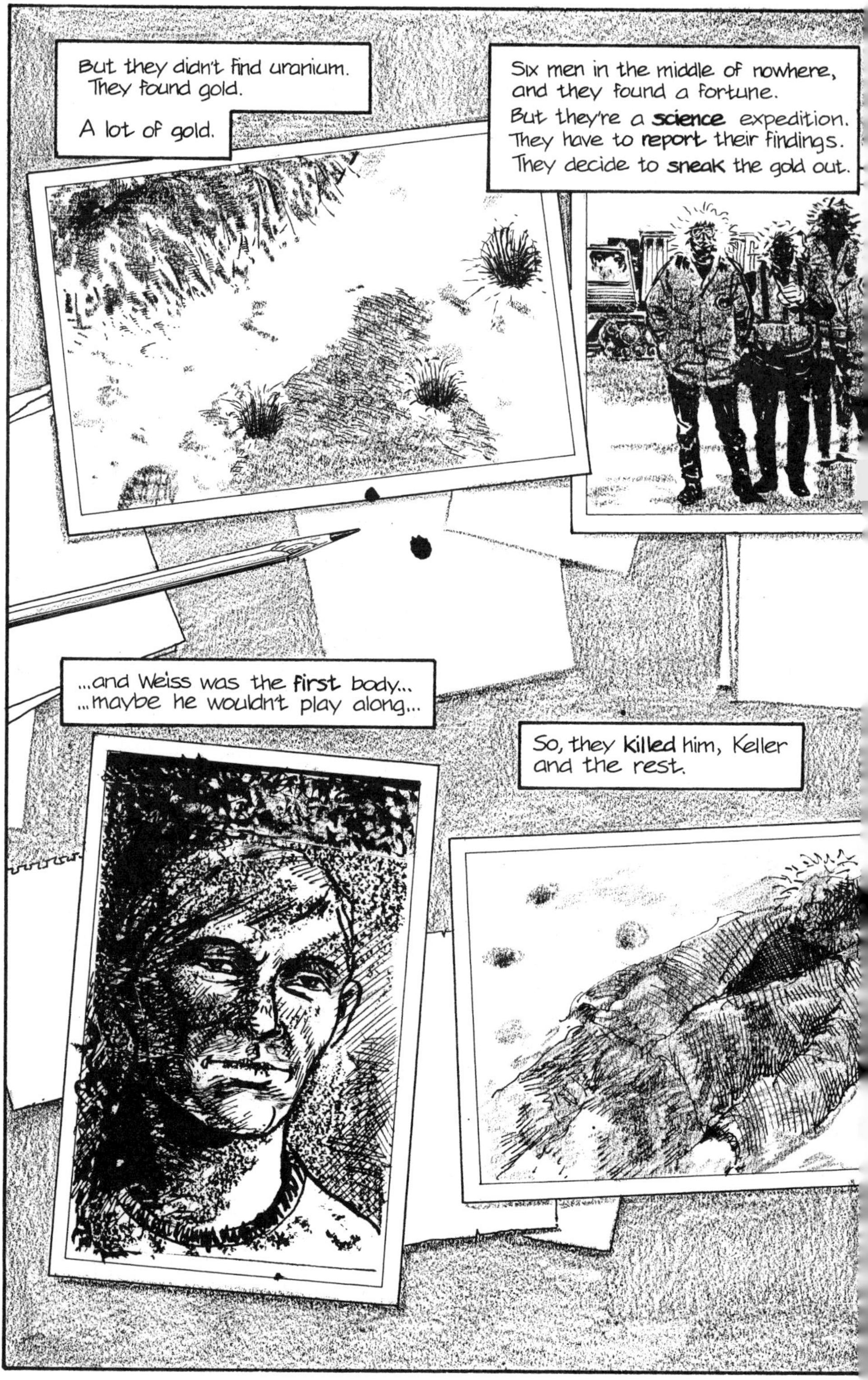
But they didn't find uranium. They found gold.
A lot of gold.
Six men in the middle of nowhere, and they found a fortune.
But they're a **science** expedition. They have to **report** their findings. They decide to **sneak** the gold out.
...and Weiss was the **first** body... ...maybe he wouldn't play along...
So, they **killed** him, Keller and the rest.

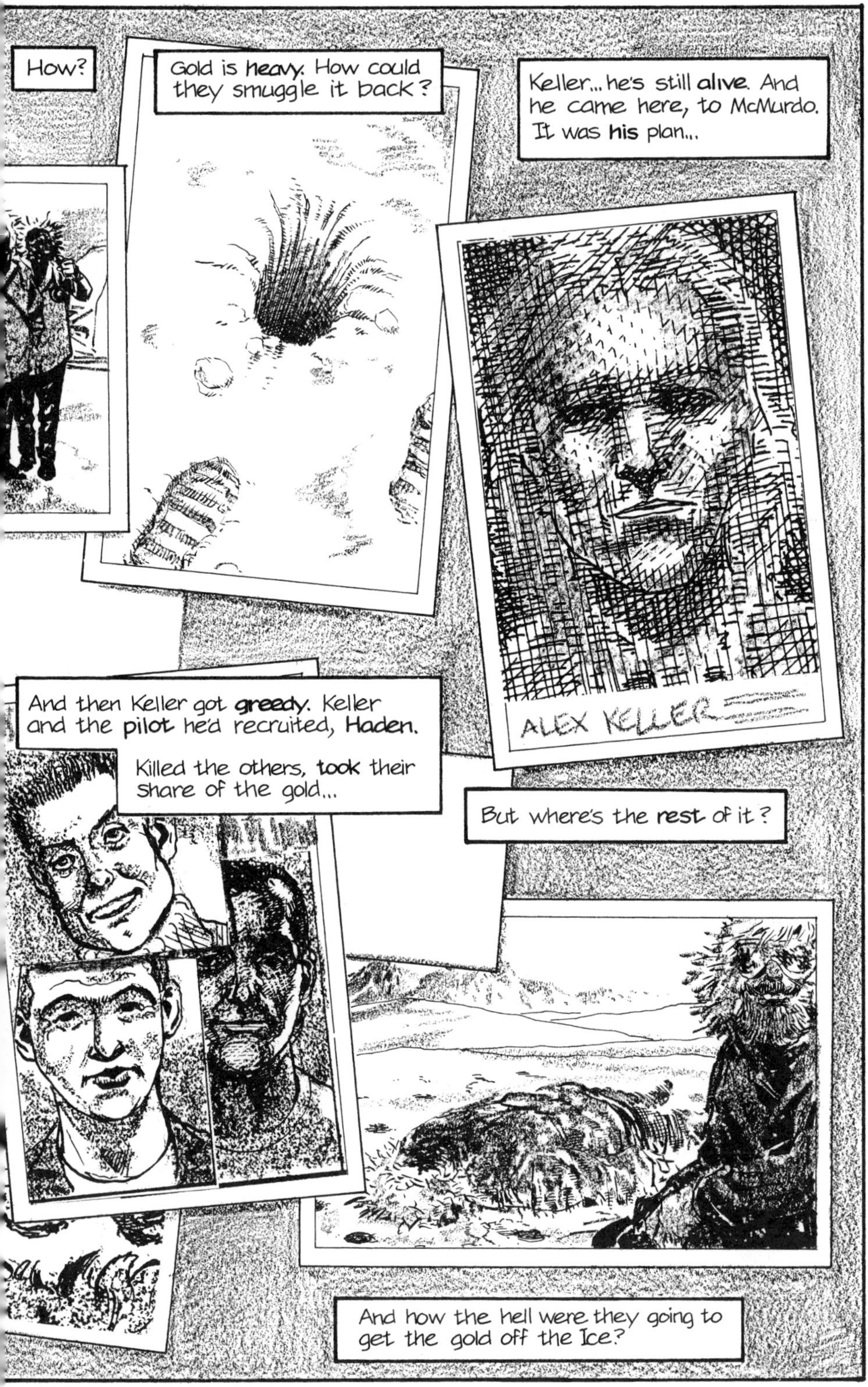
How?
Gold is heavy. How could they smuggle it back?
Keller... he's still alive. And he came here, to McMurdo. It was his plan...
ALEX KELLER
And then Keller got greedy. Keller and the pilot he'd recruited, Haden.
Killed the others, took their share of the gold...
But where's the rest of it?
And how the hell were they going to get the gold off the Ice?

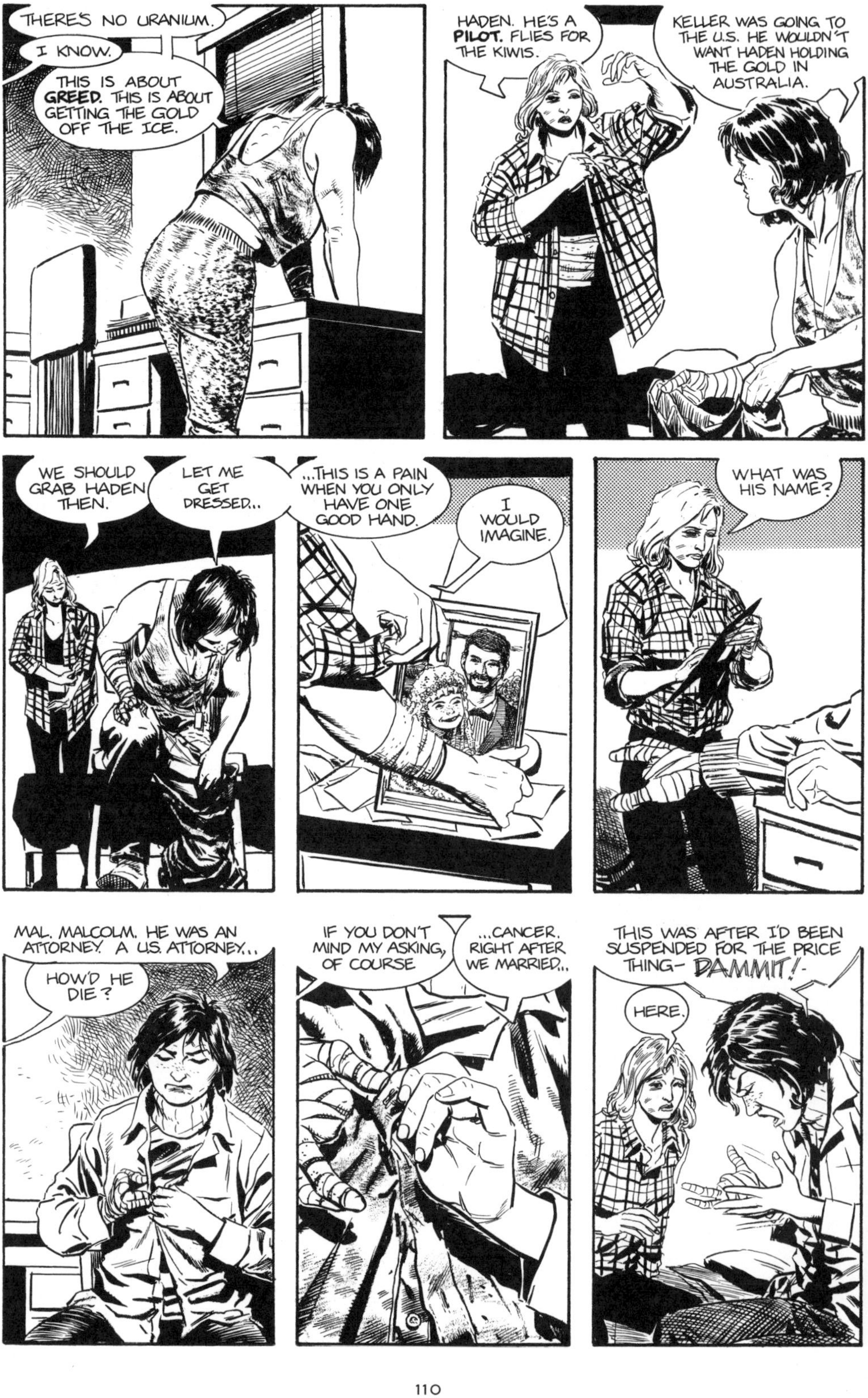
THERE'S NO URANIUM.
I KNOW.
THIS IS ABOUT GREED. THIS IS ABOUT GETTING THE GOLD OFF THE ICE.
HADEN. HE'S A PILOT. FLIES FOR THE KIWIS.
KELLER WAS GOING TO THE U.S. HE WOULDN'T WANT HADEN HOLDING THE GOLD IN AUSTRALIA.
WE SHOULD GRAB HADEN THEN.
LET ME GET DRESSED...
...THIS IS A PAIN WHEN YOU ONLY HAVE ONE GOOD HAND.
I WOULD IMAGINE.
WHAT WAS HIS NAME?
MAL. MALCOLM. HE WAS AN ATTORNEY. A U.S. ATTORNEY...
HOW'D HE DIE?
IF YOU DON'T MIND MY ASKING, OF COURSE
...CANCER. RIGHT AFTER WE MARRIED...
THIS WAS AFTER I'D BEEN SUSPENDED FOR THE PRICE THING- DAMMIT!-
HERE.

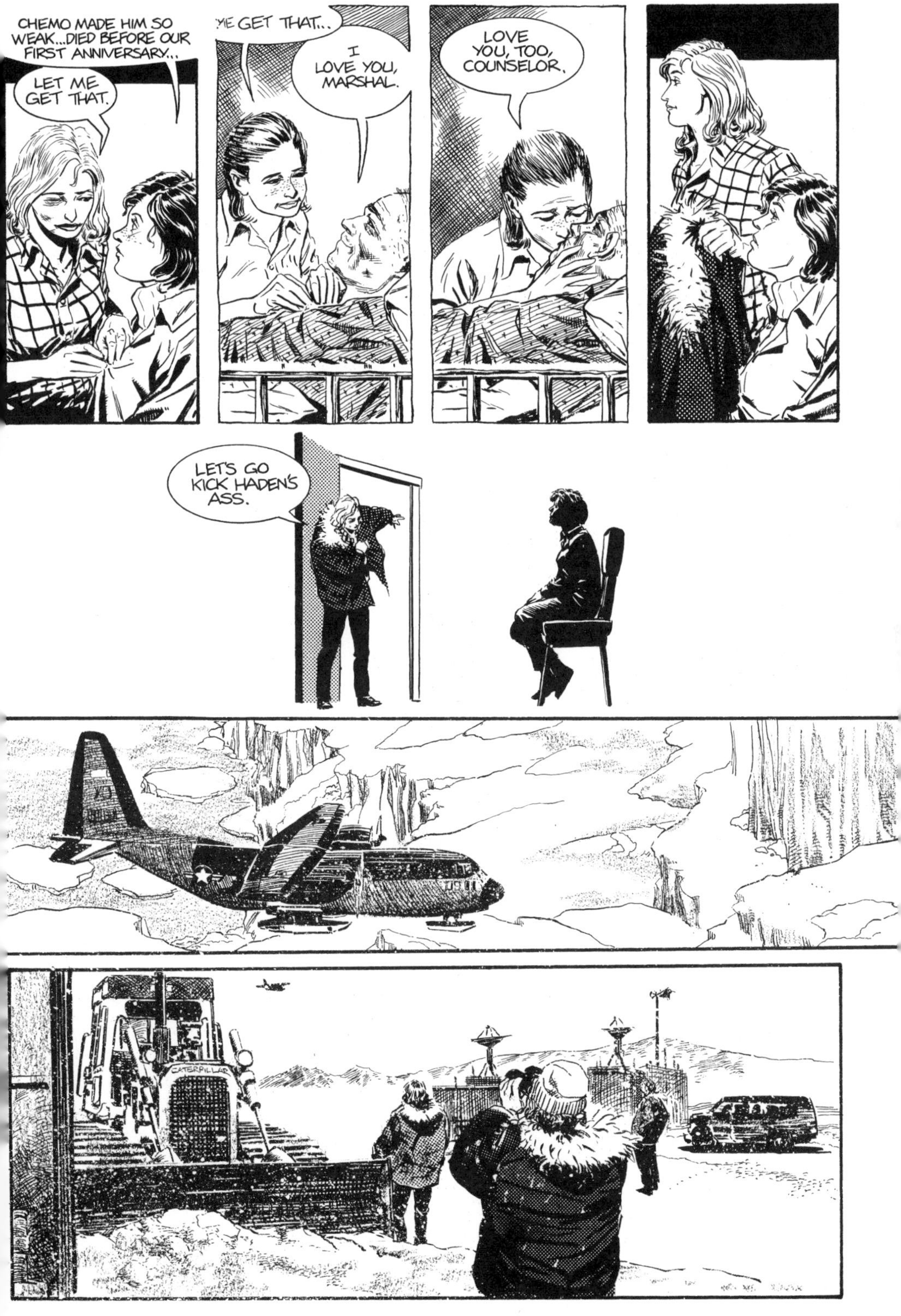

CHEMO MADE HIM SO WEAK...DIED BEFORE OUR FIRST ANNIVERSARY...
LET ME GET THAT.
ME GET THAT...
I LOVE YOU, MARSHAL.
LOVE YOU, TOO, COUNSELOR.
LET'S GO KICK HADEN'S ASS.
CATERPILLAR

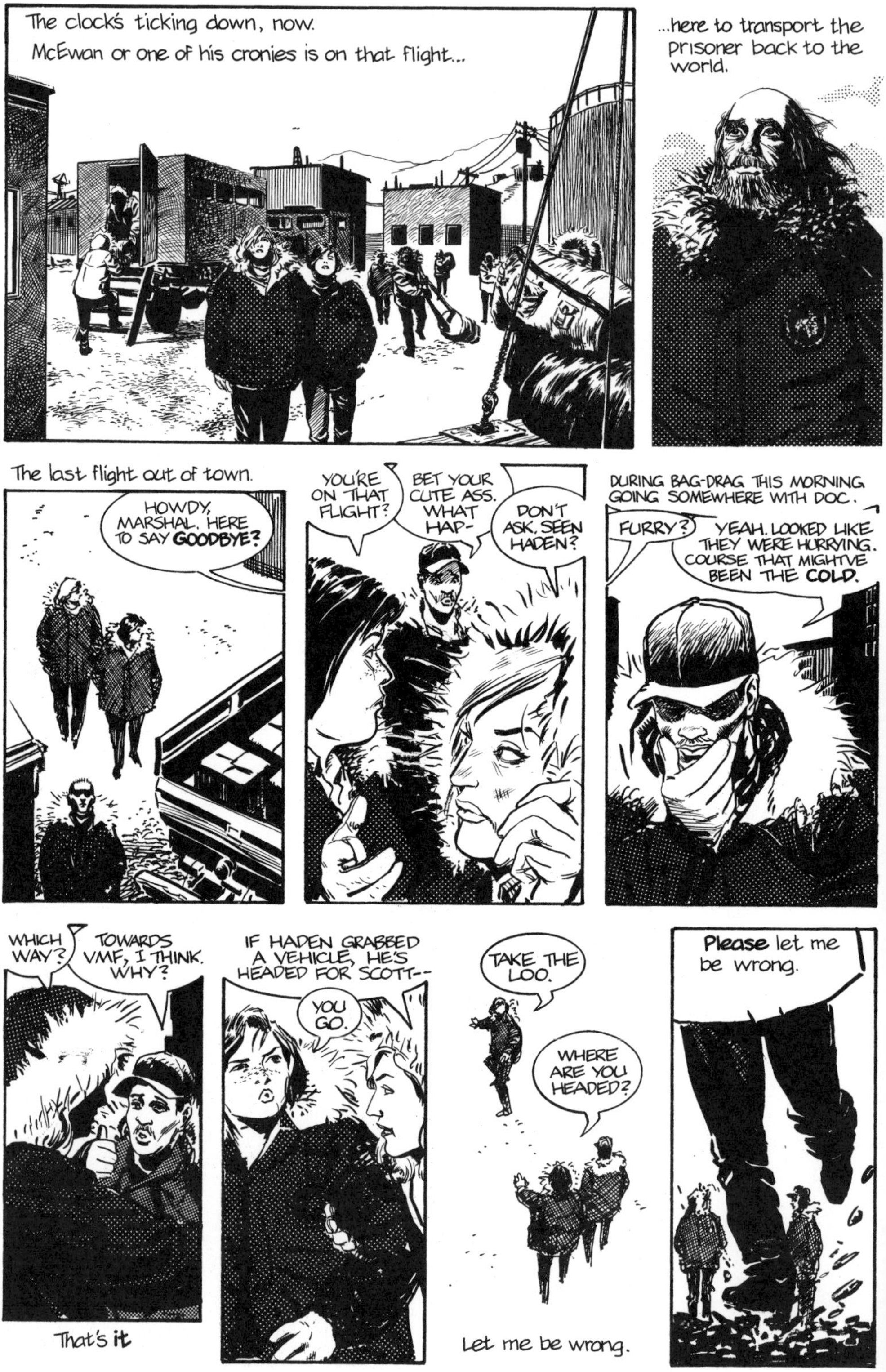

The clock's ticking down, now.
McEwan or one of his cronies is on that flight...
...here to transport the prisoner back to the world.
The last flight out of town.
HOWDY, MARSHAL. HERE TO SAY **GOODBYE?**
YOU'RE ON THAT FLIGHT?
BET YOUR CUTE ASS. WHAT HAP-
DON'T ASK. SEEN HADEN?
DURING BAG-DRAG THIS MORNING GOING SOMEWHERE WITH DOC.
FURRY?
YEAH. LOOKED LIKE THEY WERE HURRYING. COURSE THAT MIGHT'VE BEEN THE **COLD.**
WHICH WAY?
TOWARDS VMF, I THINK. WHY?
That's **it**
IF HADEN GRABBED A VEHICLE, HE'S HEADED FOR SCOTT--
YOU GO.
TAKE THE LOO.
WHERE ARE YOU HEADED?
Let me be wrong.
Please let me be wrong.

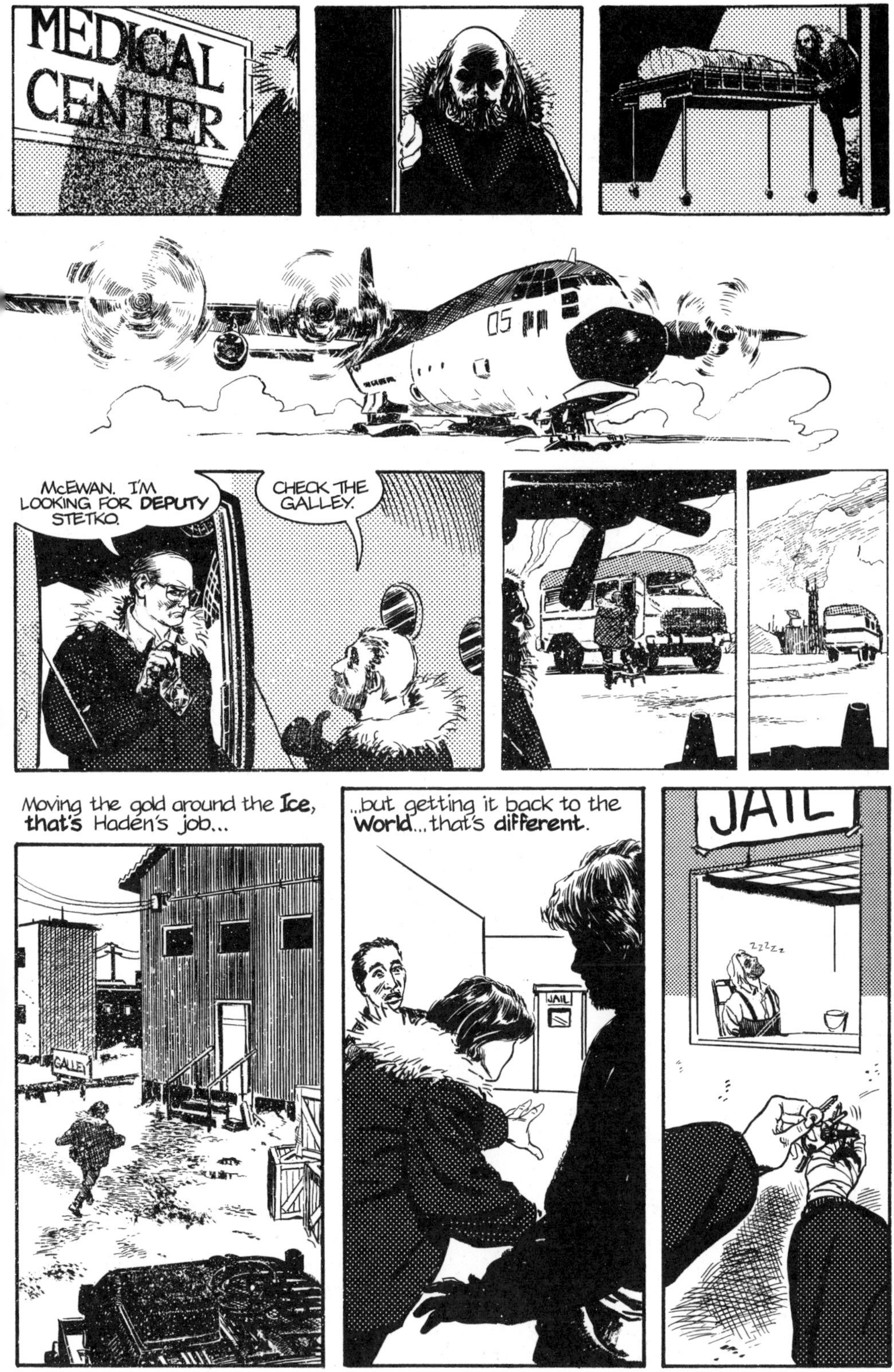
MEDICAL CENTER
05
McEWAN. I'M LOOKING FOR DEPUTY STETKO.
CHECK THE GALLEY.
Moving the gold around the Ice, that's Haden's job...
GALLEY
...but getting it back to the World... that's different.
JAIL
JAIL
ZZZzz

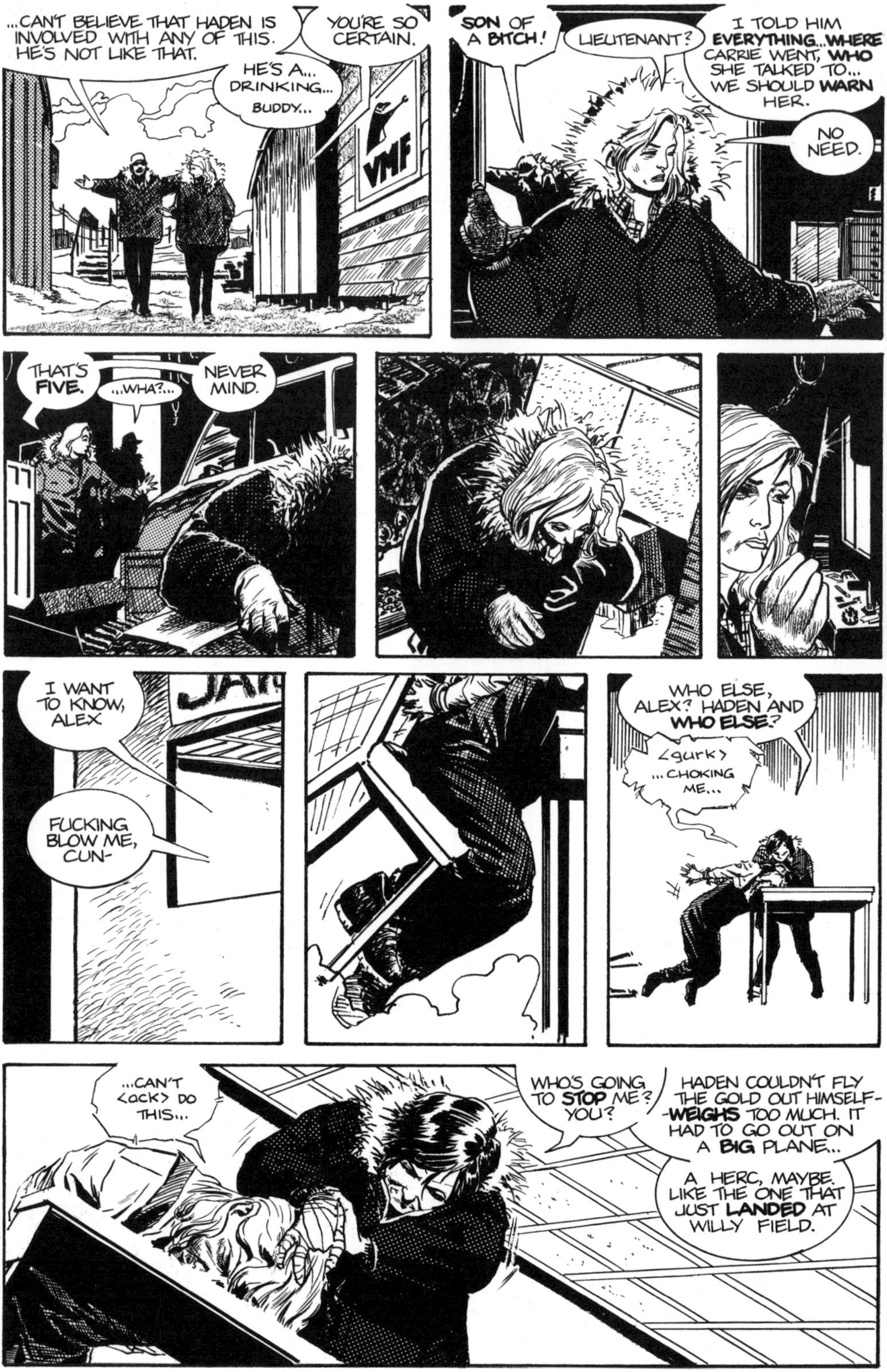

...CAN'T BELIEVE THAT HADEN IS INVOLVED WITH ANY OF THIS. HE'S NOT LIKE THAT.
YOU'RE SO CERTAIN.
HE'S A... DRINKING... BUDDY...
VMF
SON OF A BITCH!
LIEUTENANT?
I TOLD HIM EVERYTHING... WHERE CARRIE WENT, WHO SHE TALKED TO... WE SHOULD WARN HER.
NO NEED.
THAT'S FIVE.
...WHA?...
NEVER MIND.
I WANT TO KNOW, ALEX.
FUCKING BLOW ME, CUN-
WHO ELSE, ALEX? HADEN AND WHO ELSE?
<gurk> ...CHOKING ME...
...CAN'T <ack> DO THIS...
WHO'S GOING TO STOP ME? YOU?
HADEN COULDN'T FLY THE GOLD OUT HIMSELF- -WEIGHS TOO MUCH. IT HAD TO GO OUT ON A BIG PLANE...
A HERC, MAYBE. LIKE THE ONE THAT JUST LANDED AT WILLY FIELD.

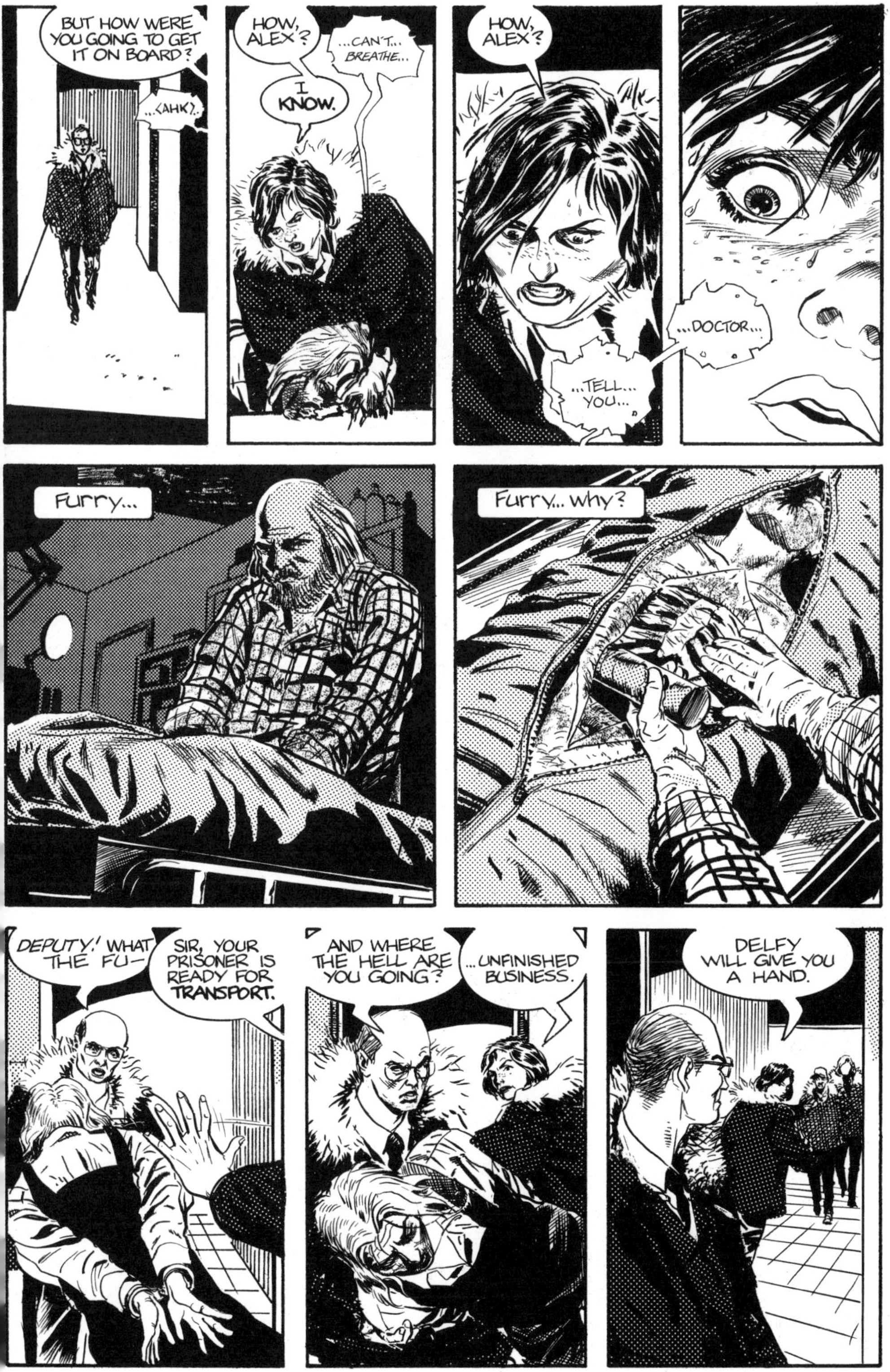
BUT HOW WERE YOU GOING TO GET IT ON BOARD?
...<AHK>...
HOW, ALEX?
...CAN'T... BREATHE...
I KNOW.
HOW, ALEX?
...TELL... YOU...
...DOCTOR...
Furry...
Furry... why?
DEPUTY! WHAT THE FU-
SIR, YOUR PRISONER IS READY FOR TRANSPORT.
AND WHERE THE HELL ARE YOU GOING?
...UNFINISHED BUSINESS.
DELFY WILL GIVE YOU A HAND.

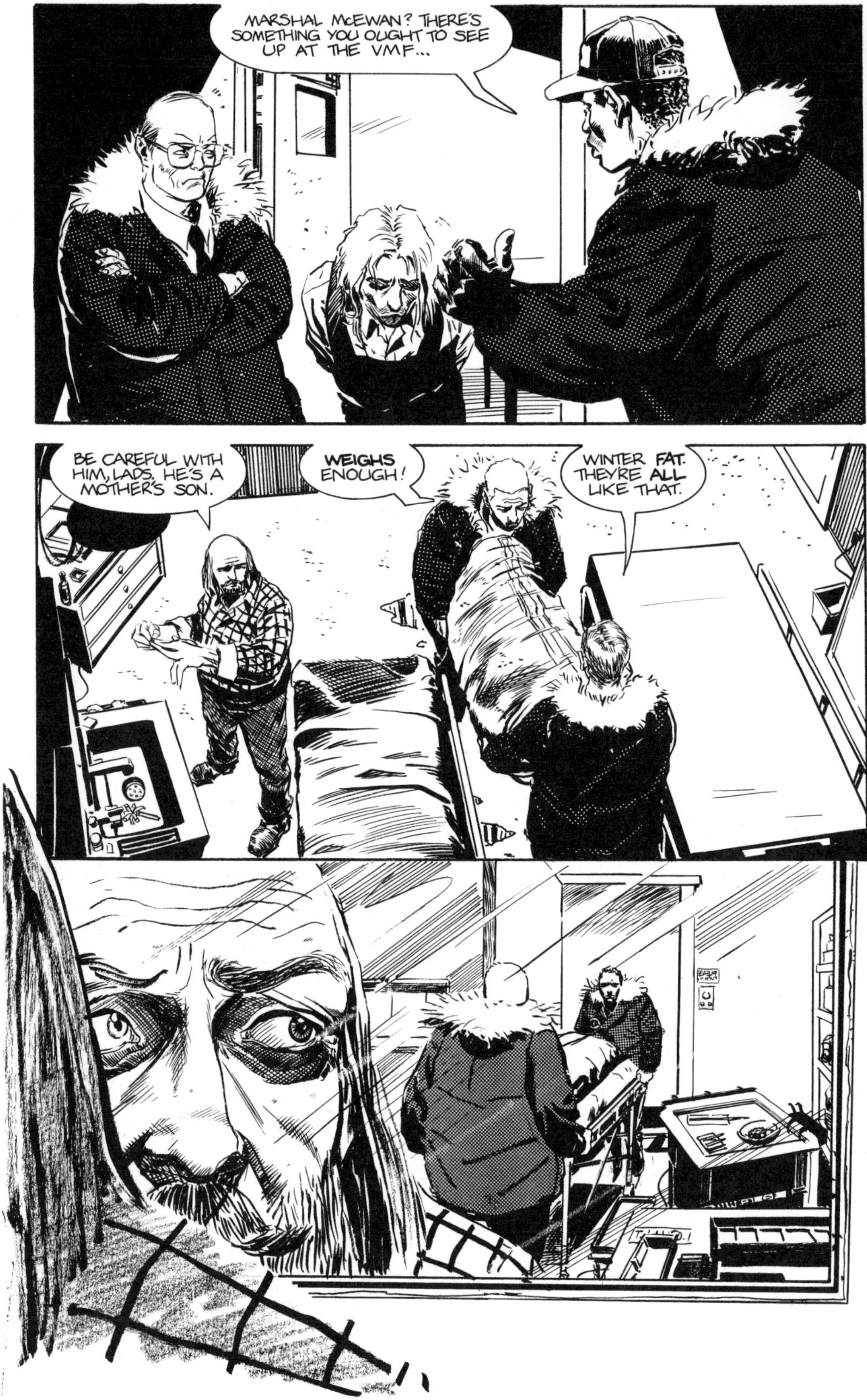
MARSHAL McEWAN? THERE'S SOMETHING YOU OUGHT TO SEE UP AT THE VMF...
BE CAREFUL WITH HIM, LADS. HE'S A MOTHER'S SON.
WEIGHS ENOUGH!
WINTER FAT. THEY'RE ALL LIKE THAT.

ZIP-GRRRRRRRR

WONDERED WHEN YOU'D GET HERE.

117

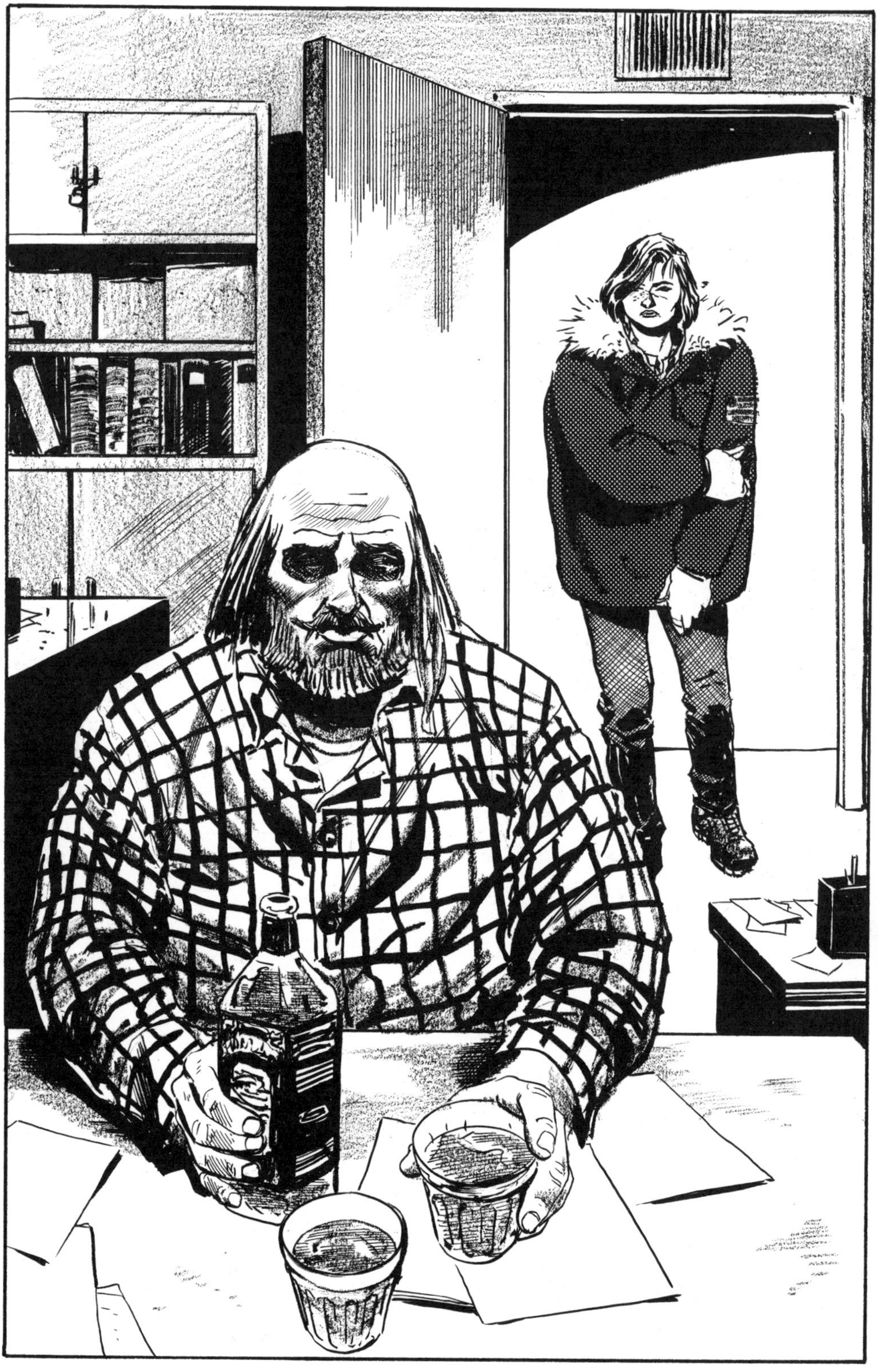

ONE LAST DRINK? FOR OLD TIME'S SAKE?

FOR OLD TIME'S SAKE, CARRIE?

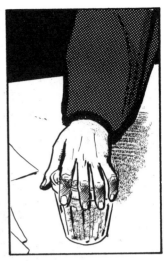

CHEERS.

YOU'VE GOT THE RIGHT TO REMAIN SILENT, HERE, FURRY.

DID KELLER FINALLY TALK, OR DID YOU FIND HADEN'S BODY?

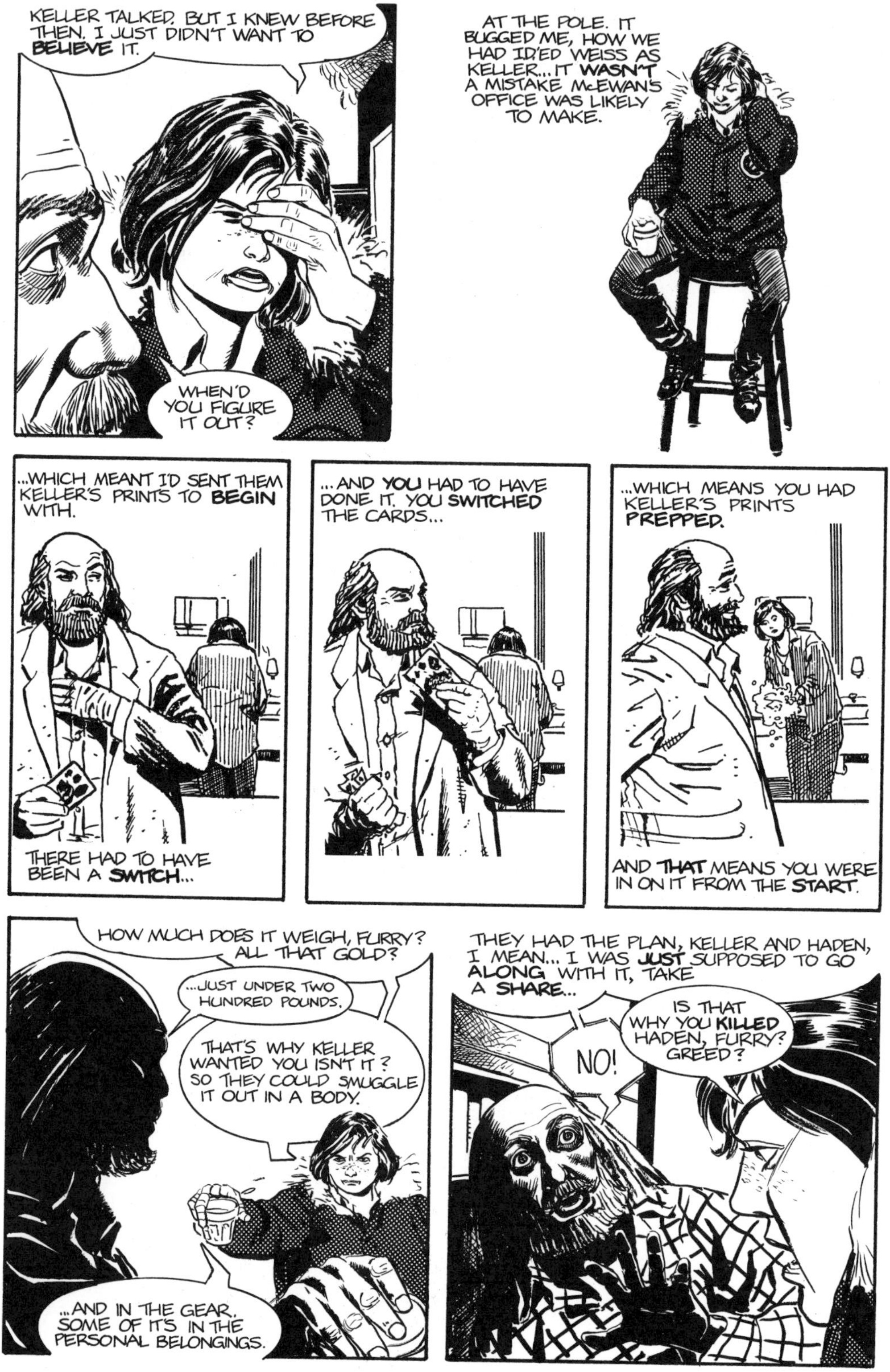
KELLER TALKED. BUT I KNEW BEFORE THEN. I JUST DIDN'T WANT TO BELIEVE IT.
WHEN'D YOU FIGURE IT OUT?
AT THE POLE. IT BUGGED ME, HOW WE HAD ID'ED WEISS AS KELLER... IT WASN'T A MISTAKE McEWAN'S OFFICE WAS LIKELY TO MAKE.
...WHICH MEANT I'D SENT THEM KELLER'S PRINTS TO BEGIN WITH.
THERE HAD TO HAVE BEEN A SWITCH...
...AND YOU HAD TO HAVE DONE IT. YOU SWITCHED THE CARDS...
...WHICH MEANS YOU HAD KELLER'S PRINTS PREPPED.
AND THAT MEANS YOU WERE IN ON IT FROM THE START.
HOW MUCH DOES IT WEIGH, FURRY? ALL THAT GOLD?
...JUST UNDER TWO HUNDRED POUNDS.
THAT'S WHY KELLER WANTED YOU ISN'T IT? SO THEY COULD SMUGGLE IT OUT IN A BODY.
...AND IN THE GEAR. SOME OF IT'S IN THE PERSONAL BELONGINGS.
THEY HAD THE PLAN, KELLER AND HADEN, I MEAN... I WAS JUST SUPPOSED TO GO ALONG WITH IT, TAKE A SHARE...
IS THAT WHY YOU KILLED HADEN, FURRY? GREED?
NO!

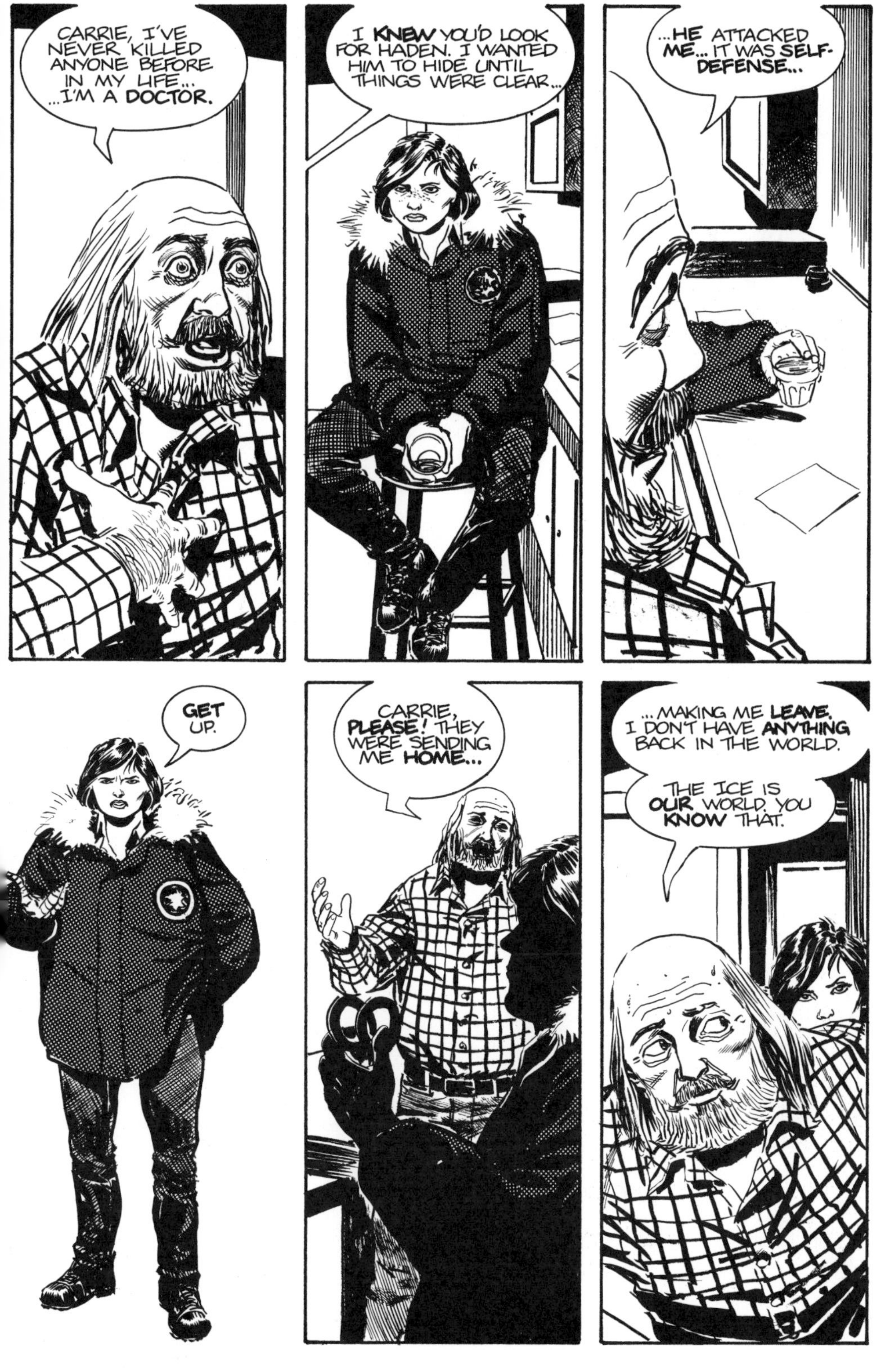
CARRIE, I'VE NEVER KILLED ANYONE BEFORE IN MY LIFE... ...I'M A DOCTOR.
I KNEW YOU'D LOOK FOR HADEN. I WANTED HIM TO HIDE UNTIL THINGS WERE CLEAR...
...HE ATTACKED ME... IT WAS SELF-DEFENSE...
GET UP.
CARRIE, PLEASE! THEY WERE SENDING ME HOME...
...MAKING ME LEAVE. I DON'T HAVE ANYTHING BACK IN THE WORLD.
THE ICE IS OUR WORLD. YOU KNOW THAT.

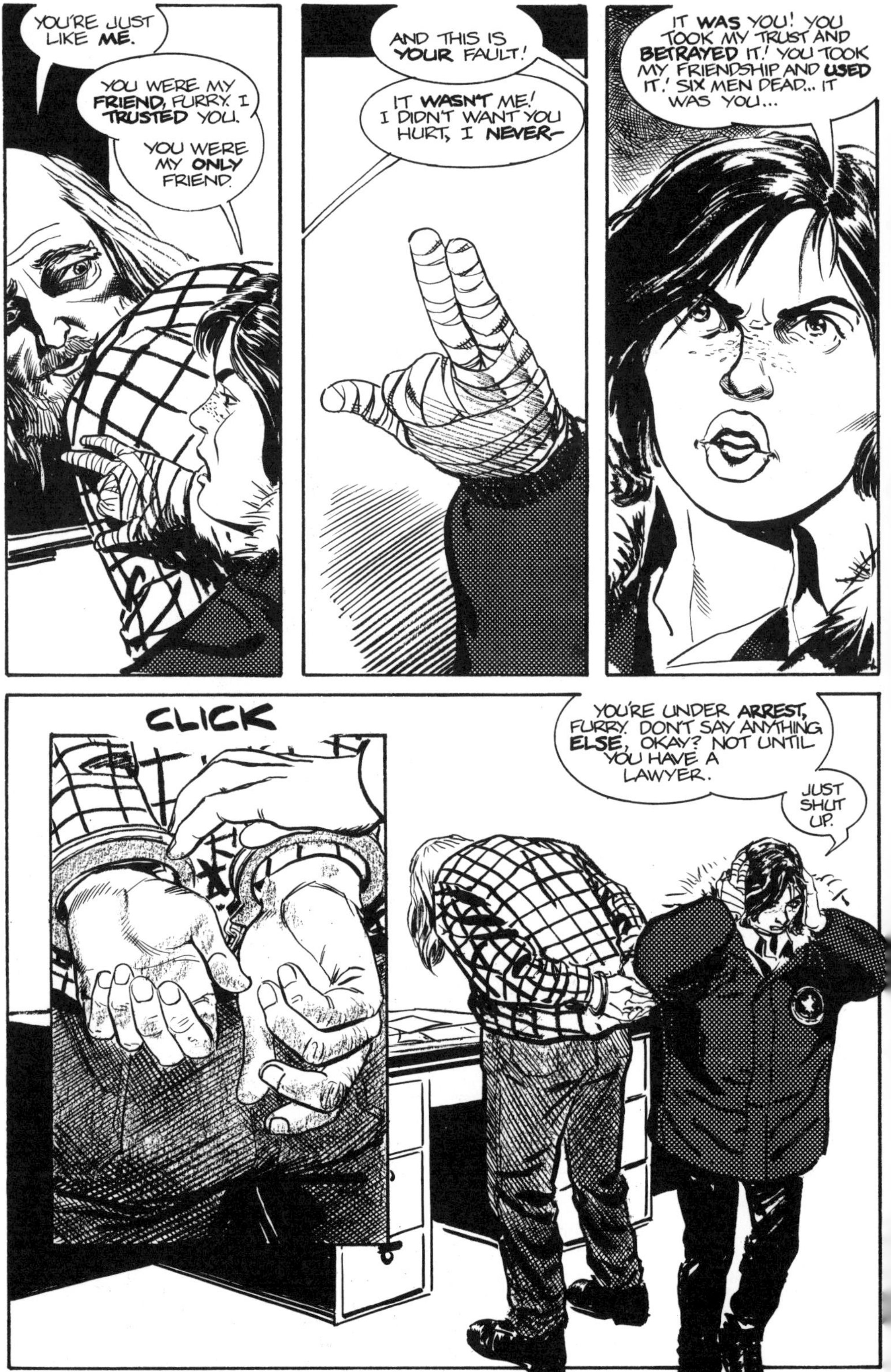
YOU'RE JUST LIKE ME.
YOU WERE MY FRIEND, FURRY. I TRUSTED YOU.
YOU WERE MY ONLY FRIEND.
AND THIS IS YOUR FAULT!
IT WASN'T ME! I DIDN'T WANT YOU HURT, I NEVER-
IT WAS YOU! YOU TOOK MY TRUST AND BETRAYED IT! YOU TOOK MY FRIENDSHIP AND USED IT! SIX MEN DEAD... IT WAS YOU...
CLICK
YOU'RE UNDER ARREST, FURRY. DON'T SAY ANYTHING ELSE, OKAY? NOT UNTIL YOU HAVE A LAWYER.
JUST SHUT UP.

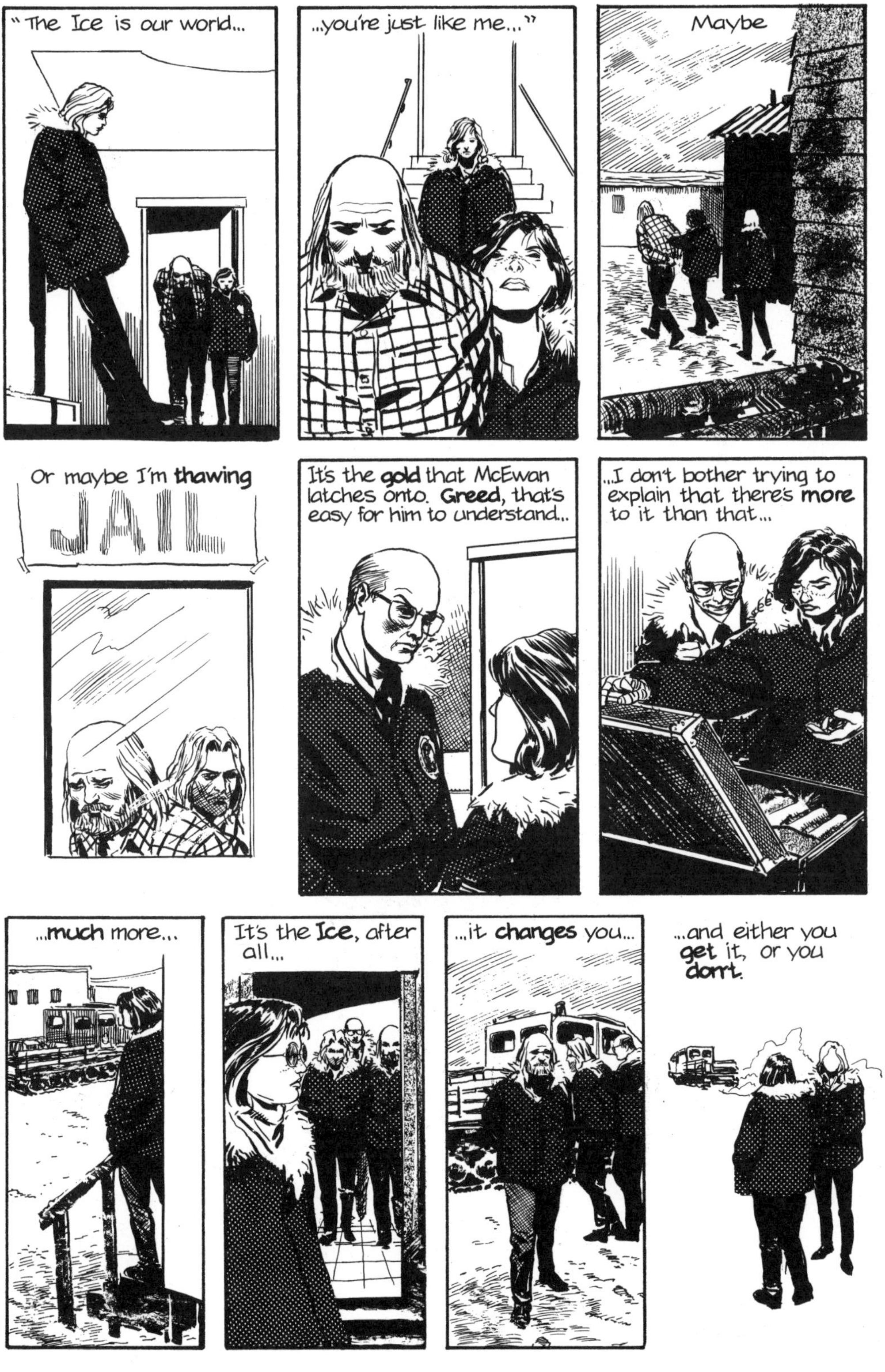

"The Ice is our world...
...you're just like me..."
Maybe
Or maybe I'm **thawing**
JAIL
It's the **gold** that McEwan latches onto. **Greed**, that's easy for him to understand...
...I don't bother trying to explain that there's **more** to it than that...
...**much** more...
It's the **Ice**, after all...
...it **changes** you...
...and either you **get** it, or you **don't**.

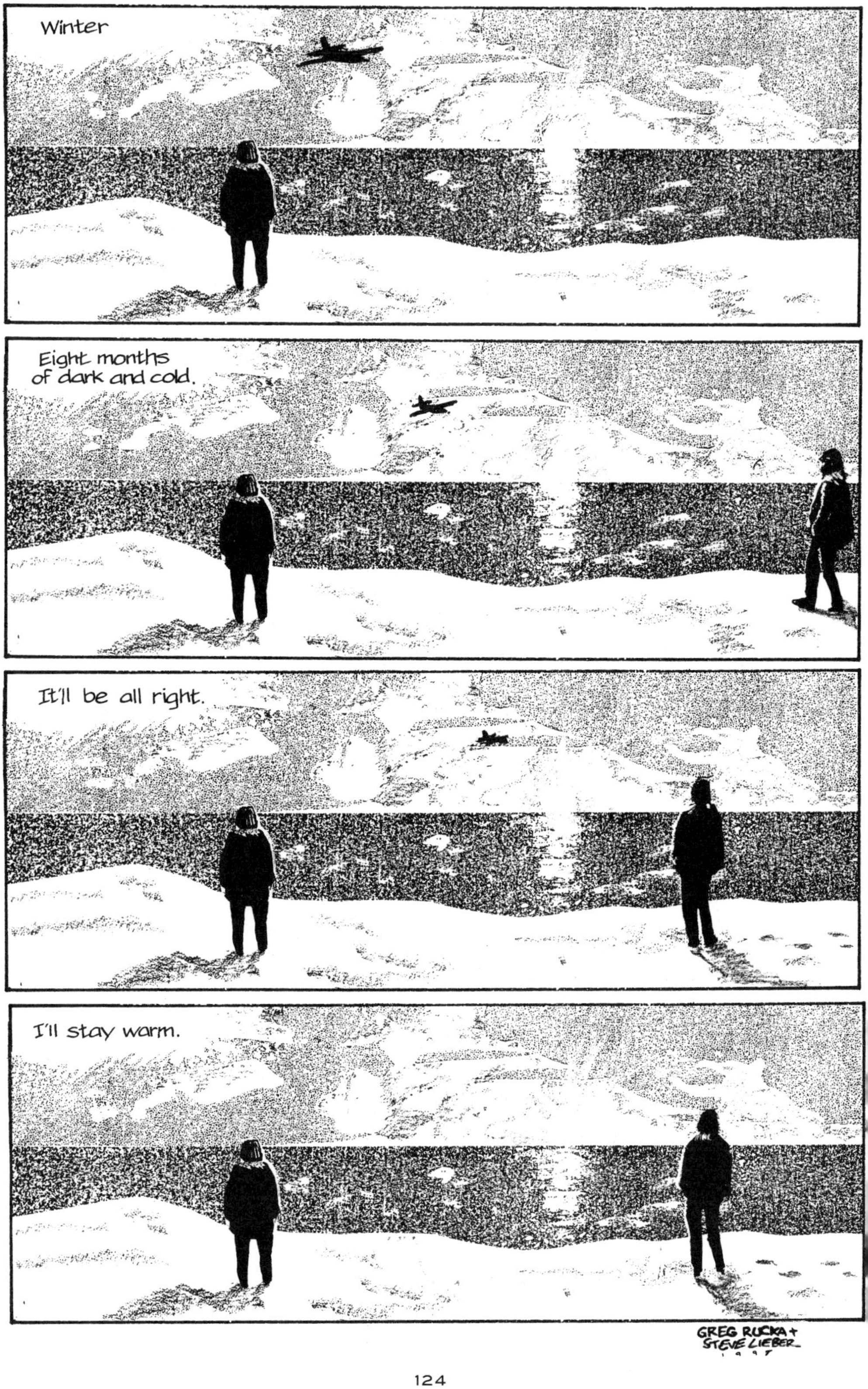
Winter
Eight months of dark and cold.
It'll be all right.
I'll stay warm.
GREG RUCKA + STEVE LIEBER

Editor's note: The following afterwords originally appeared in the Whiteout *and* Whiteout: Melt *editions released in 2007.*

AFTERWORD

Ten years ago, when Bob Schreck first handed me a copy of Greg Rucka's first novel, *Keeper,* I was convinced I'd never make anything of myself in comics. I'd been working steadily for six years, but I couldn't look at anything I'd illustrated without vague feelings of regret. I knew I was capable of solid work, and I had a big pile of sketchbooks that supported that notion, but when I looked over my hundreds of pages of published stories, there just wasn't much to shout about. I hadn't figured out how to do good work on the industry's four color assembly lines, and that was the only place anyone could make a splash, right?

That's where Schreck comes in. Bob had given me my break at Dark Horse years ago, making him the first editor at a legitimate publisher to see any potential in my stuff. He'd just started a new company called Oni Press right here in Portland, where my wife and I had just moved. Bob said that he had a script that might be right for me, written by the same guy who wrote this novel.

I took the book home and devoured it in one sitting, and I felt like someone had built a writer just for me. Greg's novel was compelling, and compulsively readable, but more importantly, he worked the rhythms of storytelling the way I was desperate to do in comics[1]. I saw that we agreed on the ways the energy and emotional pitch of a scene should rise and fall. Our attitudes about violence and heroism were in sync, as was our sense of the rules that make for believable characters and action in fiction.

Long story short, Bob sent me the script for the first issue. I said yes, and oh boy was I eager to get started. If Greg had set out to write a script just for me, he couldn't have come up with something this perfect. Carrie and Antarctica were absolutely alive in my mind. I understood her frustration and her wonder at the place she'd wound up and her determination to find out what happened. All I had to do was tell the reader the story Greg told me and we'd have a great comic. Greg's story was about a woman so frozen by anger and regret she'd found herself at home in the middle of millions of square kilometers of ice. How could I make

1 It's best not to get me started on comics as a rhythmic—as opposed to a literary—medium. I tend to judge a page of comics by how the pictures sound, and I'm very aware of what a weird sentence that is. This isn't synesthesia. I just sort of hear panels and pages in my head as if I were reading a musical score. When the rhythm is off, the page doesn't work. When it's particularly good, the work comes to life in a way that's hard to communicate. Conversations with a number of other cartoonists lead me to believe this is a fairly common experience.

that world as believable and compelling in pictures as it was in the script? Monochromatic could easily lead to monotony. Black and white comics, particularly crime stories, usually get their impact from the use of heavy areas of solid black. For obvious reasons, that wasn't going to work in this one. But those sketchbooks I mentioned earlier were full of black and white drawings where I'd played with all sorts of media and had been able to fully indulge my interest in using texture as both a color and a rhythmic element. I never worried about restricting myself to a slick comic book brushline in my sketches; I just worked to please myself. I suppose I treated the comic like it was my sketchbook, and just let myself whale away at every panel until it felt as cold, as dry, as windy, and as desolate as it needed to be. Sure, there was a danger that some panels might get overrendered, but certainly on this title I could feel okay about dealing with a bad drawing by just whiting it out.

That did it. I was free. For the first time in my career, I felt like I was producing drawings that looked like I'd drawn them. I used a dozen different brushes, any pen nib I could find, grease crayons, markers, ball points, white paint, toothbrushes, homemade zip-a-tones, xeroxes, charcoal, unerased pencil lines, sandpaper, razor blades, an electric eraser, even my own fingerprints—anything that could make or remove a mark on paper—I'd give it a try. I inhabited those panels and I think the struggle gave the pictures a lot of energy. Along the way, I tried to do what Greg had done when he wrote it—I buried myself in research, spending hours online or in the library researching Antarctica. And I'd call and fax him at all hours to discuss possible approaches to panel sequences. A twelve hour day at the board was slacking off. I drove my wife and friends insane. Greg, too, come to think of it.

Looking back, I'm grateful to everyone who was involved with this project: Greg, of course, his wife Jen Van Meter, for clarifying their concept of "hooskie" (which you, dear reader, can ask one of them about sometime); Bob Schreck, Joe Nozemack, Jamie Rich, and James Lucas Jones; graphic designers Sean Tejaratchi and Steven Birch; original cover artists Matt Wagner, Mike Mignola, Dave Gibbons, and Frank Miller; the guys at the now defunct website nextplanetover.com who gave away a metric ton of copies at the San Diego Comic-Con; the readers of rec.arts.comics.misc, who were among the first to notice that something special was going on; Jeff Parker, who told me to quit being a puss when I was over-thinking; and most of all, my wife Sara Ryan, who supported me in my obsessiveness, inspired many of Stetko's expressions and gestures, and woke up with little bits of zip-a-tone in the blankets every morning for two years. From this day forward, it's all digital, hon, I swear.

Steve Lieber

STEVE LIEBER / MAY 2007

AFTERWORD

Whiteout was catching lightning in a bottle.

Whiteout: Melt was trying to catch lightning in a bottle, twice.

Steve Lieber and I had talked about the other stories we could tell about Carrie and Antarctica while we were working on the first one, and we had realized very quickly that there was a lot more that could be shown, a lot more we had to say. But when the opportunity came to do *Melt*, I was hesitant; I didn't want to tell the same story twice. I didn't want another murder mystery. And I knew that sequels, at least to the people who buy them, are often an attempt to capture "more of the same," and that was something I wasn't sure I could do, or even wanted to do. One murder mystery in Antarctica was enough, I told myself.

I came around, obviously, and the way I came around was primarily via Steve. For all of his varied and tremendous skill as an artist, Steve is also 1) very, very smart, and 2) a tremendous collaborator. Simply talking with him about story is often all it takes to get my engine revved and to send me racing for the keyboard to start pounding away. That was how it started here. Well, that, and the fact that I love spy stories, and wanted to do something about the espionage-related history of Antarctica.

But in talking to Steve, something crystallized for me that I hadn't realized while writing the original. I found that I liked Antarctica as a character as much as—and sometimes, perhaps, more than—I liked Carrie. And I adored Carrie, and still do to this day, frankly. But, like the Marshal herself, I had fallen in love with The Ice.

Realizing that opened the floodgates, and the ideas came pouring out.

More than the original, *Melt* is a morality tale. Bad men murder fourteen people and then try to make their escape. Why they do it is, frankly, immaterial—the nukes are a very traditional MacGuffin (though, like all things in the *Whiteout* series, the theory as to how and why there would be nukes on The Ice was based firmly in fact). Fourteen men were murdered, and that is a crime against God and Man, and it must be answered.

This is why it takes four issues for Carrie and Aleks to catch the Bad Russians, and why, when they do, they practically needn't have bothered. The Ice has done their job for them. The Ice has exacted its revenge. The Ice has answered.

But (if one is willing to continue with this personalization of a continent) unlike a traditional morality tale, The Ice hasn't done this out of any sense of moral judgment or desire for justice. The Ice has done this because this is what The Ice does. It kills you; slow, fast, easy, hard, now, later, doesn't matter—The Ice kills you, because it doesn't want you there. You shouldn't be there. You weren't made to be there. And it wants you to go home. It wants you to go home, now.

In a world where the Chinese are paving the road that leads to Everest, and where space tourism is rapidly becoming a reality, and the Ross Ice Shelf is coming apart in pieces as large as the state of Rhode Island, it's sometimes good to remember our place in nature. It's sometimes right to remind ourselves of how very small we are on a very large planet.

It's sometimes right to remember to pay respect.

GREG RUCKA / JULY 19, 2007
PORTLAND, OR

MELT

CHAPTER ONE

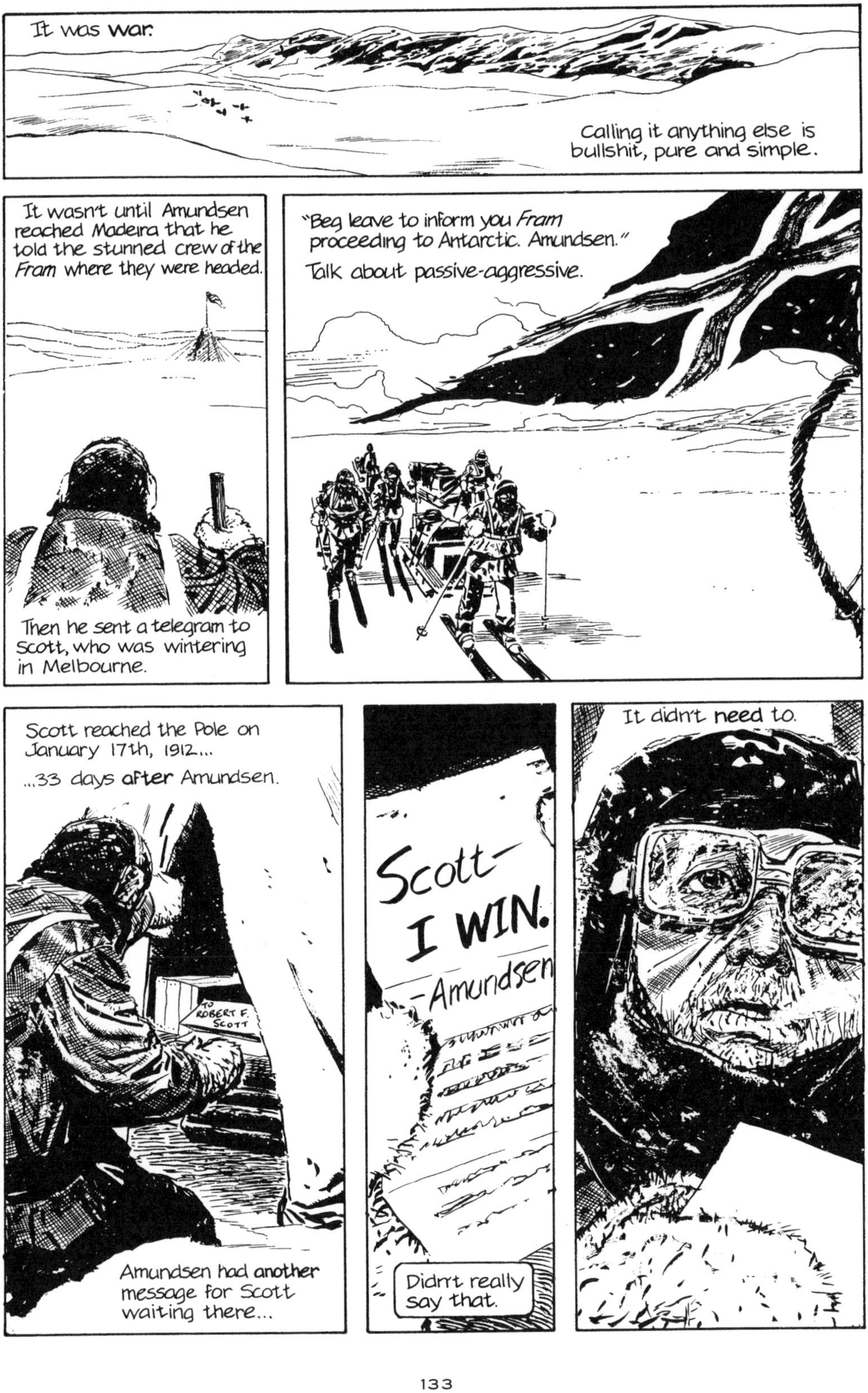

It was **war.**
Calling it anything else is bullshit, pure and simple.
It wasn't until Amundsen reached Madeira that he told the stunned crew of the *Fram* where they were headed.
Then he sent a telegram to Scott, who was wintering in Melbourne.
"Beg leave to inform you *Fram* proceeding to Antarctic. Amundsen."
Talk about passive-aggressive.
Scott reached the Pole on January 17th, 1912...
...33 days **after** Amundsen.
TO ROBERT F. SCOTT
Amundsen had **another** message for Scott waiting there...
Scott-
I WIN.
-Amundsen
Didn't really say that.
It didn't **need** to.

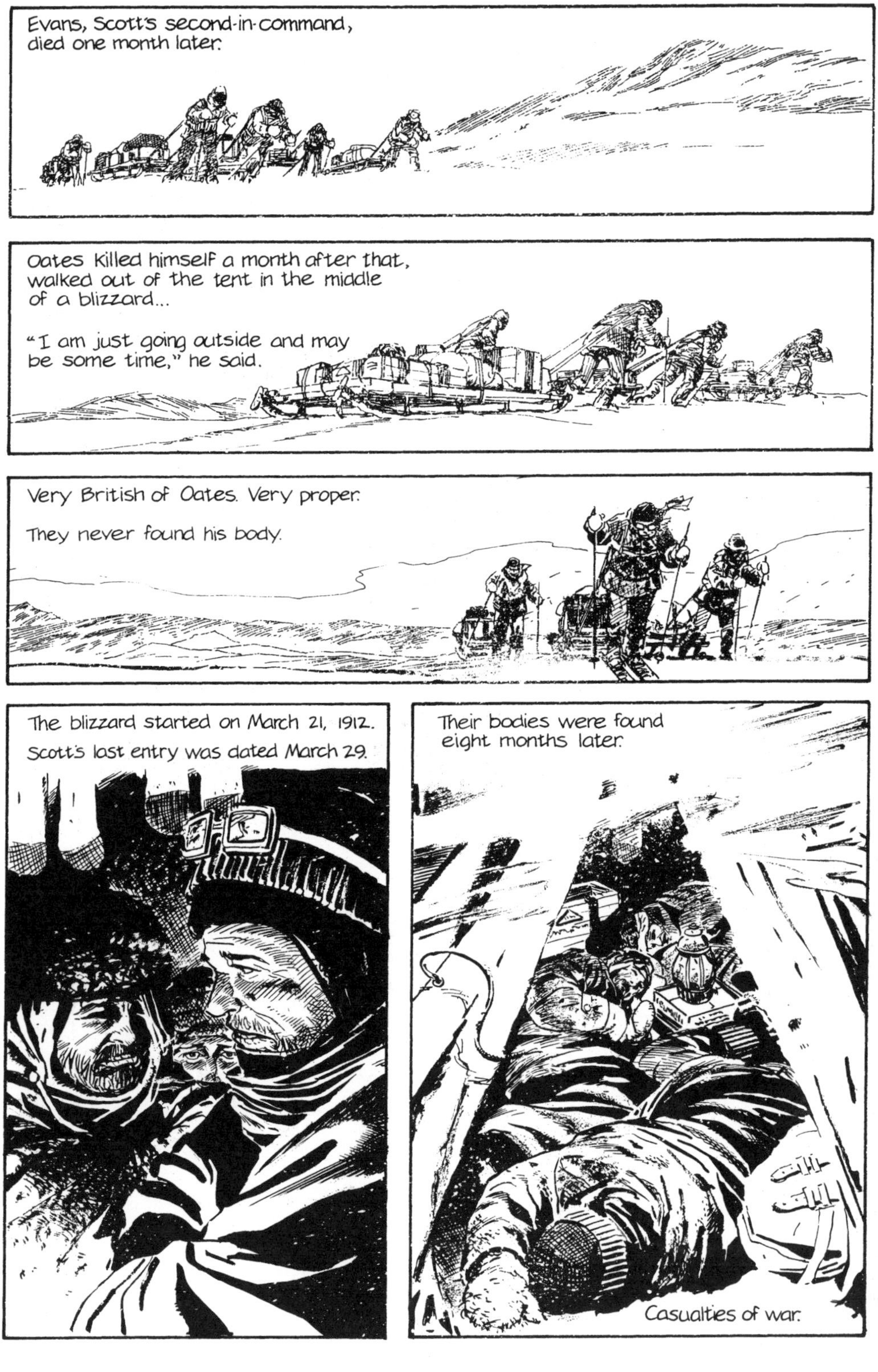

Evans, Scott's second-in-command, died one month later.
Oates killed himself a month after that, walked out of the tent in the middle of a blizzard...
"I am just going outside and may be some time," he said.
Very British of Oates. Very proper.
They never found his body.
The blizzard started on March 21, 1912.
Scott's last entry was dated March 29.
Their bodies were found eight months later.
Casualties of war.

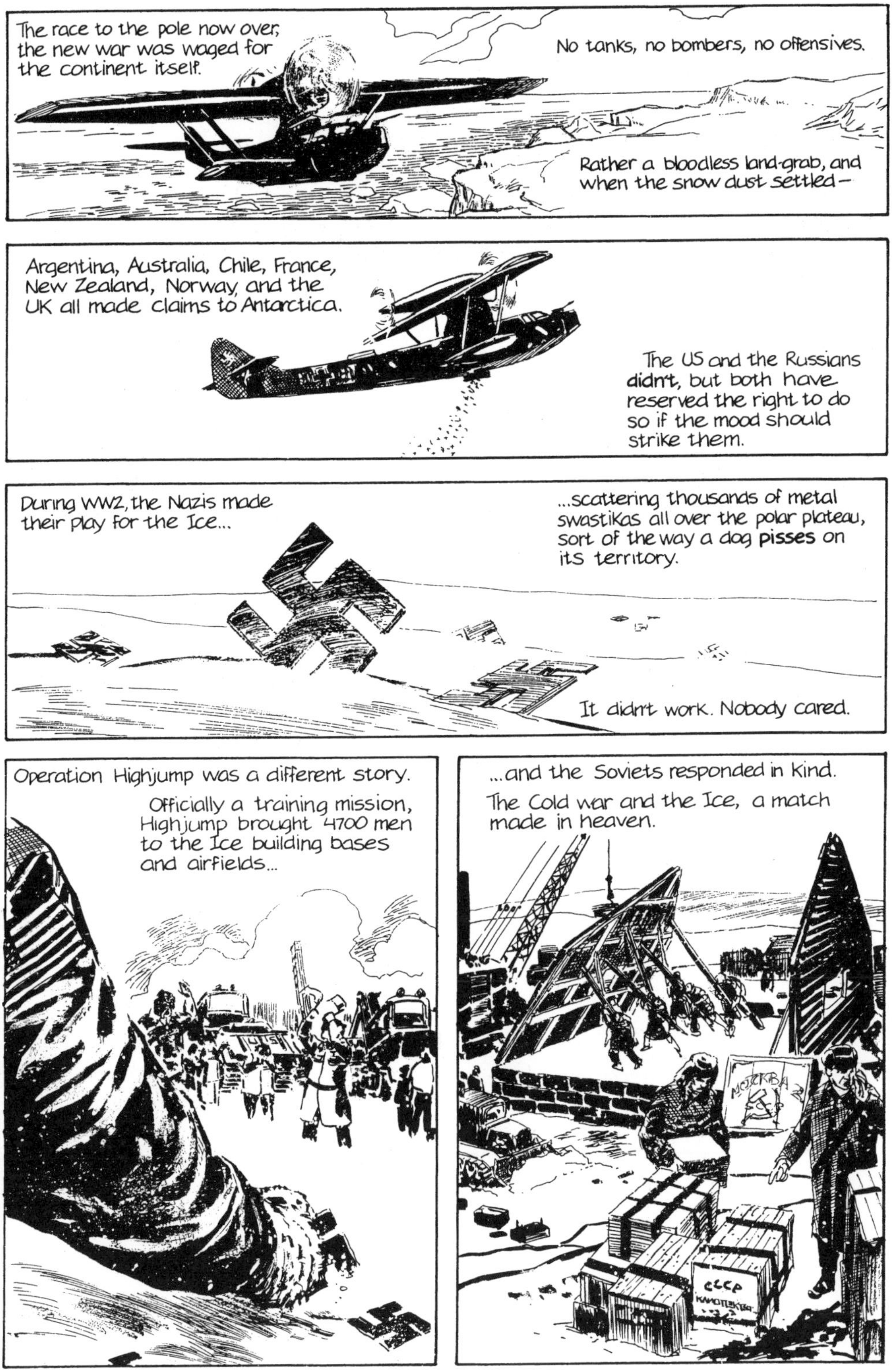
The race to the pole now over, the new war was waged for the continent itself.
No tanks, no bombers, no offensives.
Rather a bloodless land-grab, and when the snow dust settled—
Argentina, Australia, Chile, France, New Zealand, Norway, and the UK all made claims to Antarctica.
The US and the Russians **didn't**, but both have reserved the right to do so if the mood should strike them.
During WW2, the Nazis made their play for the Ice...
...scattering thousands of metal swastikas all over the polar plateau, sort of the way a dog **pisses** on its territory.
It didn't work. Nobody cared.
Operation Highjump was a different story.
Officially a training mission, Highjump brought 4700 men to the Ice building bases and airfields...
...and the Soviets responded in kind.
The Cold war and the Ice, a match made in heaven.
СССР

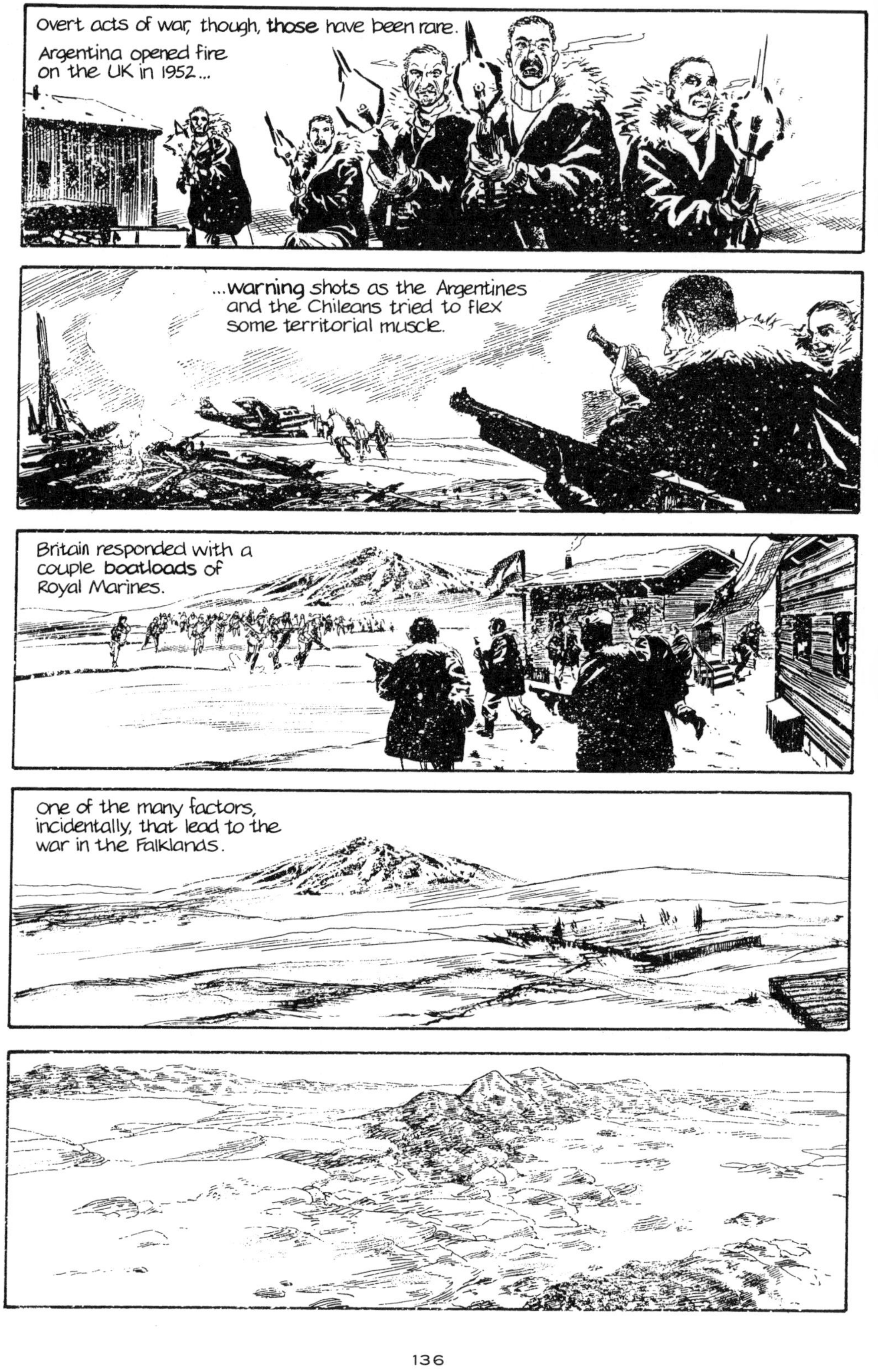
Overt acts of war, though, those have been rare.
Argentina opened fire on the UK in 1952...
...warning shots as the Argentines and the Chileans tried to flex some territorial muscle.
Britain responded with a couple boatloads of Royal Marines.
One of the many factors, incidentally, that lead to the war in the Falklands.

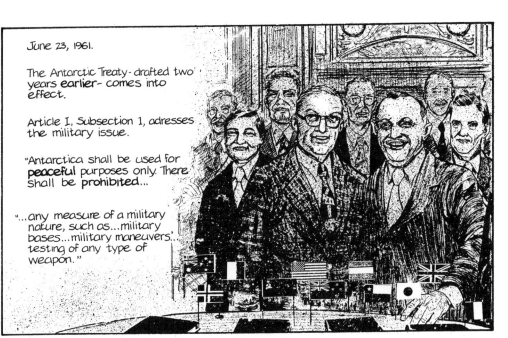

June 23, 1961.

The Antarctic Treaty- drafted two years **earlier**- comes into effect.

Article 1, Subsection 1, adresses the military issue.

"Antarctica shall be used for **peaceful** purposes only. There shall be **prohibited**...

"...any measure of a military nature, such as...military bases...military maneuvers...testing of any type of weapon."

Nearly 80% of the world's governments have added their signatures to the treaty since its ratification.

There has been no known breach of the treaty...

...no military action or violation...

...to this very day.

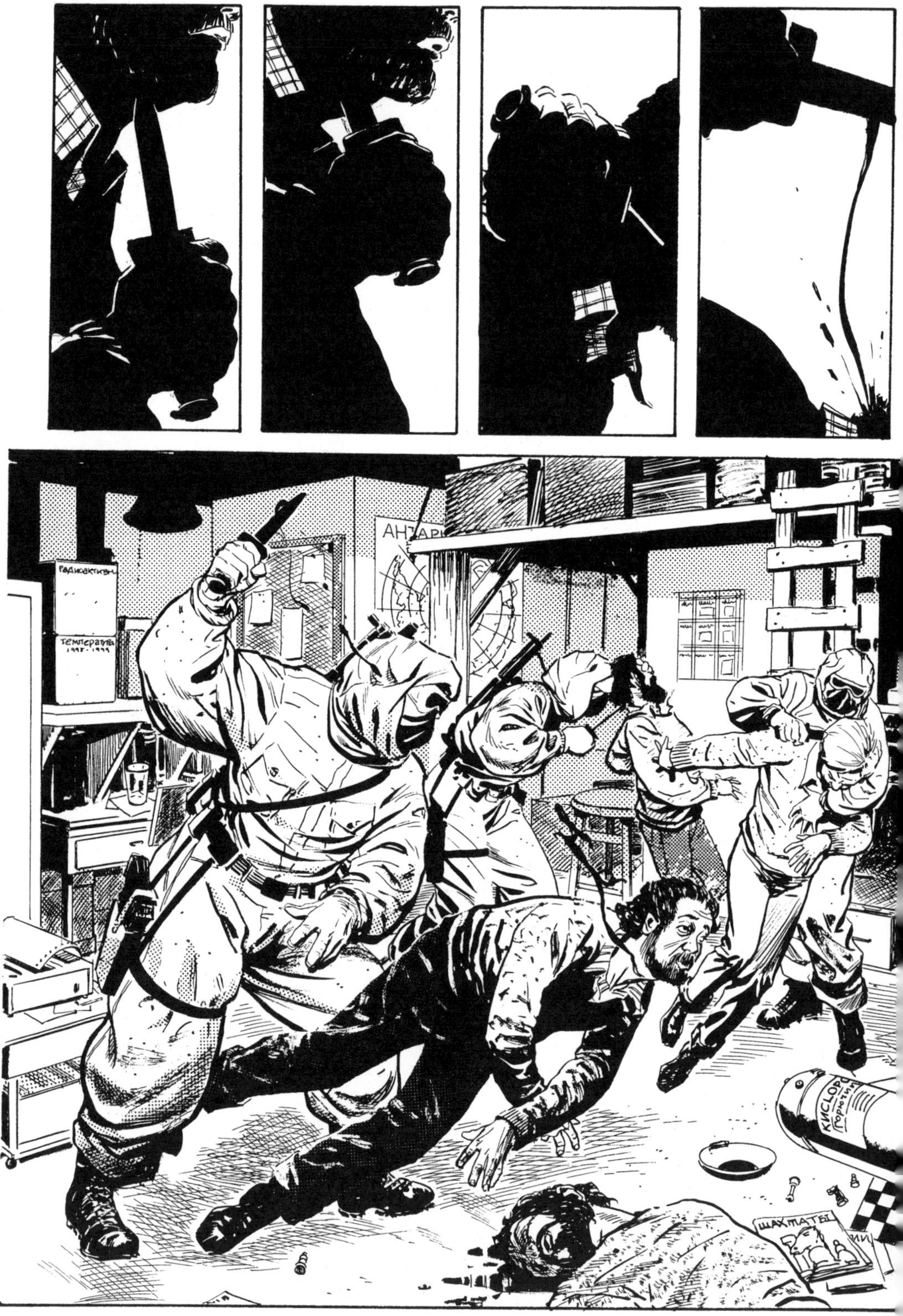
Температура
1998 - 1999
ШАХМАТЫ

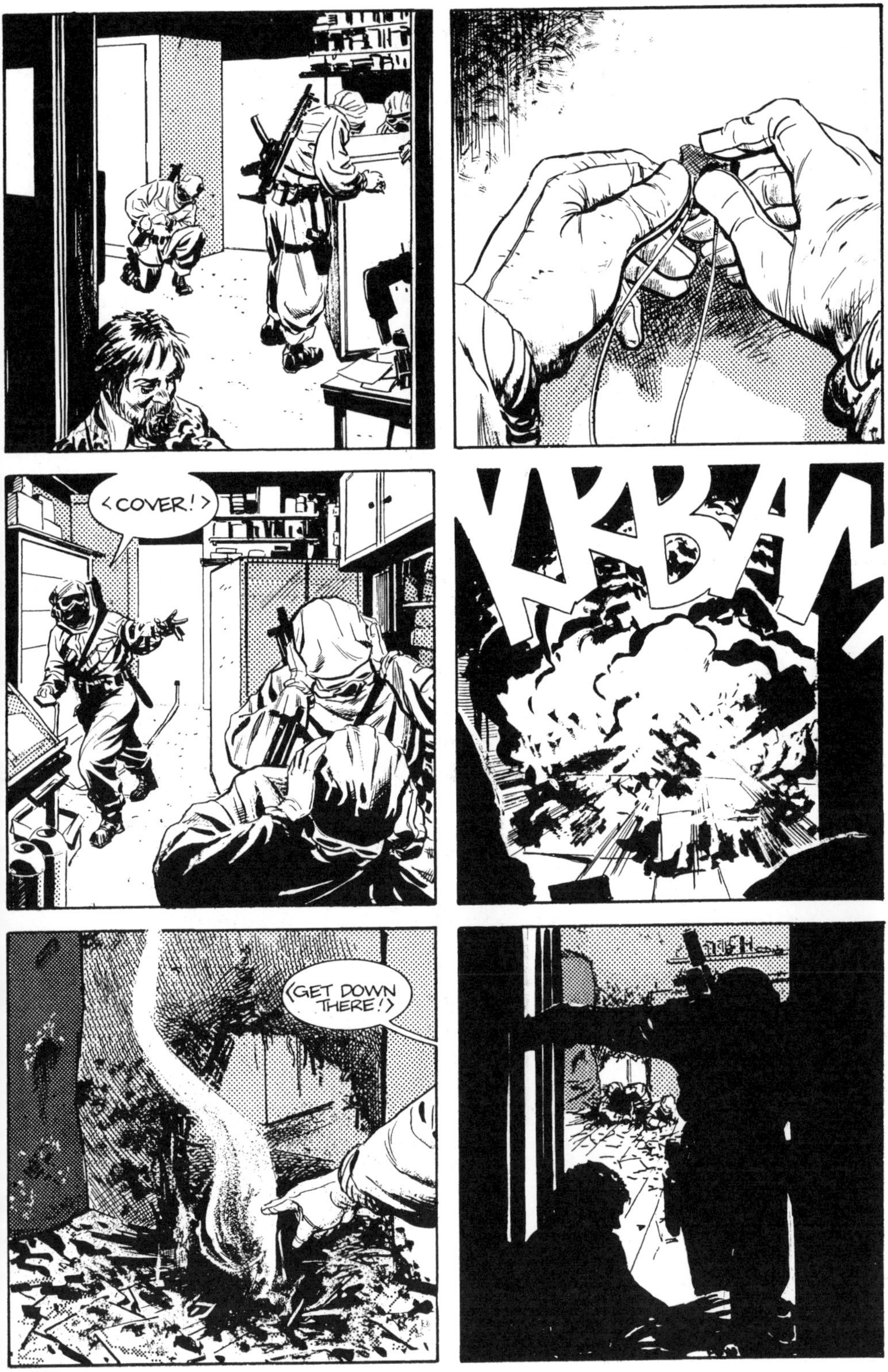
<COVER!>
<GET DOWN THERE!>

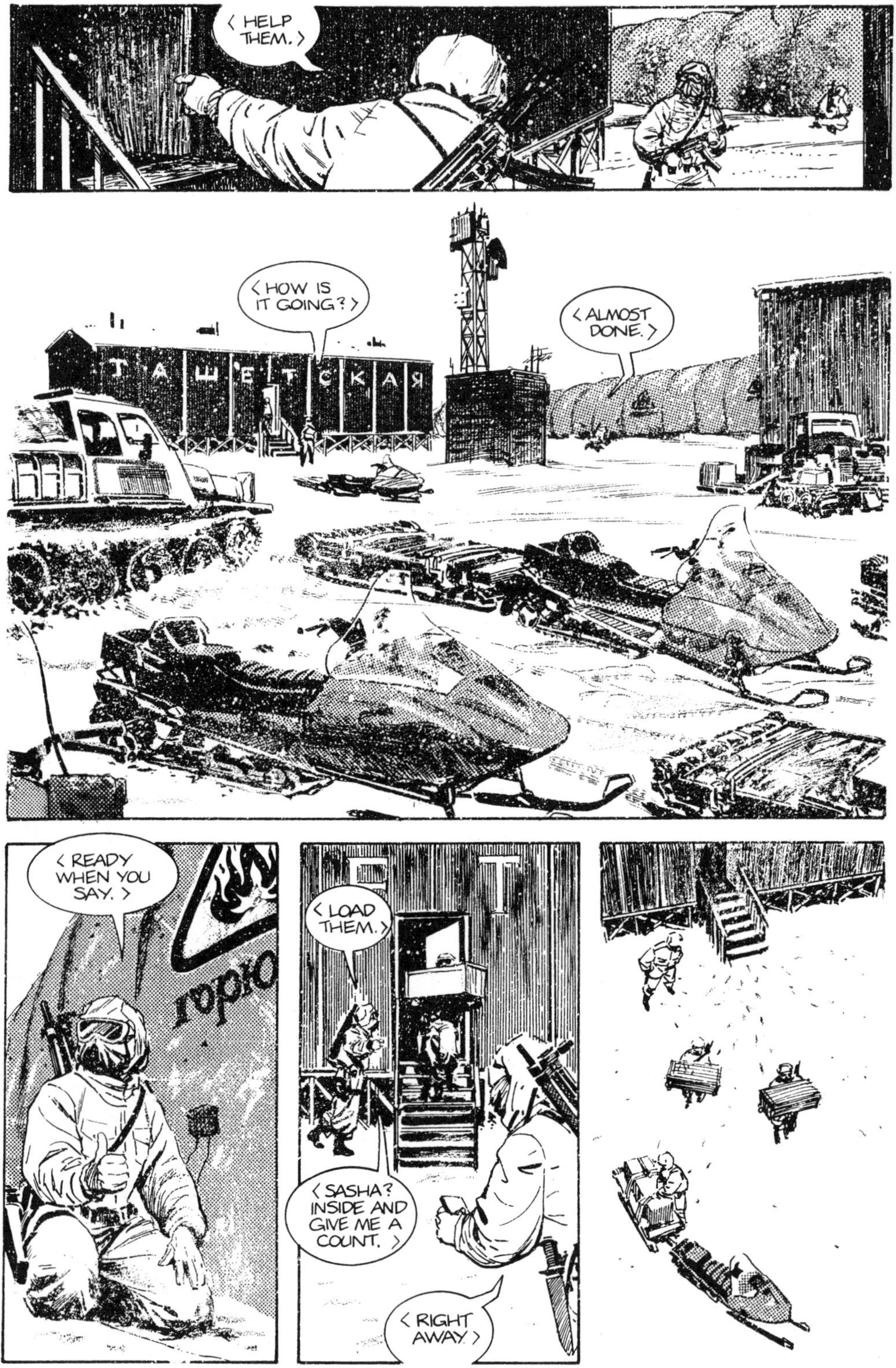
< HELP THEM. >
< HOW IS IT GOING? >
ТАШЕТСКАЯ
< ALMOST DONE. >
< READY WHEN YOU SAY. >
< LOAD THEM. >
< SASHA? INSIDE AND GIVE ME A COUNT. >
< RIGHT AWAY. >

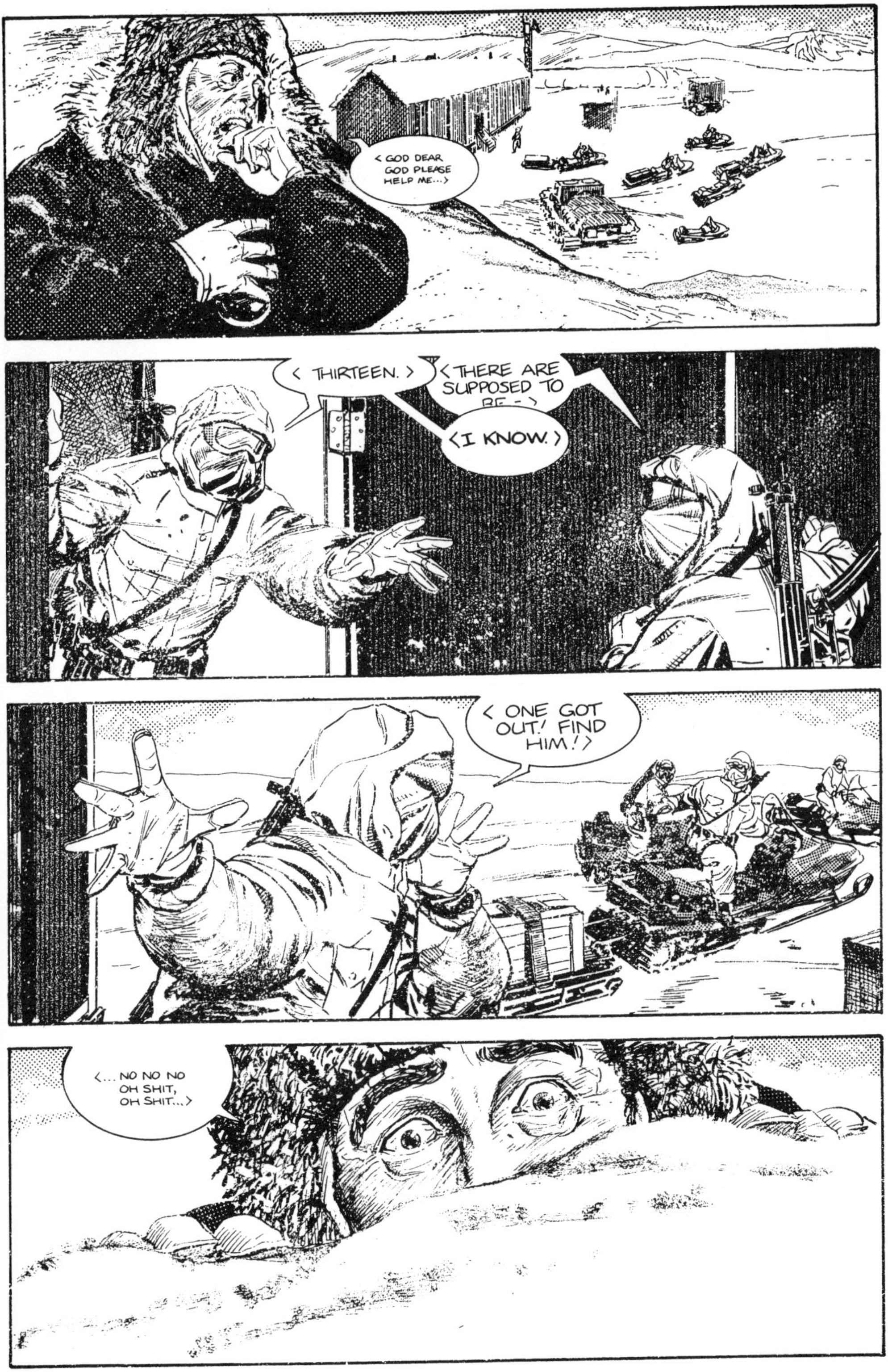

< GOD DEAR GOD PLEASE HELP ME...>
< THIRTEEN. >
< THERE ARE SUPPOSED TO BE - >
< I KNOW. >
< ONE GOT OUT! FIND HIM! >
< ... NO NO NO OH SHIT, OH SHIT... >

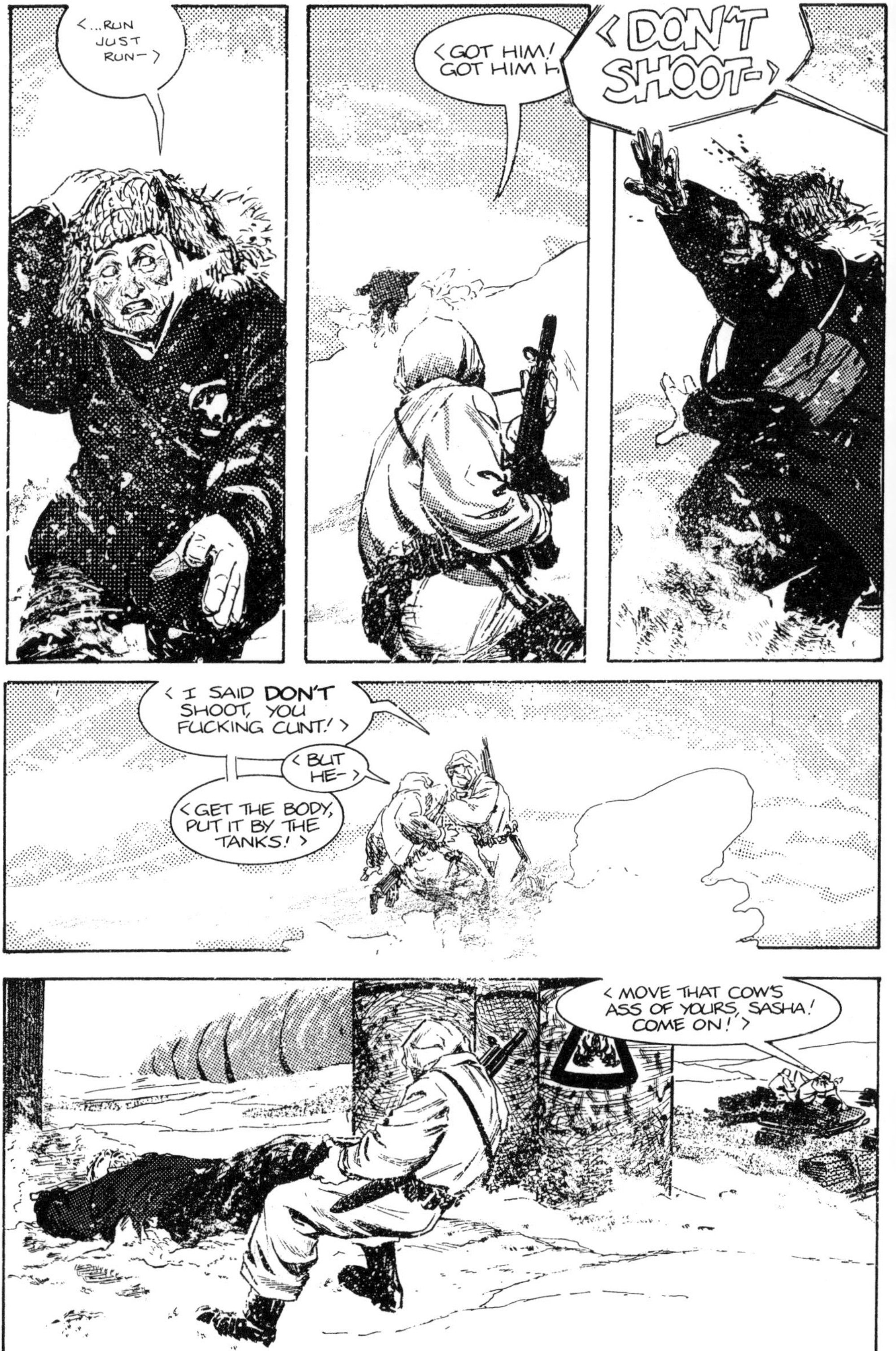

< ...RUN JUST RUN- >
< GOT HIM! GOT HIM H
< DON'T SHOOT- >
< I SAID DON'T SHOOT, YOU FUCKING CUNT! >
< BUT HE- >
< GET THE BODY, PUT IT BY THE TANKS! >
< MOVE THAT COW'S ASS OF YOURS, SASHA! COME ON! >

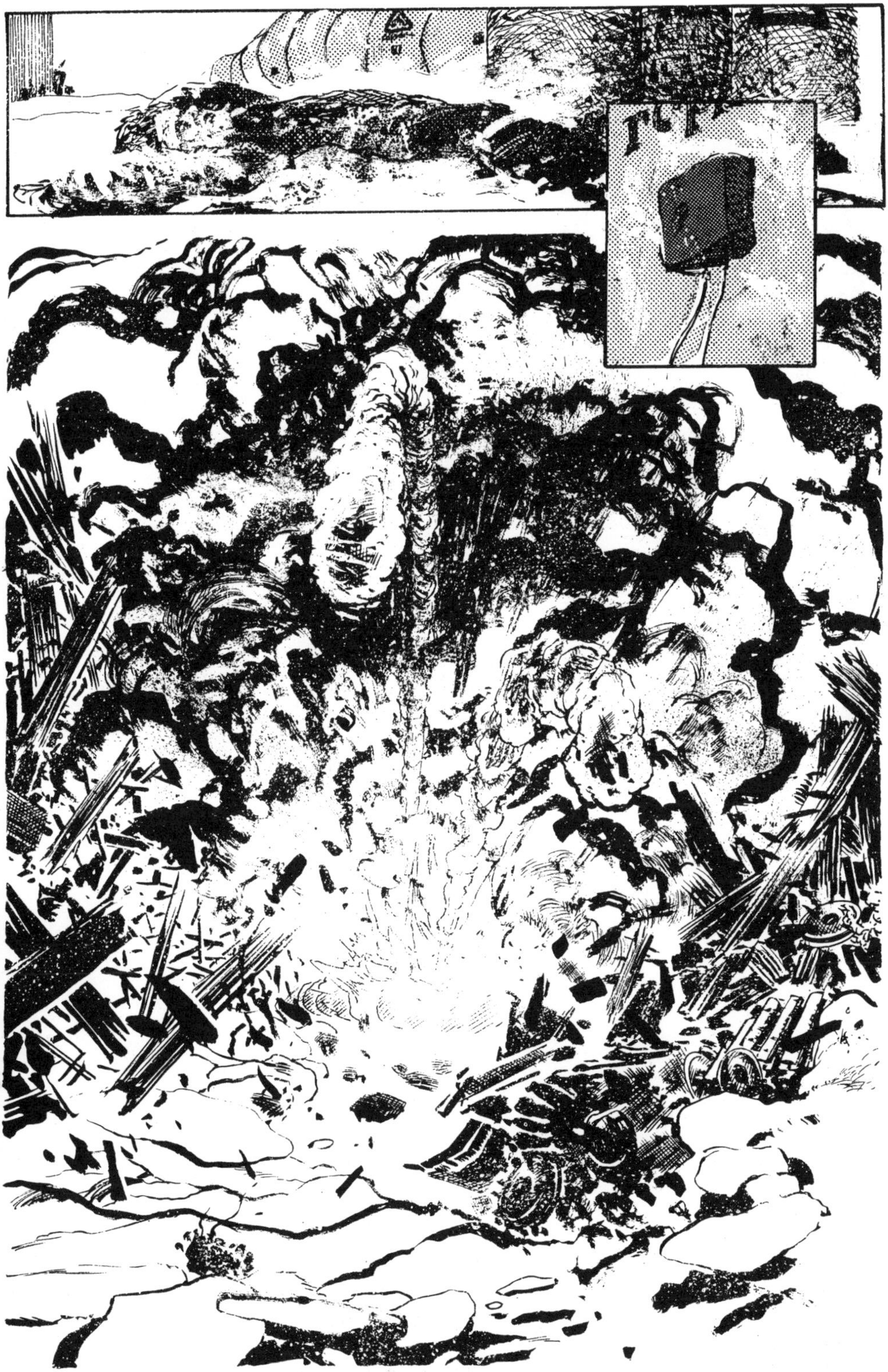

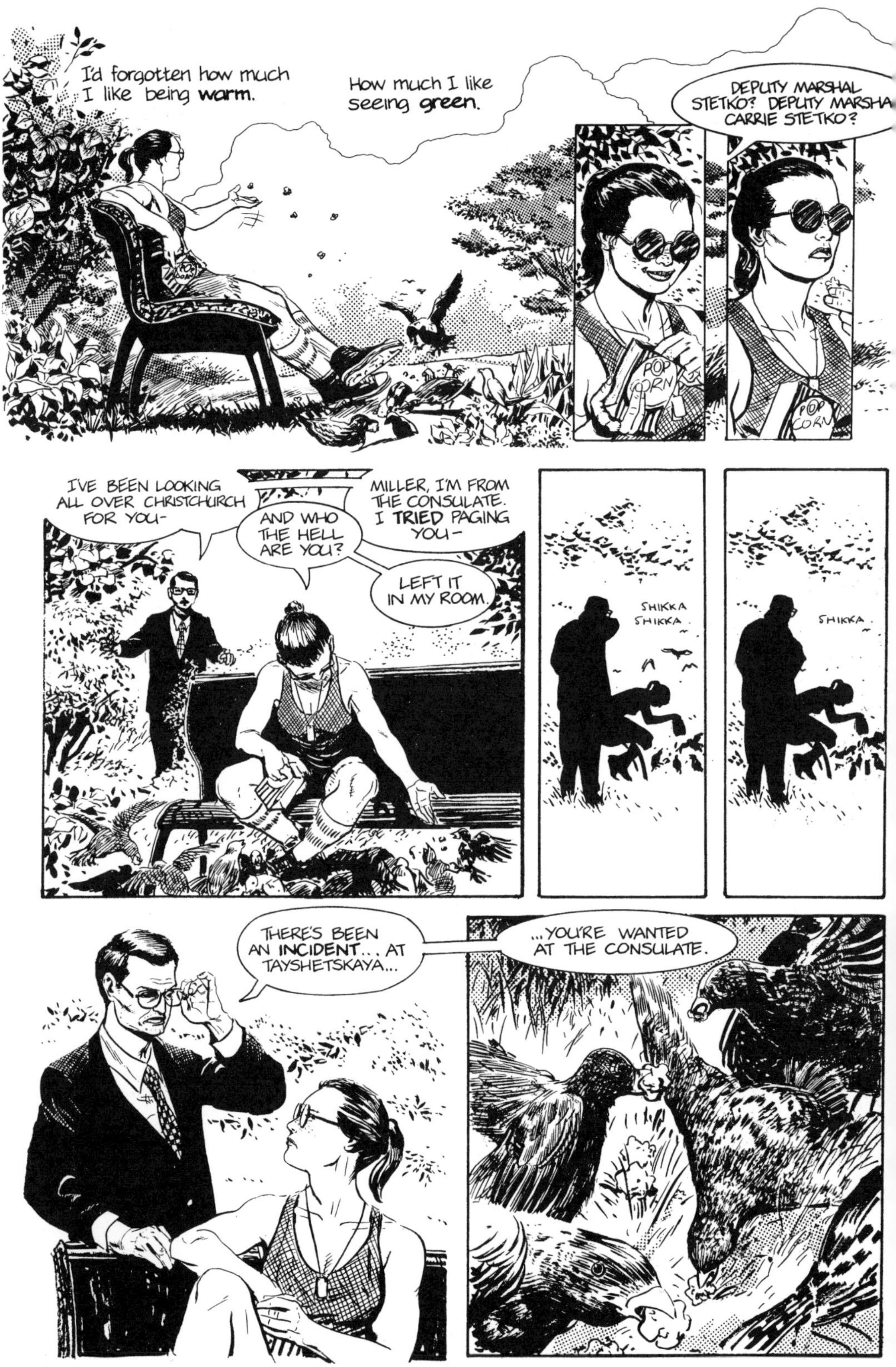
I'd forgotten how much I like being **warm**.
How much I like seeing **green**.
POP CORN
DEPUTY MARSHAL STETKO? DEPUTY MARSHA CARRIE STETKO?
POP CORN
I'VE BEEN LOOKING ALL OVER CHRISTCHURCH FOR YOU-
AND WHO THE HELL ARE YOU?
MILLER, I'M FROM THE CONSULATE. I **TRIED** PAGING YOU-
LEFT IT IN MY ROOM.
SHIKKA SHIKKA
SHIKKA
THERE'S BEEN AN **INCIDENT**... AT TAYSHETSKAYA...
...YOU'RE WANTED AT THE CONSULATE.

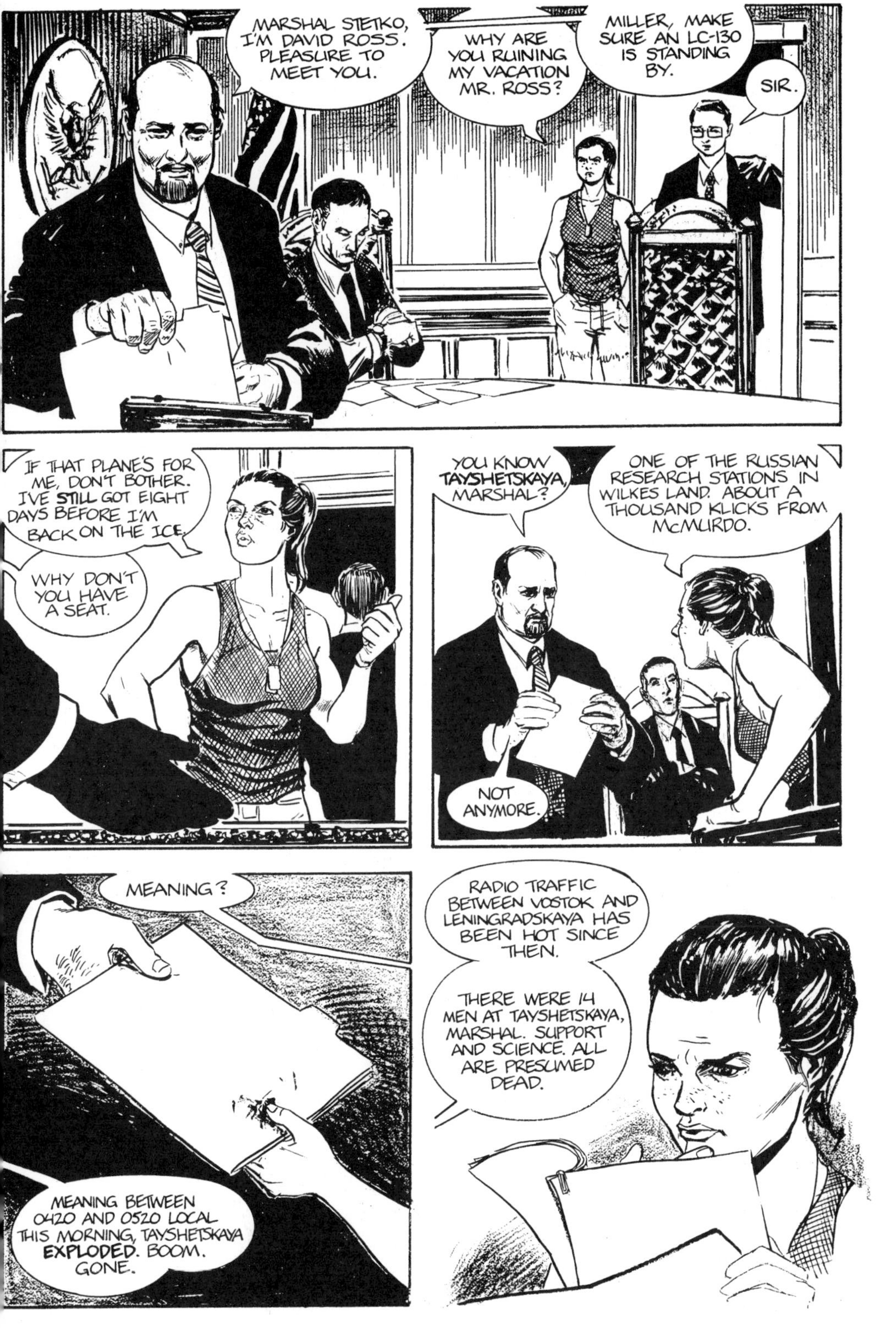
MARSHAL STETKO, I'M DAVID ROSS. PLEASURE TO MEET YOU.
WHY ARE YOU RUINING MY VACATION MR. ROSS?
MILLER, MAKE SURE AN LC-130 IS STANDING BY.
SIR.
IF THAT PLANE'S FOR ME, DON'T BOTHER. I'VE STILL GOT EIGHT DAYS BEFORE I'M BACK ON THE ICE.
WHY DON'T YOU HAVE A SEAT.
YOU KNOW TAYSHETSKAYA, MARSHAL?
ONE OF THE RUSSIAN RESEARCH STATIONS IN WILKES LAND. ABOUT A THOUSAND KLICKS FROM McMURDO.
NOT ANYMORE.
MEANING?
MEANING BETWEEN 0420 AND 0520 LOCAL THIS MORNING, TAYSHETSKAYA EXPLODED. BOOM. GONE.
RADIO TRAFFIC BETWEEN VOSTOK AND LENINGRADSKAYA HAS BEEN HOT SINCE THEN.
THERE WERE 14 MEN AT TAYSHETSKAYA, MARSHAL. SUPPORT AND SCIENCE. ALL ARE PRESUMED DEAD.

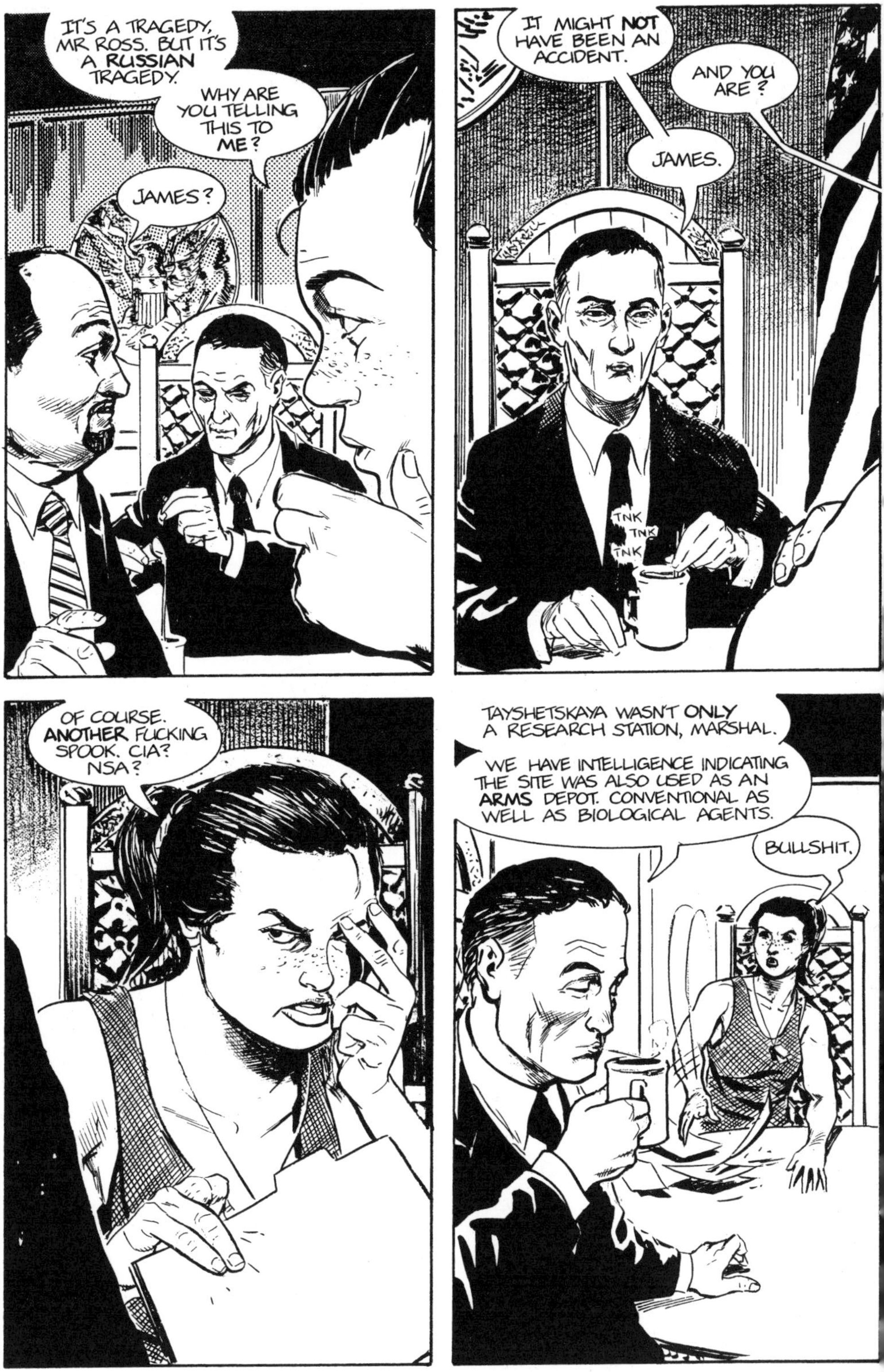
IT'S A TRAGEDY, MR ROSS. BUT IT'S A RUSSIAN TRAGEDY.
WHY ARE YOU TELLING THIS TO ME?
JAMES?
IT MIGHT NOT HAVE BEEN AN ACCIDENT.
AND YOU ARE?
JAMES.
TNK TNK TNK
OF COURSE. ANOTHER FUCKING SPOOK. CIA? NSA?
TAYSHETSKAYA WASN'T ONLY A RESEARCH STATION, MARSHAL.
WE HAVE INTELLIGENCE INDICATING THE SITE WAS ALSO USED AS AN ARMS DEPOT. CONVENTIONAL AS WELL AS BIOLOGICAL AGENTS.
BULLSHIT.

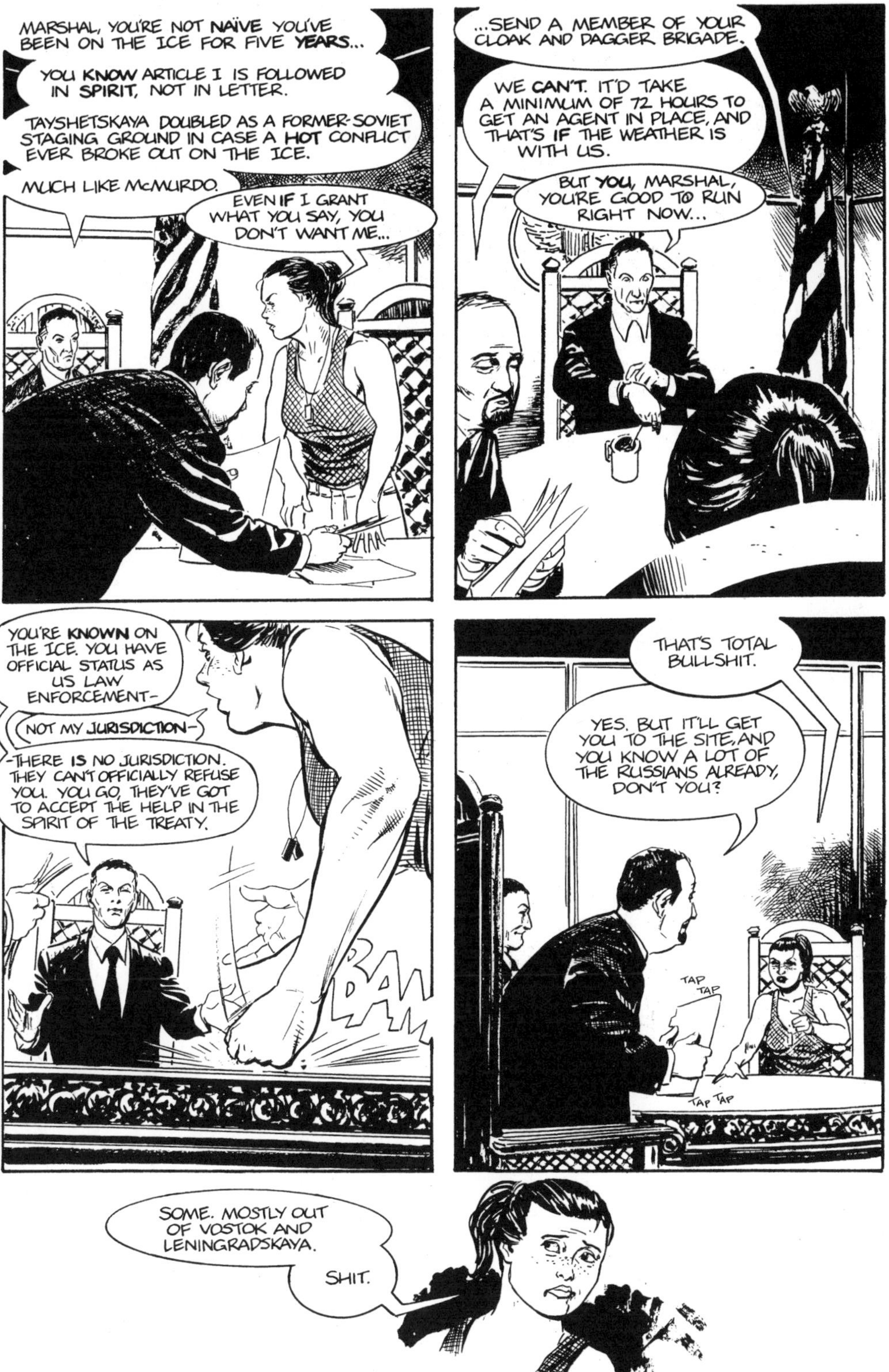
MARSHAL, YOU'RE NOT NAÏVE YOU'VE BEEN ON THE ICE FOR FIVE YEARS...
YOU KNOW ARTICLE I IS FOLLOWED IN SPIRIT, NOT IN LETTER.
TAYSHETSKAYA DOUBLED AS A FORMER-SOVIET STAGING GROUND IN CASE A HOT CONFLICT EVER BROKE OUT ON THE ICE.
MUCH LIKE McMURDO.
EVEN IF I GRANT WHAT YOU SAY, YOU DON'T WANT ME...
...SEND A MEMBER OF YOUR CLOAK AND DAGGER BRIGADE.
WE CAN'T. IT'D TAKE A MINIMUM OF 72 HOURS TO GET AN AGENT IN PLACE, AND THAT'S IF THE WEATHER IS WITH US.
BUT YOU, MARSHAL, YOU'RE GOOD TO RUN RIGHT NOW...
YOU'RE KNOWN ON THE ICE. YOU HAVE OFFICIAL STATUS AS US LAW ENFORCEMENT-
NOT MY JURISDICTION-
-THERE IS NO JURISDICTION. THEY CAN'T OFFICIALLY REFUSE YOU. YOU GO, THEY'VE GOT TO ACCEPT THE HELP IN THE SPIRIT OF THE TREATY.
BAM
THAT'S TOTAL BULLSHIT.
YES. BUT IT'LL GET YOU TO THE SITE, AND YOU KNOW A LOT OF THE RUSSIANS ALREADY, DON'T YOU?
TAP TAP
TAP TAP
SOME. MOSTLY OUT OF VOSTOK AND LENINGRADSKAYA.
SHIT.

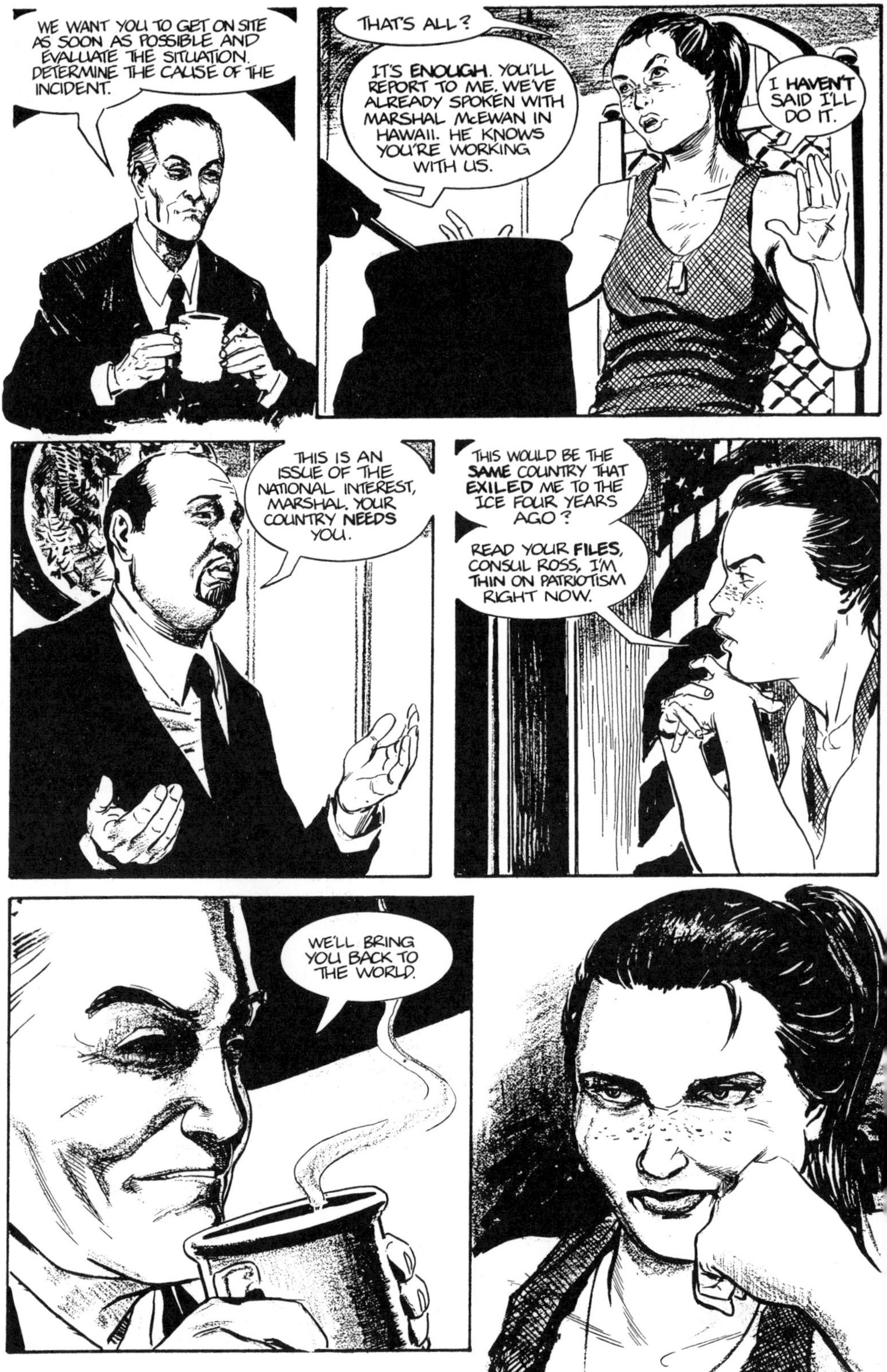
WE WANT YOU TO GET ON SITE AS SOON AS POSSIBLE AND EVALUATE THE SITUATION. DETERMINE THE CAUSE OF THE INCIDENT.
THAT'S ALL?
IT'S **ENOUGH**. YOU'LL REPORT TO ME. WE'VE ALREADY SPOKEN WITH MARSHAL McEWAN IN HAWAII. HE KNOWS YOU'RE WORKING WITH US.
I **HAVEN'T** SAID I'LL DO IT.
THIS IS AN ISSUE OF THE NATIONAL INTEREST, MARSHAL. YOUR COUNTRY **NEEDS** YOU.
THIS WOULD BE THE **SAME** COUNTRY THAT **EXILED** ME TO THE ICE FOUR YEARS AGO?
READ YOUR **FILES**, CONSUL ROSS, I'M **THIN** ON PATRIOTISM RIGHT NOW.
WE'LL BRING YOU BACK TO THE WORLD.

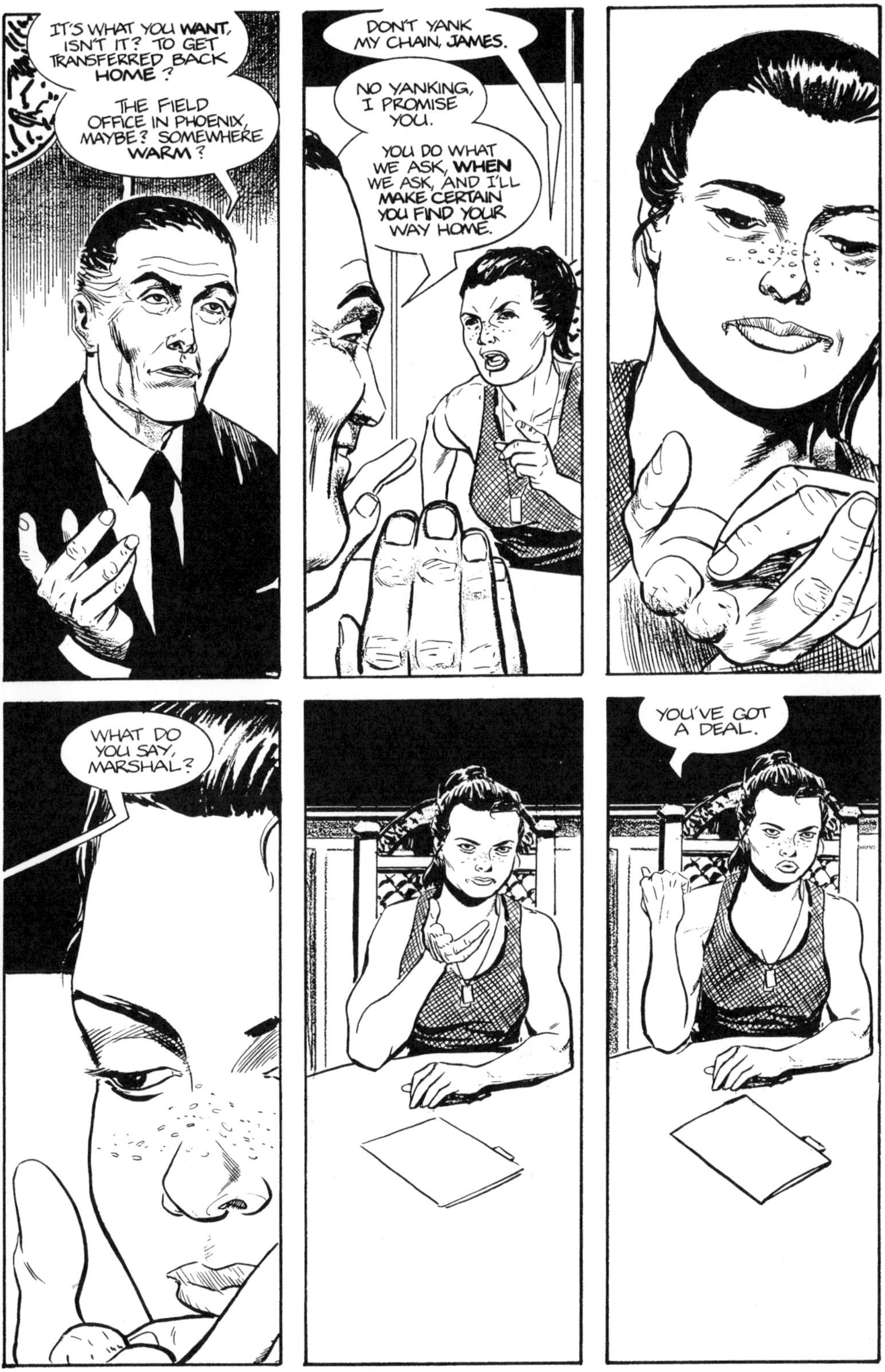

IT'S WHAT YOU WANT, ISN'T IT? TO GET TRANSFERRED BACK HOME?
THE FIELD OFFICE IN PHOENIX, MAYBE? SOMEWHERE WARM?
DON'T YANK MY CHAIN, JAMES.
NO YANKING, I PROMISE YOU.
YOU DO WHAT WE ASK, WHEN WE ASK, AND I'LL MAKE CERTAIN YOU FIND YOUR WAY HOME.
WHAT DO YOU SAY, MARSHAL?
YOU'VE GOT A DEAL.

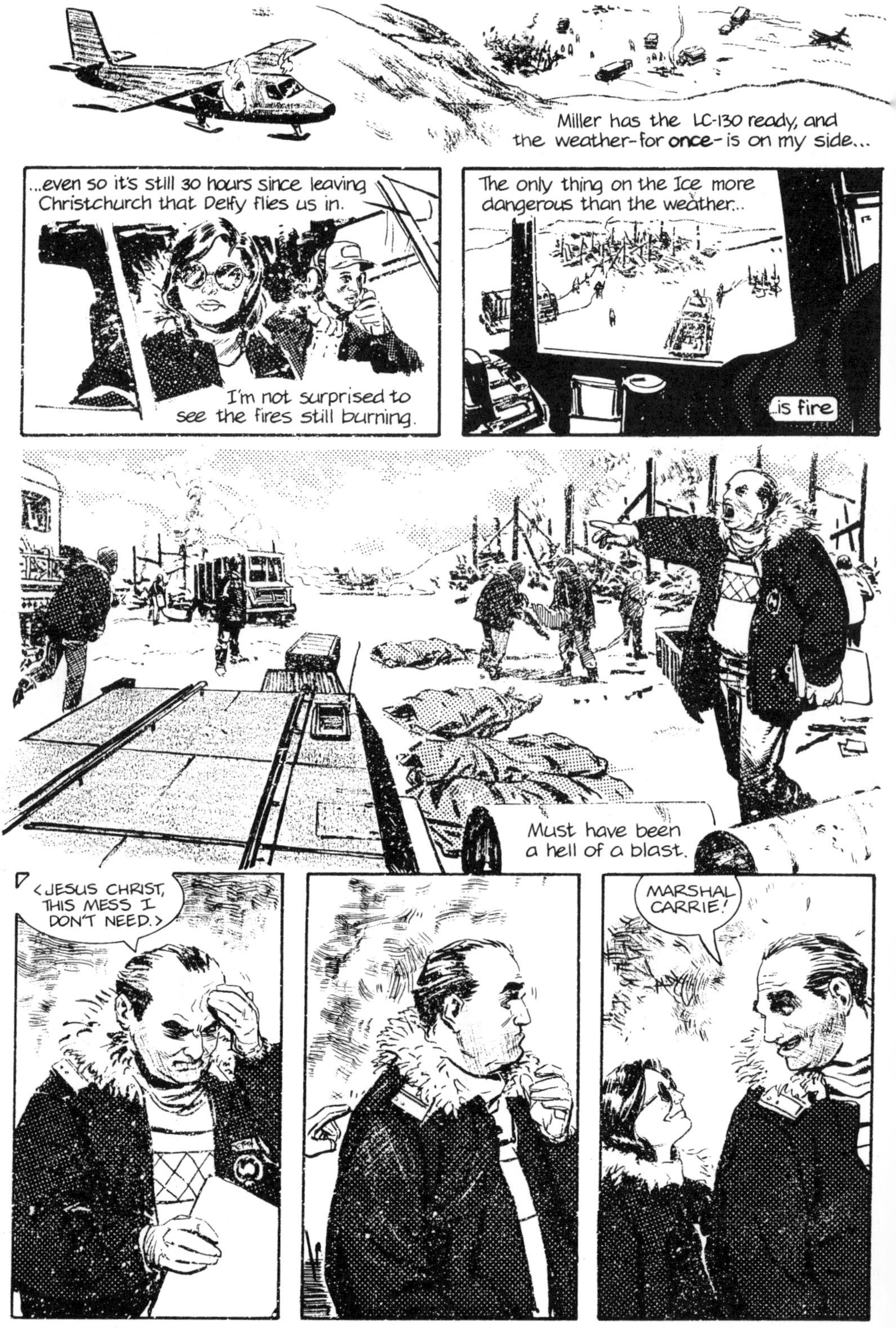

Miller has the LC-130 ready, and the weather-for once- is on my side...
...even so it's still 30 hours since leaving Christchurch that Delfy flies us in.
I'm not surprised to see the fires still burning.
The only thing on the Ice more dangerous than the weather...
..is fire
Must have been a hell of a blast.
<JESUS CHRIST, THIS MESS I DON'T NEED.>
MARSHAL CARRIE!

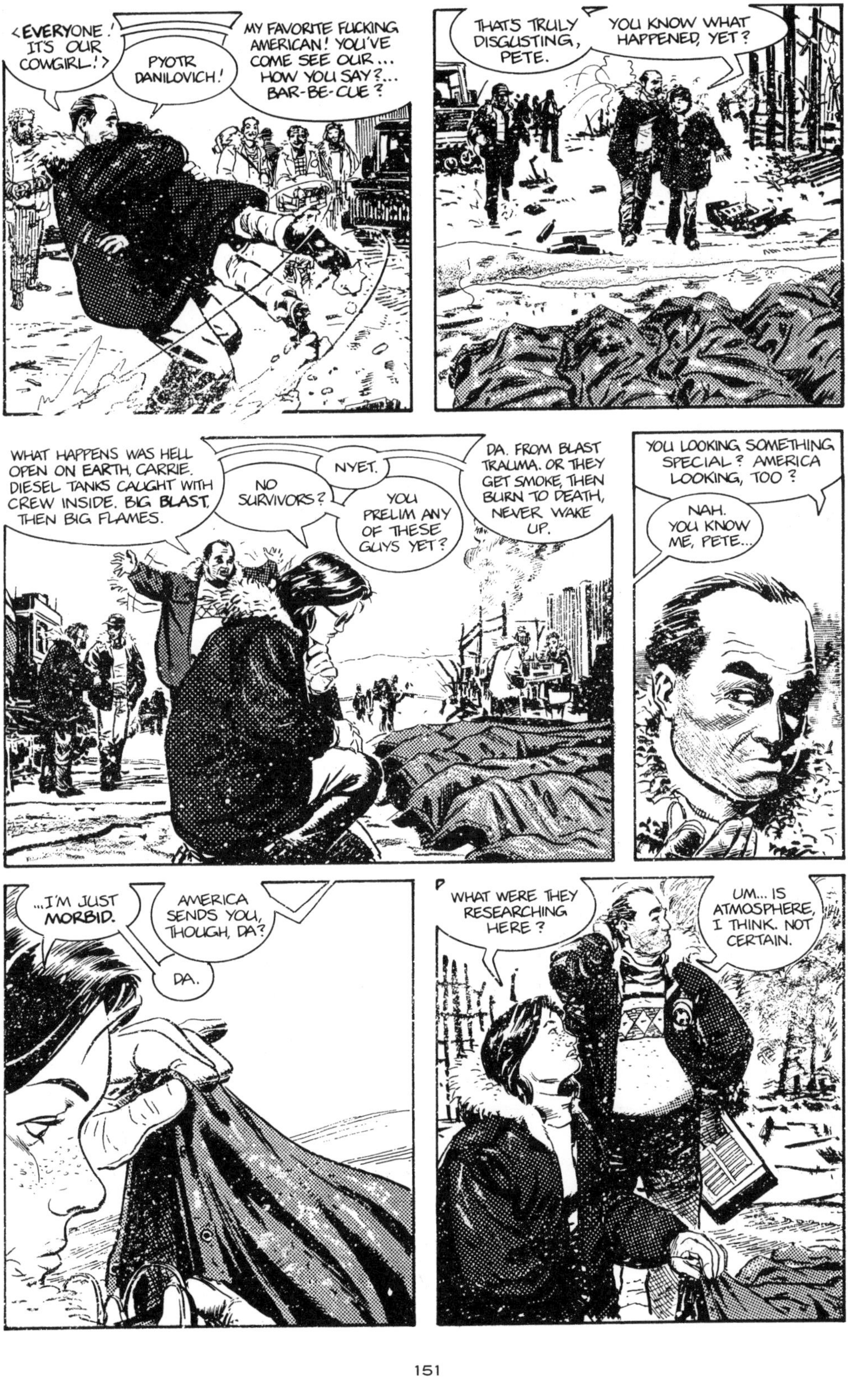

<EVERYONE! IT'S OUR COWGIRL!>
PYOTR DANILOVICH!
MY FAVORITE FUCKING AMERICAN! YOU'VE COME SEE OUR... HOW YOU SAY?... BAR-BE-CUE?
THAT'S TRULY DISGUSTING, PETE.
YOU KNOW WHAT HAPPENED, YET?
WHAT HAPPENS WAS HELL OPEN ON EARTH, CARRIE. DIESEL TANKS CAUGHT WITH CREW INSIDE. BIG BLAST, THEN BIG FLAMES.
NO SURVIVORS?
NYET.
YOU PRELIM ANY OF THESE GUYS YET?
DA. FROM BLAST TRAUMA. OR THEY GET SMOKE, THEN BURN TO DEATH, NEVER WAKE UP.
YOU LOOKING SOMETHING SPECIAL? AMERICA LOOKING, TOO?
NAH. YOU KNOW ME, PETE...
...I'M JUST MORBID.
AMERICA SENDS YOU, THOUGH, DA?
DA.
WHAT WERE THEY RESEARCHING HERE?
UM... IS ATMOSPHERE, I THINK. NOT CERTAIN.

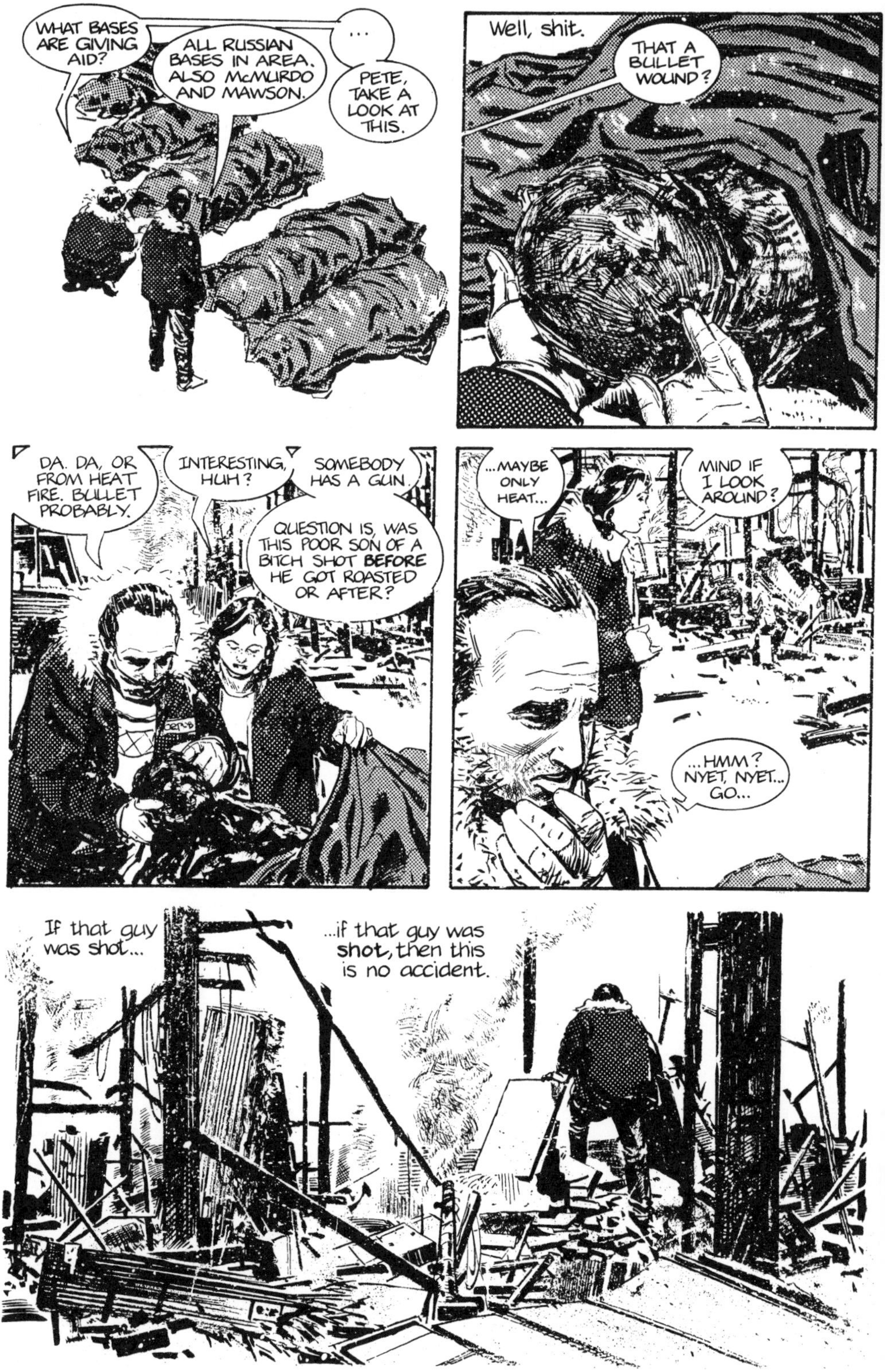
WHAT BASES ARE GIVING AID?
ALL RUSSIAN BASES IN AREA. ALSO McMURDO AND MAWSON.
...
PETE, TAKE A LOOK AT THIS.
Well, shit.
THAT A BULLET WOUND?
DA. DA, OR FROM HEAT FIRE. BULLET PROBABLY.
INTERESTING, HUH?
SOMEBODY HAS A GUN.
QUESTION IS, WAS THIS POOR SON OF A BITCH SHOT BEFORE HE GOT ROASTED OR AFTER?
...MAYBE ONLY HEAT...
MIND IF I LOOK AROUND?
...HMM? NYET, NYET... GO...
If that guy was shot...
...if that guy was shot, then this is no accident.

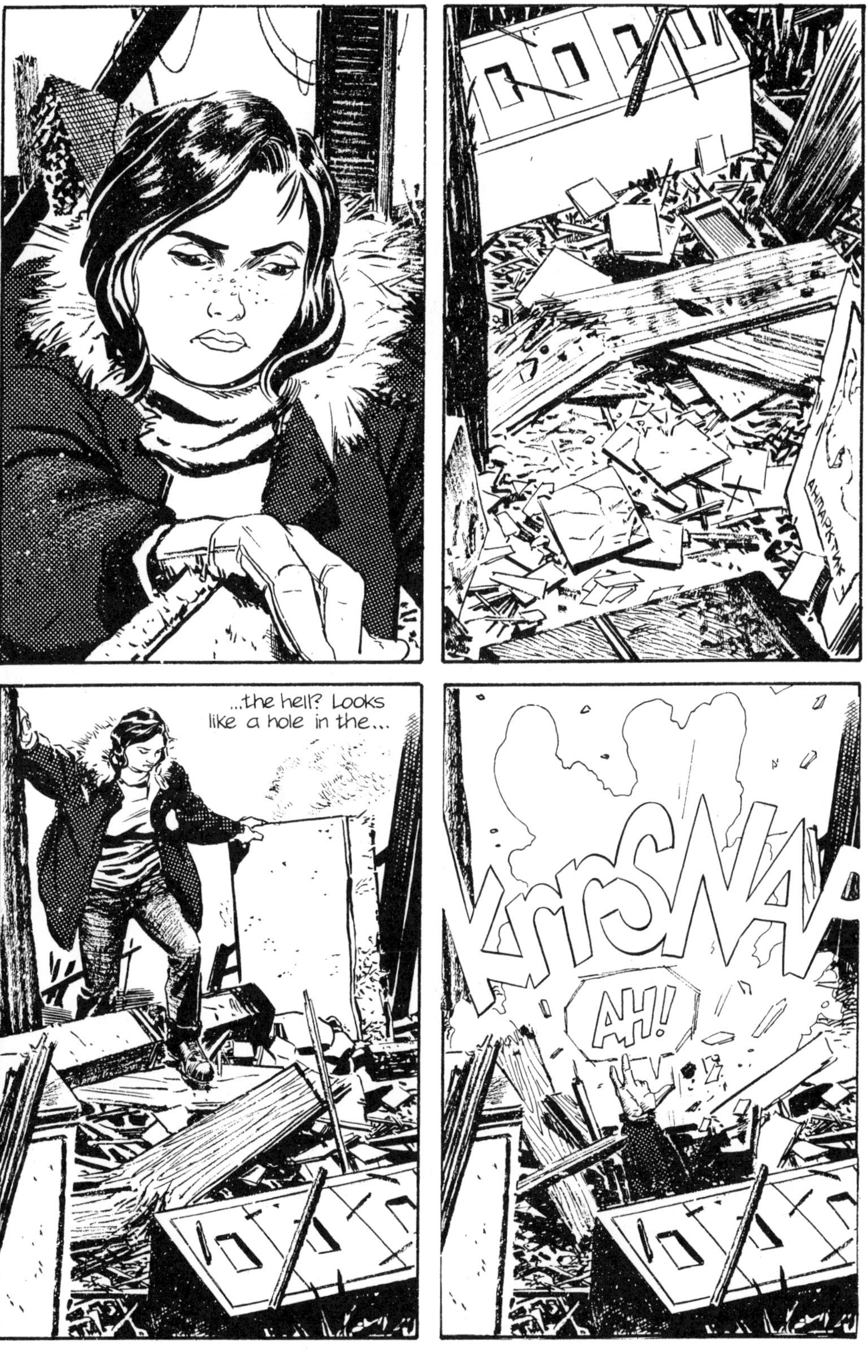

...the hell? Looks like a hole in the...
KRRRSNAP
AH!

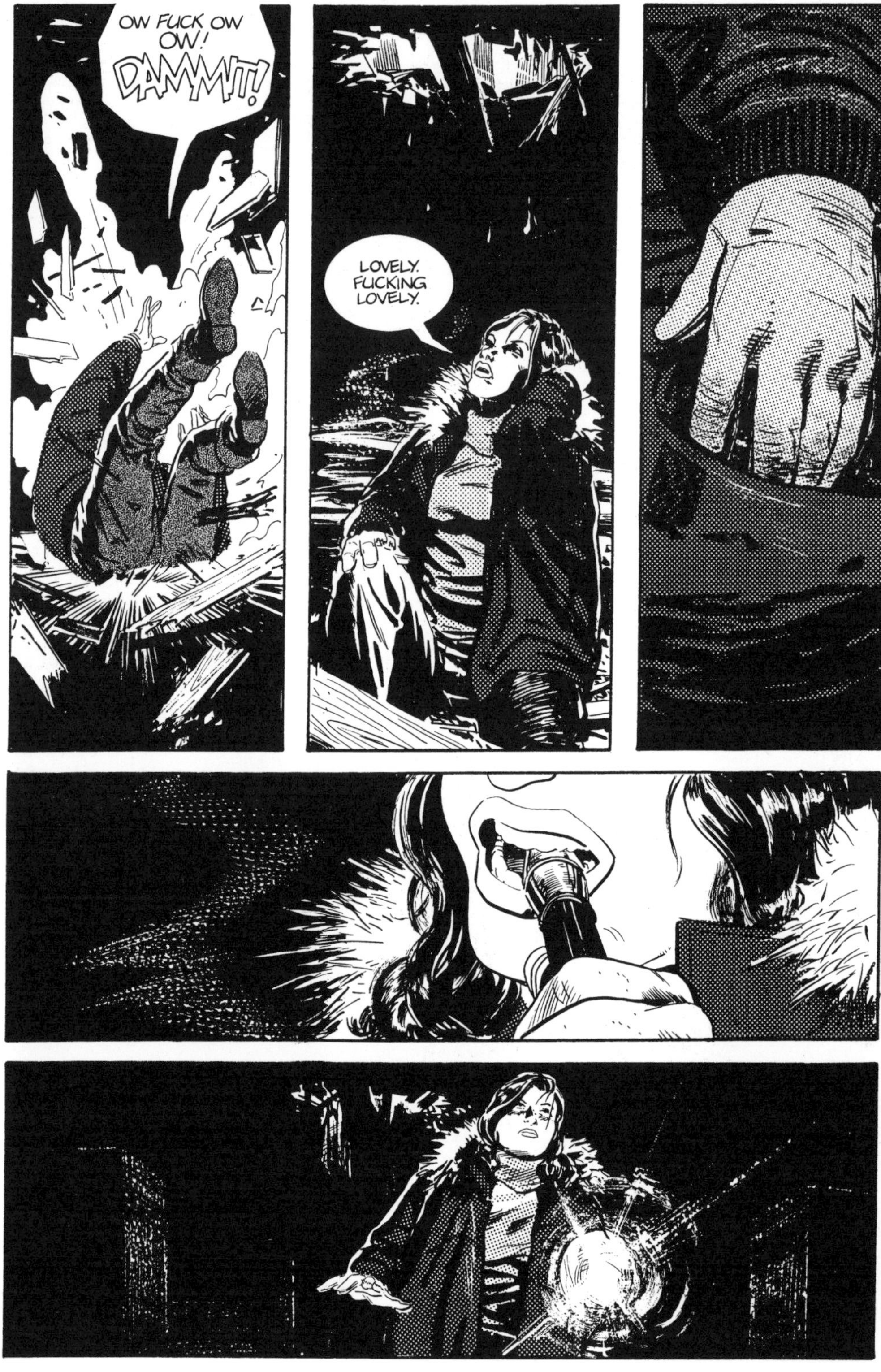
OW FUCK OW OW! DAMMIT!
LOVELY. FUCKING LOVELY.

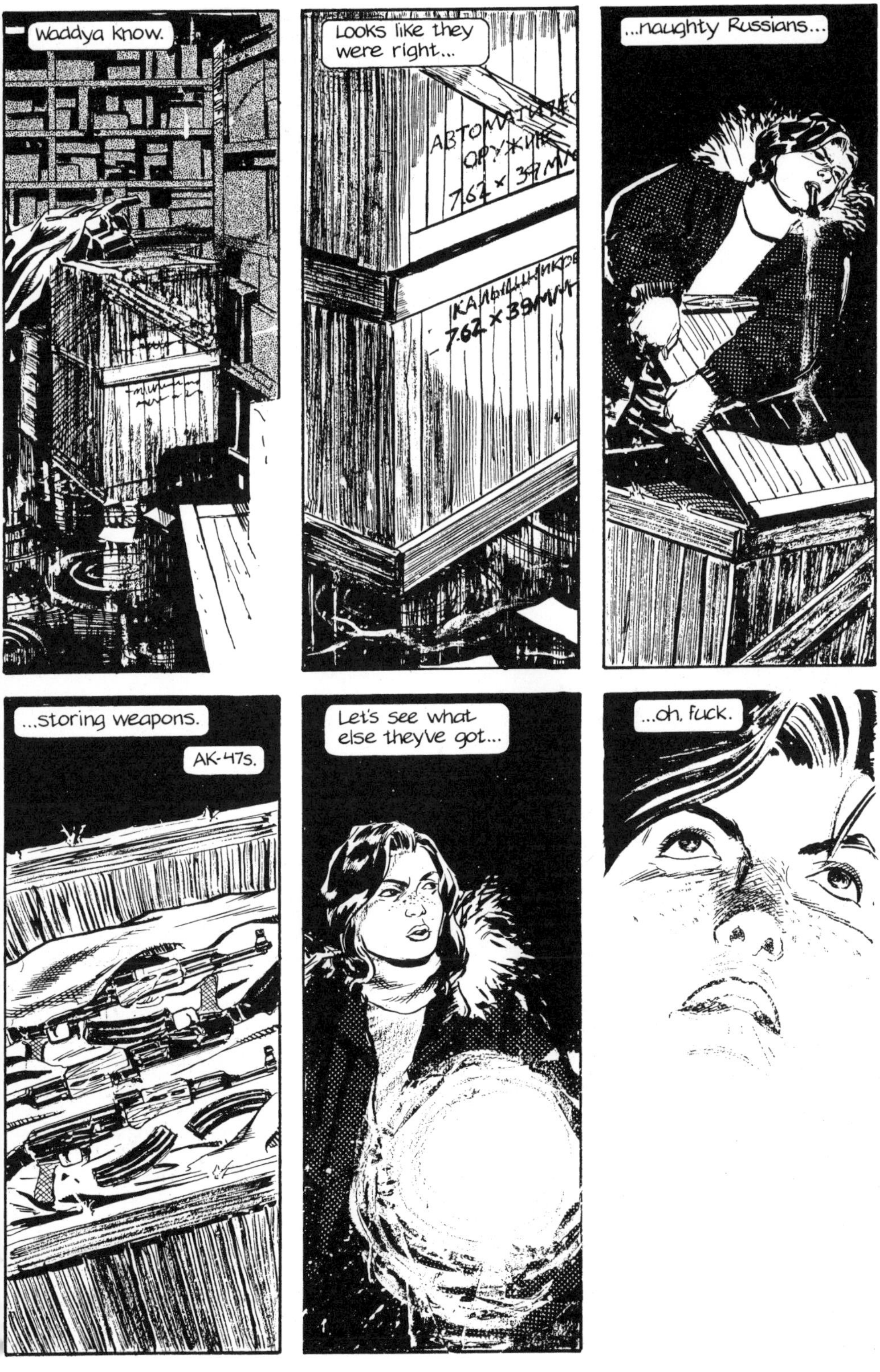
Waddya know.
Looks like they were right...
...naughty Russians...
...storing weapons.
AK-47s.
Let's see what else they've got...
...oh, fuck.

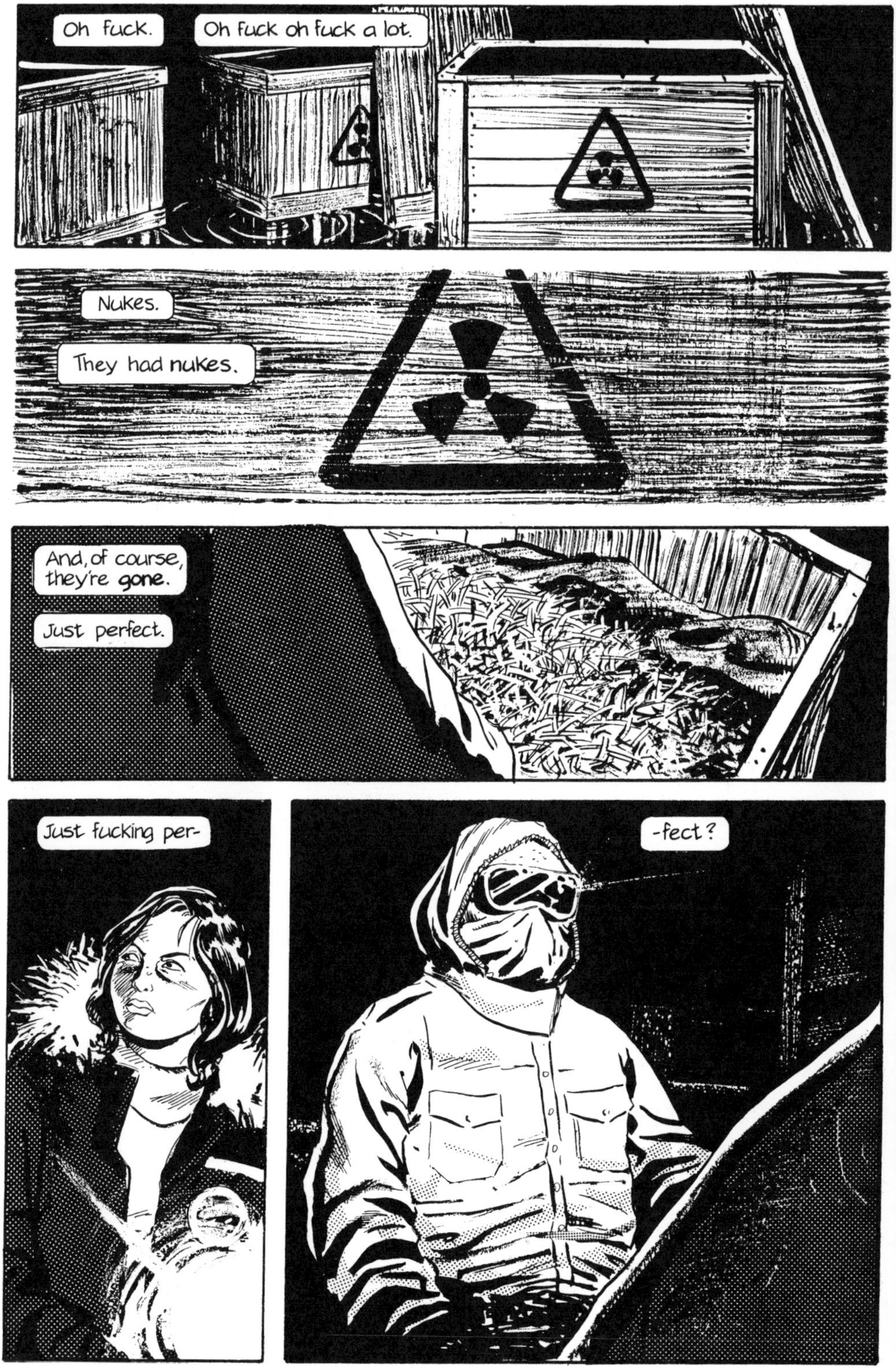

Oh fuck.
Oh fuck oh fuck a lot.
Nukes.
They had nukes.
And, of course, they're gone.
Just perfect.
Just fucking per-
-fect?

CHAPTER TWO

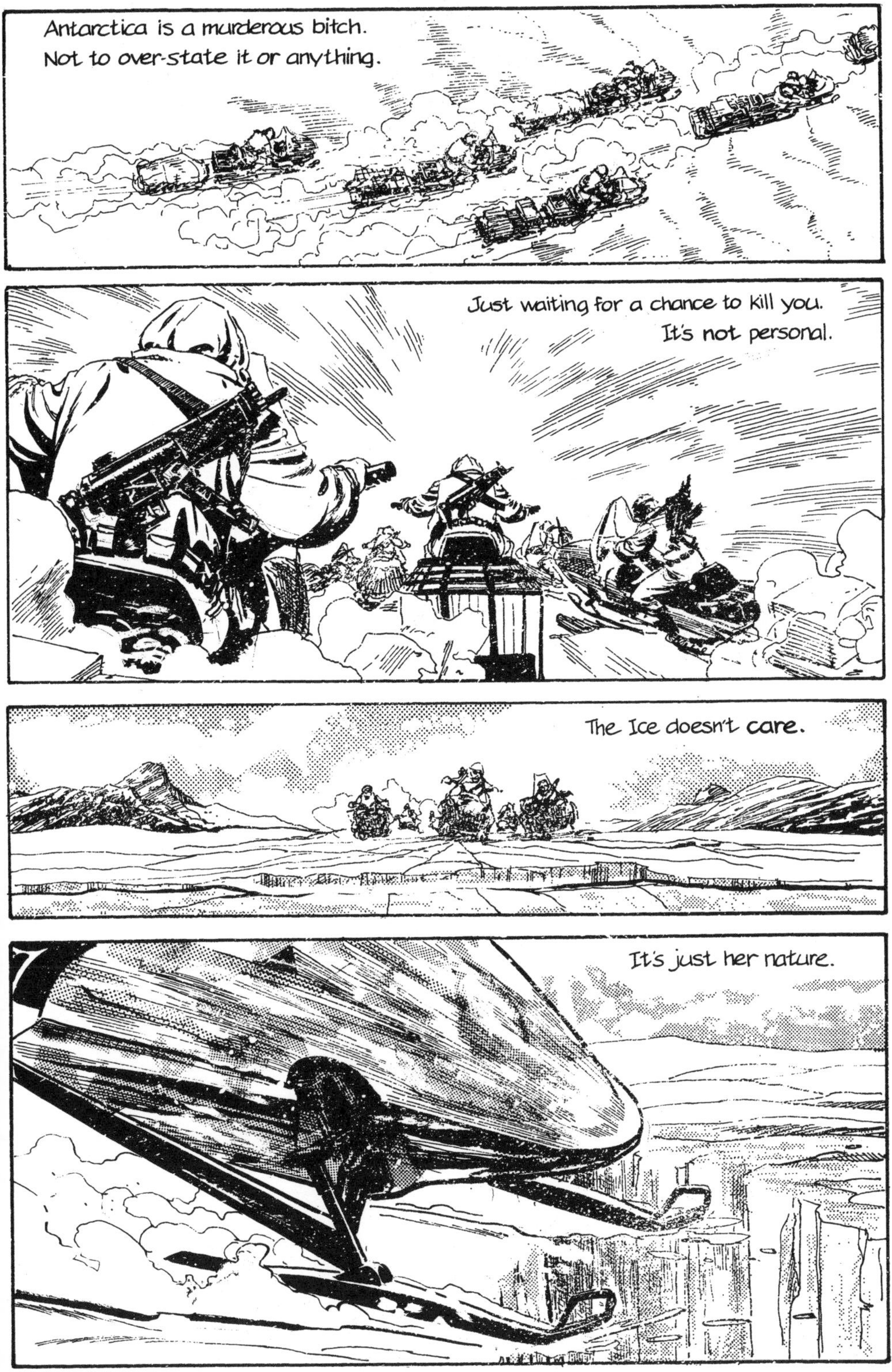
Antarctica is a murderous bitch.
Not to over-state it or anything.
Just waiting for a chance to kill you.
It's not personal.
The Ice doesn't care.
It's just her nature.

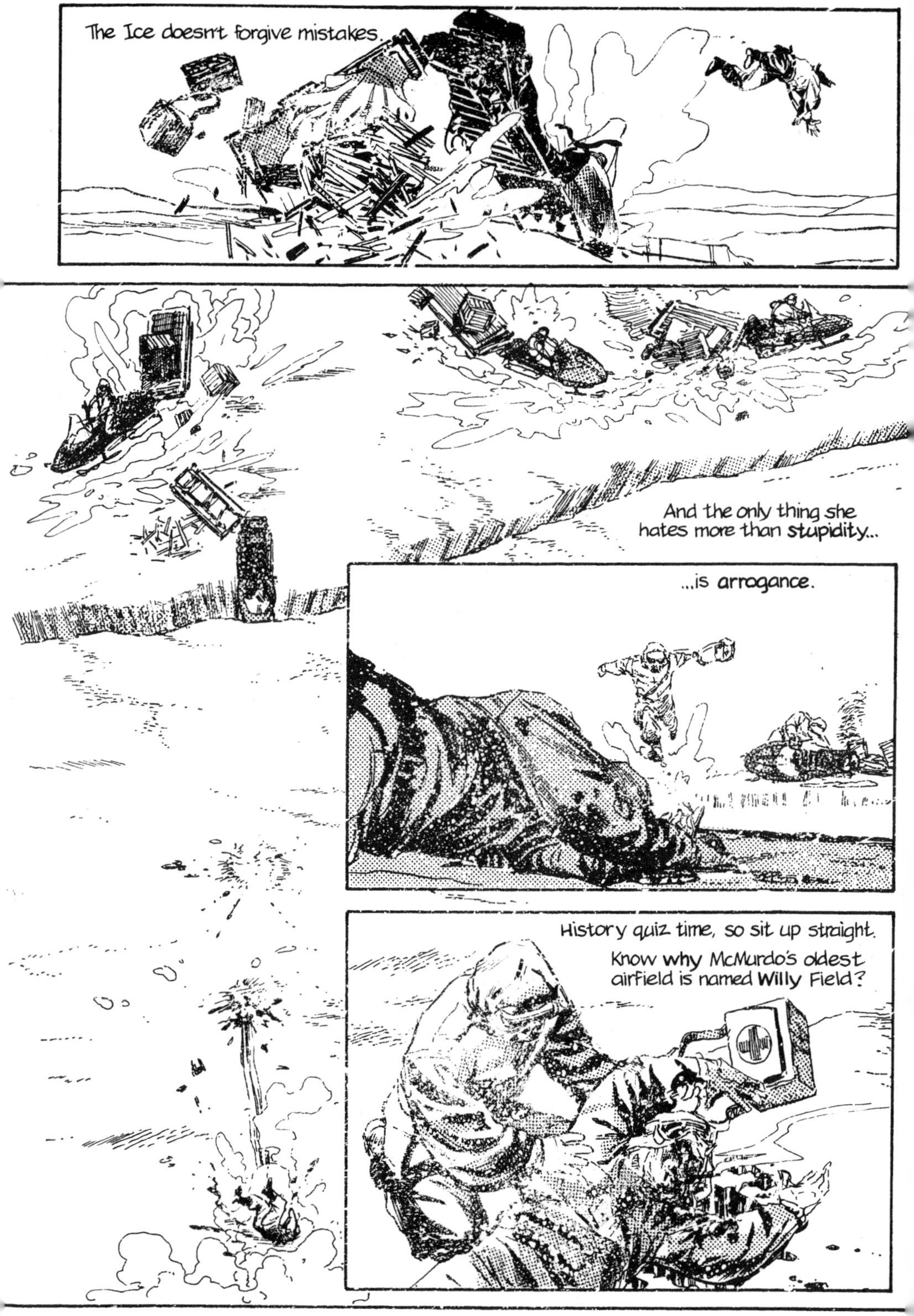

The Ice doesn't forgive mistakes.
And the only thing she hates more than stupidity...
...is arrogance.
History quiz time, so sit up straight.
Know why McMurdo's oldest airfield is named Willy Field?

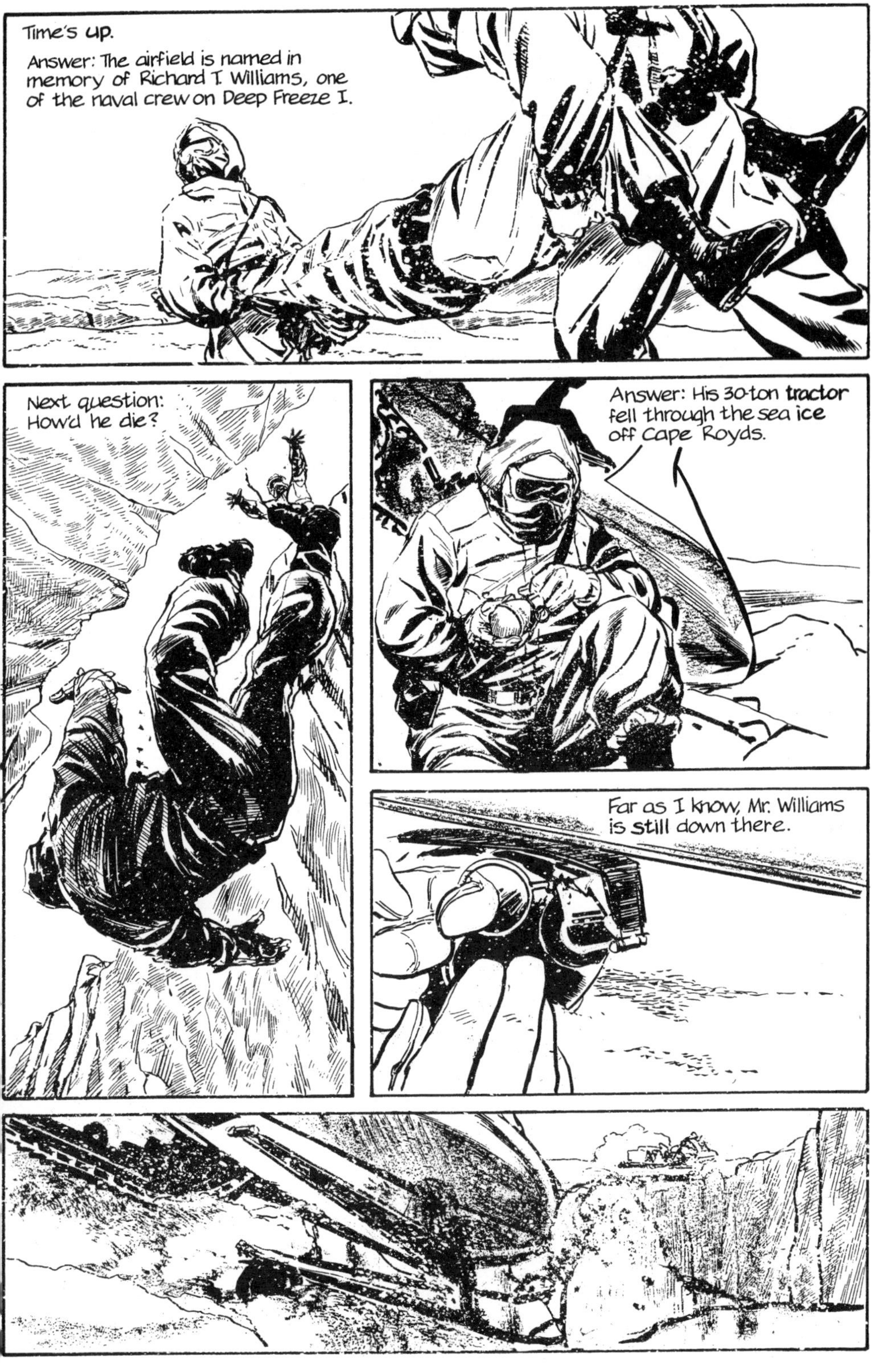
Time's up.
Answer: The airfield is named in memory of Richard T. Williams, one of the naval crew on Deep Freeze I.
Next question: How'd he die?
Answer: His 30-ton tractor fell through the sea ice off Cape Royds.
Far as I know, Mr. Williams is still down there.

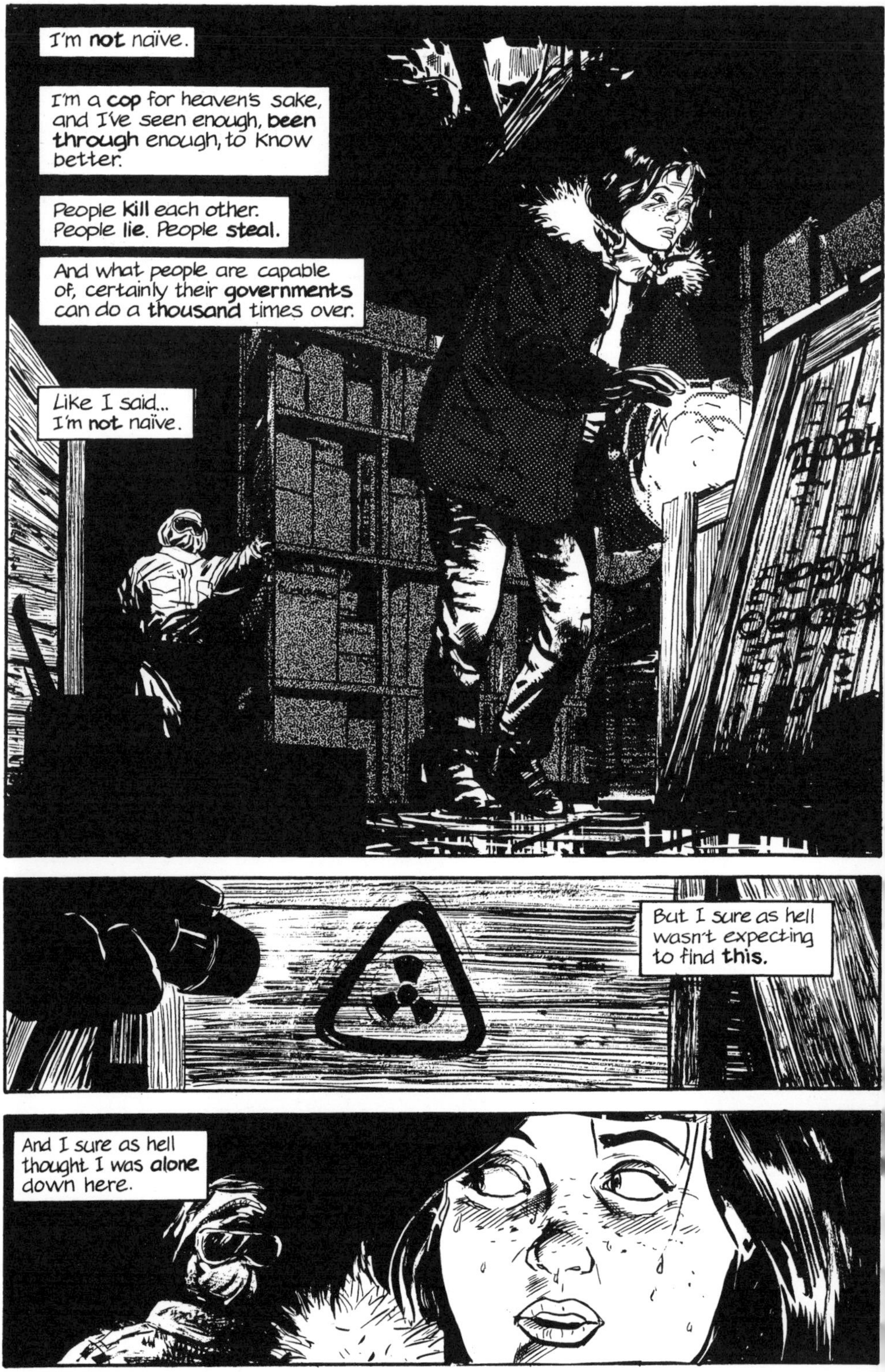
I'm **not** naïve.
I'm a **cop** for heaven's sake, and I've seen enough, **been through** enough, to know better.
People **kill** each other. People **lie**. People **steal**.
And what people are capable of, certainly their **governments** can do a **thousand** times over.
Like I said... I'm **not** naïve.
But I sure as hell wasn't expecting to find **this.**
And I sure as hell thought I was **alone** down here.

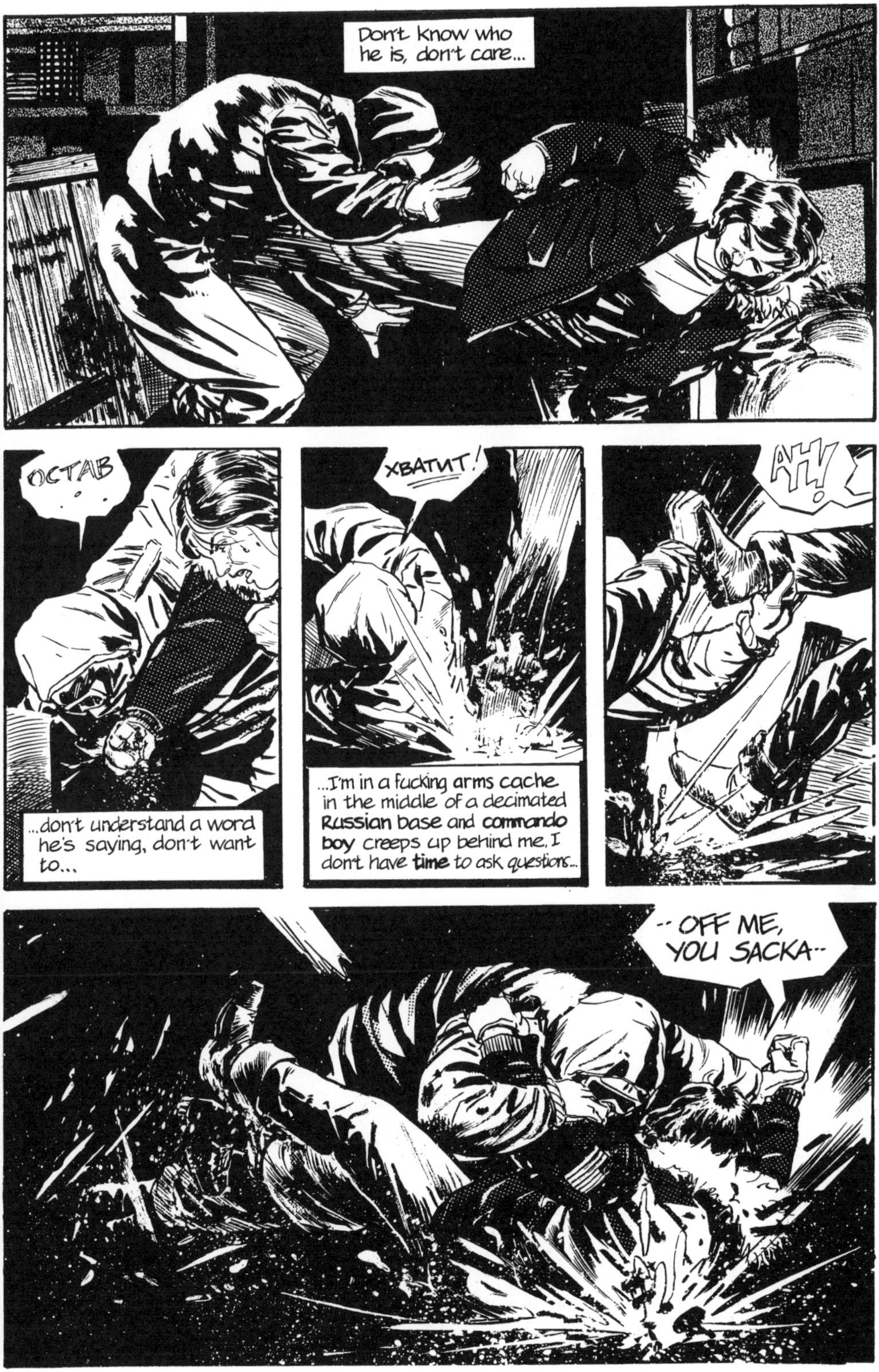
Don't know who he is, don't care...
ОСТАВ
...don't understand a word he's saying, don't want to...
ХВАТИТ!
...I'm in a fucking **arms cache** in the middle of a decimated **Russian** base and **commando boy** creeps up behind me, I don't have **time** to ask questions...
AH!
-- OFF ME, YOU SACKA--

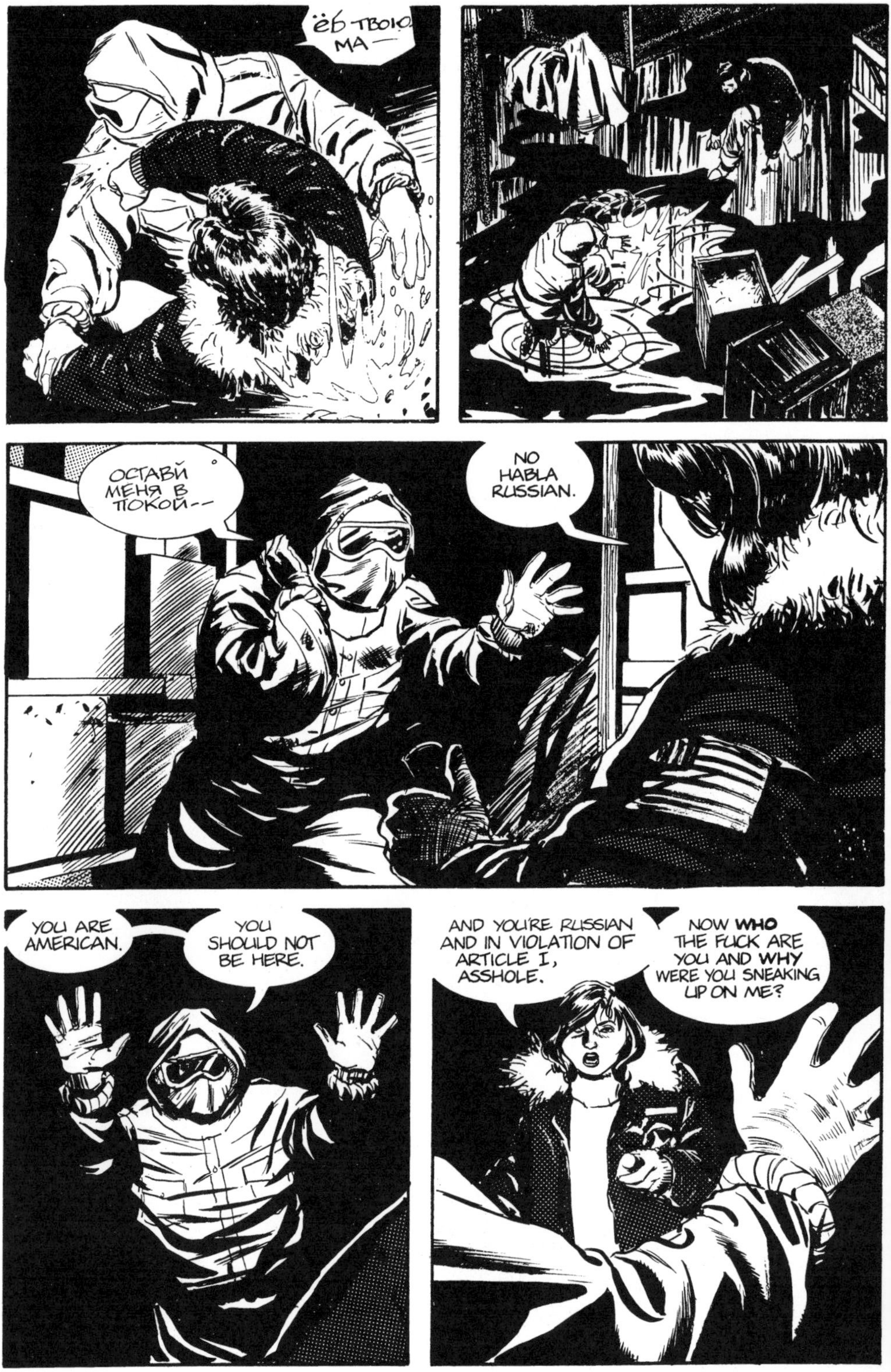

ЁБ ТВОЮ МА—
ОСТАВЬ МЕНЯ В ПОКОЙ--
NO HABLA RUSSIAN.
YOU ARE AMERICAN.
YOU SHOULD NOT BE HERE.
AND YOU'RE RUSSIAN AND IN VIOLATION OF ARTICLE I, ASSHOLE.
NOW **WHO** THE FUCK ARE YOU AND **WHY** WERE YOU SNEAKING UP ON ME?

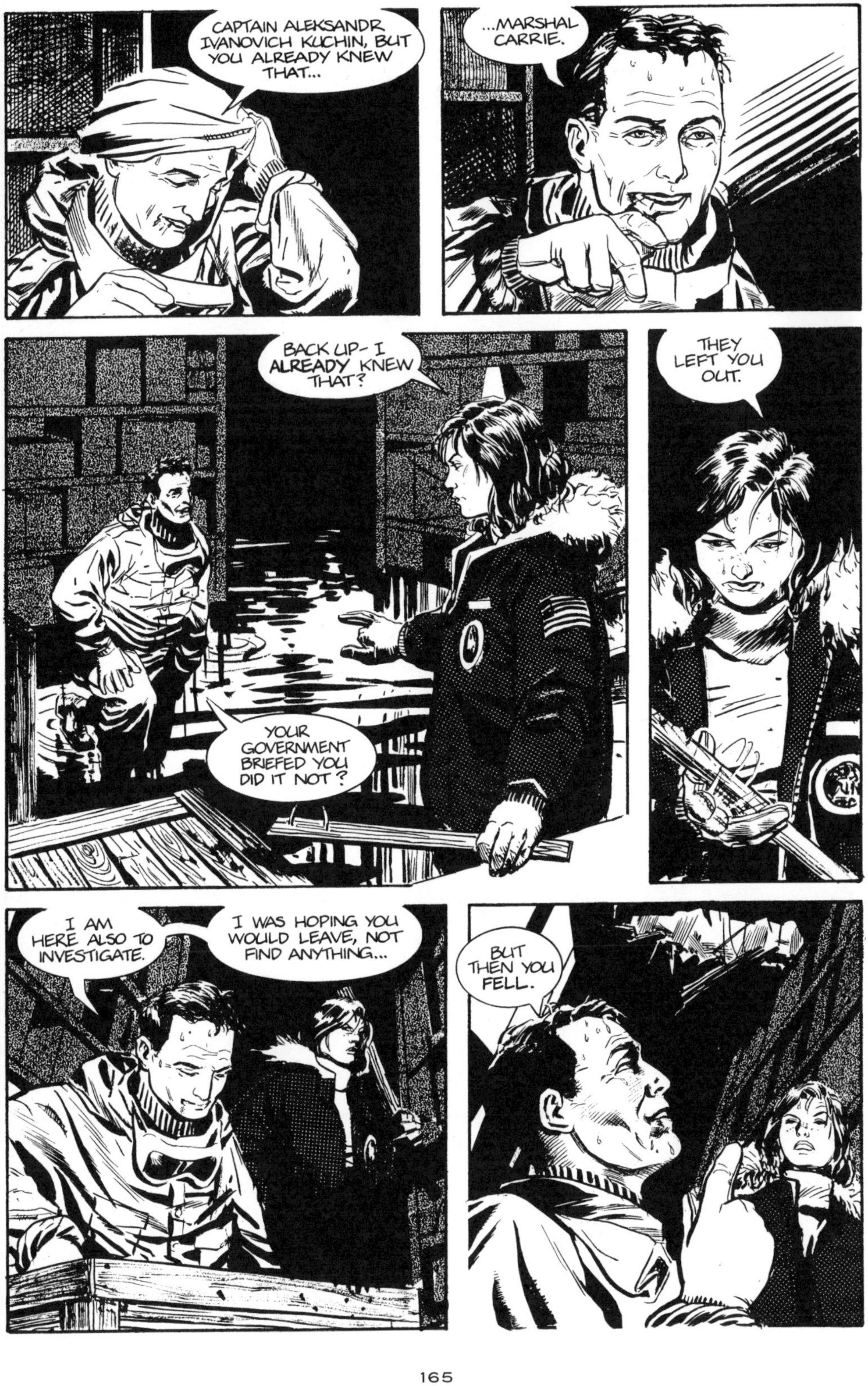
CAPTAIN ALEKSANDR IVANOVICH KUCHIN, BUT YOU ALREADY KNEW THAT...
...MARSHAL CARRIE.
BACK UP- I ALREADY KNEW THAT?
YOUR GOVERNMENT BRIEFED YOU DID IT NOT?
THEY LEFT YOU OUT.
I AM HERE ALSO TO INVESTIGATE.
I WAS HOPING YOU WOULD LEAVE, NOT FIND ANYTHING...
BUT THEN YOU FELL.

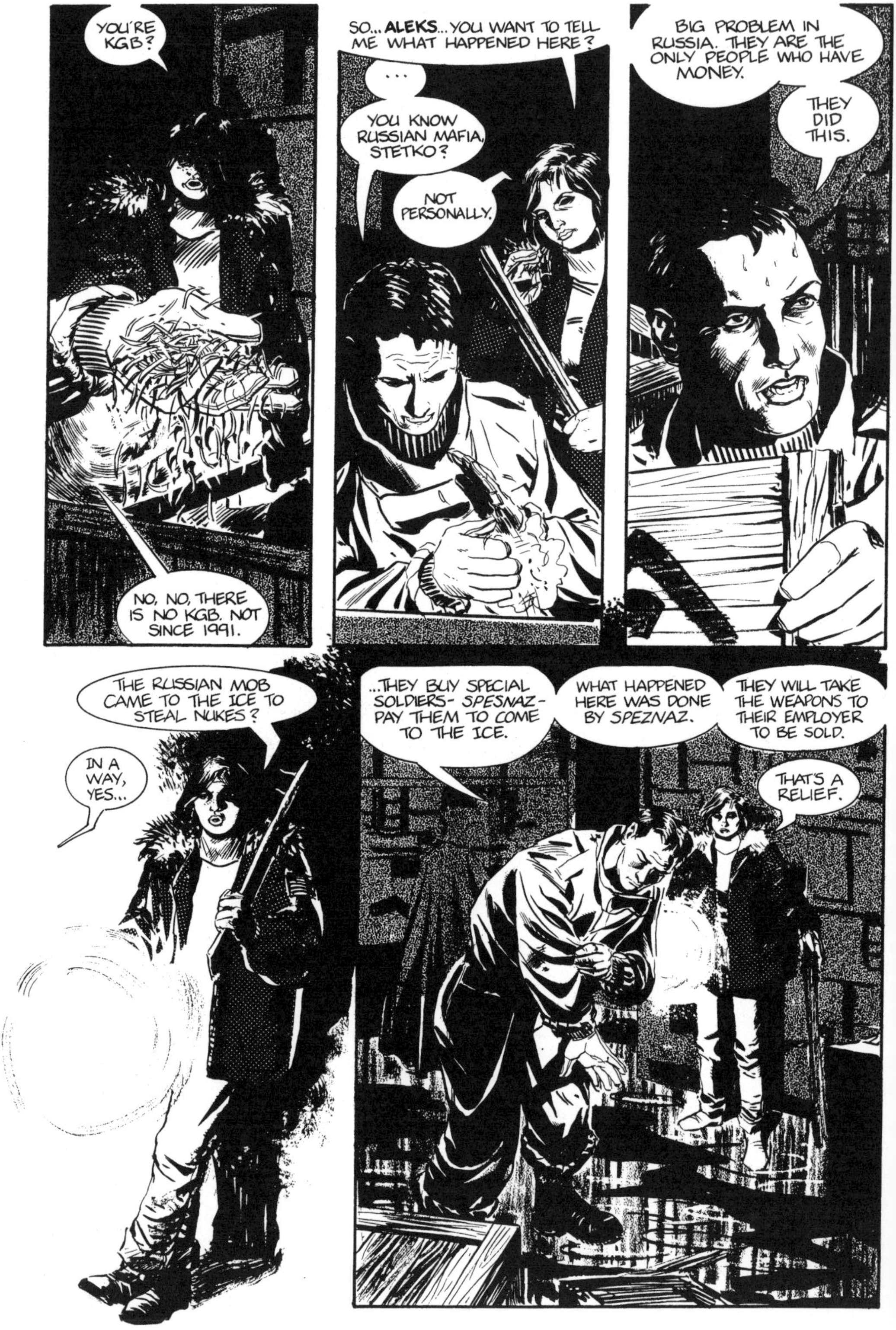
YOU'RE KGB?
NO, NO, THERE IS NO KGB. NOT SINCE 1991.
SO... ALEKS... YOU WANT TO TELL ME WHAT HAPPENED HERE?
...
YOU KNOW RUSSIAN MAFIA, STETKO?
NOT PERSONALLY.
BIG PROBLEM IN RUSSIA. THEY ARE THE ONLY PEOPLE WHO HAVE MONEY.
THEY DID THIS.
THE RUSSIAN MOB CAME TO THE ICE TO STEAL NUKES?
IN A WAY, YES...
...THEY BUY SPECIAL SOLDIERS- SPESNAZ- PAY THEM TO COME TO THE ICE.
WHAT HAPPENED HERE WAS DONE BY SPEZNAZ.
THEY WILL TAKE THE WEAPONS TO THEIR EMPLOYER TO BE SOLD.
THAT'S A RELIEF.

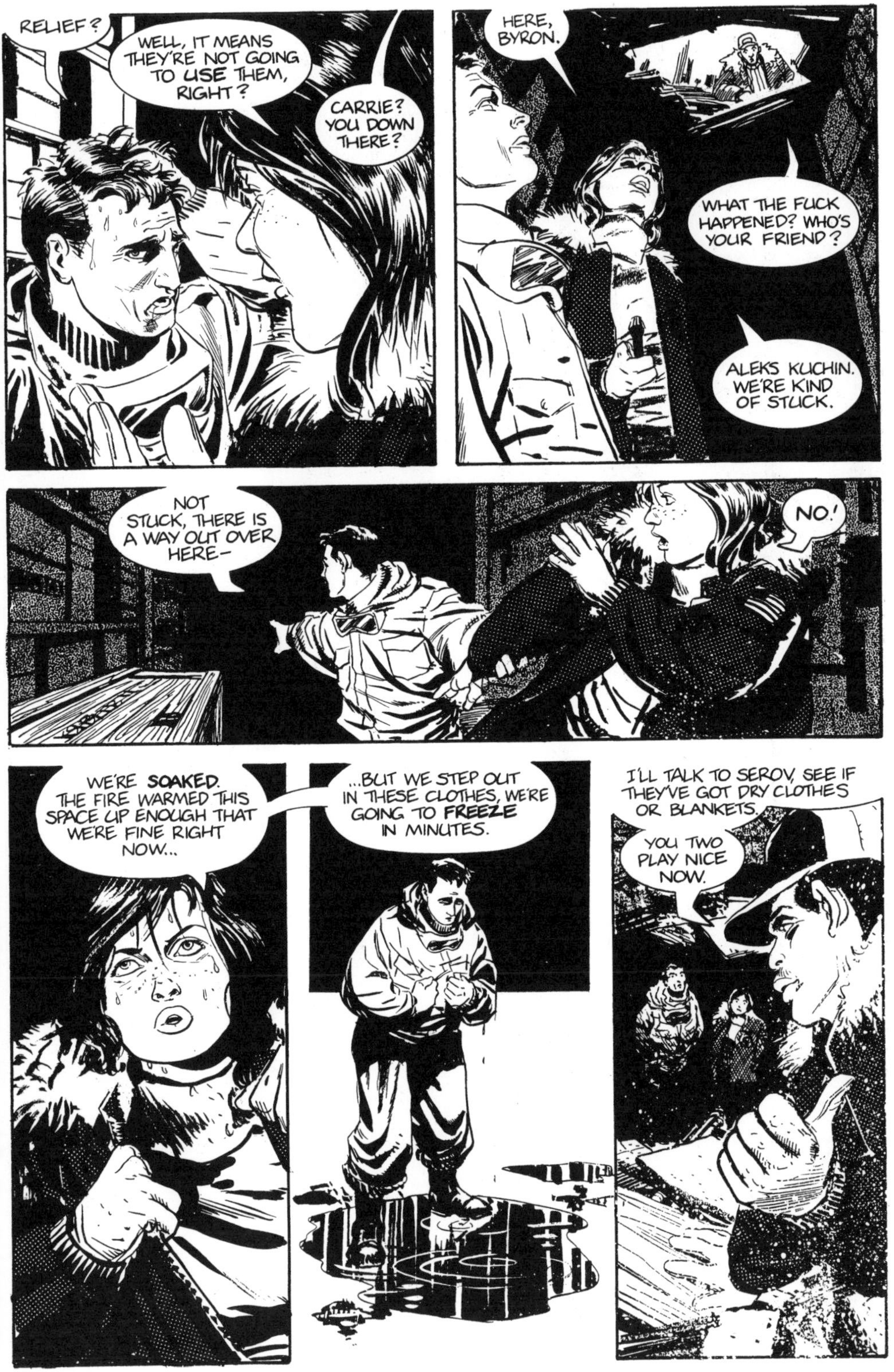
RELIEF?
WELL, IT MEANS THEY'RE NOT GOING TO USE THEM, RIGHT?
CARRIE? YOU DOWN THERE?
HERE, BYRON.
WHAT THE FUCK HAPPENED? WHO'S YOUR FRIEND?
ALEKS KUCHIN. WE'RE KIND OF STUCK.
NOT STUCK, THERE IS A WAY OUT OVER HERE–
NO!
WE'RE SOAKED. THE FIRE WARMED THIS SPACE UP ENOUGH THAT WE'RE FINE RIGHT NOW...
...BUT WE STEP OUT IN THESE CLOTHES, WE'RE GOING TO FREEZE IN MINUTES.
I'LL TALK TO SEROV, SEE IF THEY'VE GOT DRY CLOTHES OR BLANKETS.
YOU TWO PLAY NICE NOW.

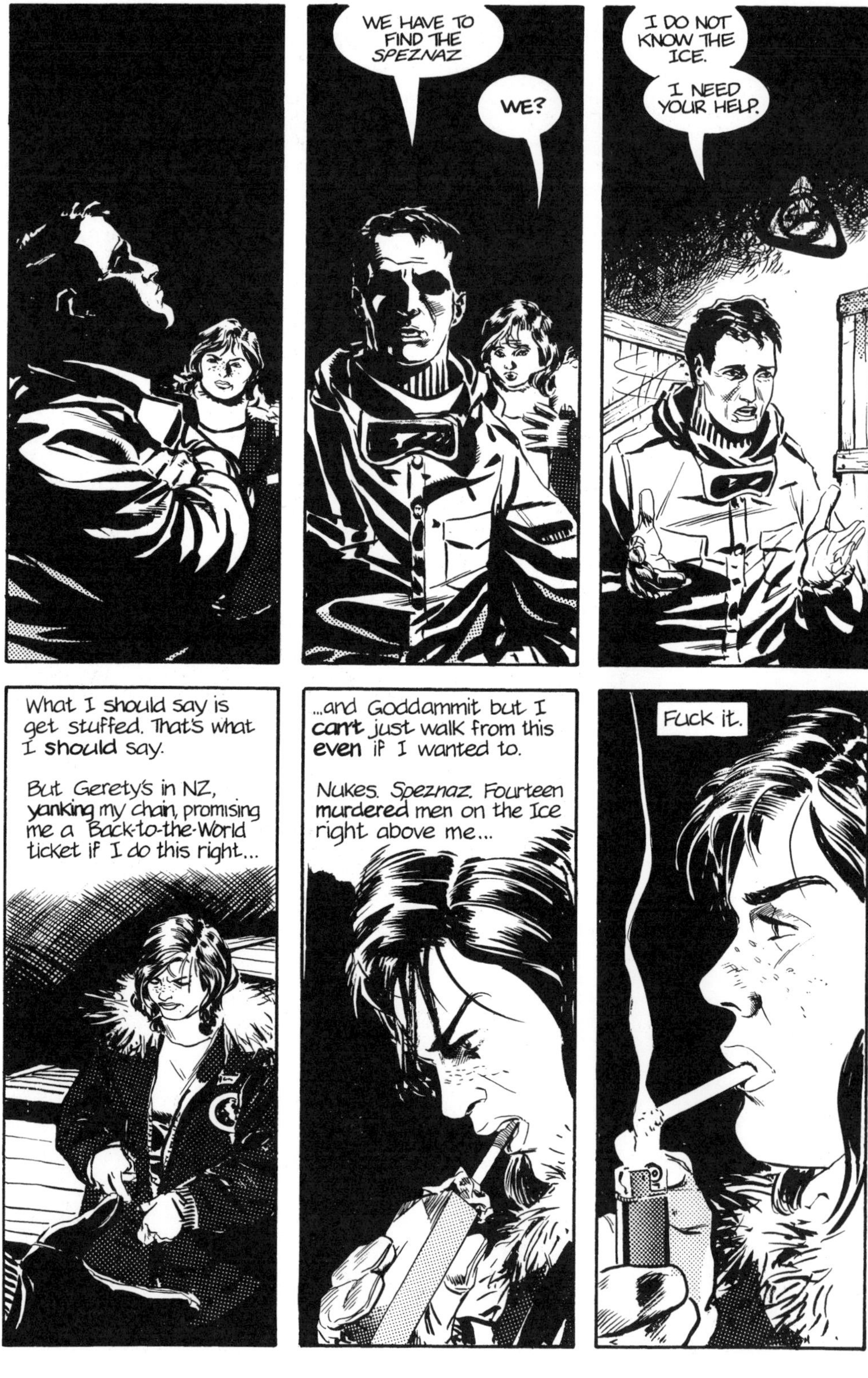
WE HAVE TO FIND THE *SPEZNAZ*
WE?
I DO NOT KNOW THE ICE.
I NEED YOUR HELP.
What I should say is get stuffed. That's what I **should** say.
But Gerety's in NZ, **yanking** my chain, promising me a Back-to-the-World ticket if I do this right...
...and Goddammit but I **can't** just walk from this **even** if I wanted to.
Nukes. *Speznaz.* Fourteen **murdered** men on the Ice right above me...
Fuck it.

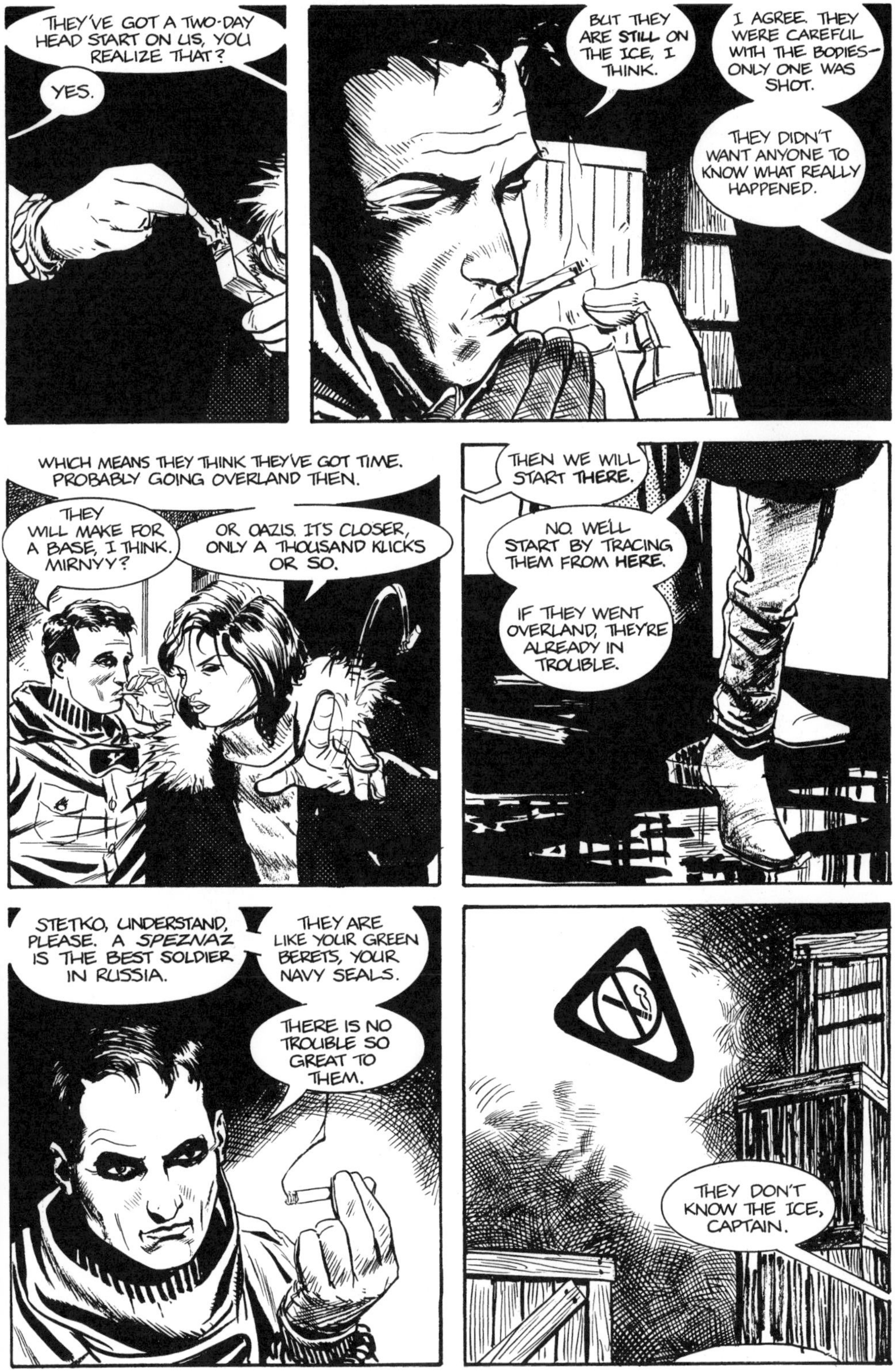
THEY'VE GOT A TWO-DAY HEAD START ON US, YOU REALIZE THAT?
YES.
BUT THEY ARE STILL ON THE ICE, I THINK.
I AGREE. THEY WERE CAREFUL WITH THE BODIES- ONLY ONE WAS SHOT.
THEY DIDN'T WANT ANYONE TO KNOW WHAT REALLY HAPPENED.
WHICH MEANS THEY THINK THEY'VE GOT TIME. PROBABLY GOING OVERLAND THEN.
THEY WILL MAKE FOR A BASE, I THINK. MIRNYY?
OR OAZIS. IT'S CLOSER, ONLY A THOUSAND KLICKS OR SO.
THEN WE WILL START THERE.
NO. WE'LL START BY TRACING THEM FROM HERE.
IF THEY WENT OVERLAND, THEY'RE ALREADY IN TROUBLE.
STETKO, UNDERSTAND, PLEASE. A *SPEZNAZ* IS THE BEST SOLDIER IN RUSSIA.
THEY ARE LIKE YOUR GREEN BERETS, YOUR NAVY SEALS.
THERE IS NO TROUBLE SO GREAT TO THEM.
THEY DON'T KNOW THE ICE, CAPTAIN.

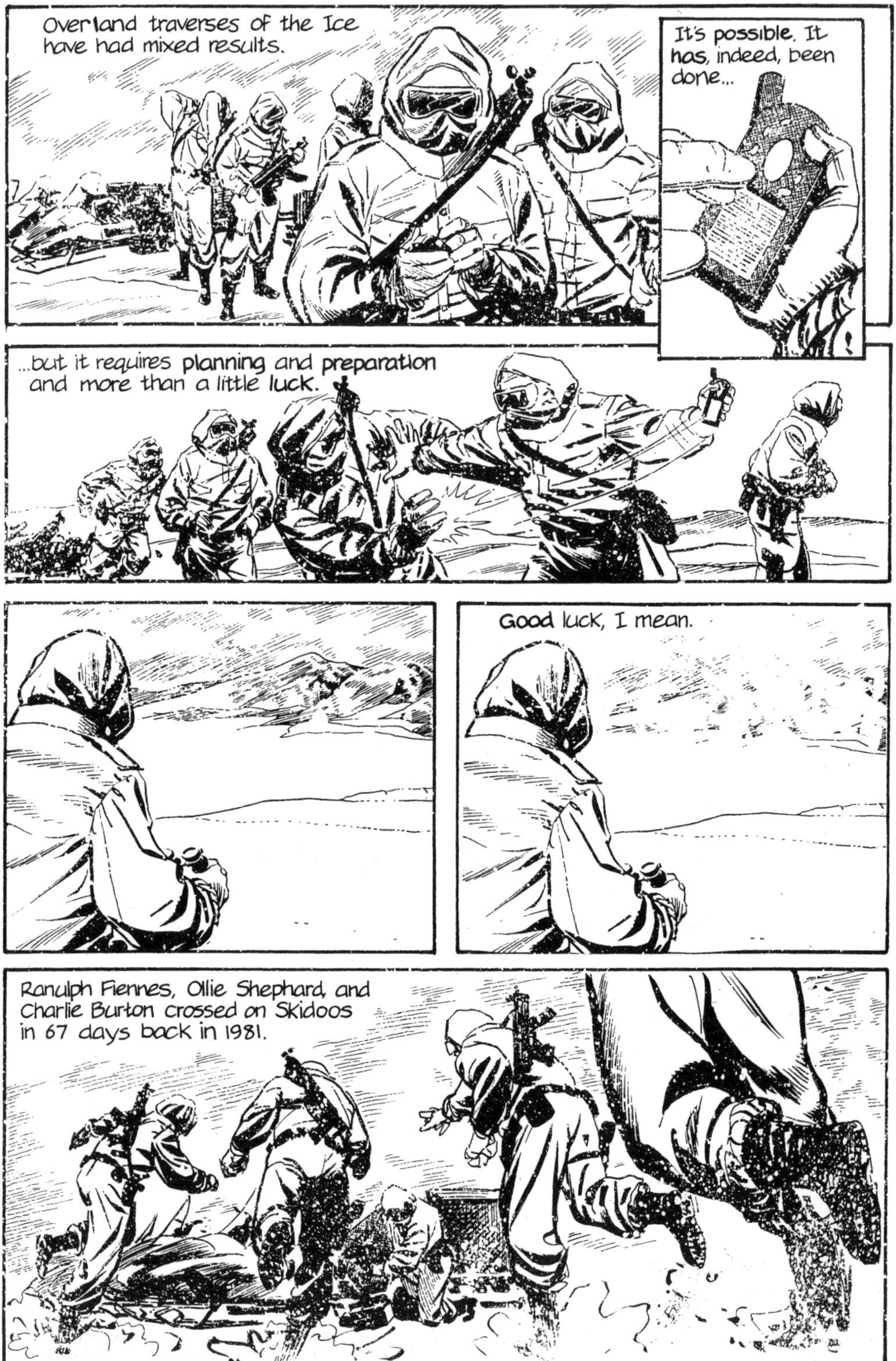

Overland traverses of the Ice have had mixed results.
It's possible. It has, indeed, been done...
...but it requires planning and preparation and more than a little luck.
Good luck, I mean.
Ranulph Fiennes, Ollie Shephard, and Charlie Burton crossed on Skidoos in 67 days back in 1981.

That's an example of **good** luck.

Maybe it went to his head...

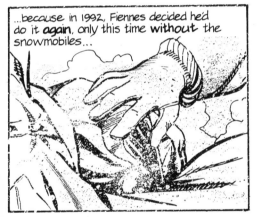

...because in 1992, Fiennes decided he'd do it **again**, only this time **without** the snowmobiles...

...planning to manhaul sledges with Mike Stroud.

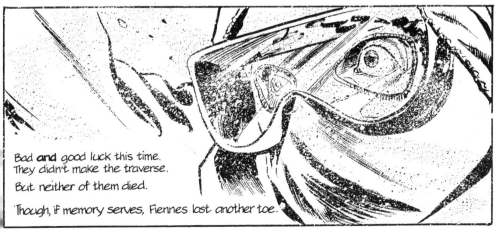

Bad **and** good luck this time. They didn't make the traverse.

But neither of them died.

Though, if memory serves, Fiennes lost another toe.

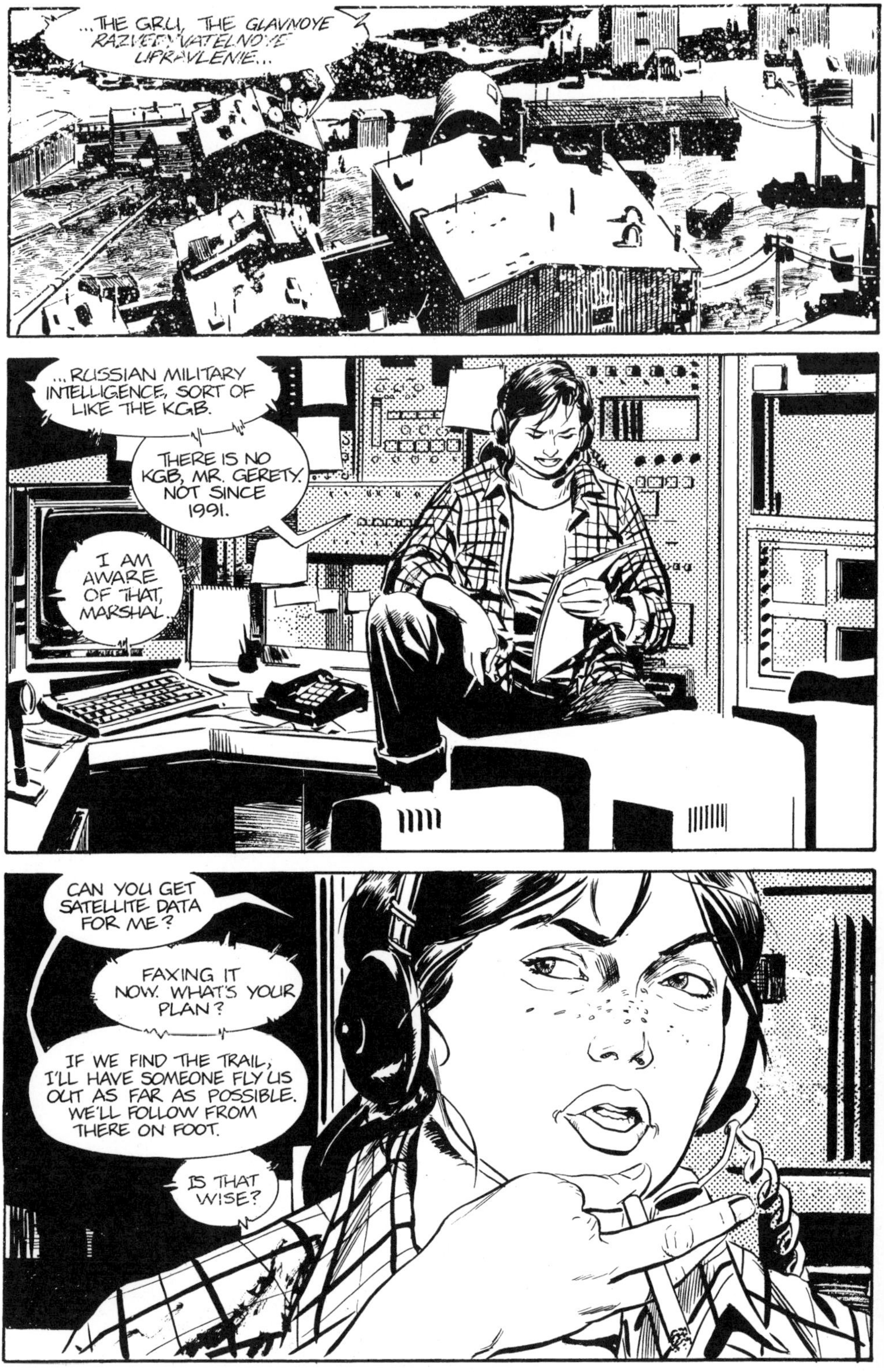
...THE GRU, THE GLAVNOYE RAZVEDYVATELNOYE UPRAVLENIE...
...RUSSIAN MILITARY INTELLIGENCE, SORT OF LIKE THE KGB.
THERE IS NO KGB, MR. GERETY. NOT SINCE 1991.
I AM AWARE OF THAT, MARSHAL.
CAN YOU GET SATELLITE DATA FOR ME?
FAXING IT NOW. WHAT'S YOUR PLAN?
IF WE FIND THE TRAIL, I'LL HAVE SOMEONE FLY US OUT AS FAR AS POSSIBLE. WE'LL FOLLOW FROM THERE ON FOOT.
IS THAT WISE?

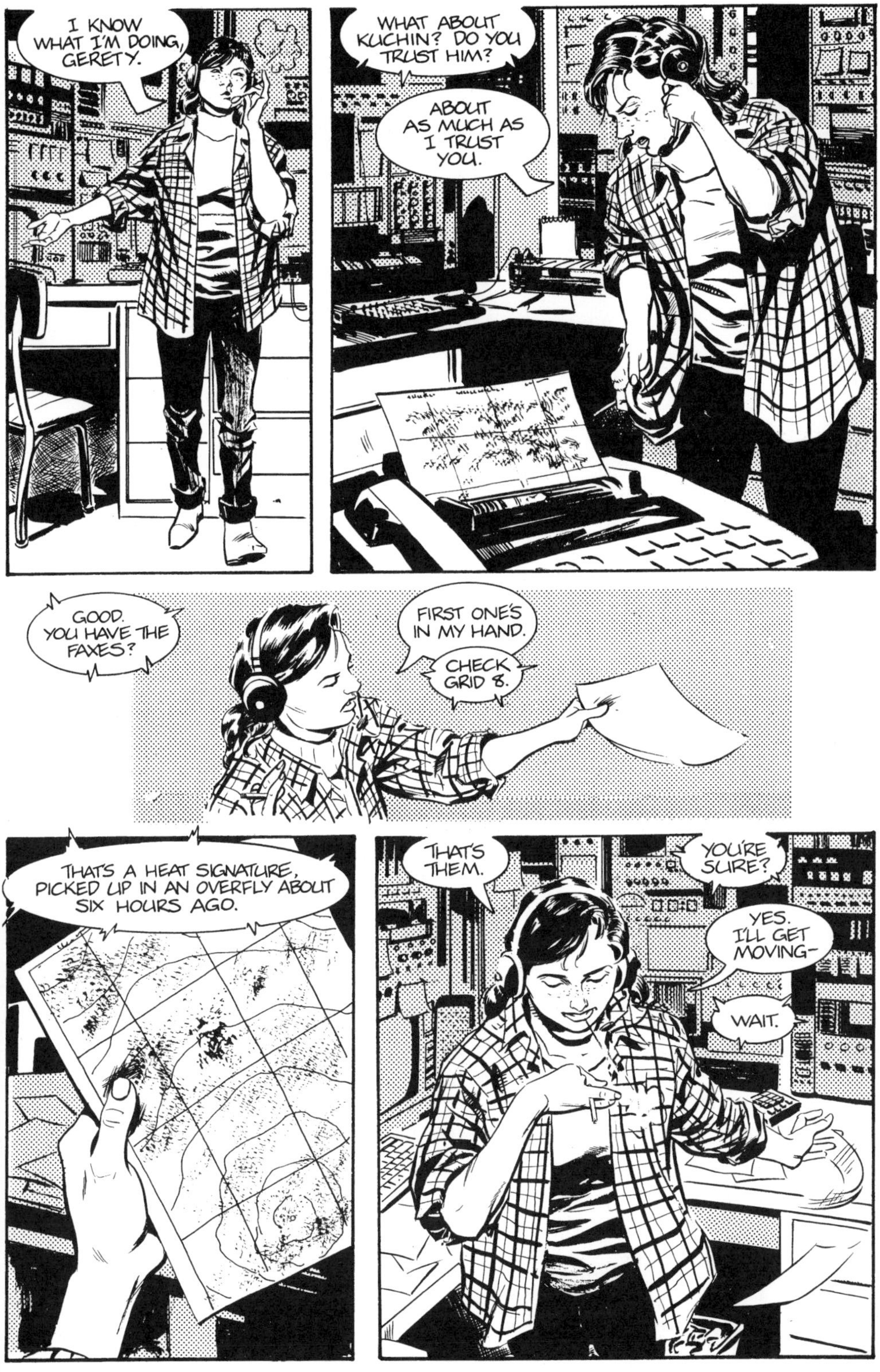
I KNOW WHAT I'M DOING, GERETY.
WHAT ABOUT KUCHIN? DO YOU TRUST HIM?
ABOUT AS MUCH AS I TRUST YOU.
GOOD. YOU HAVE THE FAXES?
FIRST ONE'S IN MY HAND.
CHECK GRID 8.
THAT'S A HEAT SIGNATURE, PICKED UP IN AN OVERFLY ABOUT SIX HOURS AGO.
THAT'S THEM.
YOU'RE SURE?
YES. I'LL GET MOVING-
WAIT.

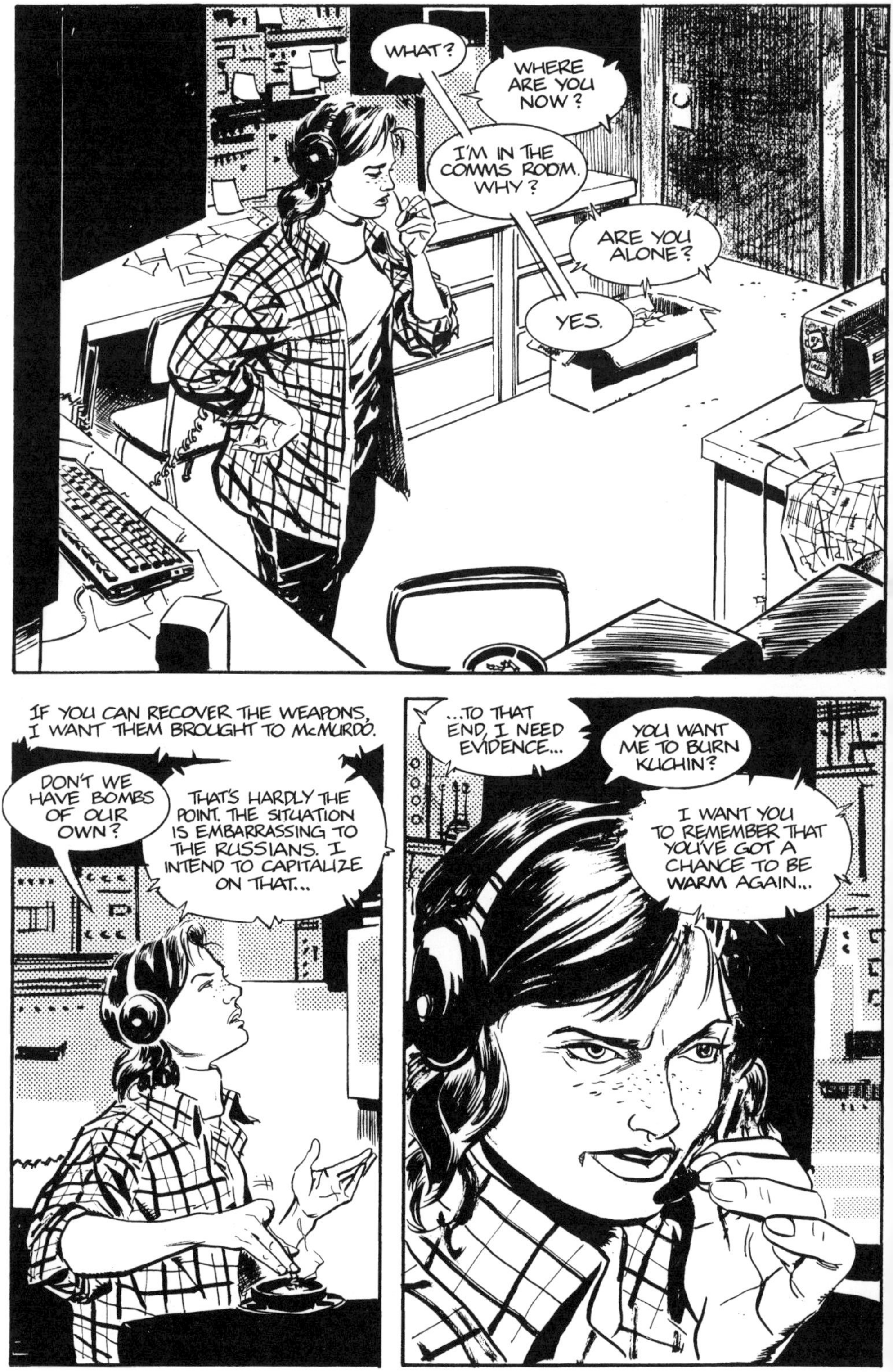
WHAT?
WHERE ARE YOU NOW?
I'M IN THE COMMS ROOM. WHY?
ARE YOU ALONE?
YES.
IF YOU CAN RECOVER THE WEAPONS, I WANT THEM BROUGHT TO McMURDO.
DON'T WE HAVE BOMBS OF OUR OWN?
THAT'S HARDLY THE POINT. THE SITUATION IS EMBARRASSING TO THE RUSSIANS. I INTEND TO CAPITALIZE ON THAT...
...TO THAT END, I NEED EVIDENCE...
YOU WANT ME TO BURN KUCHIN?
I WANT YOU TO REMEMBER THAT YOU'VE GOT A CHANCE TO BE WARM AGAIN...

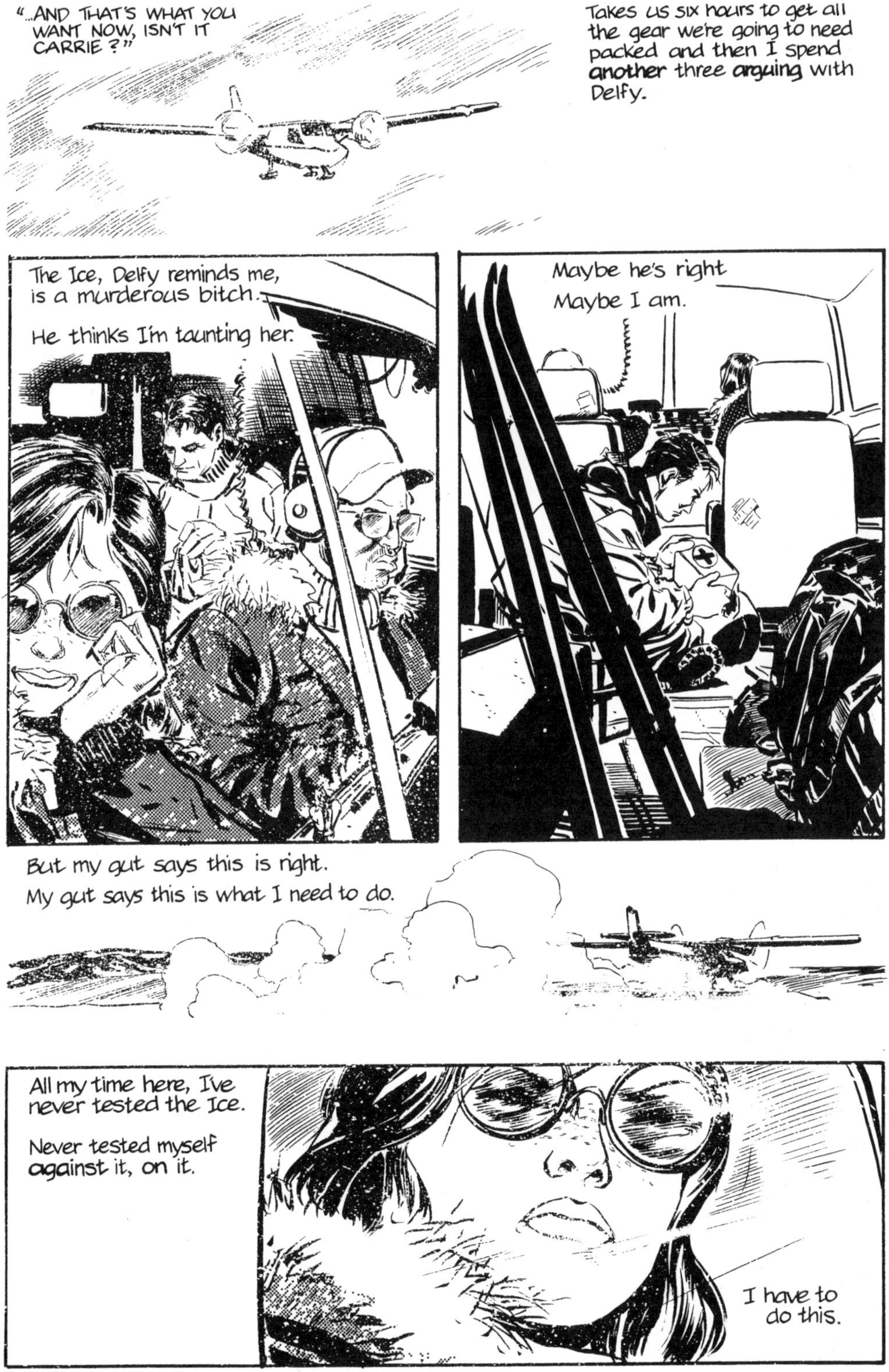
"...AND THAT'S WHAT YOU WANT NOW, ISN'T IT CARRIE?"
Takes us six hours to get all the gear we're going to need packed and then I spend **another** three **arguing** with Delfy.
The Ice, Delfy reminds me, is a murderous bitch.
He thinks I'm taunting her.
Maybe he's right
Maybe I am.
But my gut says this is right.
My gut says this is what I need to do.
All my time here, I've never tested the Ice.
Never tested myself **against** it, on it.
I have to do this.

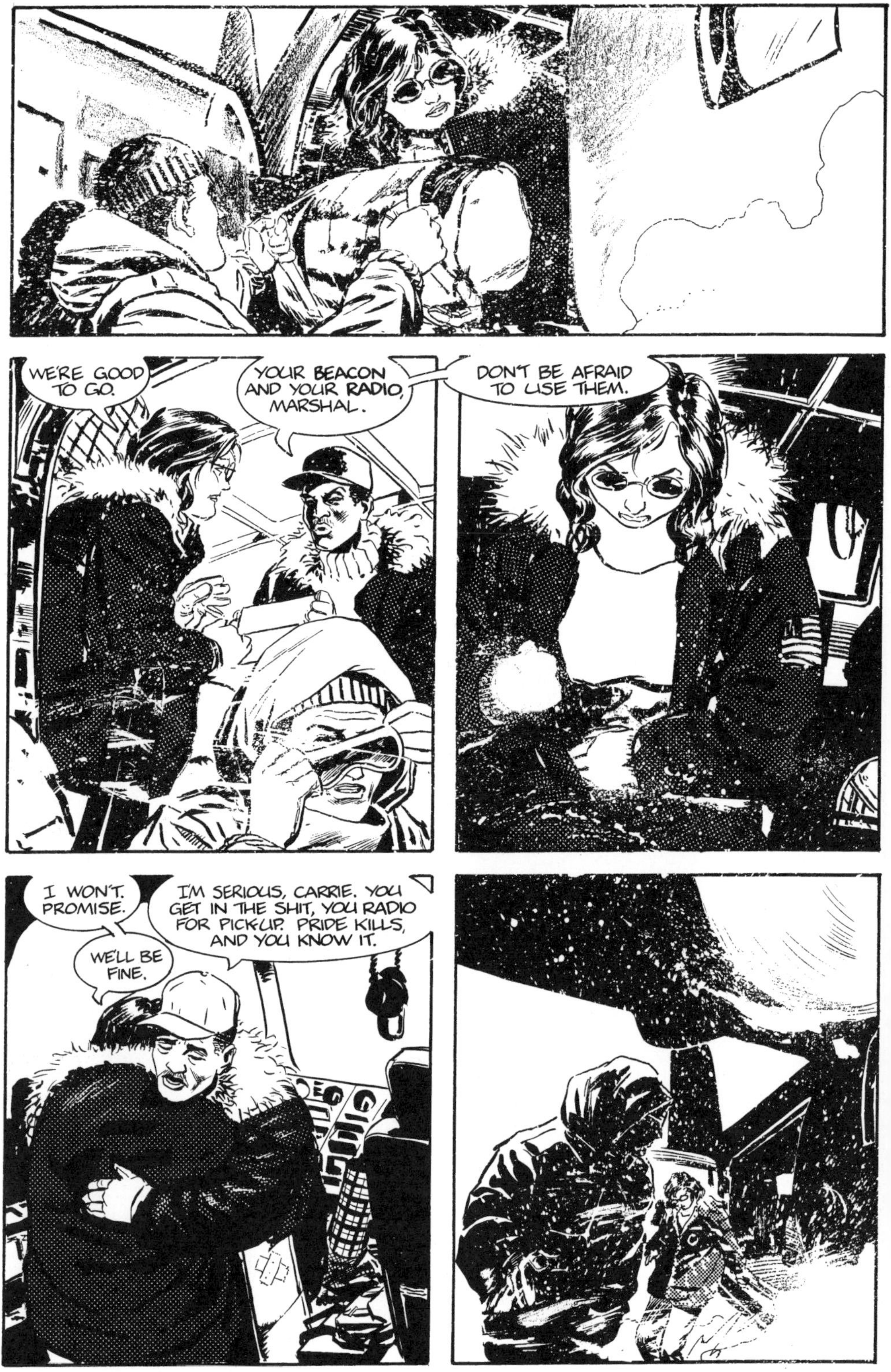
WE'RE GOOD TO GO.
YOUR BEACON AND YOUR RADIO, MARSHAL.
DON'T BE AFRAID TO USE THEM.
I WON'T. PROMISE.
I'M SERIOUS, CARRIE. YOU GET IN THE SHIT, YOU RADIO FOR PICK-UP. PRIDE KILLS, AND YOU KNOW IT.
WE'LL BE FINE.

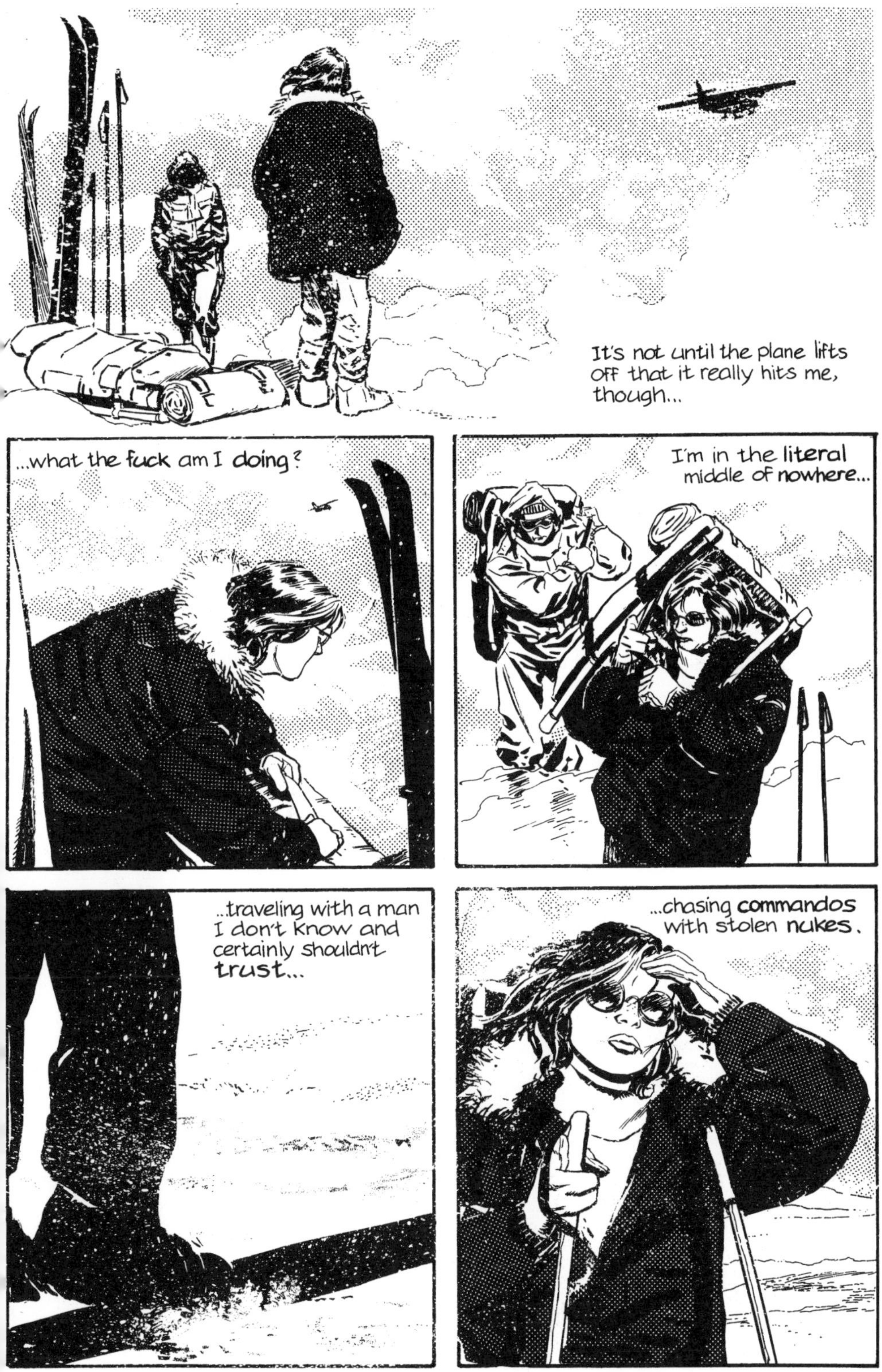
It's not until the plane lifts off that it really hits me, though...
...what the fuck am I doing?
I'm in the literal middle of nowhere...
...traveling with a man I don't know and certainly shouldn't trust...
...chasing commandos with stolen nukes.

HA HA
SOMETHING IS FUNNY?
HA OH... OH, yeah.. HEE-HEE...
TELL ME YOU DON'T THINK THIS IS FUNNY.
YOU, ME, HERE... I MEAN...
I DON'T THINK IT IS FUNNY.
WE SHOULD BE MOVING.
Heh.

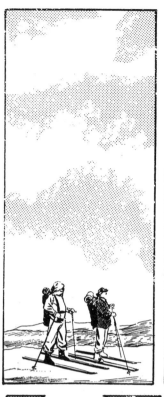

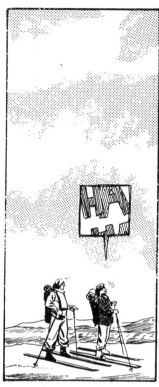

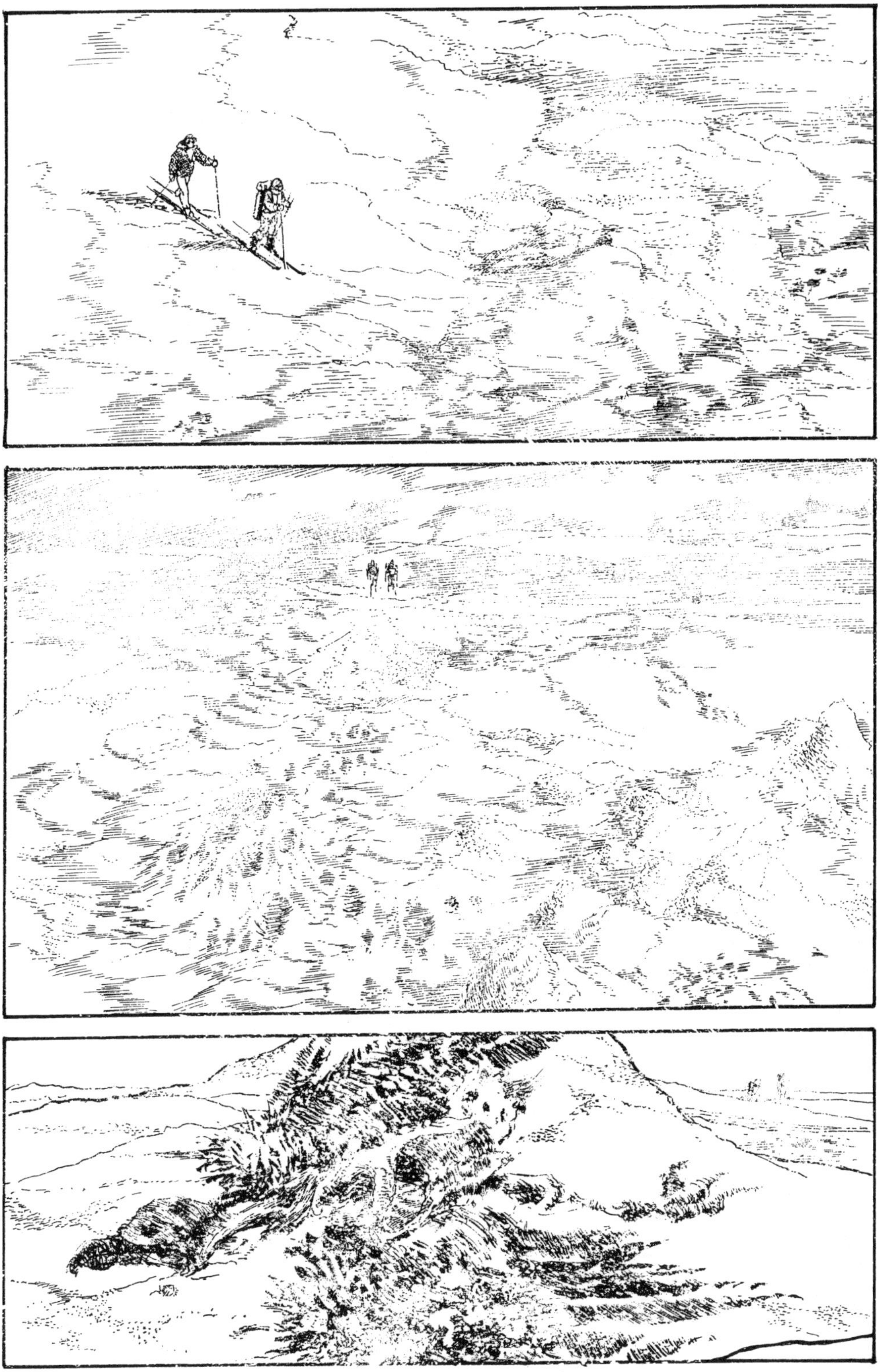

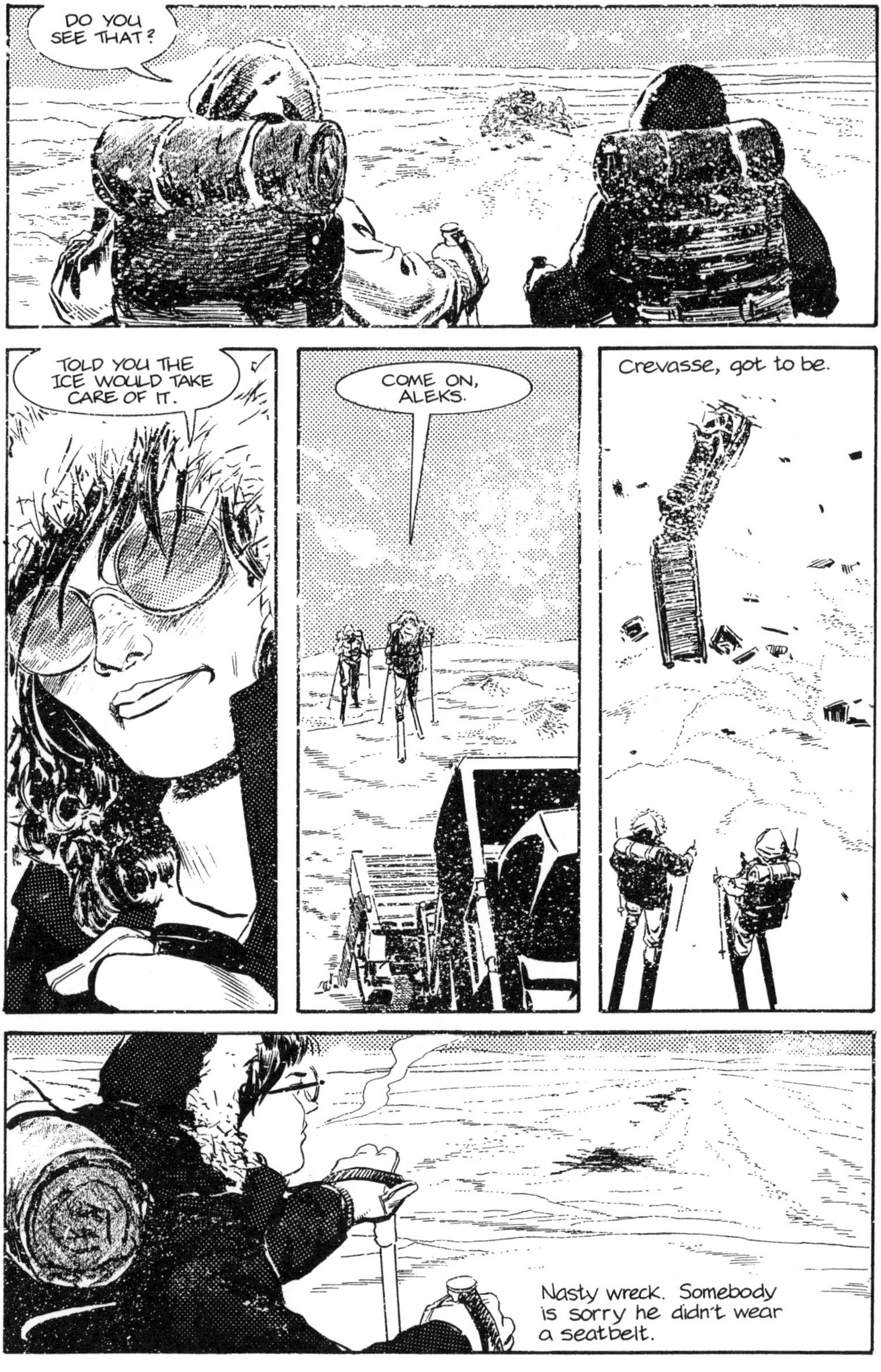
DO YOU SEE THAT?
TOLD YOU THE ICE WOULD TAKE CARE OF IT.
COME ON, ALEKS.
Crevasse, got to be.
Nasty wreck. Somebody is sorry he didn't wear a seatbelt.

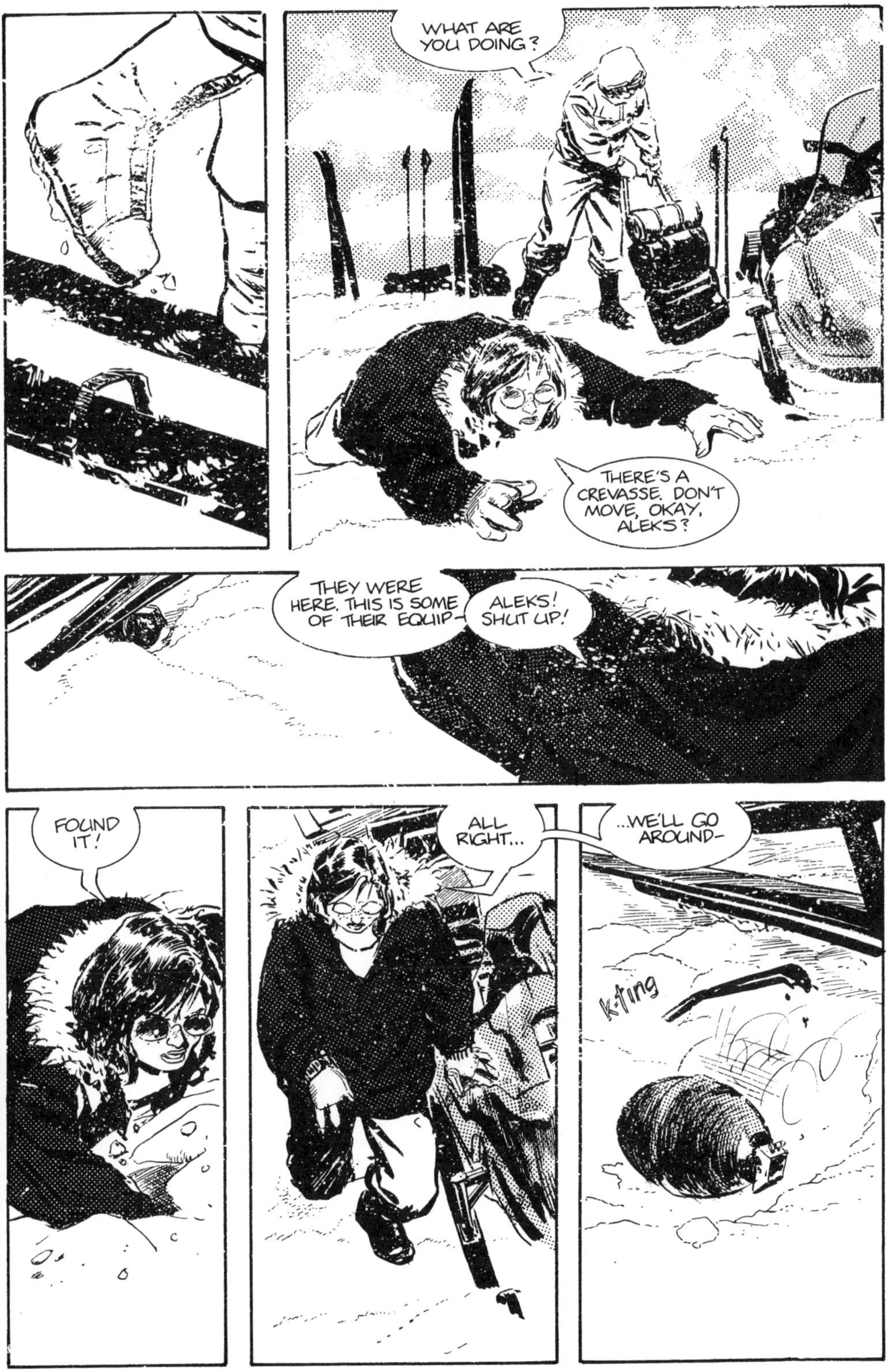
WHAT ARE YOU DOING?
THERE'S A CREVASSE. DON'T MOVE, OKAY, ALEKS?
THEY WERE HERE. THIS IS SOME OF THEIR EQUIP-
ALEKS! SHUT UP!
FOUND IT!
ALL RIGHT...
...WE'LL GO AROUND-
k-ting

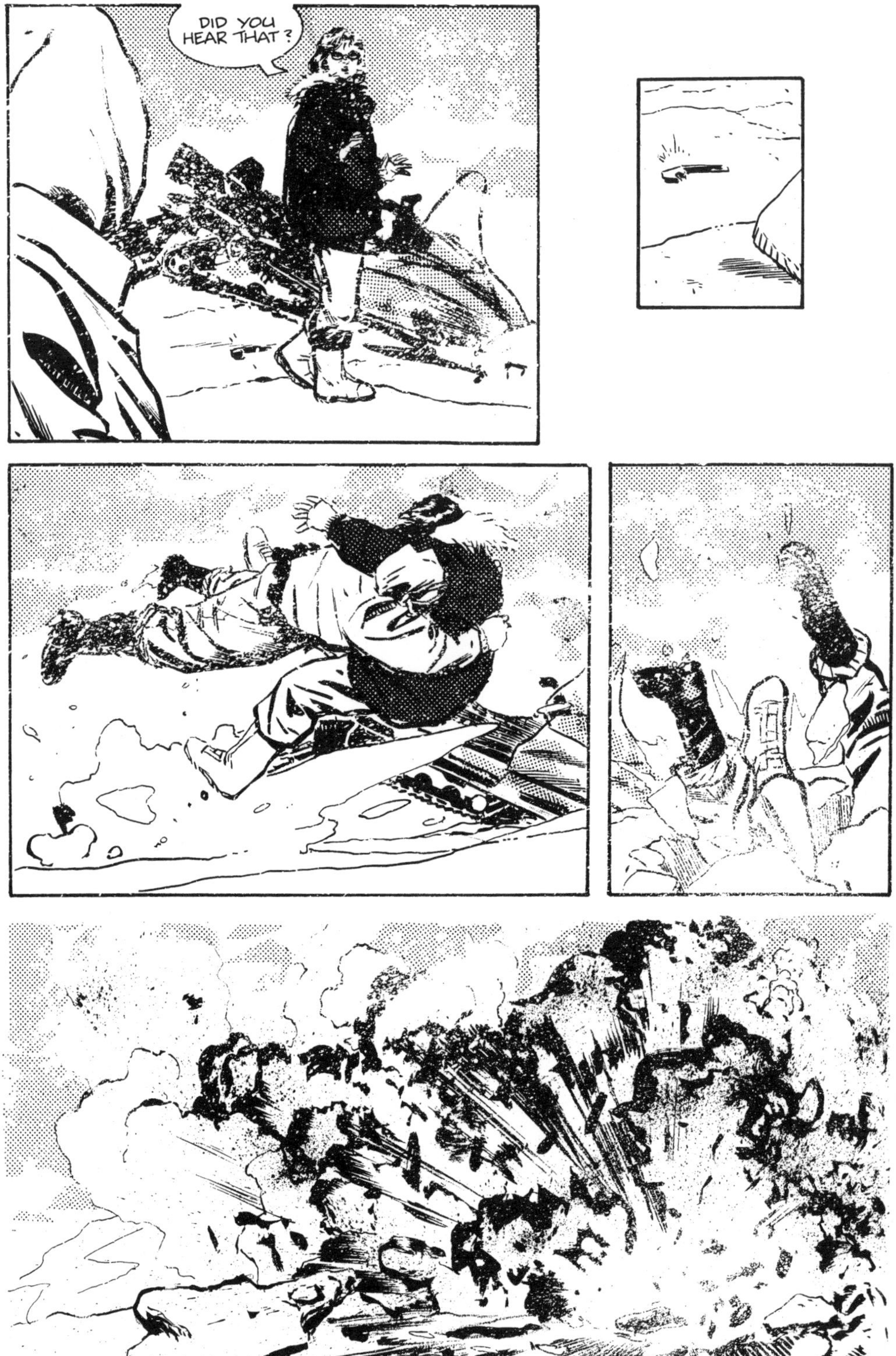
DID YOU HEAR THAT ?

CHAPTER THREE

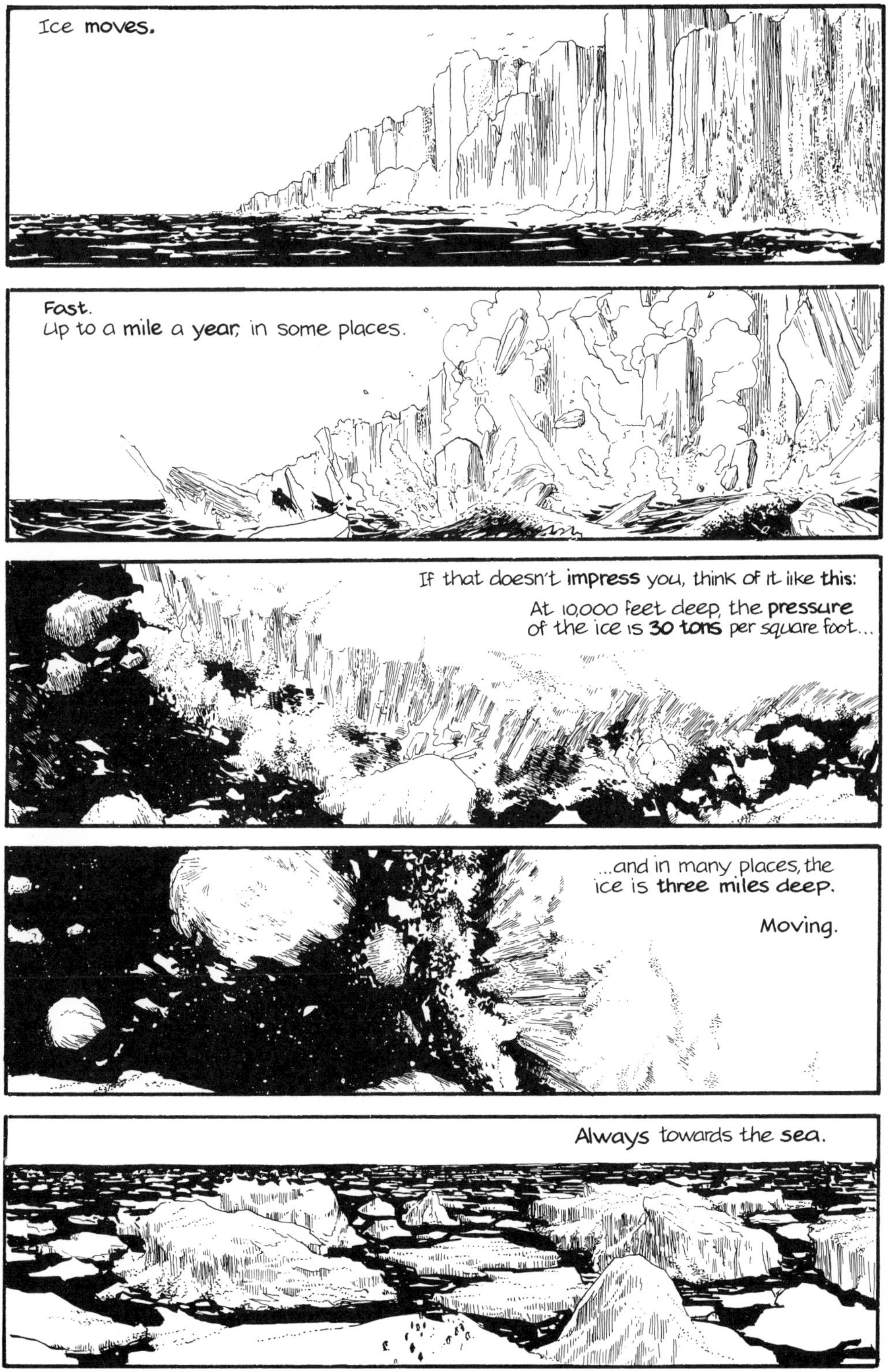
Ice moves.
Fast.
Up to a mile a year, in some places.
If that doesn't impress you, think of it like this:
At 10,000 feet deep, the pressure of the ice is 30 tons per square foot...
...and in many places, the ice is three miles deep.
Moving.
Always towards the sea.

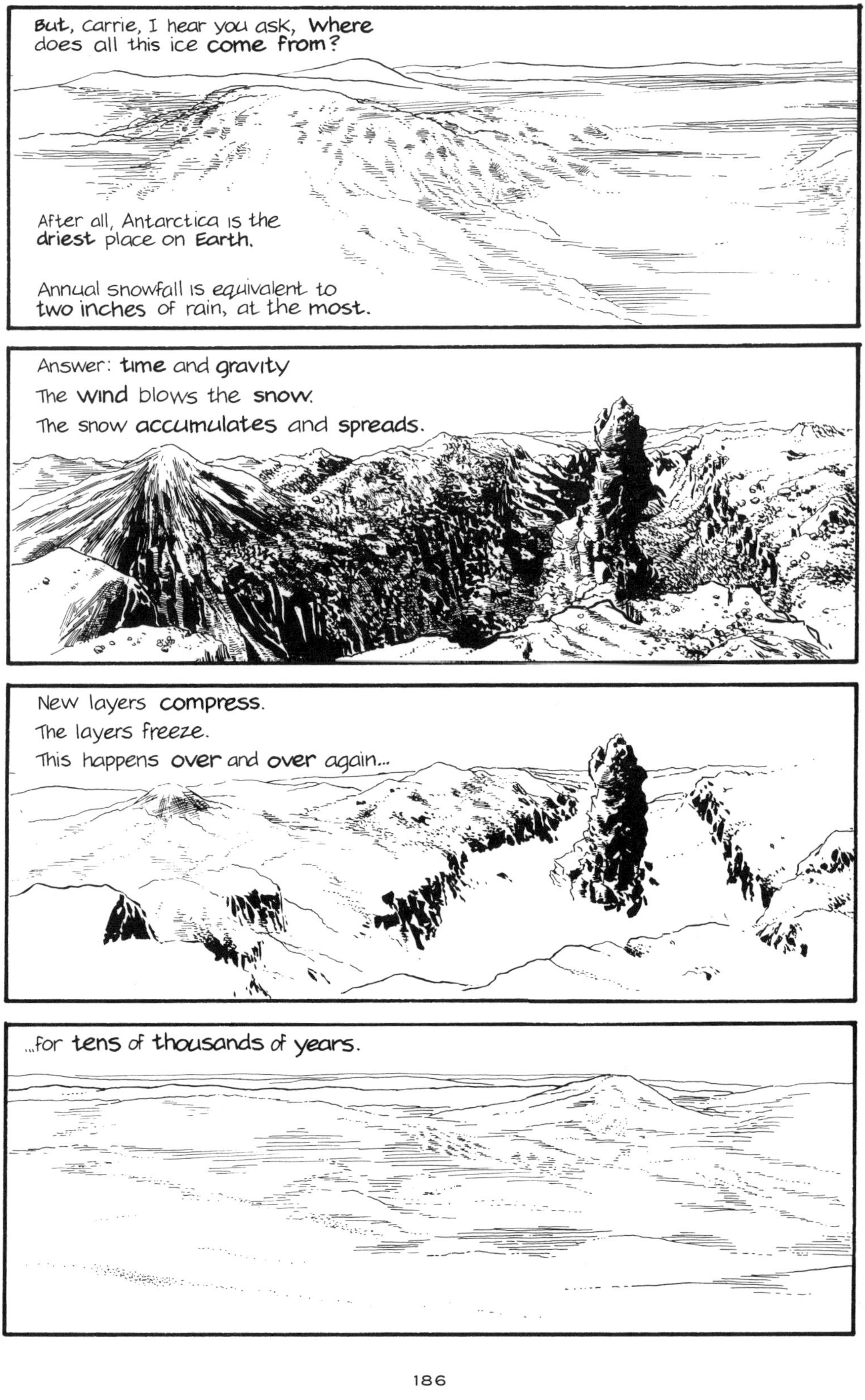
But, Carrie, I hear you ask, Where does all this ice come from?
After all, Antarctica is the driest place on Earth.
Annual snowfall is equivalent to two inches of rain, at the most.
Answer: time and gravity
The wind blows the snow.
The snow accumulates and spreads.
New layers compress.
The layers freeze.
This happens over and over again...
...for tens of thousands of years.

There **is** a **point** to this, bear with me.
That point is called a **crevasse**.

One of the Ice's **nastier** surprises.
Friction from moving ice opens
cracks on the surface.

...cracks that can be **hundreds** of **feet** deep.

That's **not** the problem.

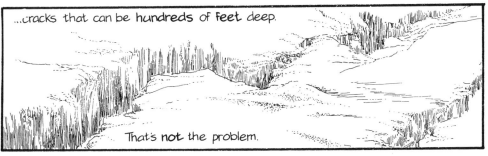

Remember the whole **wind** and **snow** equation?
That's the problem.

The Ice **hides** crevasses.
And people **fall**...

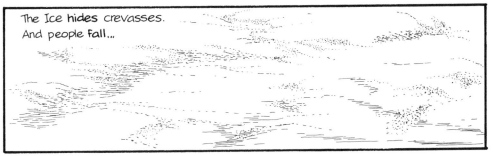

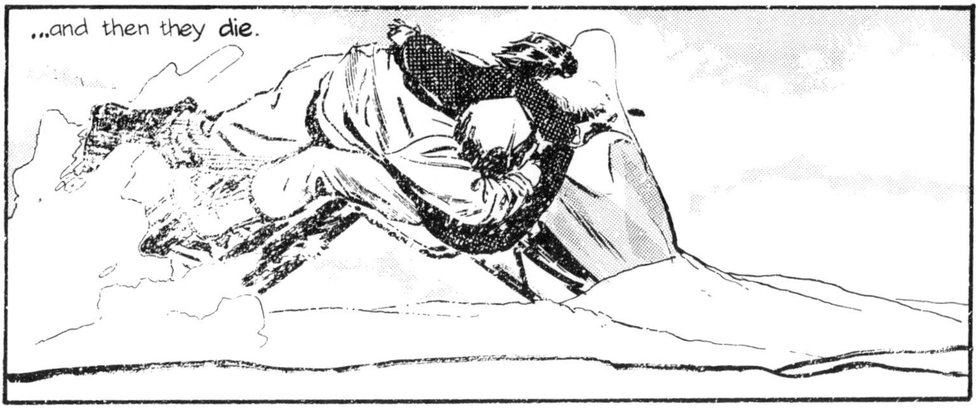
...and then they die.

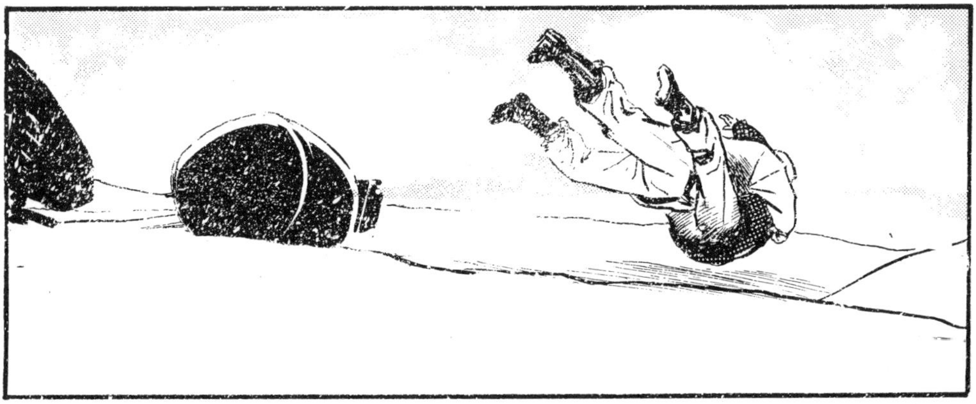

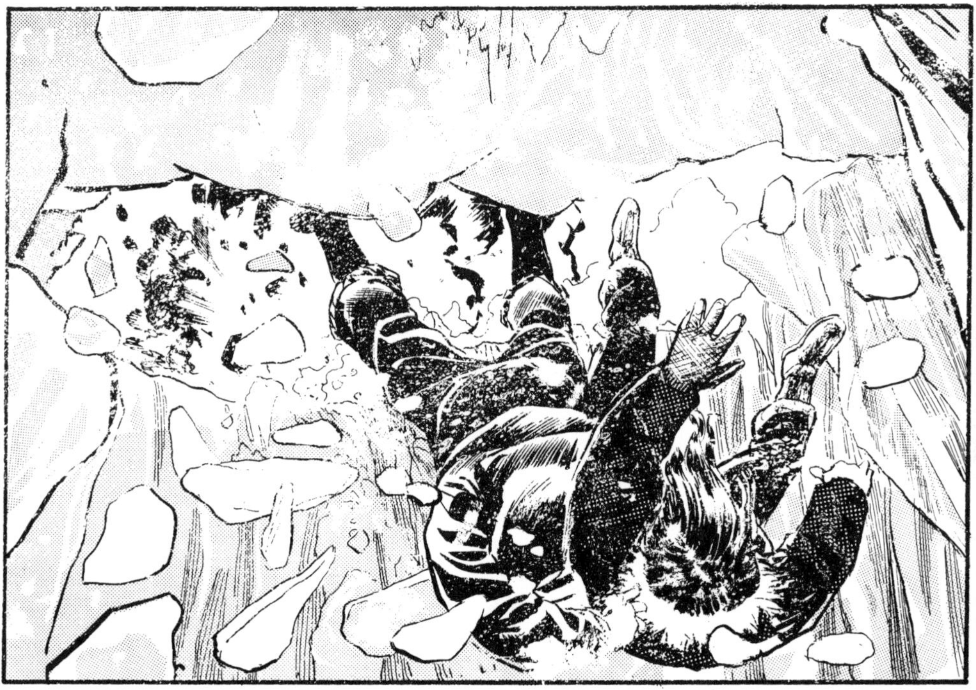

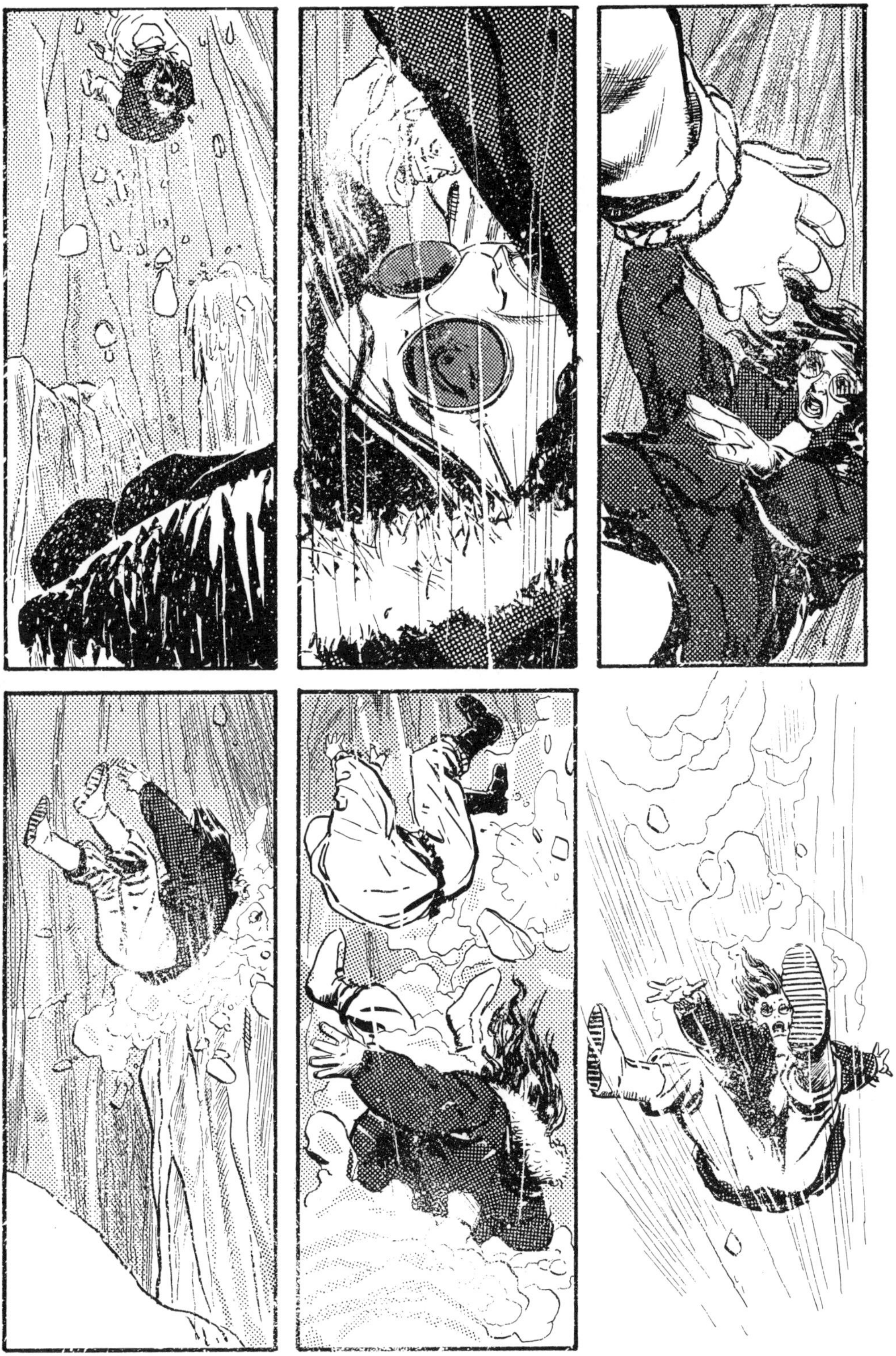

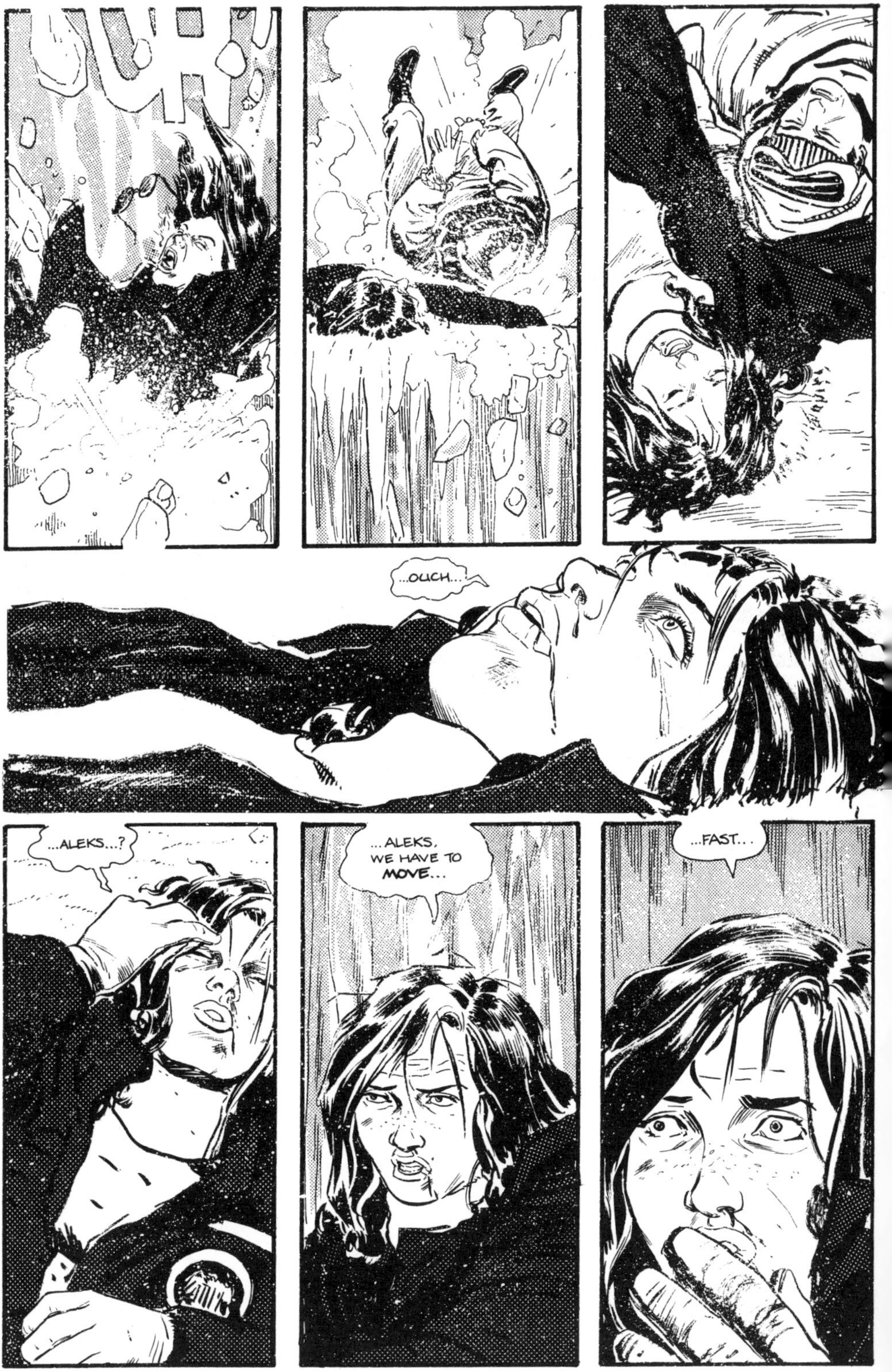
...OUCH...
...ALEKS...?
...ALEKS, WE HAVE TO MOVE...
...FAST...

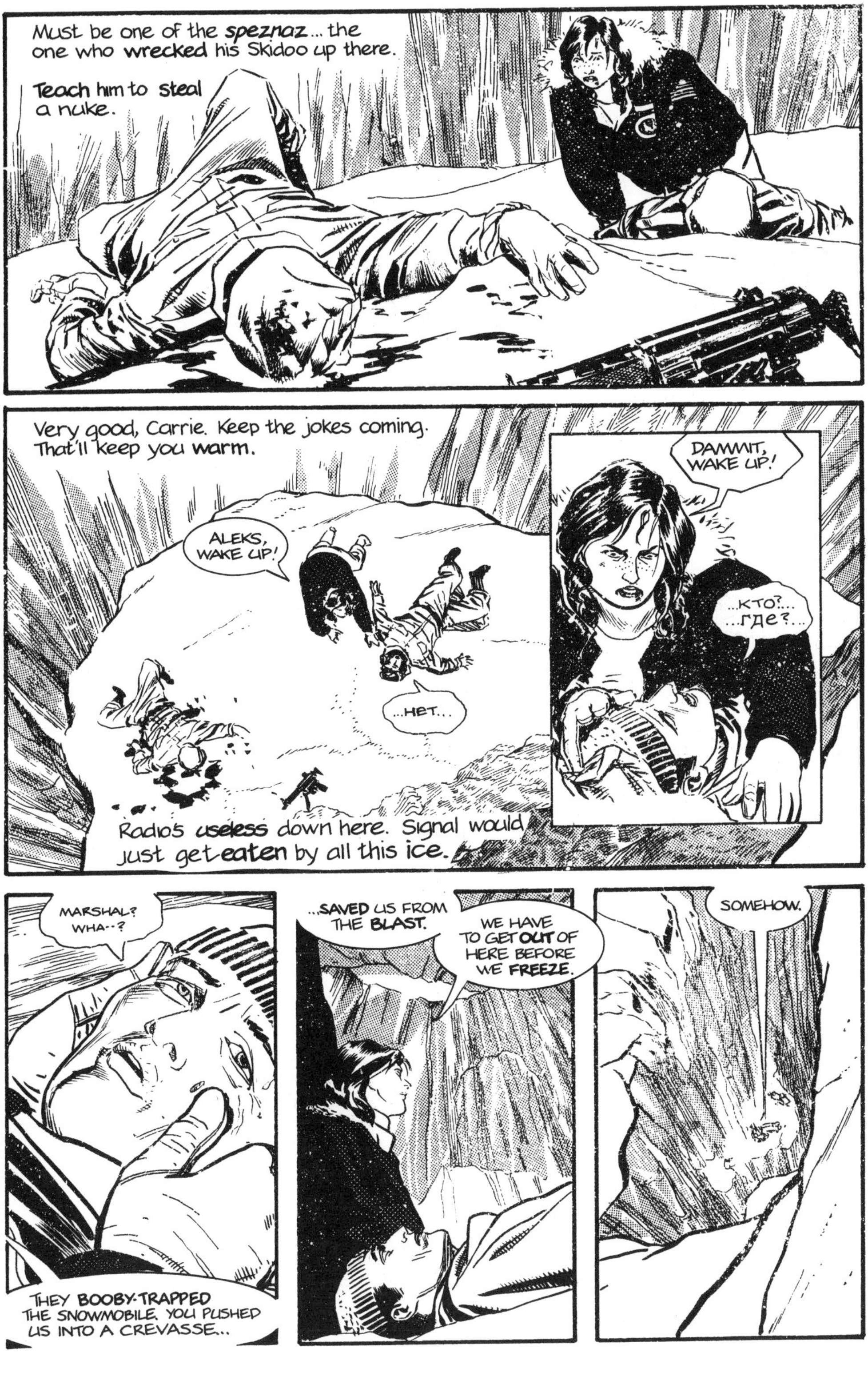

Must be one of the spetsnaz... the one who wrecked his Skidoo up there.
Teach him to steal a nuke.
Very good, Carrie. Keep the jokes coming. That'll keep you warm.
ALEKS, WAKE UP!
...HET...
DAMMIT, WAKE UP!
...КТО?... ...ГДЕ?...
Radio's useless down here. Signal would just get eaten by all this ice.
MARSHAL? WHA--?
THEY BOOBY-TRAPPED THE SNOWMOBILE. YOU PUSHED US INTO A CREVASSE...
...SAVED US FROM THE BLAST.
WE HAVE TO GET OUT OF HERE BEFORE WE FREEZE.
SOMEHOW.

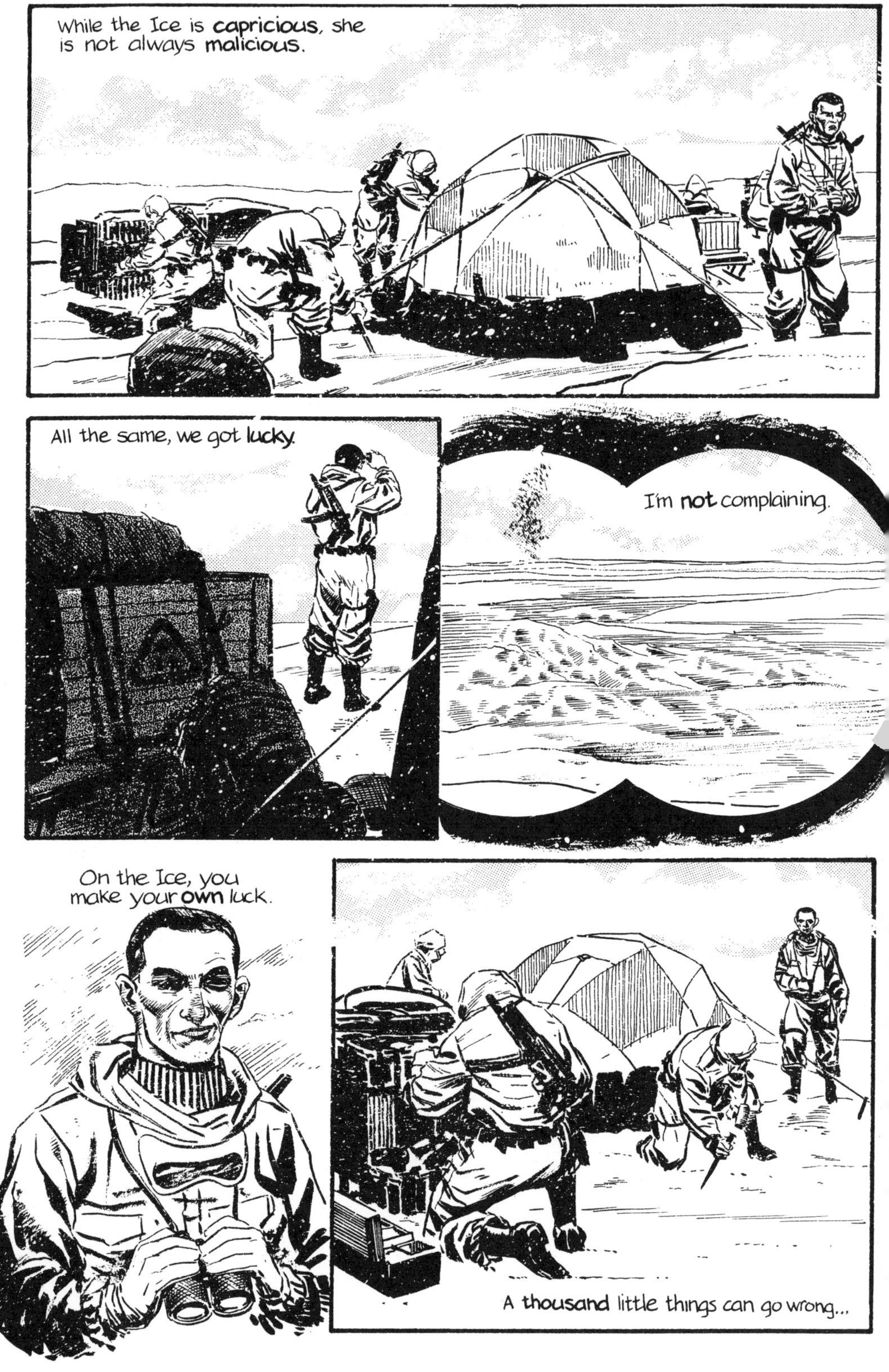
While the Ice is capricious, she is not always malicious.
All the same, we got lucky.
I'm not complaining.
On the Ice, you make your own luck.
A thousand little things can go wrong...

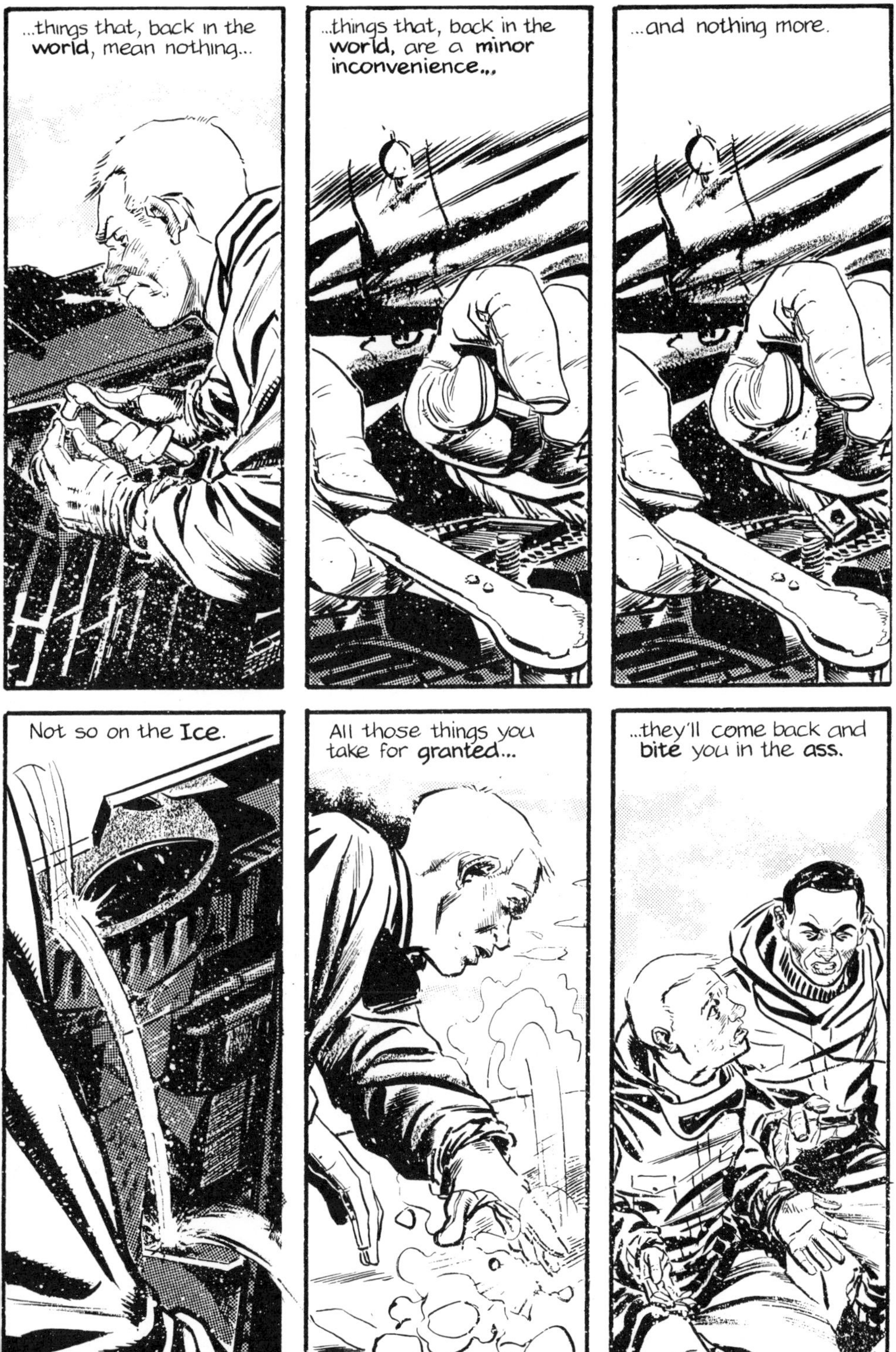
...things that, back in the world, mean nothing...
...things that, back in the world, are a minor inconvenience...
...and nothing more.
Not so on the Ice.
All those things you take for granted...
...they'll come back and bite you in the ass.

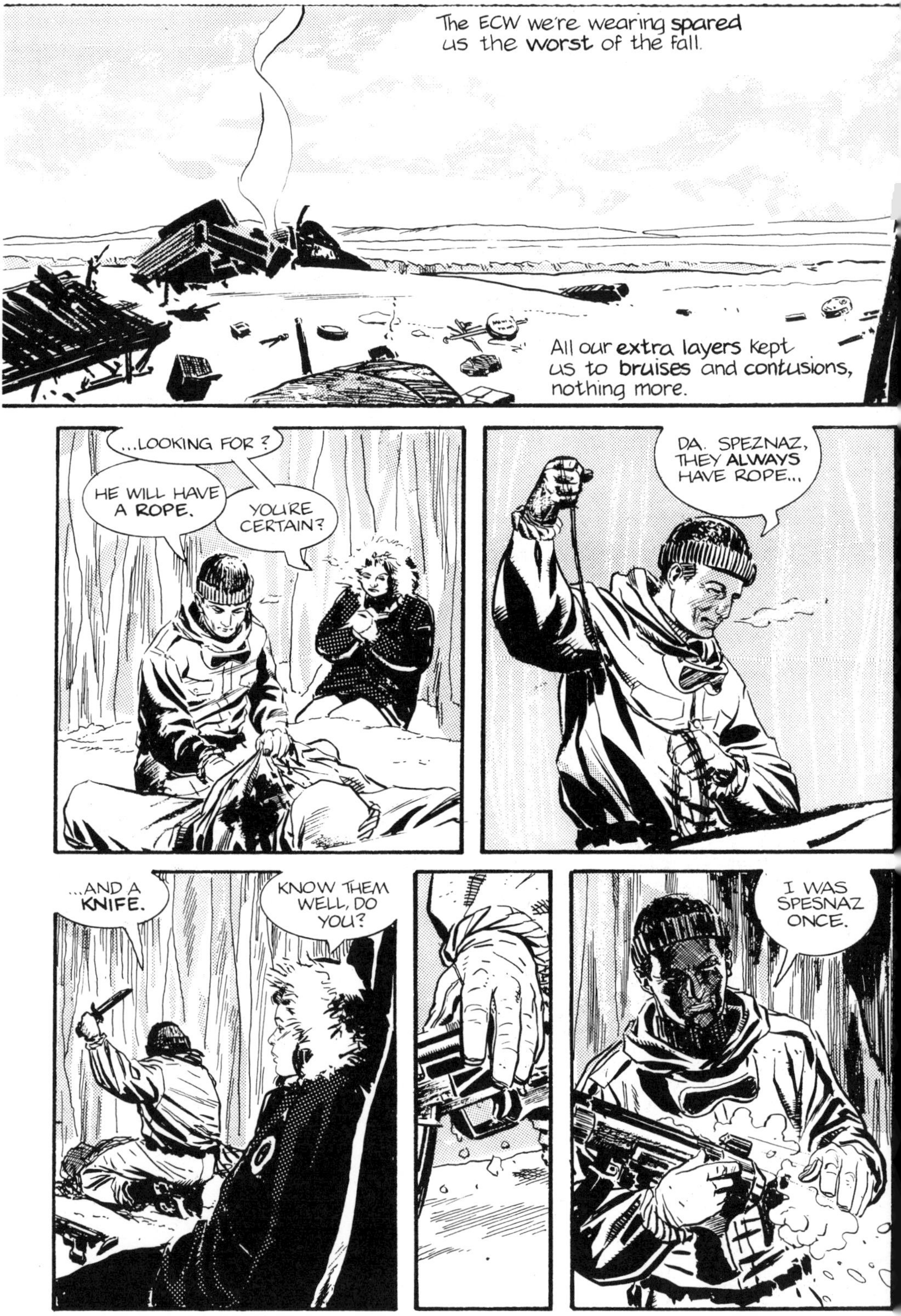

The ECW we're wearing **spared** us the **worst** of the fall.
All our **extra layers** kept us to **bruises** and **contusions**, nothing more.
...LOOKING FOR?
HE WILL HAVE A **ROPE**.
YOU'RE CERTAIN?
DA. SPEZNAZ, THEY **ALWAYS** HAVE ROPE...
...AND A **KNIFE**.
KNOW THEM WELL, DO YOU?
I WAS SPESNAZ ONCE.

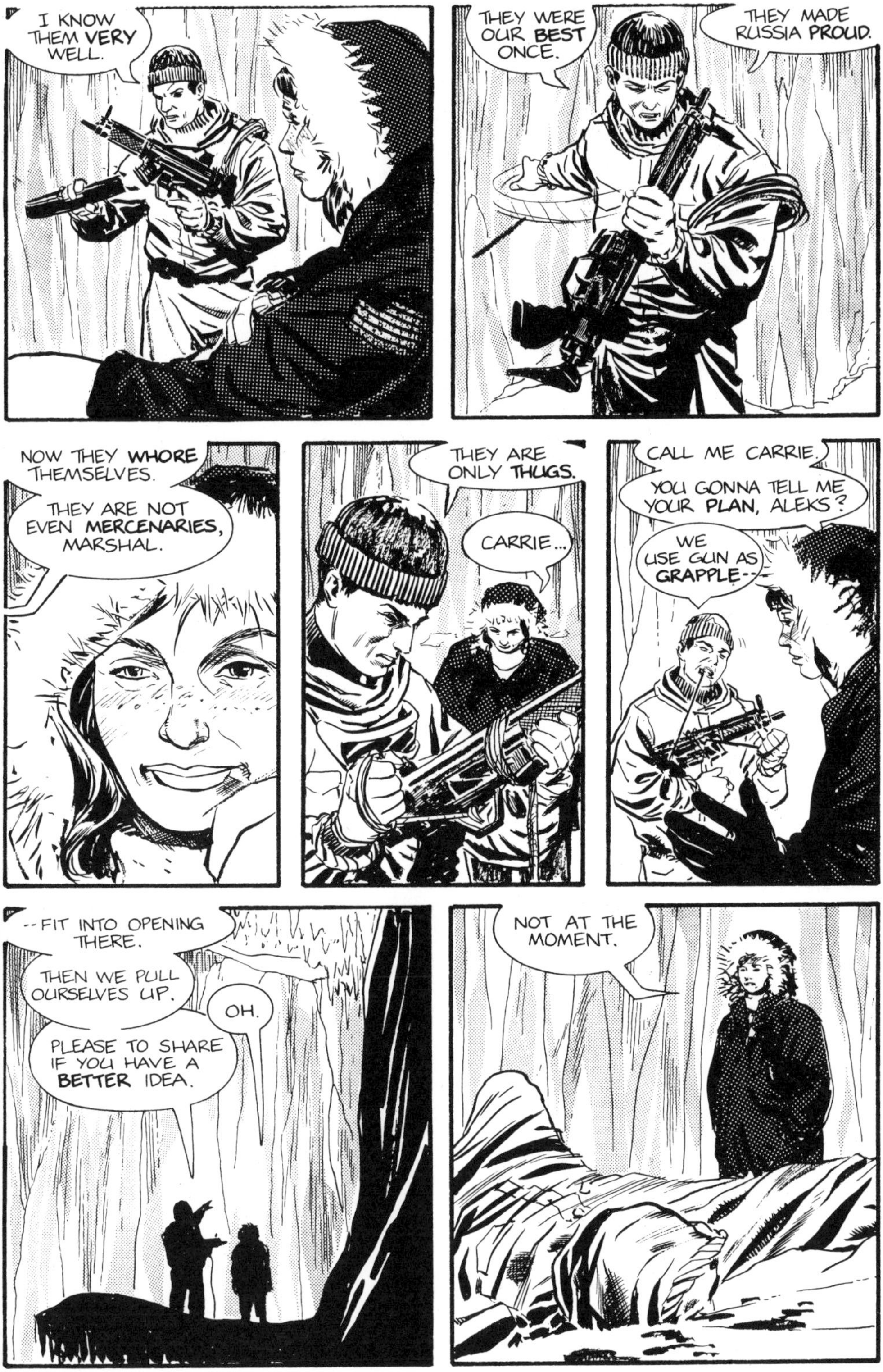
I KNOW THEM VERY WELL.
THEY WERE OUR BEST ONCE.
THEY MADE RUSSIA PROUD.
NOW THEY WHORE THEMSELVES.
THEY ARE NOT EVEN MERCENARIES, MARSHAL.
THEY ARE ONLY THUGS.
CARRIE...
CALL ME CARRIE.
YOU GONNA TELL ME YOUR PLAN, ALEKS?
WE USE GUN AS GRAPPLE--
--FIT INTO OPENING THERE.
THEN WE PULL OURSELVES UP.
OH.
PLEASE TO SHARE IF YOU HAVE A BETTER IDEA.
NOT AT THE MOMENT.

Eight tries before Aleks makes a throw that holds...

...all the while I'm reminding myself that we're **freezing.**

We need **shelter.** We need **heat.**

He offers to let me go first, and I show him my hand...

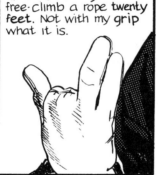

...there's **no way** I can free-climb a rope **twenty feet.** Not with my **grip** what it is.

So Aleks **goes,** planning to **hoist** me **after** him.

Then he's **gone.**

And I've **never felt** more **alone** in my life.

I'm scared.

I'm really scared.

I was **stupid**, I think.
Delfy was **right**.

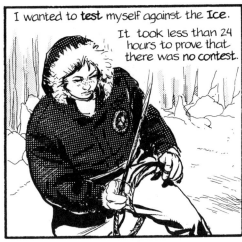

I wanted to **test** myself against the **Ice**.
It took less than 24 hours to prove that there was **no contest**.

Tough as I am, **hard** as I am, **experienced** as I am...
...the Ice is going to **kick** my ass **every** time.

Then he comes back...

...and I'm thinking all the way **up**...

...Aleks **drops** me, I'm **dead**.
And **no one** would **know** it was **murder**.

197

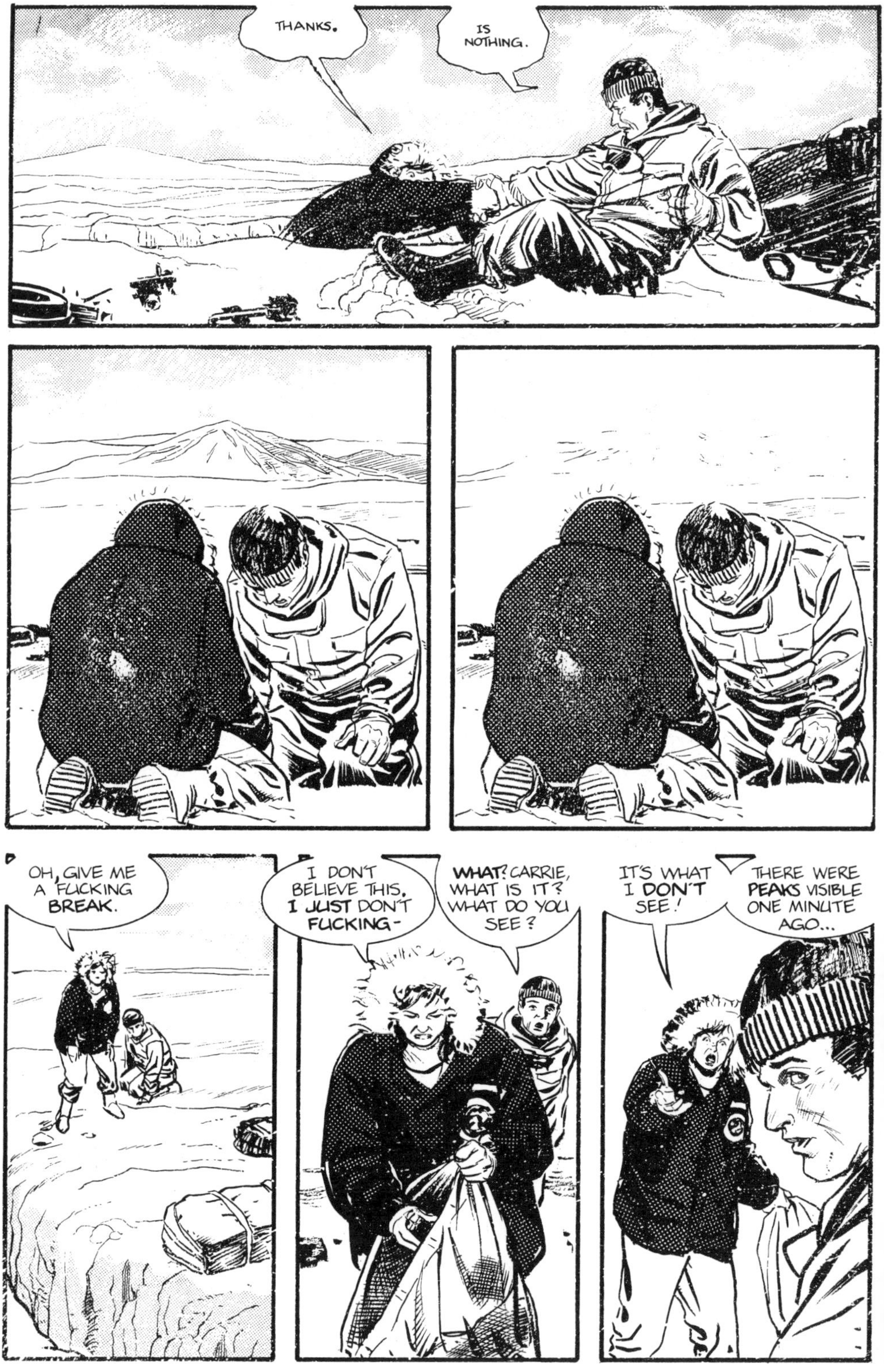
THANKS.
IS NOTHING.
OH, GIVE ME A FUCKING BREAK.
I DON'T BELIEVE THIS. I JUST DON'T FUCKING-
WHAT? CARRIE, WHAT IS IT? WHAT DO YOU SEE?
IT'S WHAT I DON'T SEE!
THERE WERE PEAKS VISIBLE ONE MINUTE AGO...

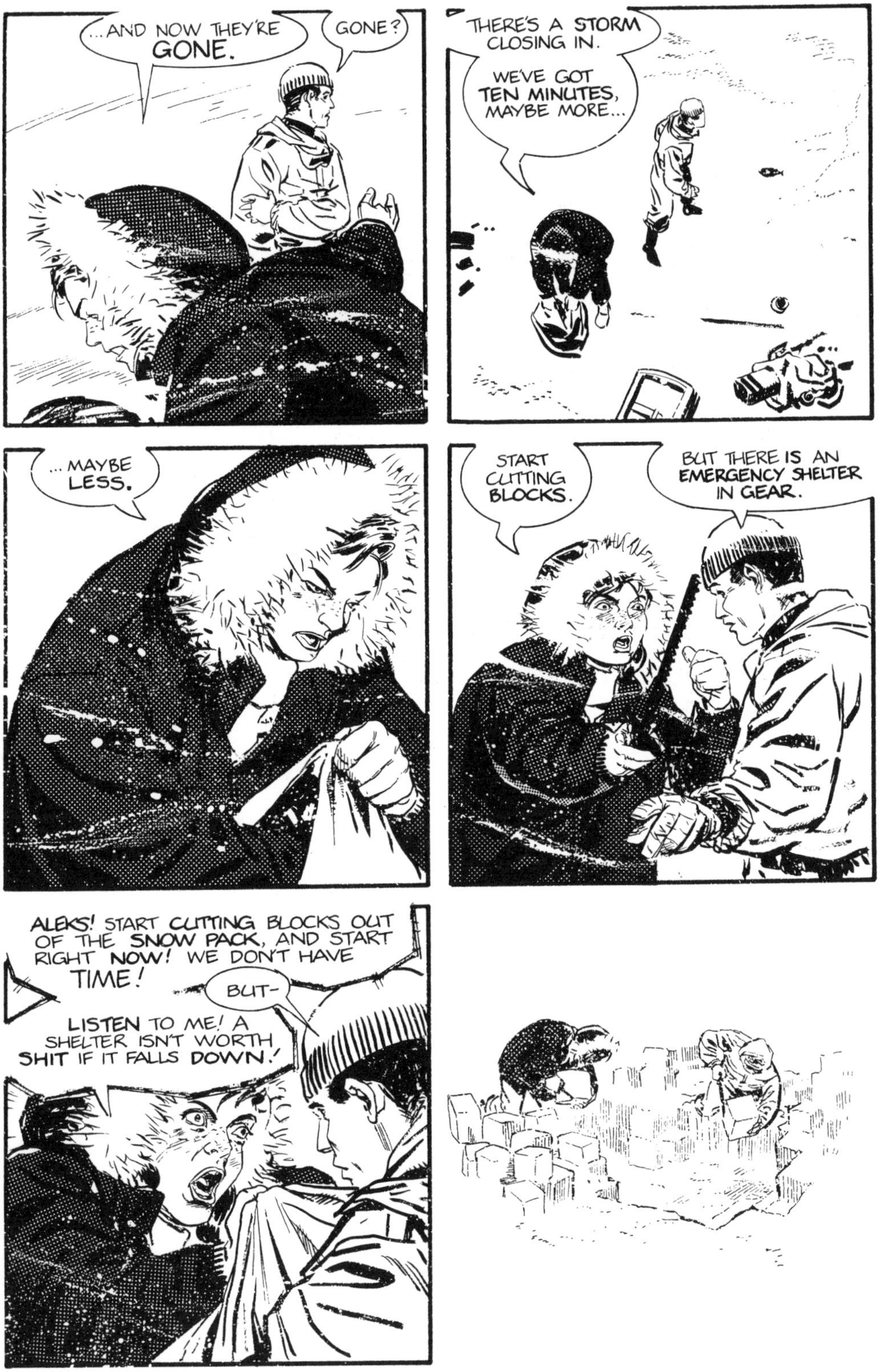
...AND NOW THEY'RE GONE.
GONE?
THERE'S A STORM CLOSING IN.
WE'VE GOT TEN MINUTES, MAYBE MORE...
...MAYBE LESS.
START CUTTING BLOCKS.
BUT THERE IS AN EMERGENCY SHELTER IN GEAR.
ALEKS! START CUTTING BLOCKS OUT OF THE SNOW PACK, AND START RIGHT NOW! WE DON'T HAVE TIME!
BUT-
LISTEN TO ME! A SHELTER ISN'T WORTH SHIT IF IT FALLS DOWN!

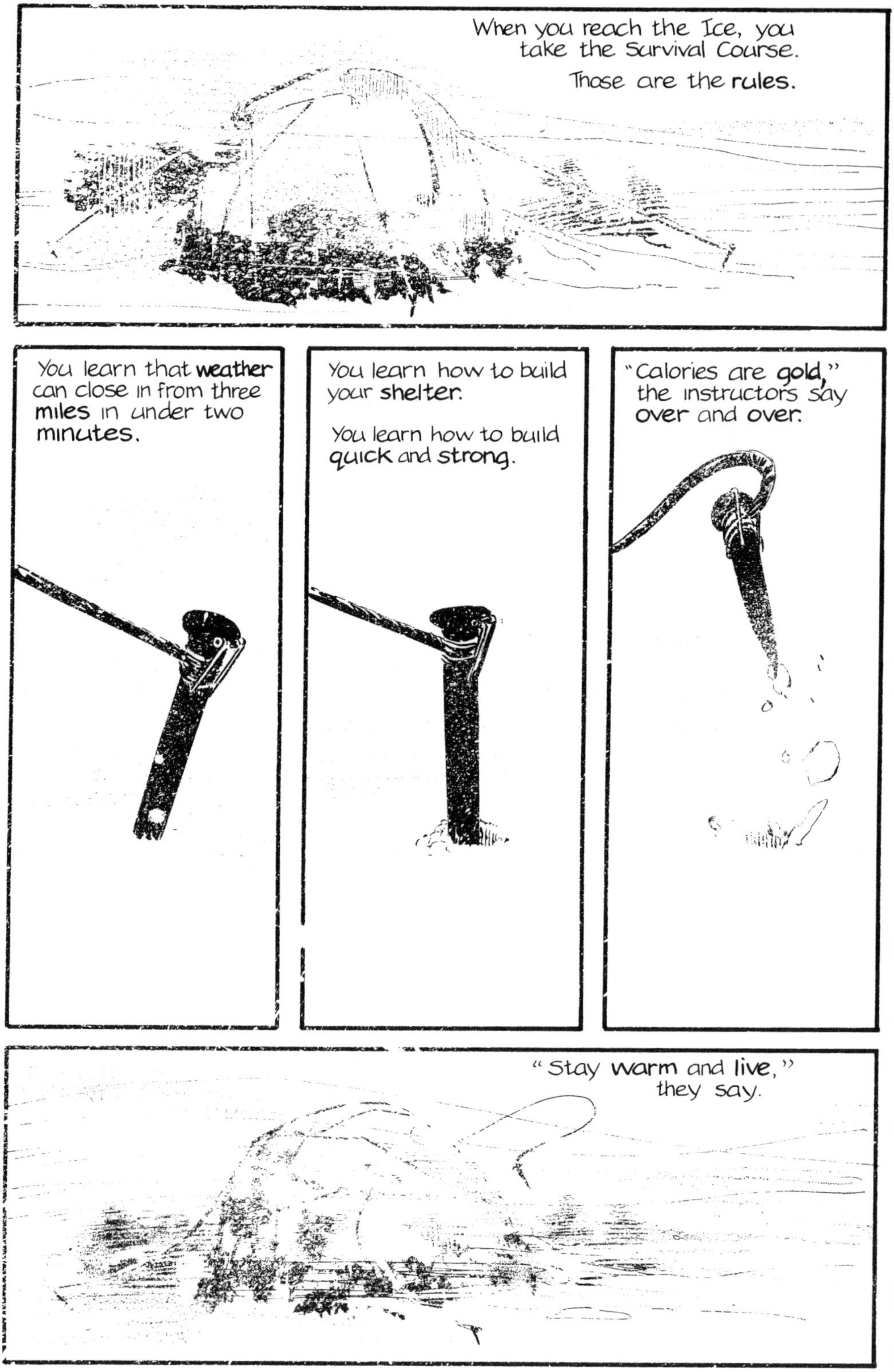
When you reach the Ice, you take the Survival Course.
Those are the rules.
You learn that weather can close in from three miles in under two minutes.
You learn how to build your shelter.
You learn how to build quick and strong.
"Calories are gold," the instructors say over and over.
"Stay warm and live," they say.

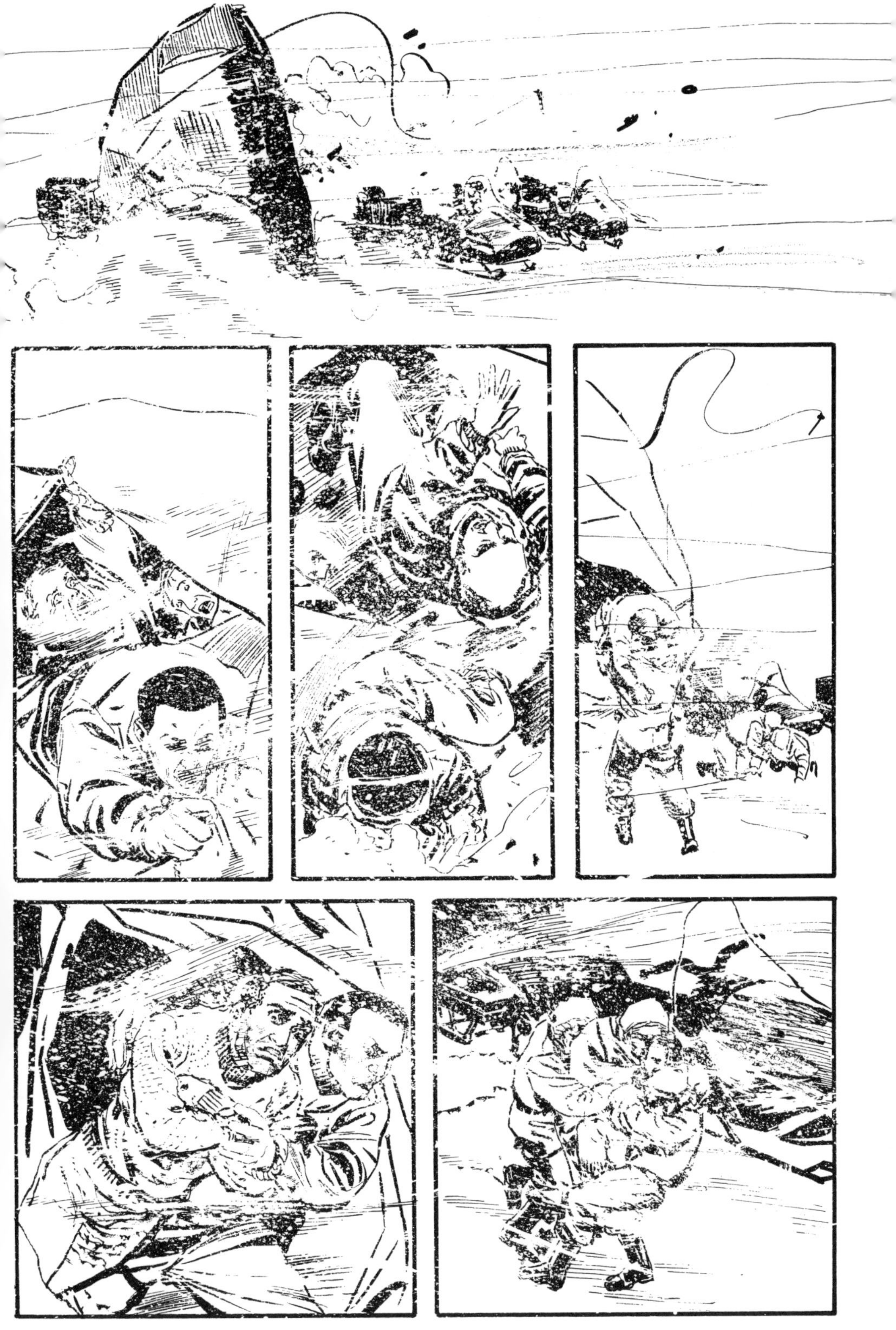

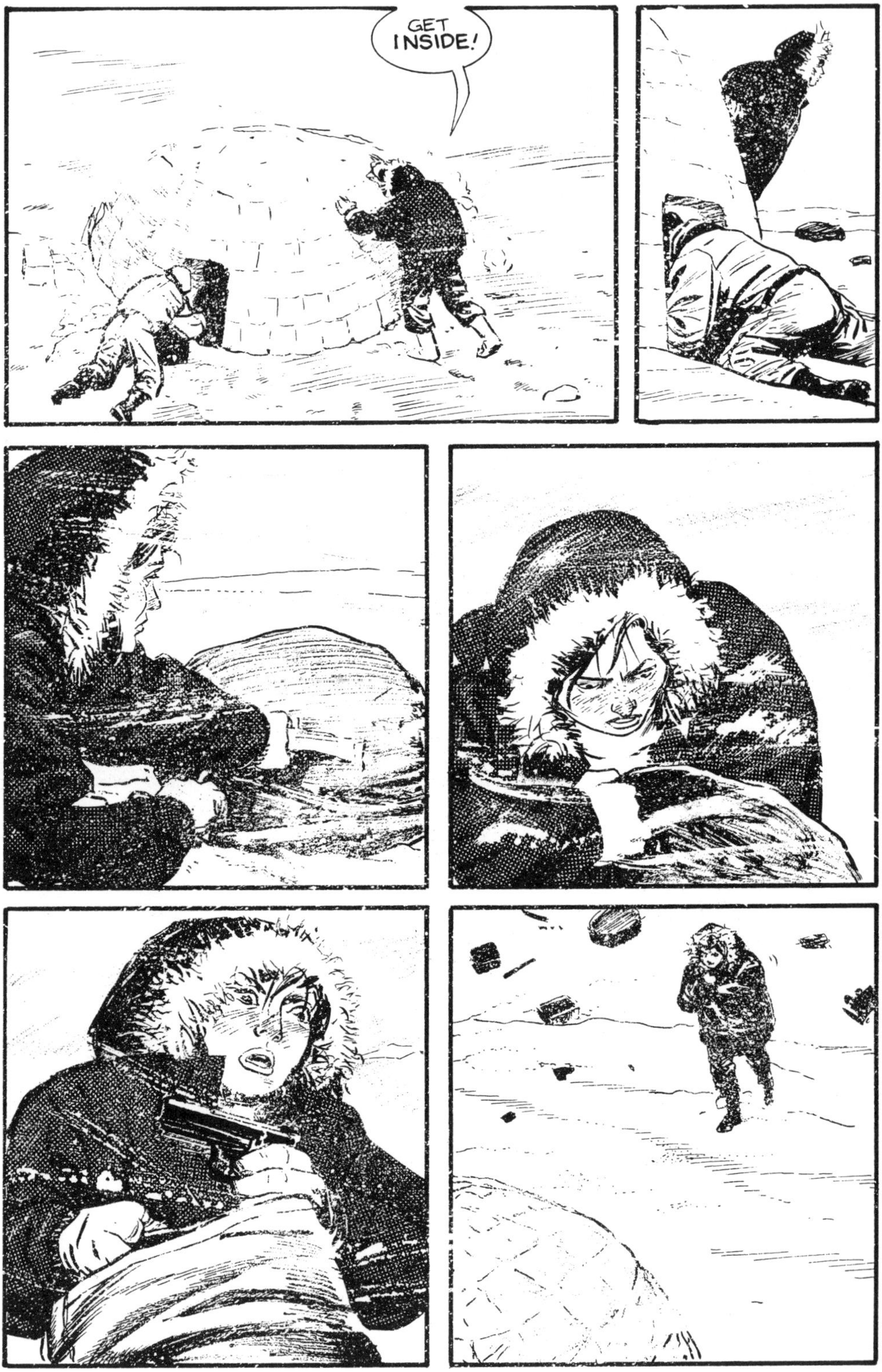
GET INSIDE!

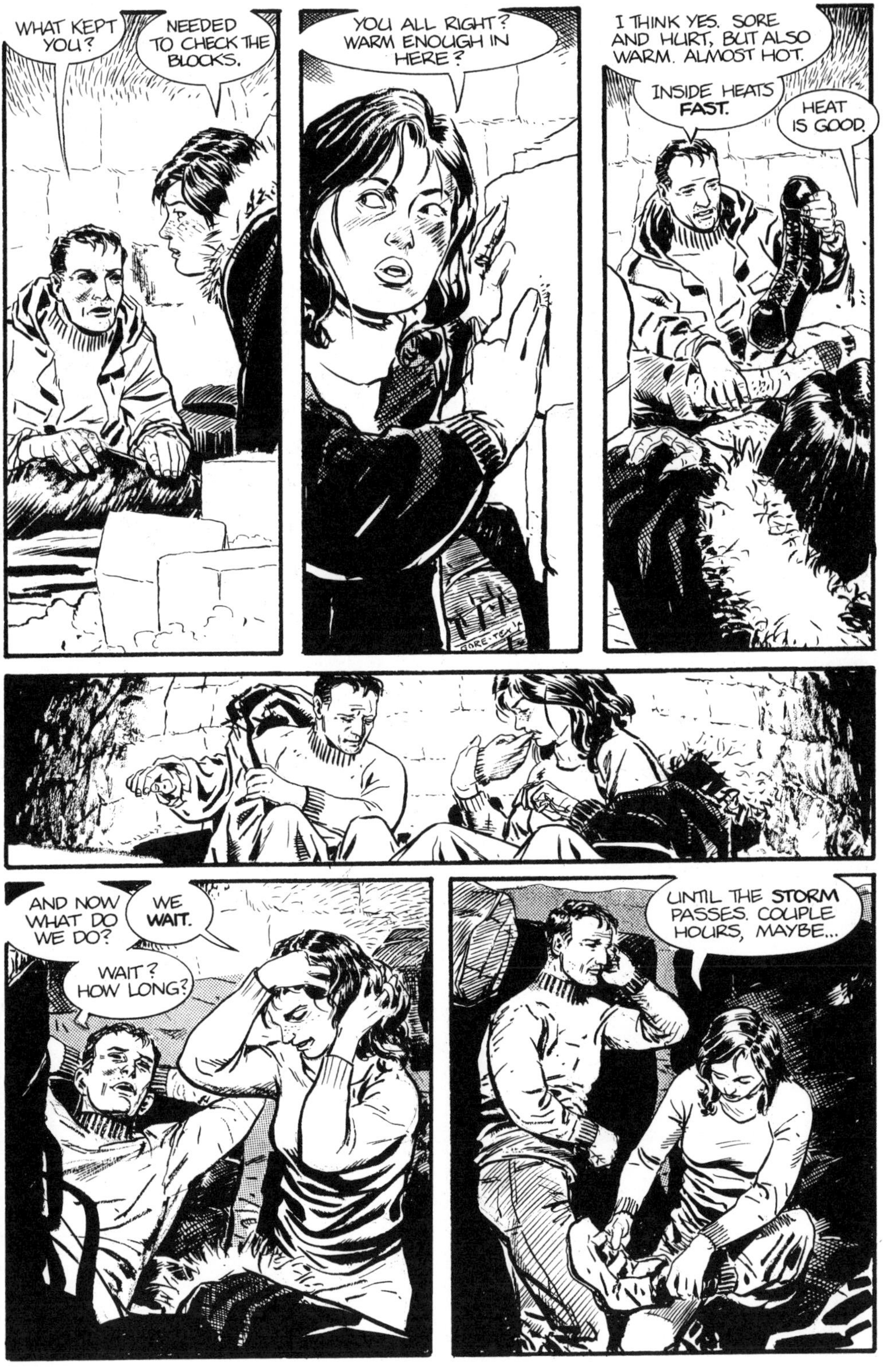
WHAT KEPT YOU?
NEEDED TO CHECK THE BLOCKS.
YOU ALL RIGHT? WARM ENOUGH IN HERE?
I THINK YES. SORE AND HURT, BUT ALSO WARM. ALMOST HOT.
INSIDE HEATS **FAST.**
HEAT IS GOOD.
AND NOW WHAT DO WE DO?
WE **WAIT.**
WAIT? HOW LONG?
UNTIL THE **STORM** PASSES. COUPLE HOURS, MAYBE...

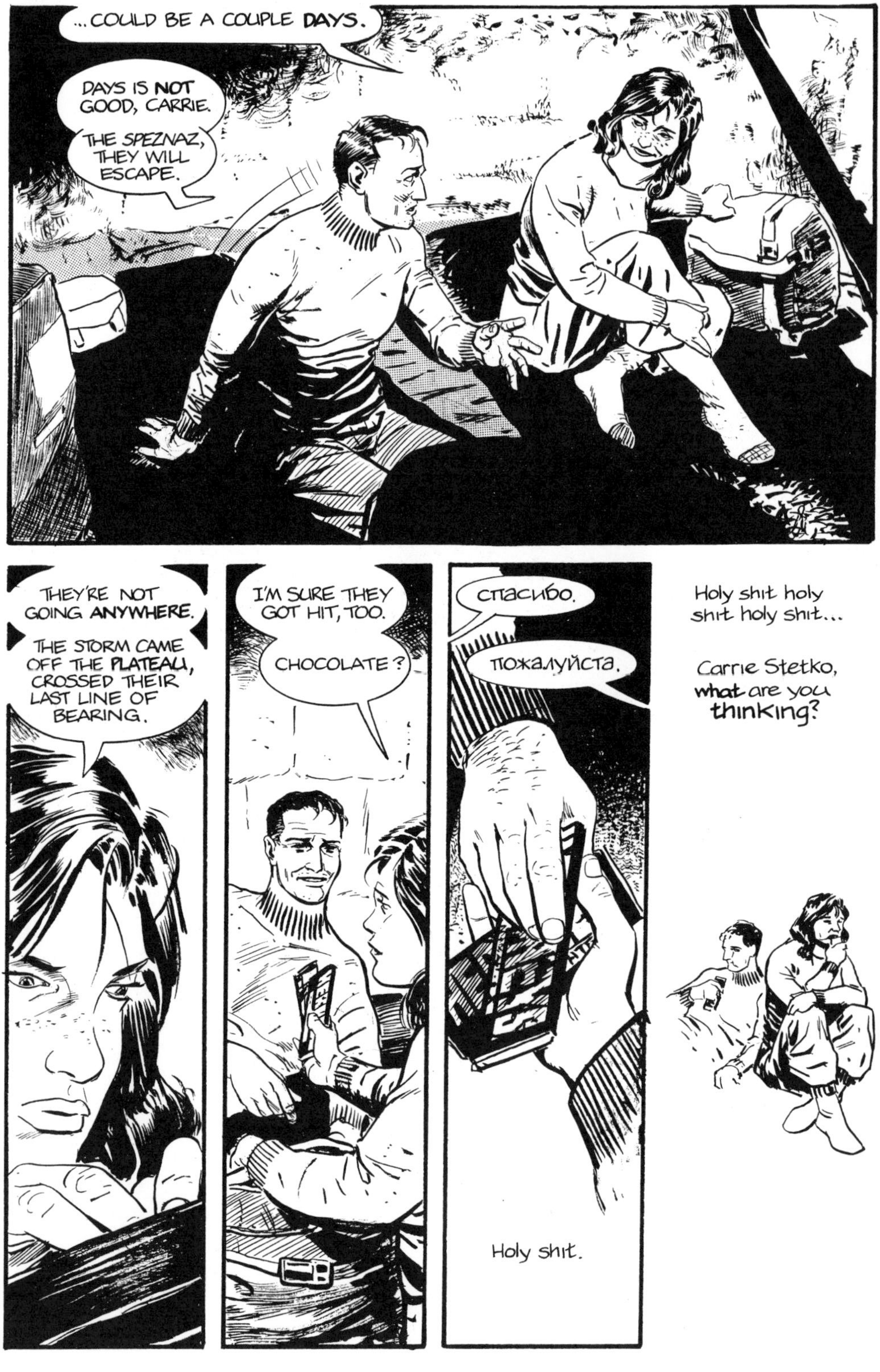

...COULD BE A COUPLE DAYS.
DAYS IS NOT GOOD, CARRIE.
THE SPEZNAZ, THEY WILL ESCAPE.
THEY'RE NOT GOING ANYWHERE.
THE STORM CAME OFF THE PLATEAU, CROSSED THEIR LAST LINE OF BEARING.
I'M SURE THEY GOT HIT, TOO.
CHOCOLATE?
спасибо.
пожалуйста.
Holy shit.
Holy shit holy shit holy shit...
Carrie Stetko, what are you thinking?

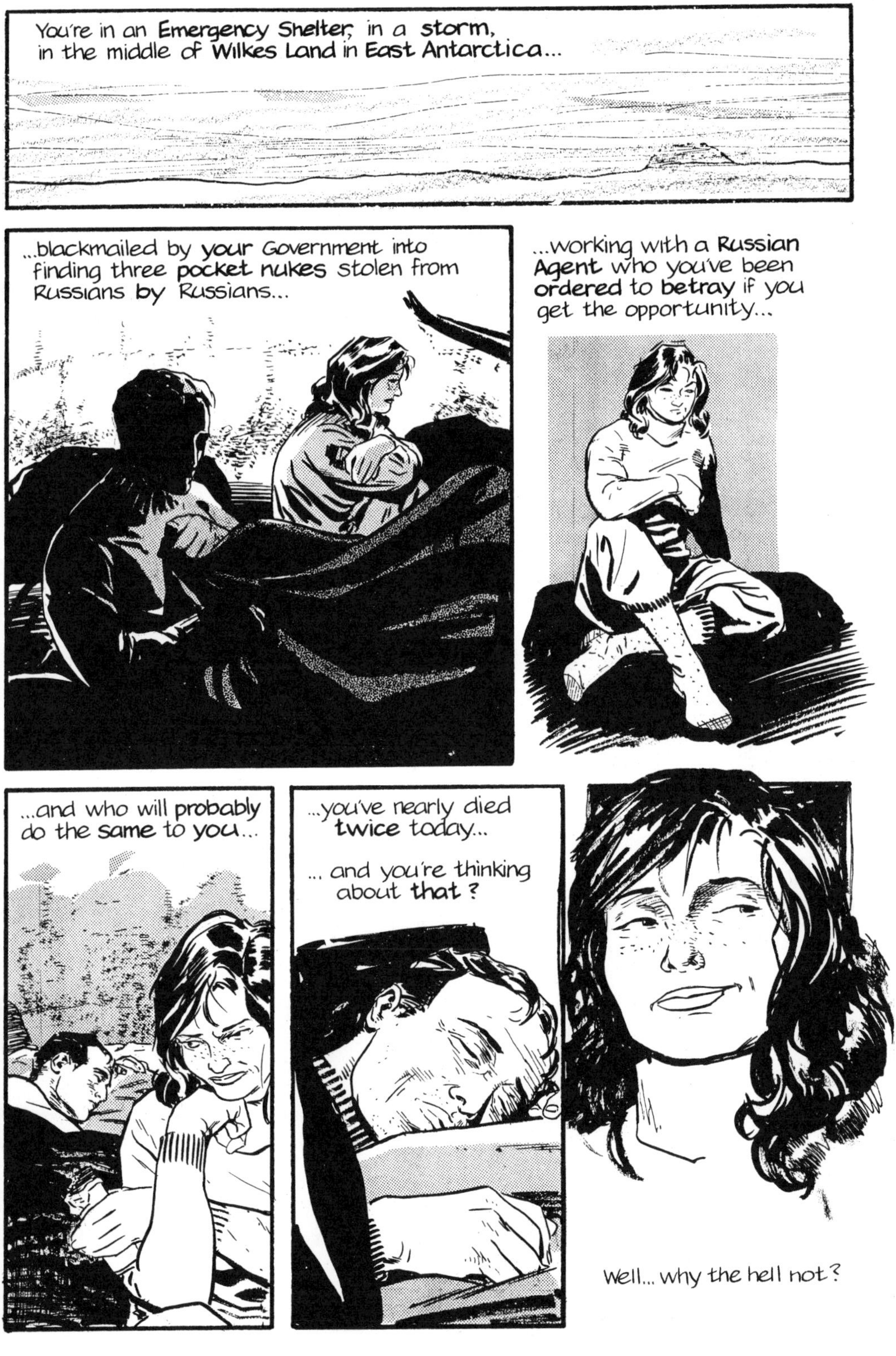
You're in an Emergency Shelter, in a storm, in the middle of Wilkes Land in East Antarctica...
...blackmailed by your Government into finding three pocket nukes stolen from Russians by Russians...
...working with a Russian Agent who you've been ordered to betray if you get the opportunity...
...and who will probably do the same to you...
...you've nearly died twice today...
... and you're thinking about that?
Well... why the hell not?

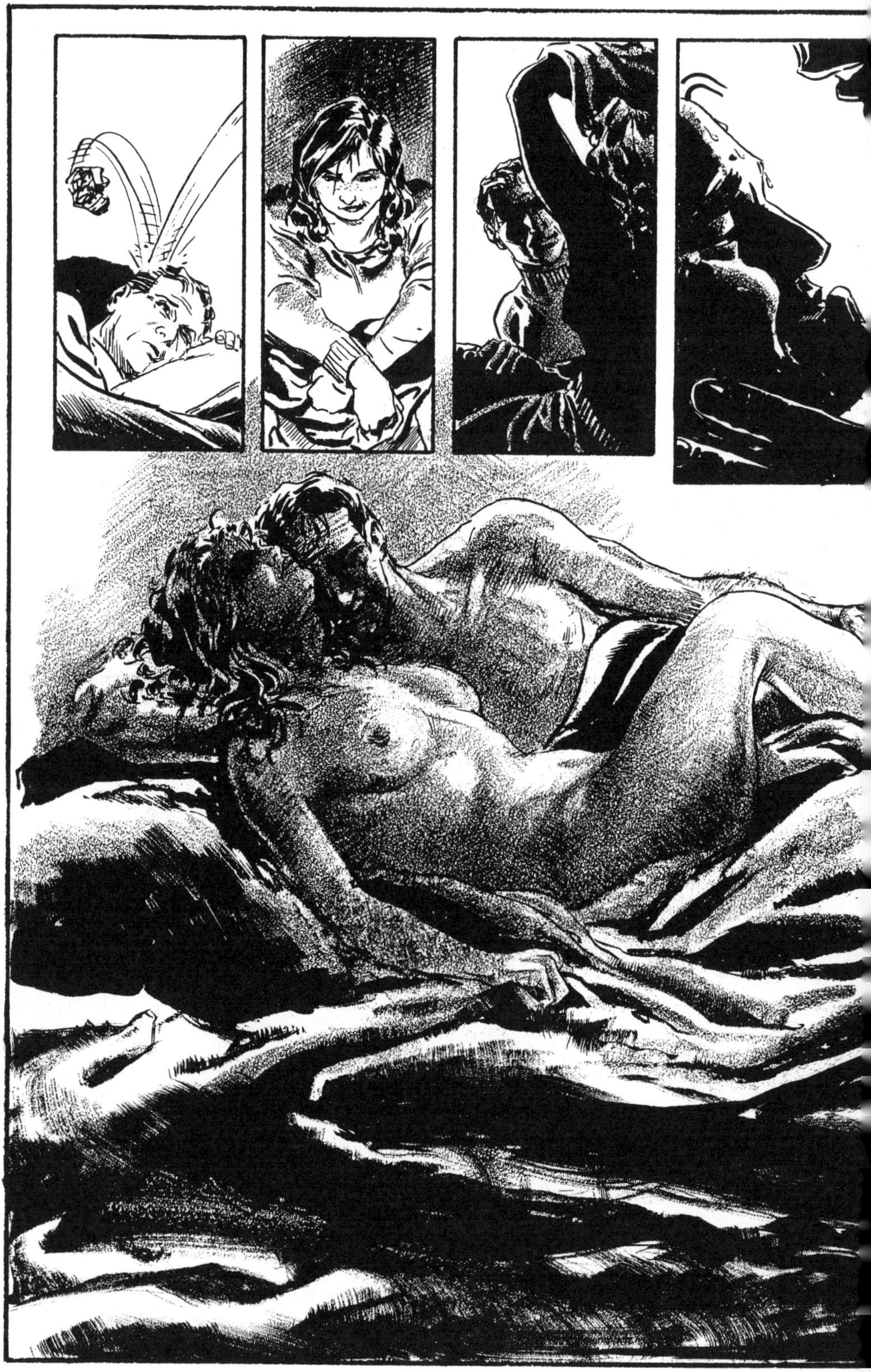

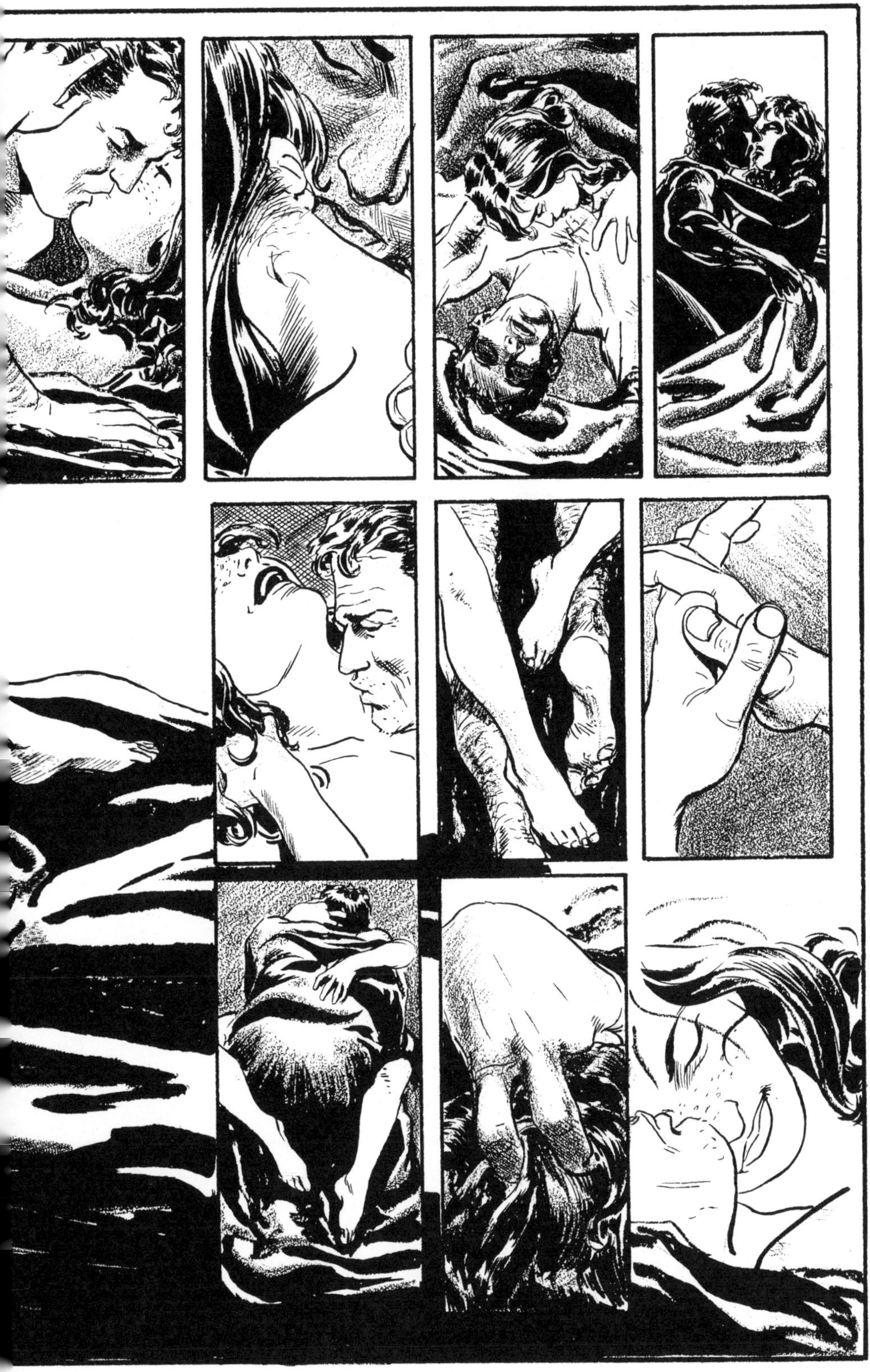

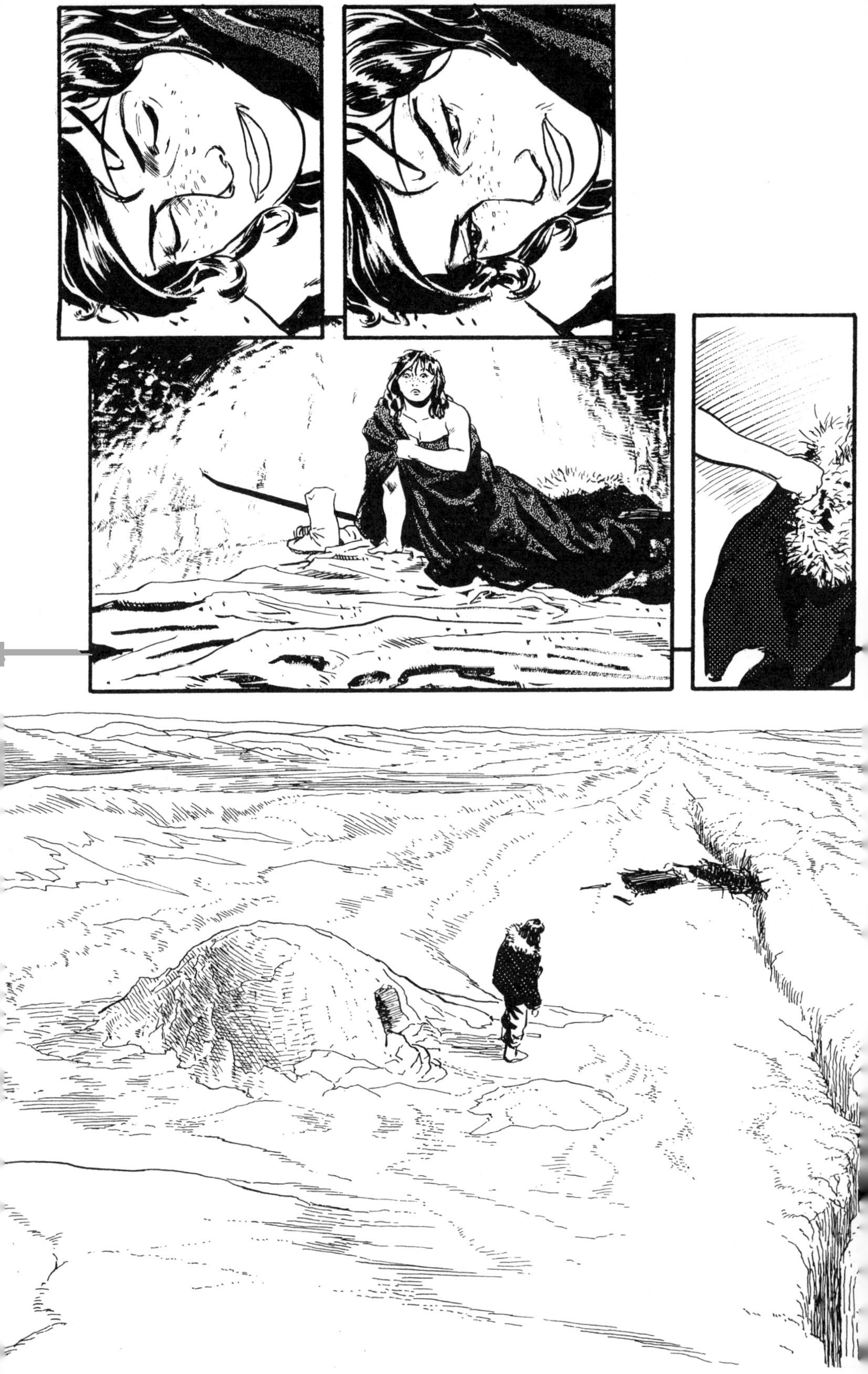

CHAPTER FOUR

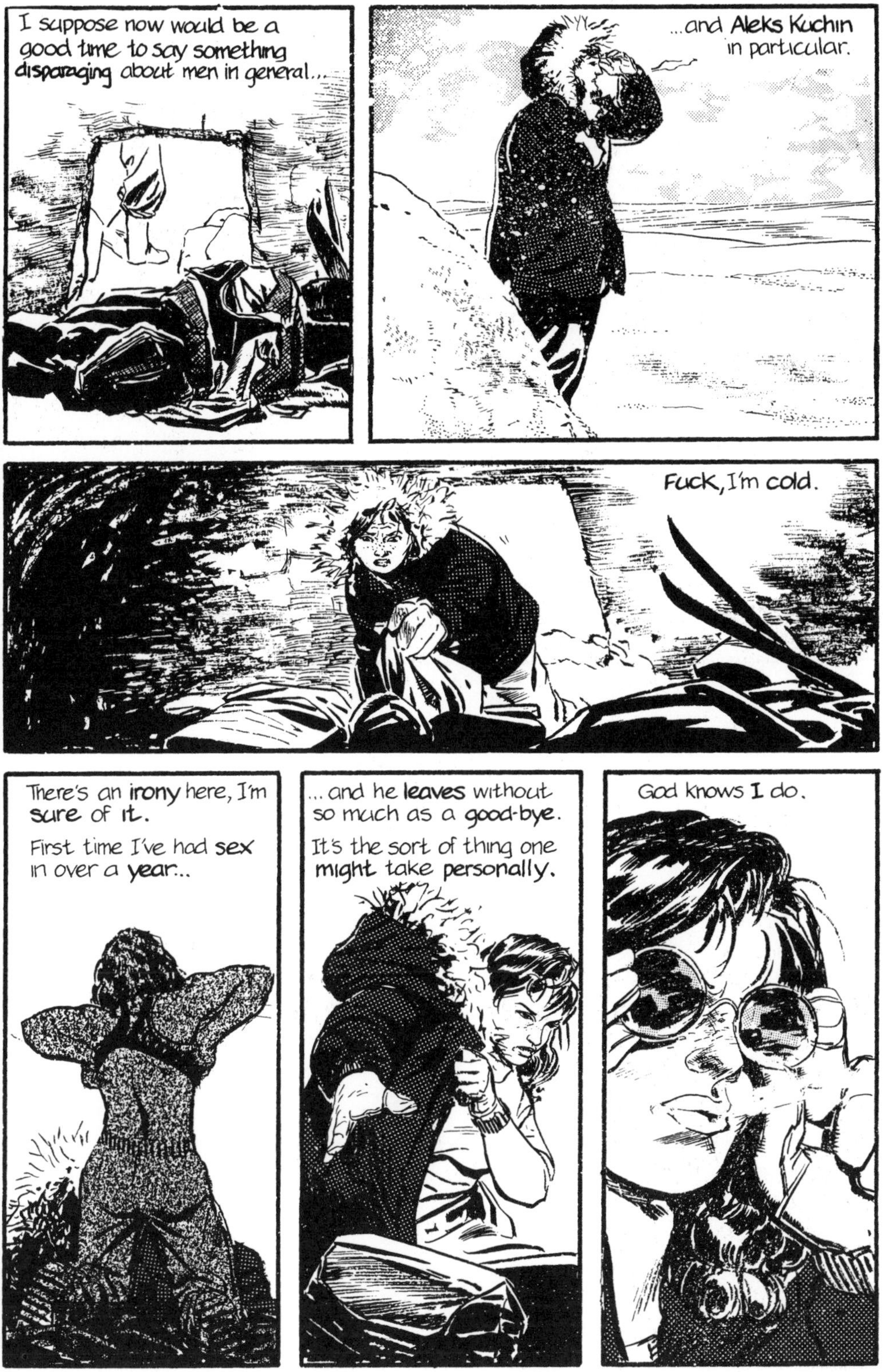
I suppose now would be a good time to say something disparaging about men in general...
...and Aleks Kuchin in particular.
Fuck, I'm cold.
There's an irony here, I'm sure of it.
First time I've had sex in over a year...
...and he leaves without so much as a good-bye.
It's the sort of thing one might take personally.
God knows I do.

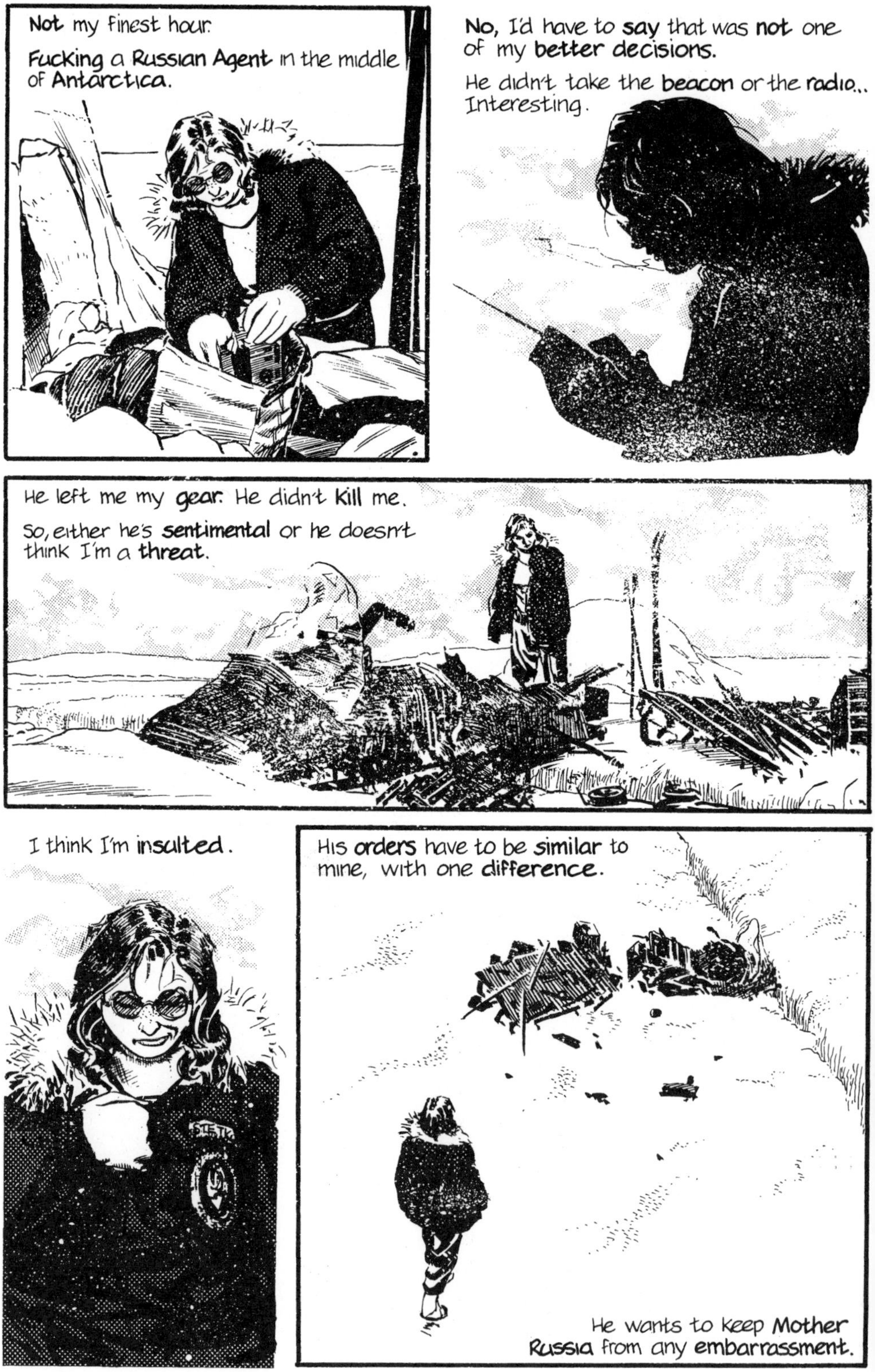
Not my finest hour.
Fucking a Russian Agent in the middle of Antarctica.
No, I'd have to say that was not one of my better decisions.
He didn't take the beacon or the radio... Interesting.
He left me my gear. He didn't kill me.
So, either he's sentimental or he doesn't think I'm a threat.
I think I'm insulted.
S.I.E.T.K.
His orders have to be similar to mine, with one difference.
He wants to keep Mother Russia from any embarrassment.

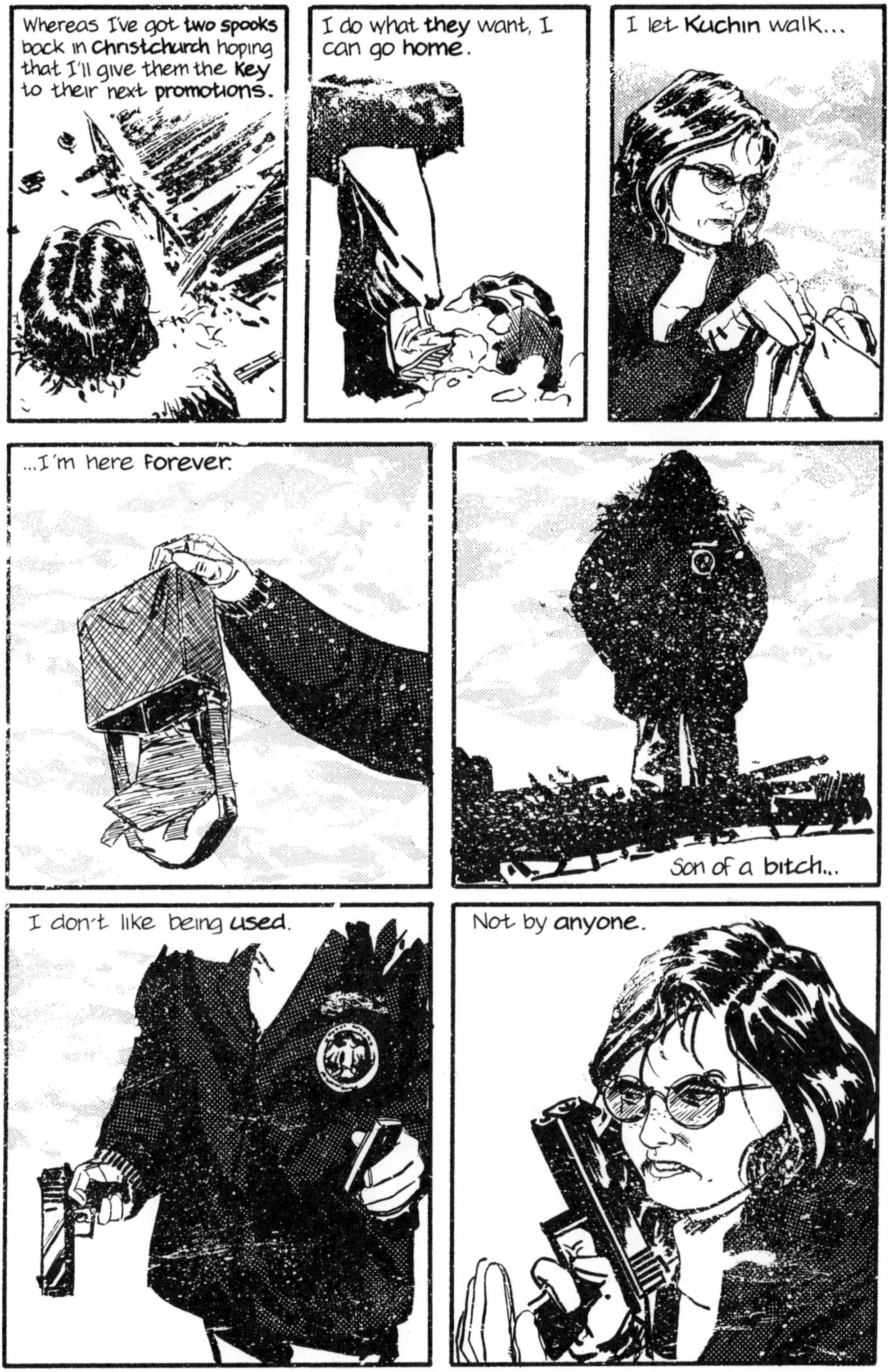
Whereas I've got two spooks back in Christchurch hoping that I'll give them the key to their next promotions.
I do what they want, I can go home.
I let Kuchin walk...
...I'm here forever.
Son of a bitch...
I don't like being used.
Not by anyone.

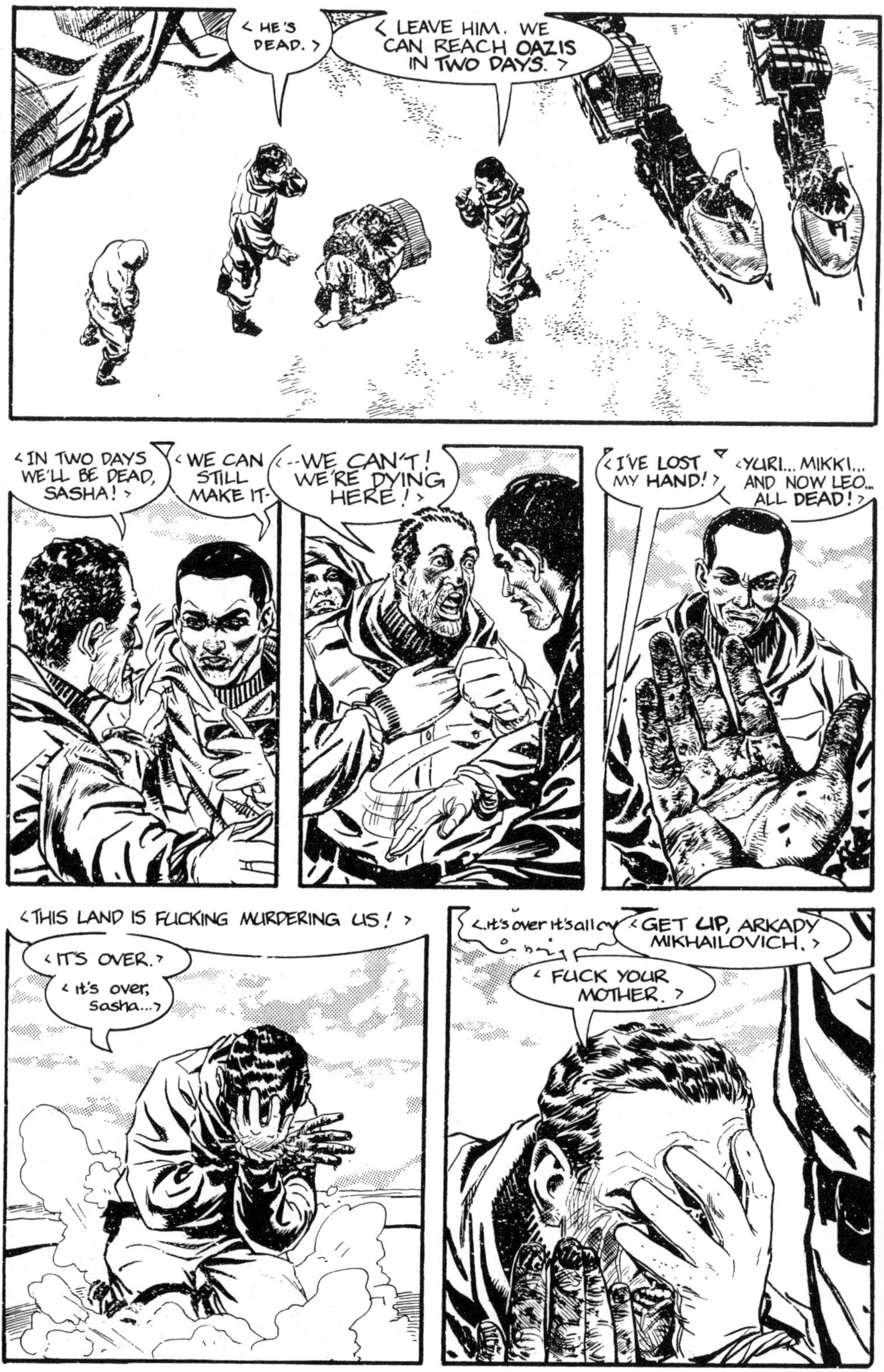
< HE'S DEAD. >
< LEAVE HIM. WE CAN REACH OAZIS IN TWO DAYS. >
< IN TWO DAYS WE'LL BE DEAD, SASHA! >
< WE CAN STILL MAKE IT-
< --WE CAN'T! WE'RE DYING HERE! >
< I'VE LOST MY HAND! >
< YURI... MIKKI... AND NOW LEO... ALL DEAD! >
< THIS LAND IS FUCKING MURDERING US! >
< IT'S OVER. >
< it's over, sasha... >
<..It's over It's all ov
< GET UP, ARKADY MIKHAILOVICH. >
< FUCK YOUR MOTHER. >

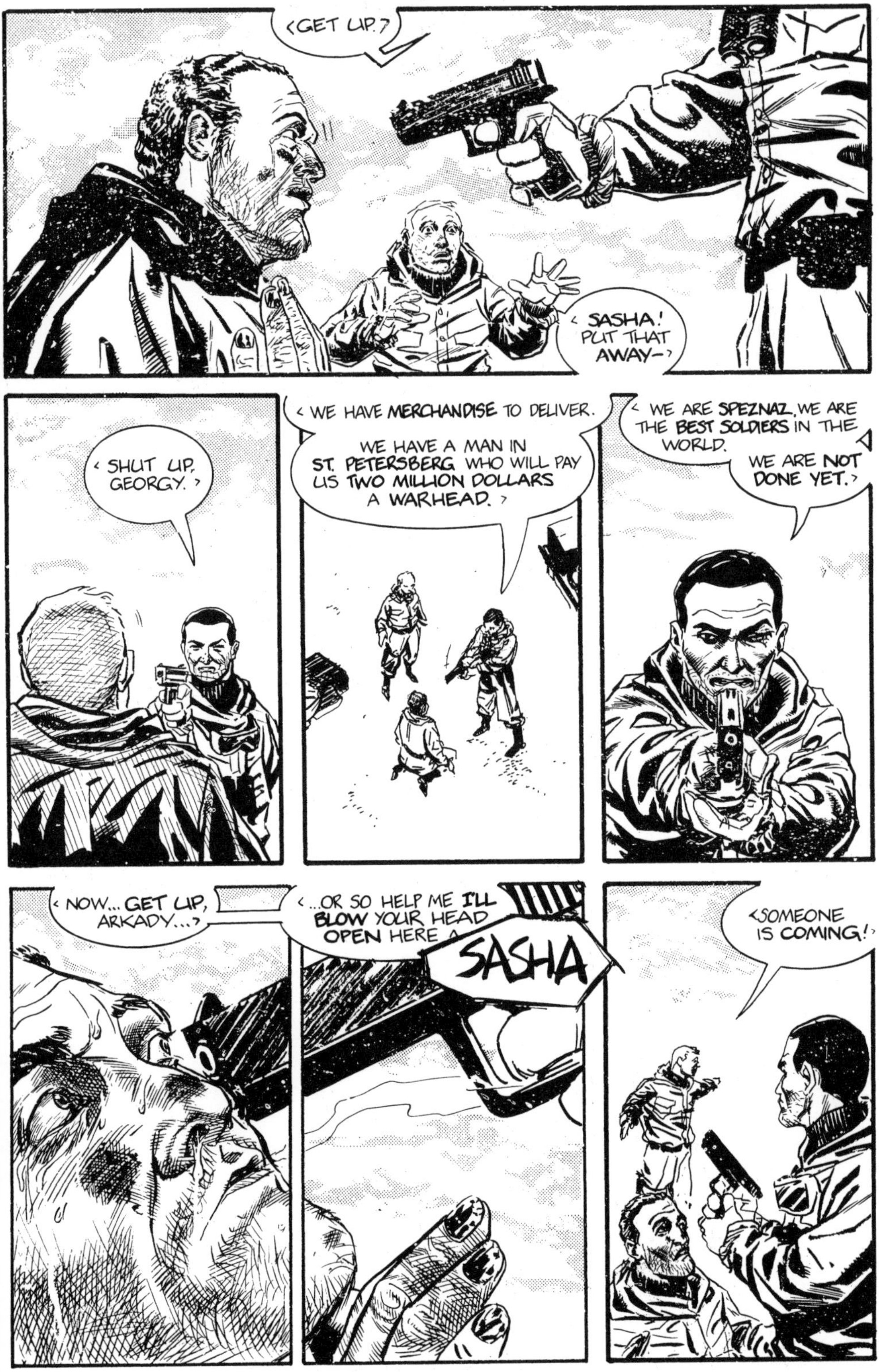

<GET UP.>
< SASHA! PUT THAT AWAY- >
< SHUT UP, GEORGY. >
< WE HAVE MERCHANDISE TO DELIVER.
WE HAVE A MAN IN ST. PETERSBERG WHO WILL PAY US TWO MILLION DOLLARS A WARHEAD. >
< WE ARE SPEZNAZ, WE ARE THE BEST SOLDIERS IN THE WORLD.
WE ARE NOT DONE YET. >
< NOW... GET UP, ARKADY... >
< ...OR SO HELP ME I'LL BLOW YOUR HEAD OPEN HERE A
SASHA
<SOMEONE IS COMING!>

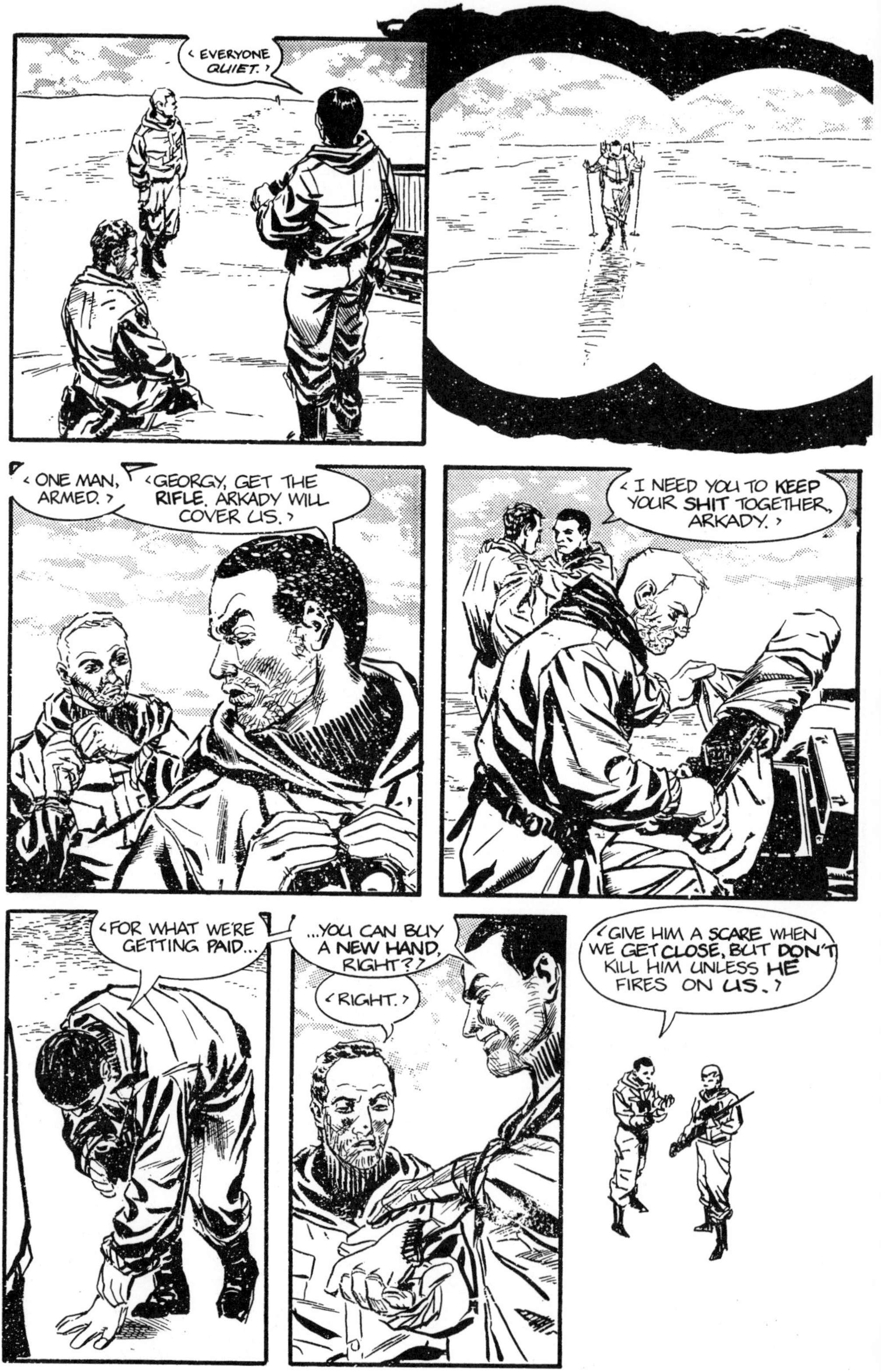
‹ EVERYONE QUIET. ›
‹ ONE MAN, ARMED. ›
‹ GEORGY, GET THE RIFLE. ARKADY WILL COVER US. ›
‹ I NEED YOU TO KEEP YOUR SHIT TOGETHER, ARKADY. ›
‹ FOR WHAT WE'RE GETTING PAID...
...YOU CAN BUY A NEW HAND, RIGHT? ›
‹ RIGHT. ›
‹ GIVE HIM A SCARE WHEN WE GET CLOSE, BUT DON'T KILL HIM UNLESS HE FIRES ON US. ›

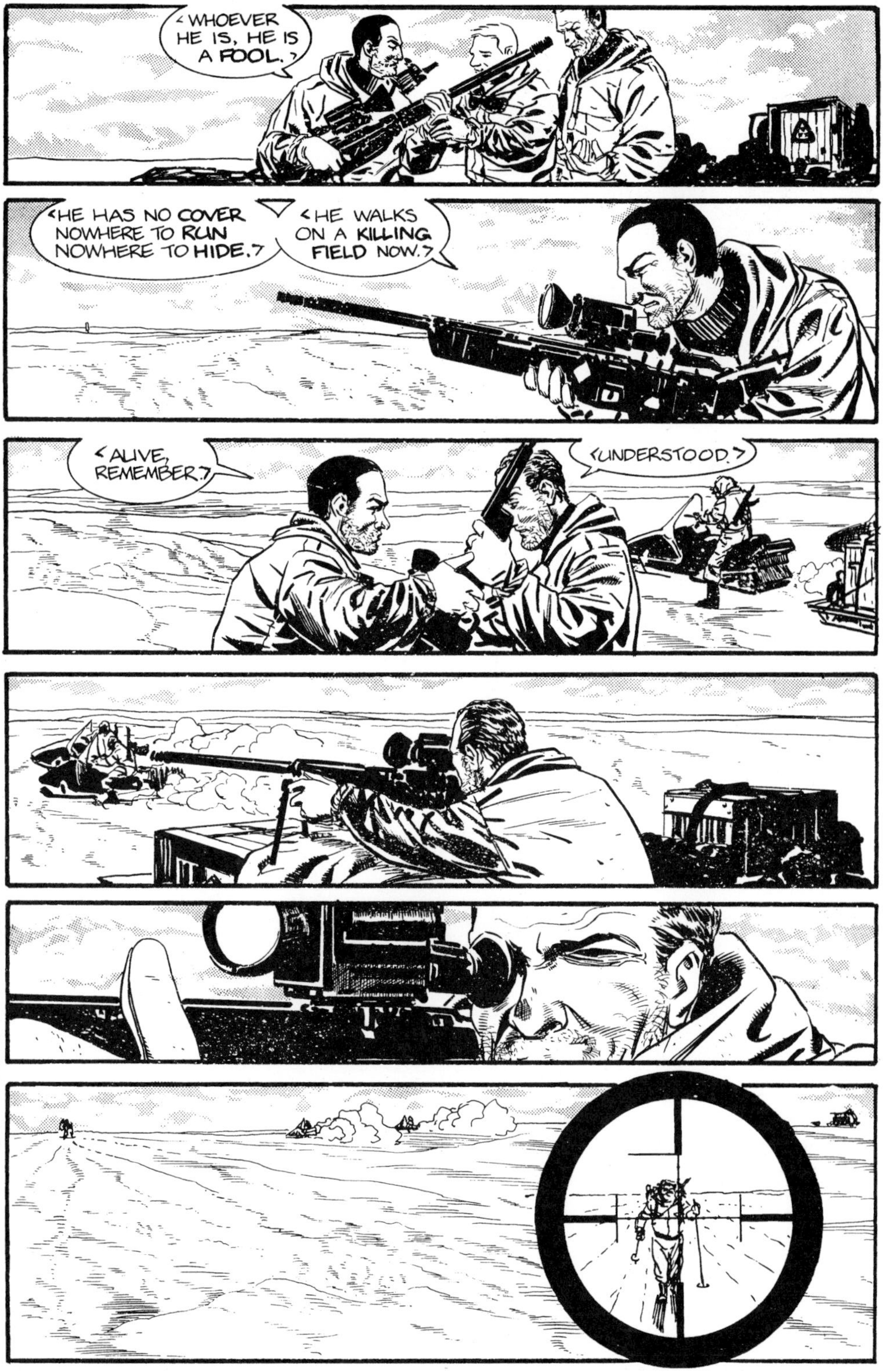

‹WHOEVER HE IS, HE IS A FOOL.›
‹HE HAS NO COVER NOWHERE TO RUN NOWHERE TO HIDE.›
‹HE WALKS ON A KILLING FIELD NOW.›
‹ALIVE, REMEMBER.›
‹UNDERSTOOD.›

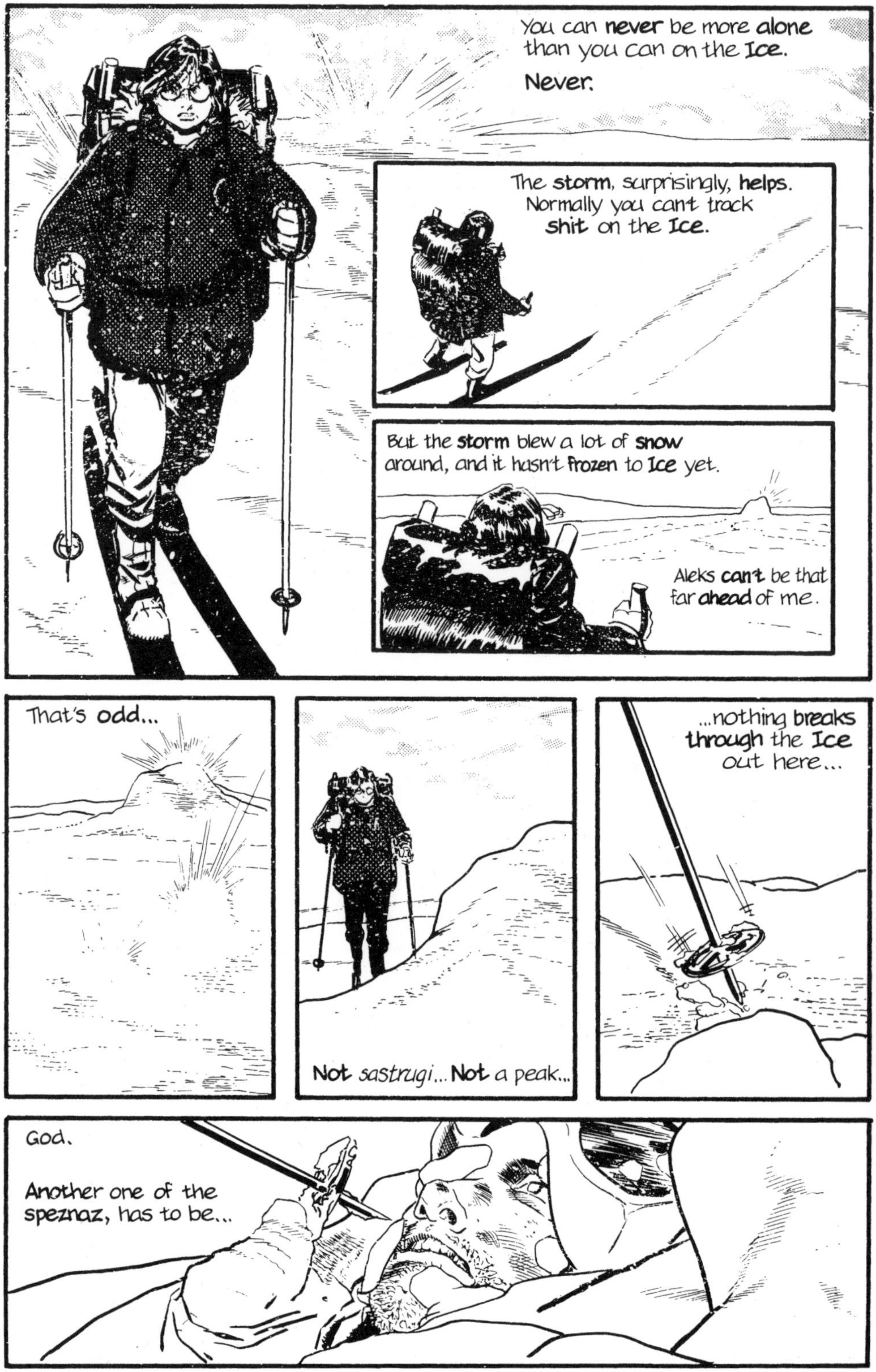
You can never be more alone than you can on the Ice.
Never.
The storm, surprisingly, helps. Normally you can't track shit on the Ice.
But the storm blew a lot of snow around, and it hasn't frozen to Ice yet.
Aleks can't be that far ahead of me.
That's odd...
Not sastrugi... Not a peak...
...nothing breaks through the Ice out here...
God.
Another one of the speznaz, has to be...

...must have gotten **separated** from the **others** somehow.

Well, it's not like **he** needs them any longer.

And at least this way I don't stick out like a nun in a whorehouse.

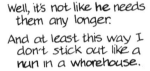

Separated from the rest. Froze to death.

So, where's your transport, hmm?

Figure one snowmobile for **each** of you...

...just like at the crevasse...

219

Come to momma, come on...

...a little transportation and I'm—

MOTHERFUCK!

They scuttled it

MOTHERFUCK!

MOTHERFUCK
MOTHERFUCK
MOTHERFUCK

MOTHERFUCK

WAIT A MINUTE...

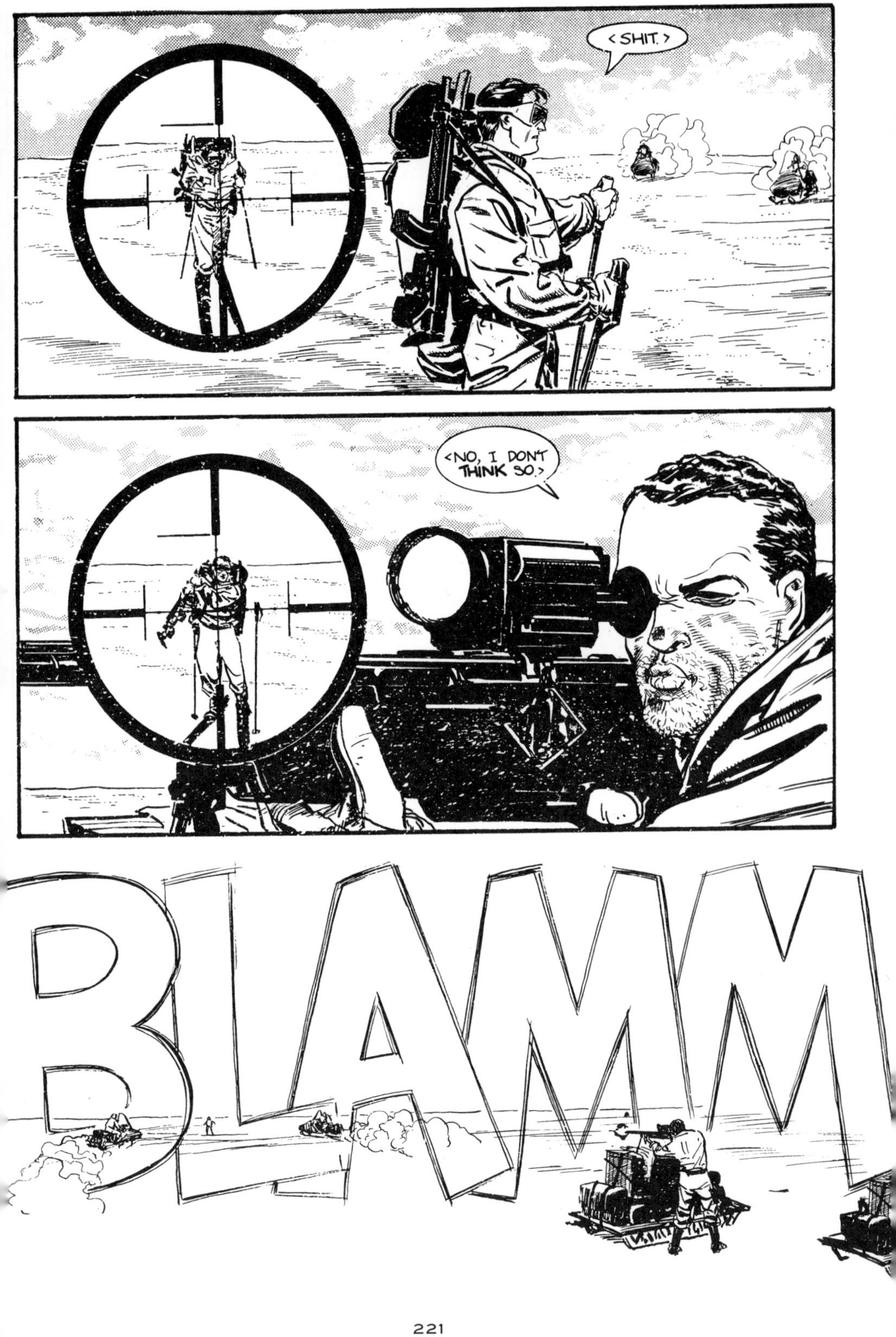

< SHIT. >
<NO, I DON'T THINK SO.>
BLAMM

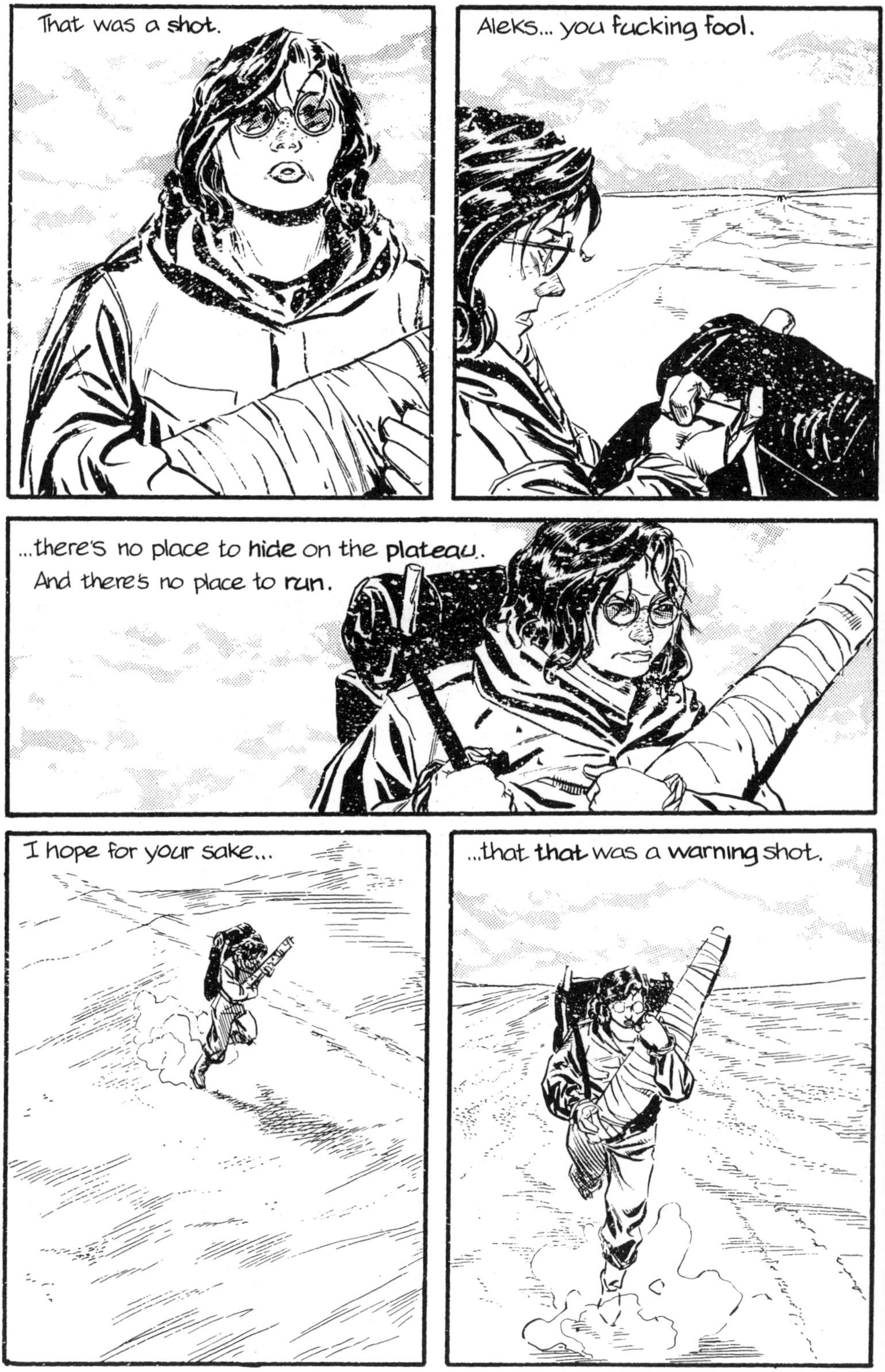

That was a shot.
Aleks... you fucking fool.
...there's no place to hide on the plateau.
And there's no place to run.
I hope for your sake...
...that that was a warning shot.

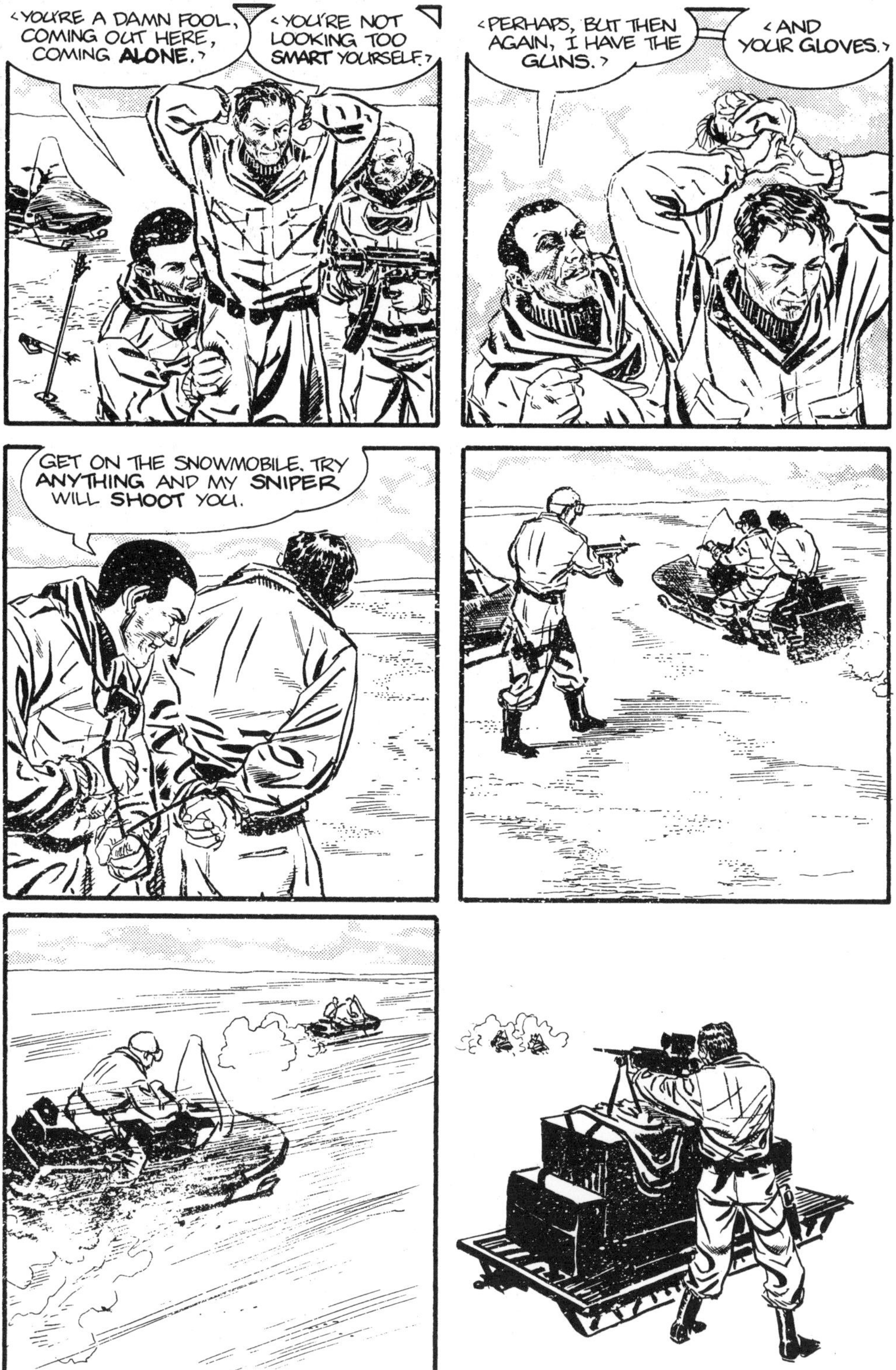

<YOU'RE A DAMN FOOL, COMING OUT HERE, COMING ALONE.>
<YOU'RE NOT LOOKING TOO SMART YOURSELF.>
<PERHAPS, BUT THEN AGAIN, I HAVE THE GUNS.>
<AND YOUR GLOVES.>
GET ON THE SNOWMOBILE. TRY ANYTHING AND MY SNIPER WILL SHOOT YOU.

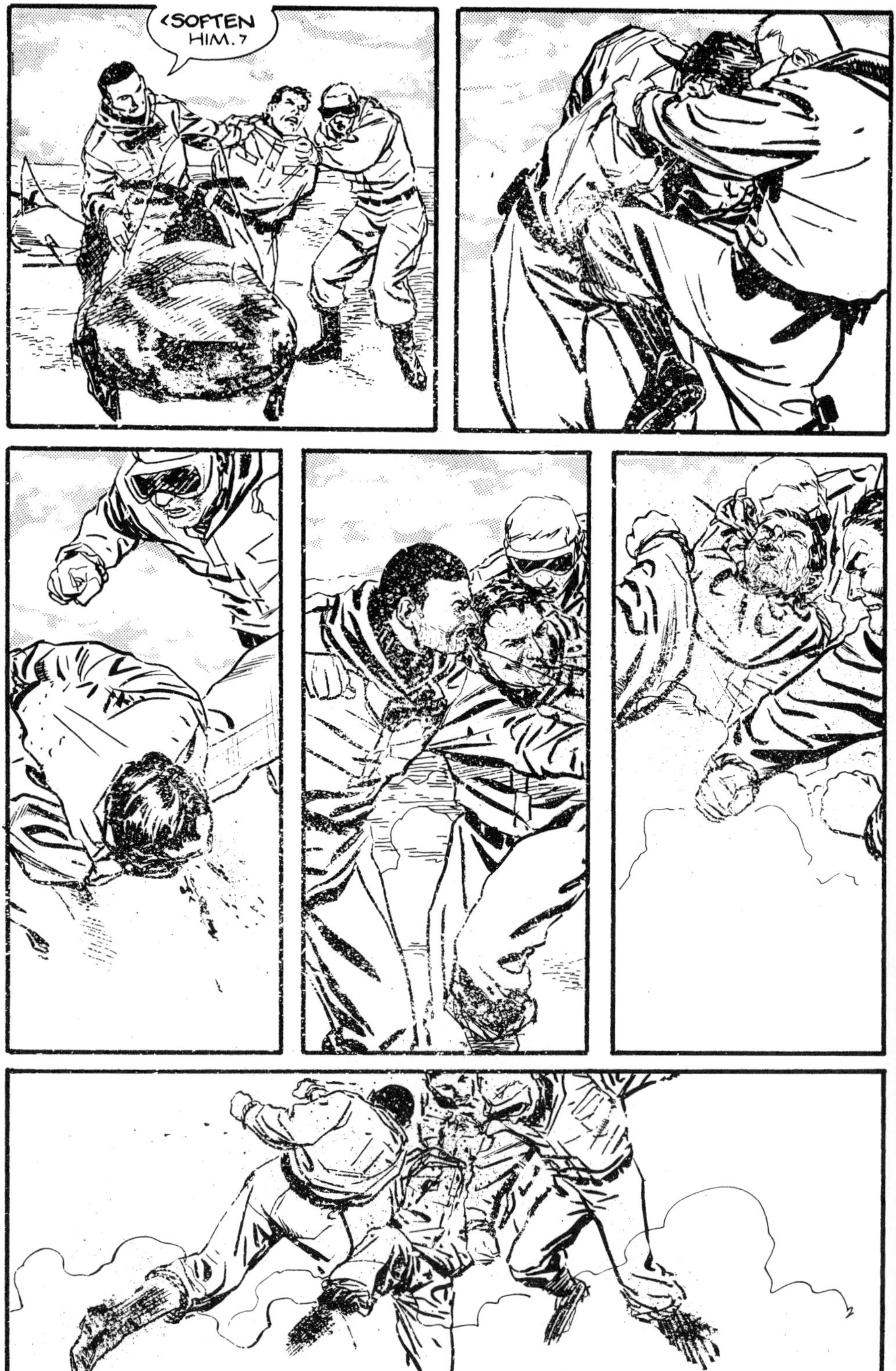
‹SOFTEN HIM.›

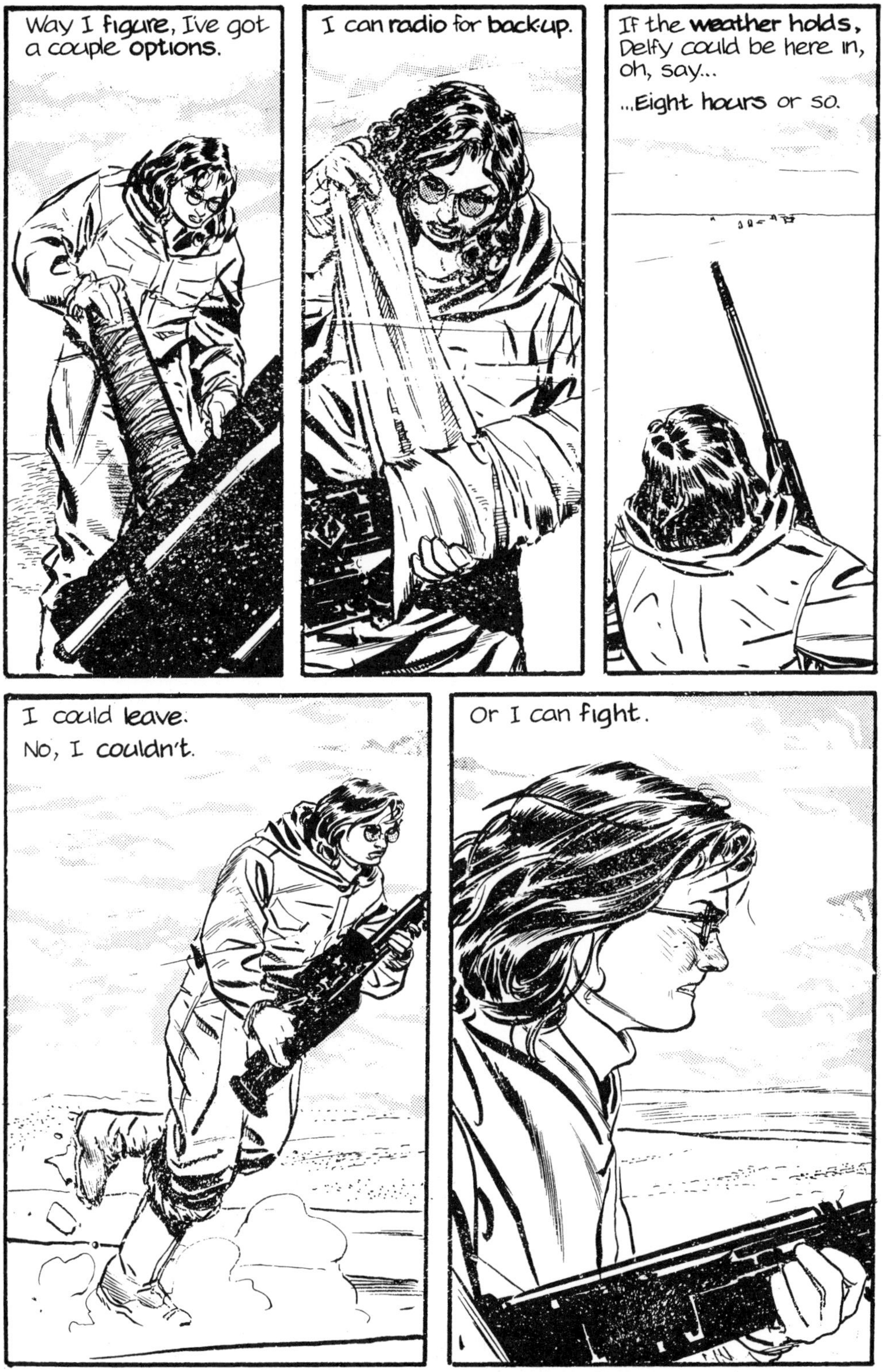
Way I figure, I've got a couple options.
I can radio for back-up.
If the weather holds, Delfy could be here in, oh, say...
...Eight hours or so.
I could leave.
No, I couldn't.
Or I can fight.

I've got **two** advantages.

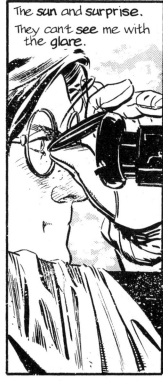

The **sun** and **surprise**. They can't **see** me with the **glare**.

I've got **several** more **disadvantages**. Not the least of them being I'm not a **sniper**...

...and I'm **lying** on **ice**.

Here goes nothing.

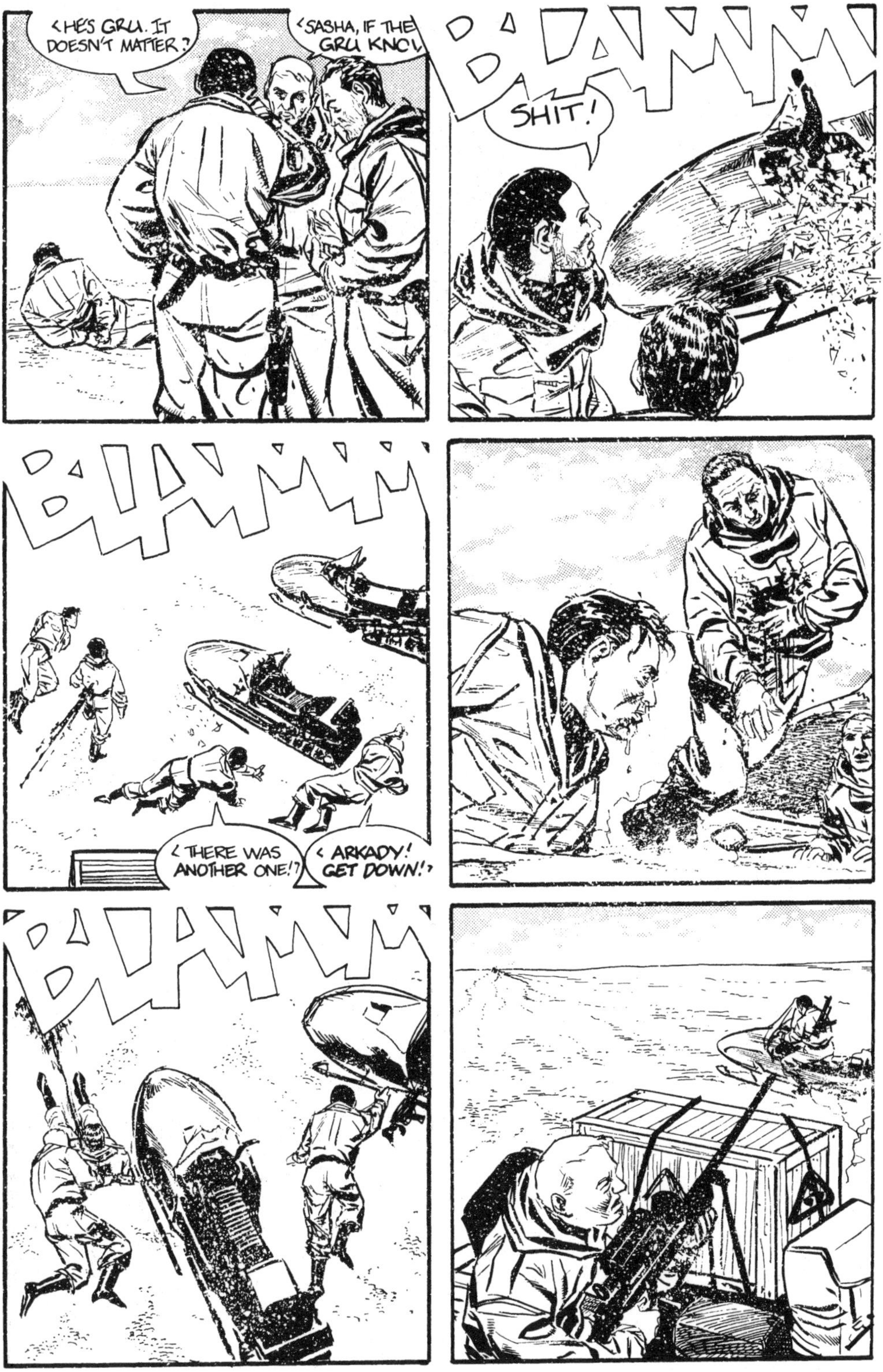
<HE'S GRU. IT DOESN'T MATTER.>
<SASHA, IF THE GRU KNO
BLAMM
SHIT!
BLAMM
<THERE WAS ANOTHER ONE!>
<ARKADY! GET DOWN!>
BLAMM

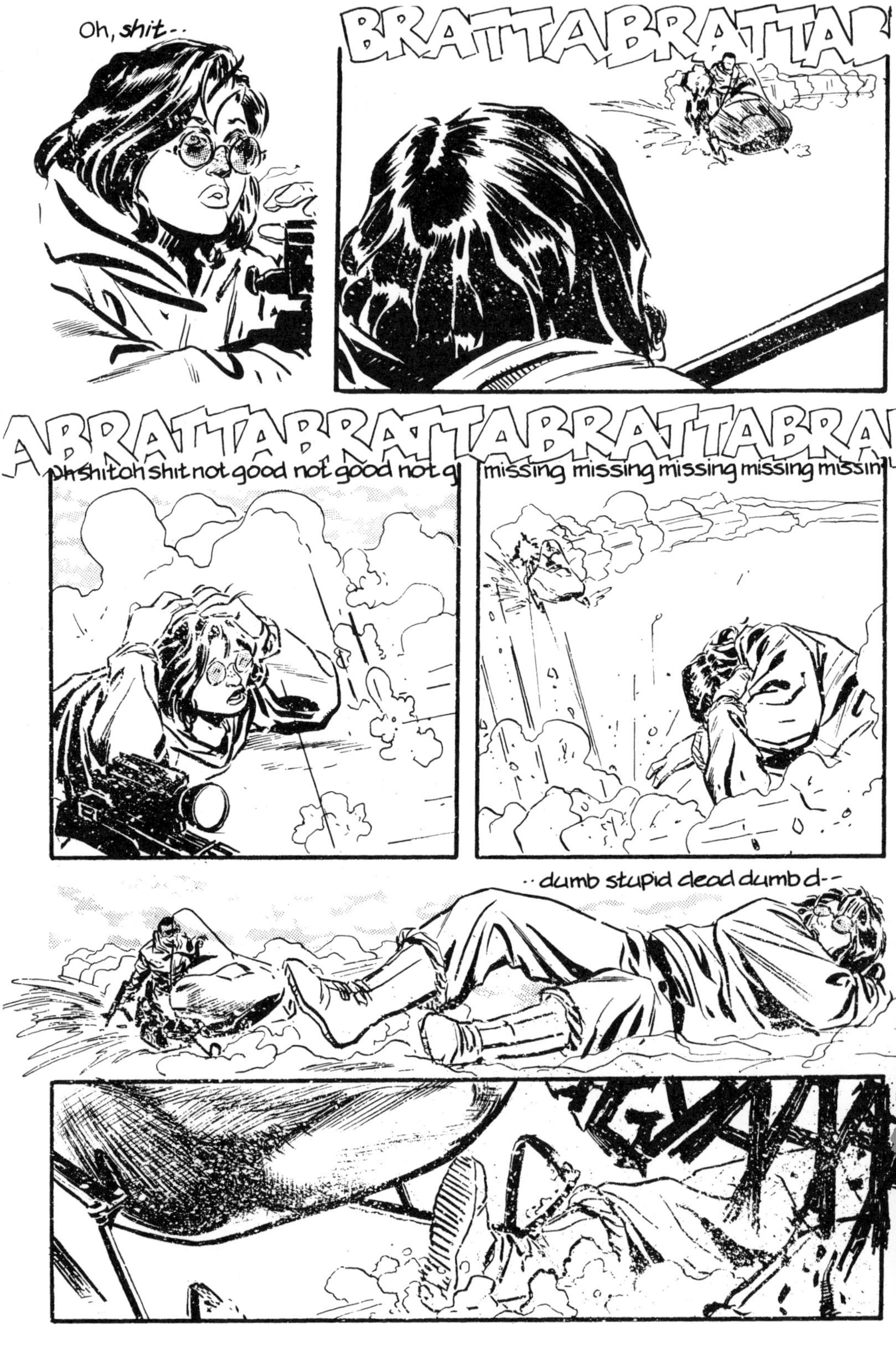
Oh, shit..
BRATTABRATTAB
ABRATTABRATTABRATTABRA
oh shit oh shit not good not good not g
missing missing missing missing missin
..dumb stupid dead dumb d--

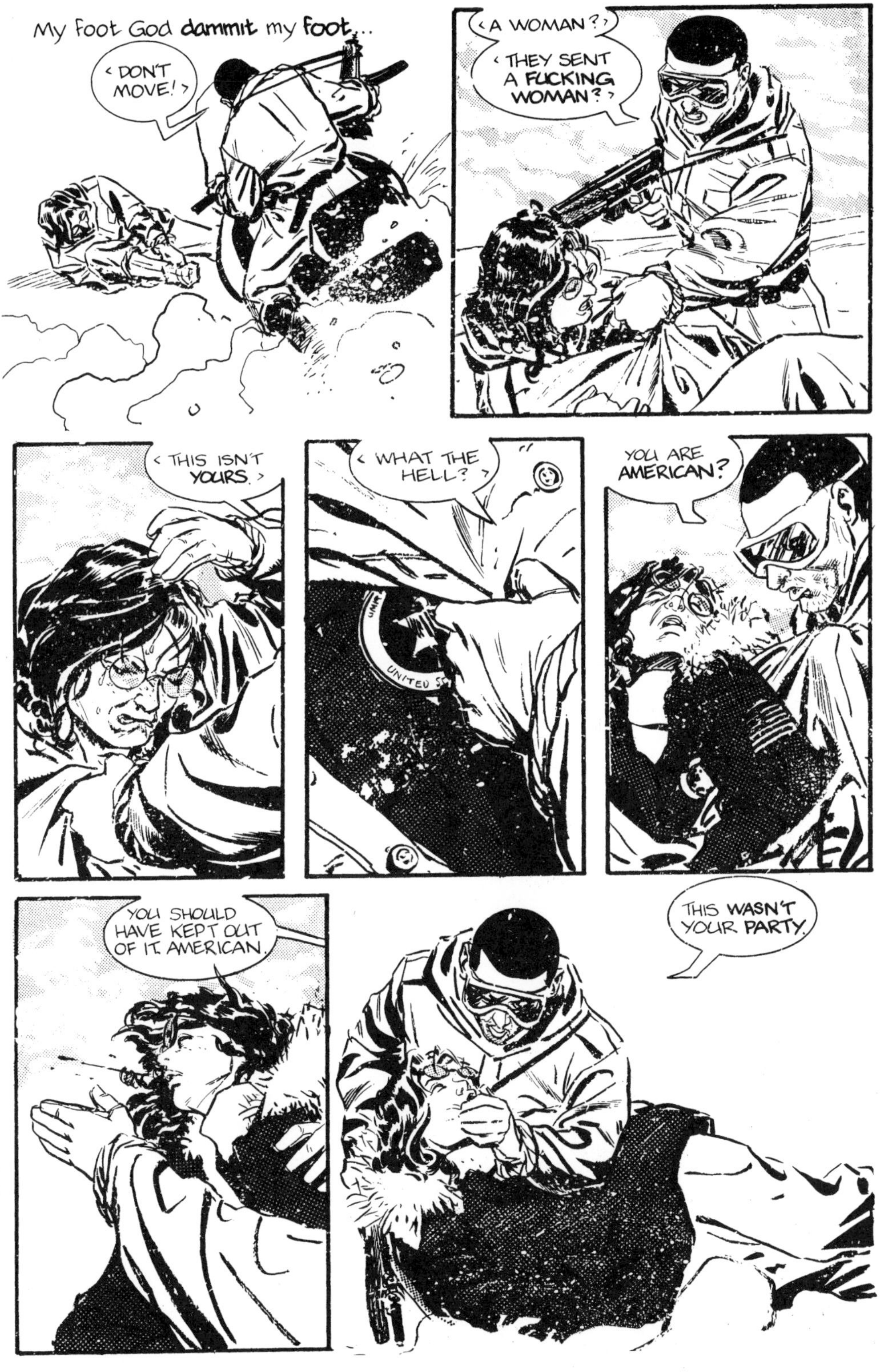
My foot God dammit my foot...
‹ DON'T MOVE! ›
‹ A WOMAN? ›
‹ THEY SENT A FUCKING WOMAN? ›
‹ THIS ISN'T YOURS. ›
‹ WHAT THE HELL? ›
YOU ARE AMERICAN?
YOU SHOULD HAVE KEPT OUT OF IT, AMERICAN.
THIS WASN'T YOUR PARTY.

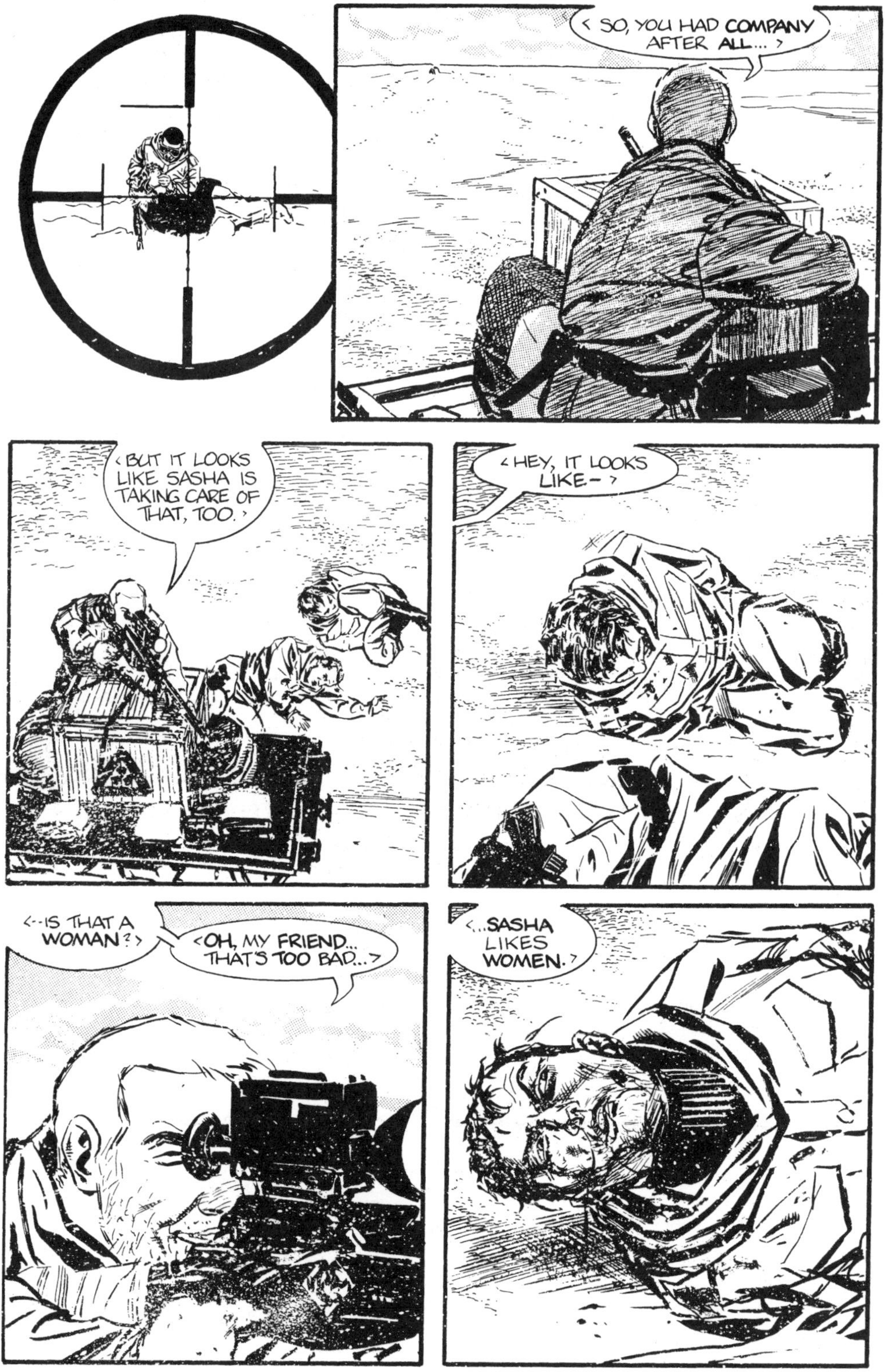
< SO, YOU HAD COMPANY AFTER ALL... >
< BUT IT LOOKS LIKE SASHA IS TAKING CARE OF THAT, TOO. >
< HEY, IT LOOKS LIKE-- >
< --IS THAT A WOMAN? >
< OH, MY FRIEND... THAT'S TOO BAD... >
< ...SASHA LIKES WOMEN. >

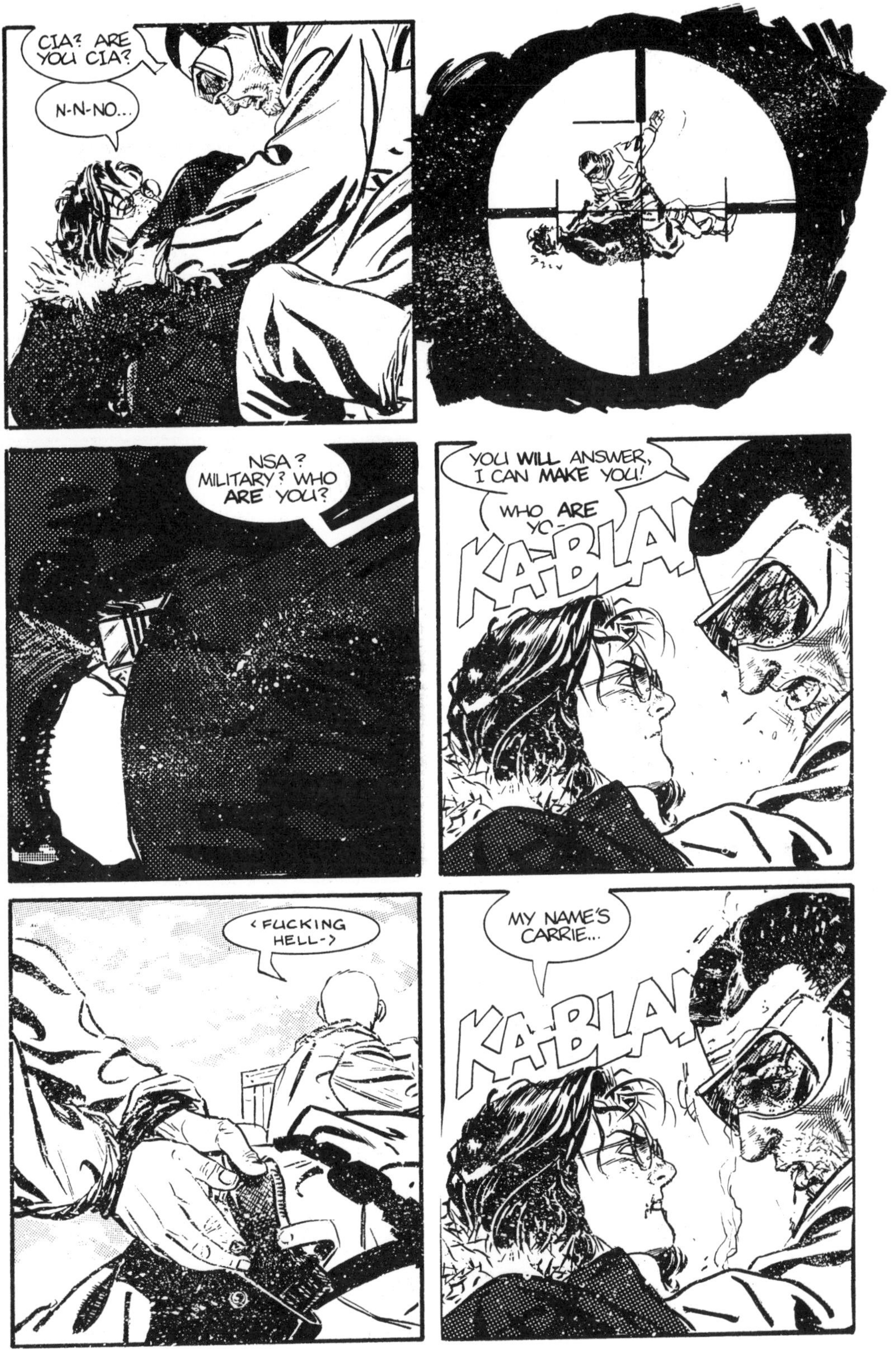
CIA? ARE YOU CIA?
N-N-NO...
NSA? MILITARY? WHO ARE YOU?
YOU WILL ANSWER, I CAN MAKE YOU!
WHO ARE YO-
KA-BLAM
‹FUCKING HELL-›
MY NAME'S CARRIE...
KA-BLAM

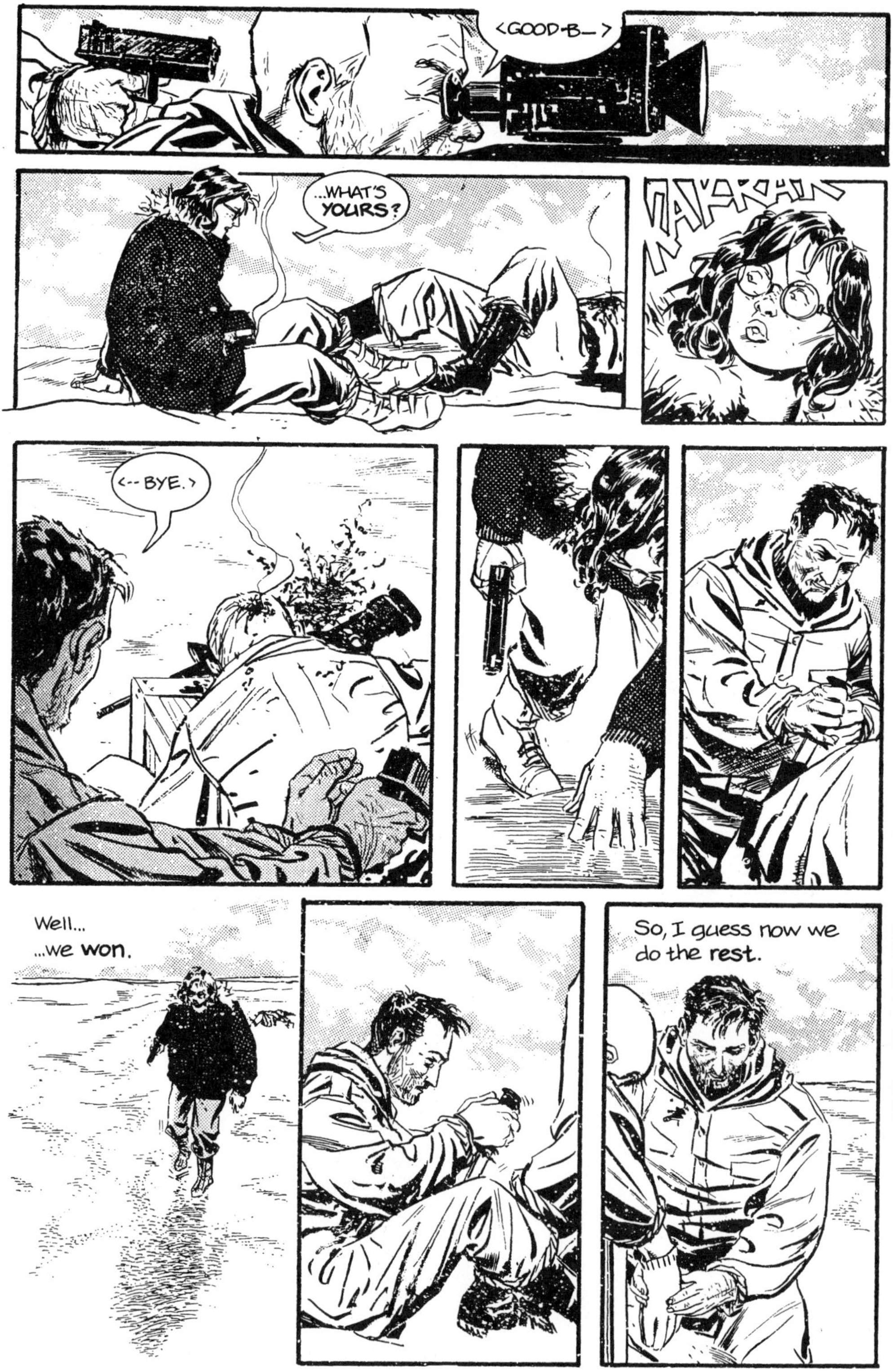
<GOOD-B_>
...WHAT'S YOURS?
<--BYE.>
Well...
...we won.
So, I guess now we do the rest.

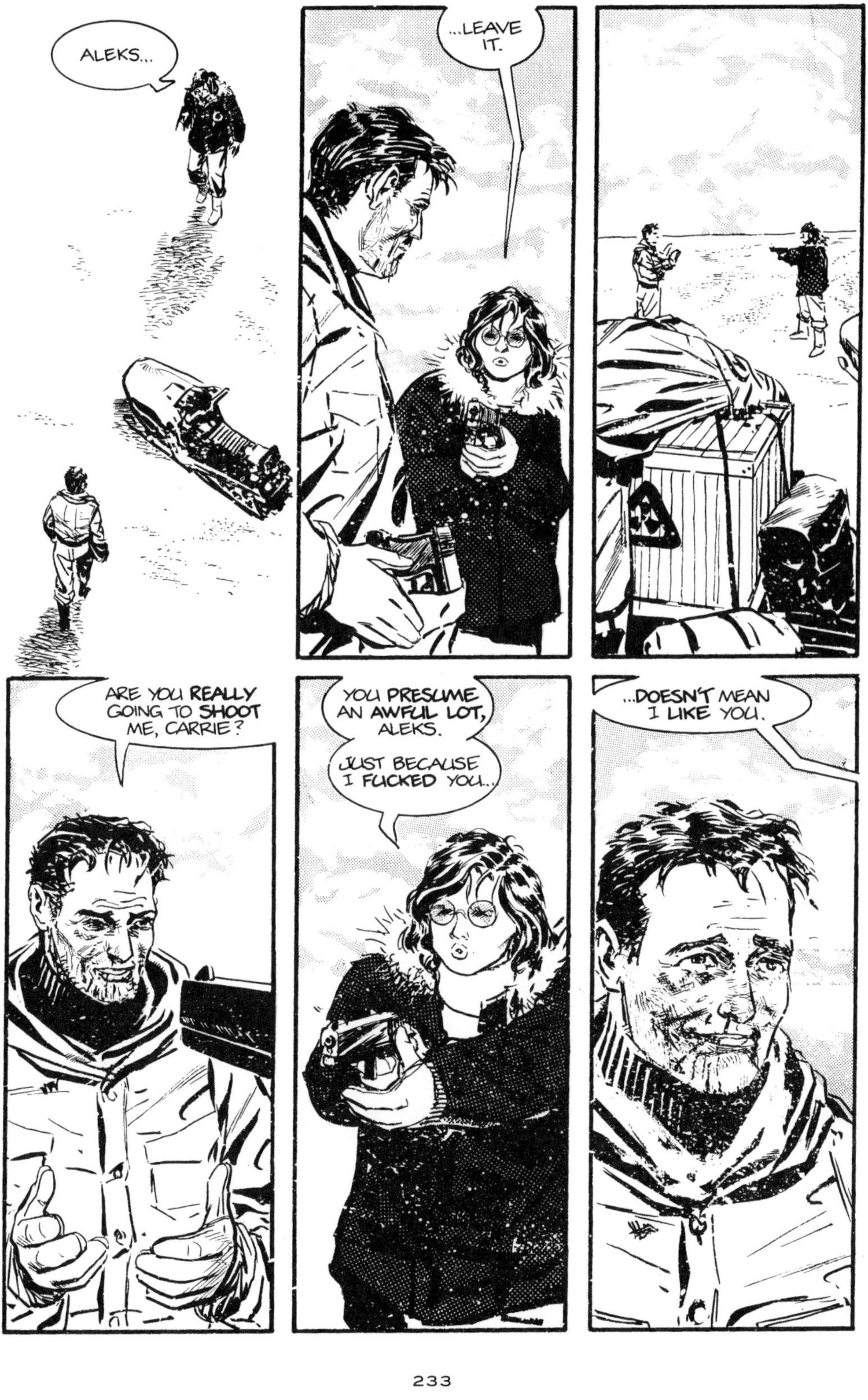
ALEKS...
...LEAVE IT.
ARE YOU **REALLY** GOING TO **SHOOT** ME, CARRIE?
YOU **PRESUME** AN **AWFUL LOT**, ALEKS.
JUST BECAUSE I **FUCKED** YOU...
...**DOESN'T** MEAN I **LIKE** YOU.

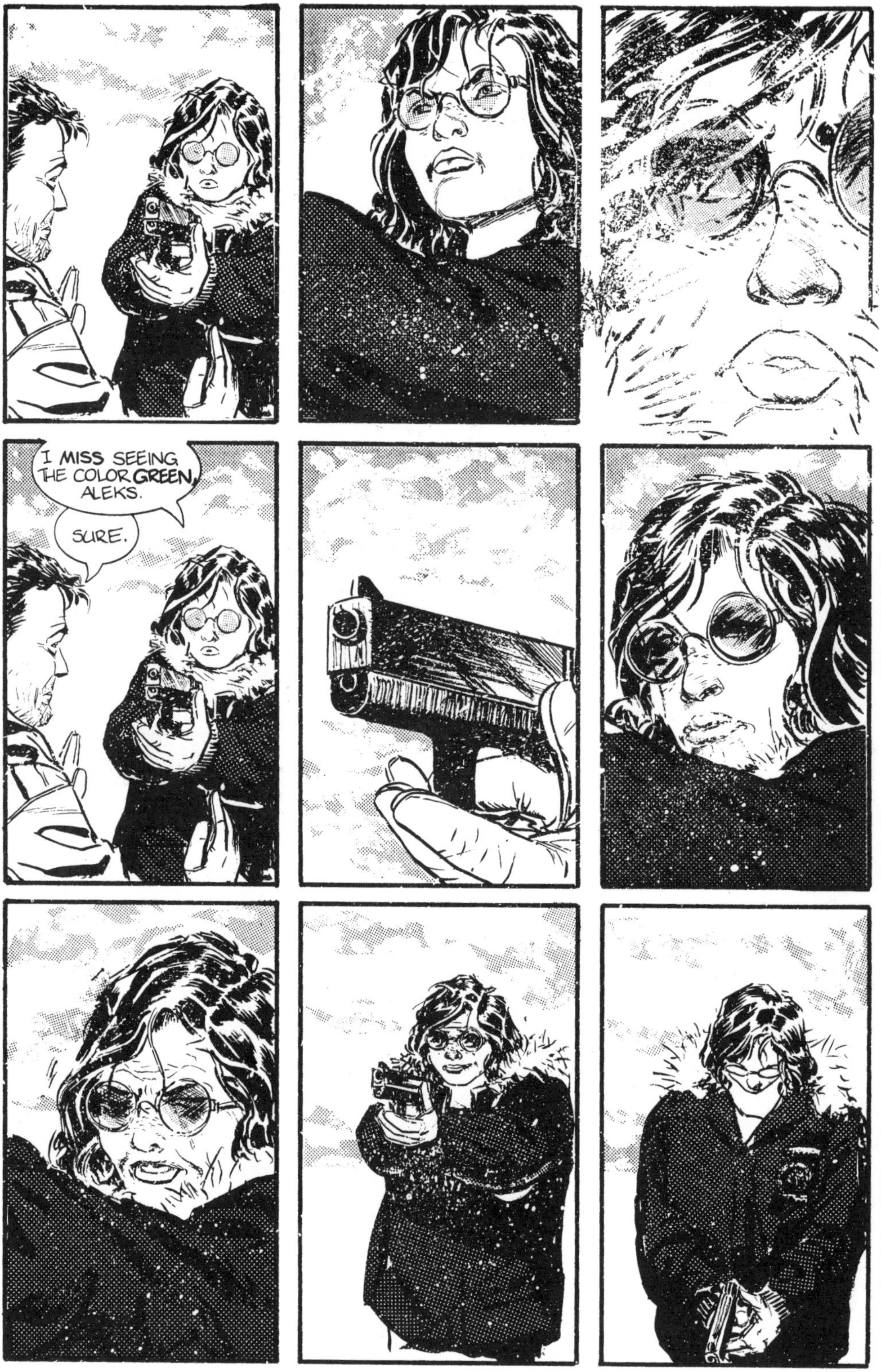
I MISS SEEING THE COLOR GREEN, ALEKS.
SURE.

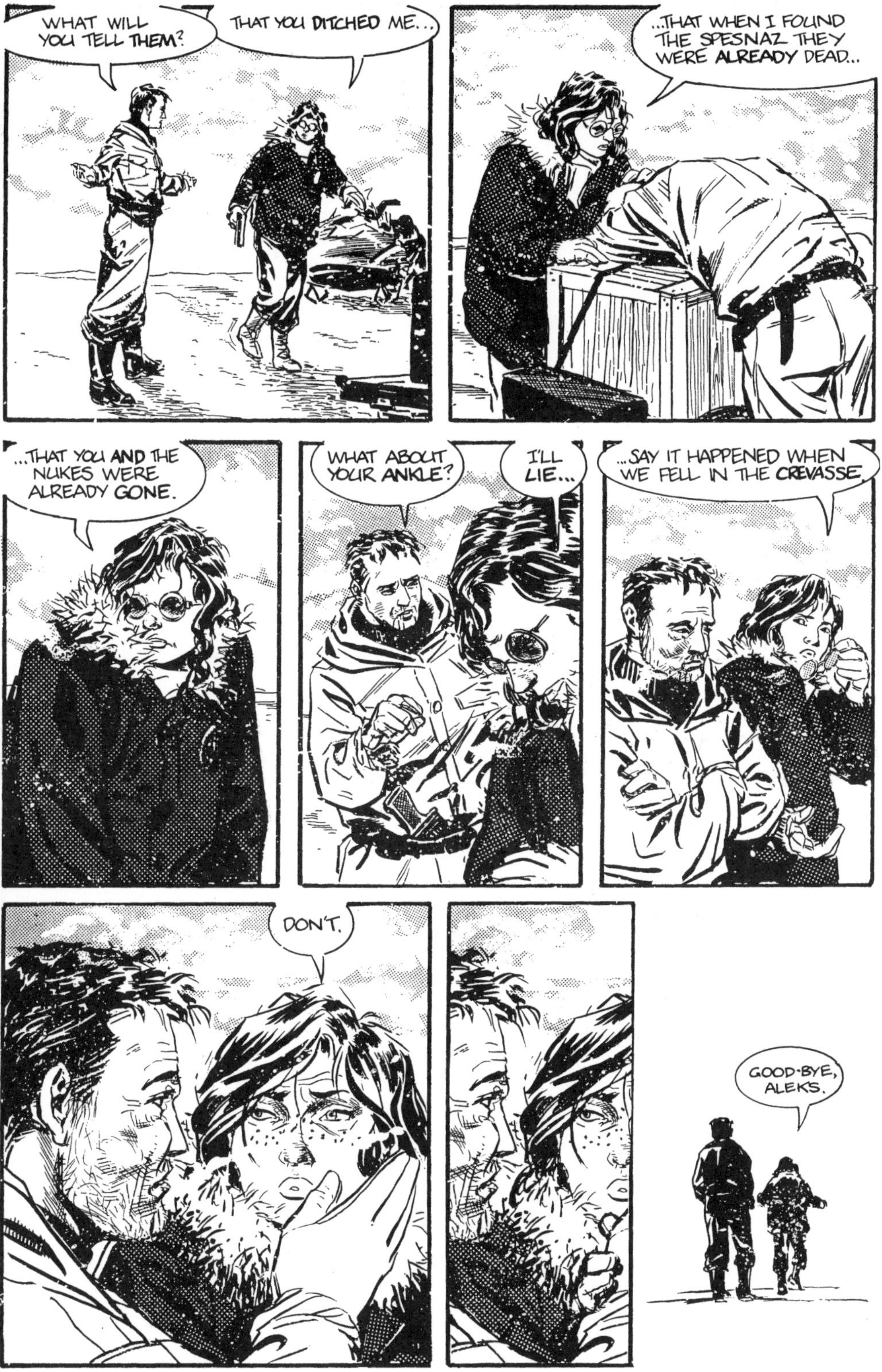
WHAT WILL YOU TELL THEM?
THAT YOU DITCHED ME...
...THAT WHEN I FOUND THE SPESNAZ THEY WERE ALREADY DEAD...
...THAT YOU AND THE NUKES WERE ALREADY GONE.
WHAT ABOUT YOUR ANKLE?
I'LL LIE...
...SAY IT HAPPENED WHEN WE FELL IN THE CREVASSE.
DON'T.
GOOD-BYE, ALEKS.

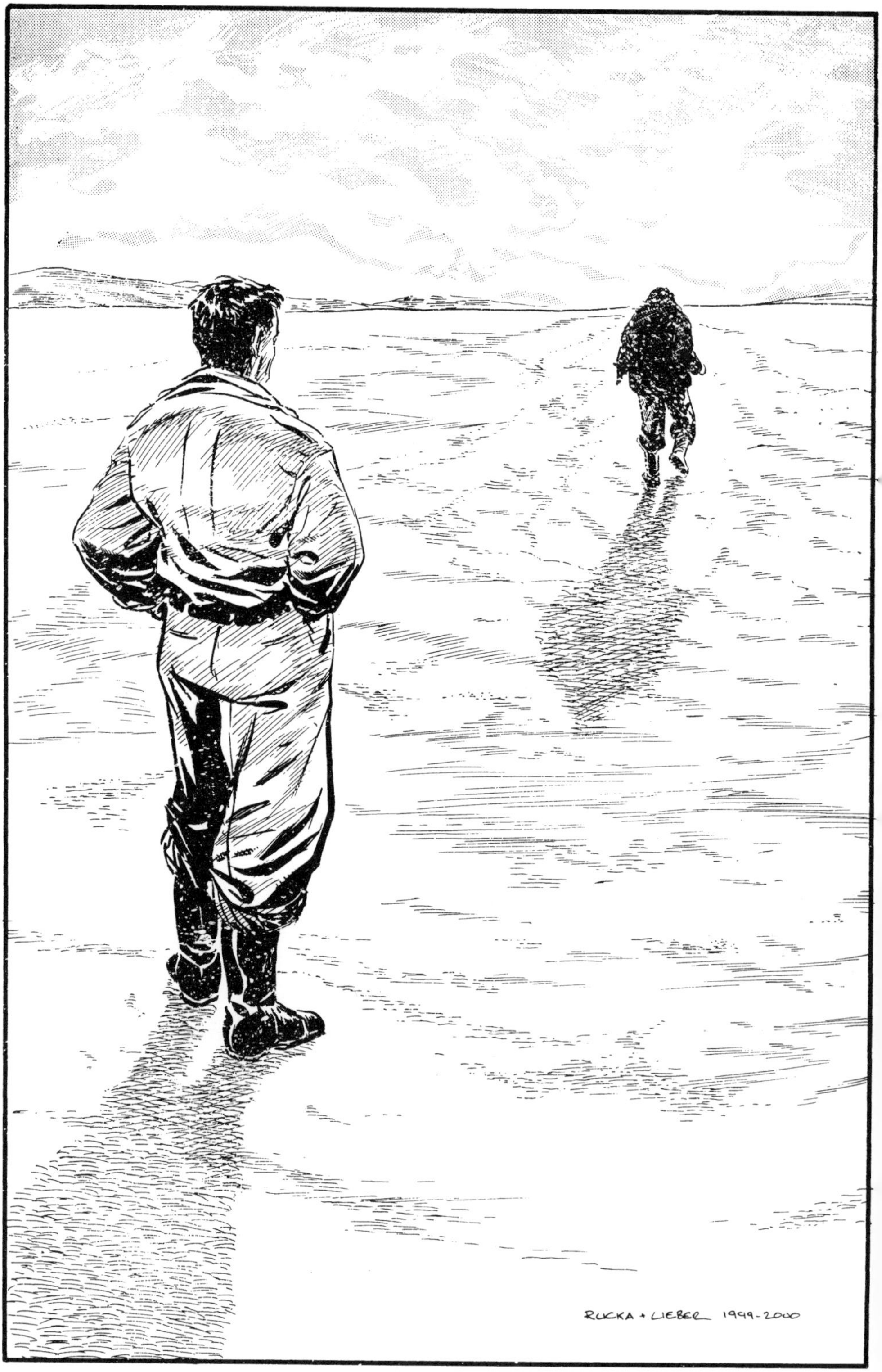
RUCKA + LIEBER 1999-2000

AFTERWORD

It's the sign that does it.

It's an emergency evacuation sign, an "in case of fire" sign, with a map of escape routes and with all the nearest exits clearly marked, neatly lettered, crisp, clean. It is exactly what you would expect it to be.

Except it's on the wall of Amundsen-Scott base at the South Pole.

Except it's not, because it's on the wall of the set of Amundsen-Scott on a sound stage in Montreal.

I arrived on set a couple days before Steve, if memory serves. Memory doesn't serve me well here, frankly. This was a lifetime ago, it seems, a decade at least. But I remember that I'd arrived ahead of Steve, and that when Steve came to the set I just had to show him this detail, this piece of set dressing on the wall in this sound stage where they— "they" being the people who were making this movie—were trying to take the comic we'd created a decade prior and turn it into a feature film. This detail, this thing on the wall, so small, something that nobody would see in the movie, that they'd likely never notice, but I had to show it to Steve.

We wandered the sets for a while that day. Visited the fake Vostok and the storeroom where Carrie would seek shelter after her line had been cut. Admired the icicles that looked like icicles and were, instead, some manner of rubber or plastic or gelatin or I don't-even-know-what. We talked to the actors and the crew, and we took photographs, and I'm pretty certain each of us had these stupid, dopey grins on our faces, as much amused and bemused by what was going on around us as anything else.

The fact that—and we can be honest here, we're amongst friends—the movie wasn't very good doesn't diminish the memories for me. The movie is what it is, and what you've just finished reading (or rereading, perhaps) is the comic, and they exist as separate things, and that's as it should be. Twenty years later, this comic is still a living, thriving work, one that Steve and I both cherish, one that we both remain very proud of, and—speaking for myself alone, now—a little baffled by, to be honest.

Twenty years is a long time. Twenty years is a *remarkably* long time, to tell the truth. Twenty years is long enough for the world to fundamentally change, for us to go from desktops to laptops to computers in our pockets that we call "phones." It's long enough to go from having no children to having two of them, and to see one of them entering his last year of high school as the other one is set to begin it. It's long enough to have a career. It's long enough to have several.

Whiteout began with me marveling at two facts. The first was, simply, that there was no actual law enforcement in Antarctica—the continent didn't have a cop; but what they did have was—at least at that time—the station manager at McMurdo deputized as a US Marshal. The second was that, again back in 1998, the ratio of men to women on The Ice was 200:1, and during winterover it became 400:1.

And being a writer, I looked at those two facts and decided that with a little nudging of the truth, there was a hell of a story one could tell.

I look back over these pages and I suffer the Writer's Curse of *seeing every single thing I did wrong*. Every mistake. I see the clumsiness of a writer trying to transition from novels to comics, I see how young I was, I see the overwriting and the telegraphing and the ham-fistedness and all the things I know now but didn't know then. I see how I've grown in my craft, with experience, with my art. I would be wildly surprised if Steve didn't say the same. All the things we did wrong, all the things we just *didn't know*, and still, people return to these stories, people ask for sketches of Carrie and ask if I'll write another one, people still read *Whiteout*.

This is the work that launched my career in comics. Without this there is no *Queen & Country* or *Stumptown*. There is no *Gotham Central* or *Wonder Woman* or *Batwoman*. There is no *Lazarus* or *The Old Guard* or *Black Magick*. Without this work, and the fearless collaboration of Steve Lieber, I am not here writing this, now.

All of that is obvious enough, I suppose. But how many of us can say, with certainty, that they can pinpoint the moment, the decision, the single meeting, that dictated so much of their life? Certainly I'd have continued writing if *Whiteout* hadn't happened. I was three novels in and setting up for the fourth when I started writing *Whiteout*. The odds are good that my career, in that respect at least, would've continued on its established trajectory.

But I most certainly wouldn't have the life I have now. And I am very, very lucky in that it is, all things being equal, a pretty damn good life.

So, the moment. *That* moment. As with all things, it's never just *one* instance. I could pick Patty Jeres introducing me to Bob Schreck at San Diego Comic Con back in 1997. I could pick the meeting with Bob that followed, where I showed him my novels and he looked at me with near-panic in his eyes, praying that I wasn't about to ask to adapt them. I could pick the party I was invited to that night, where I got to meet Joe Nozemack.

But if I'm honest, it was the moment I met Steve.

The story of how Steve and I first met, and how he came aboard *Whiteout*, has been told many times in many places, and I won't tell it again here. What I *will* share is that he and I have been through a lot in these past two decades, and not all of it was pleasant. There was a time when we were actively avoiding one another. There was a time when the thought of speaking together, let alone working together, was—if not difficult—shall we say, unlikely. I am grateful, and I am happy, to say that such a time has since passed. Twenty years is a long time. It's time enough to reveal things which, in their moment seemed so big, and that with perspective and age are uncovered to be small to the point of inconsequential, that were never worth the blood and sweat they exacted.

In twenty years, Steve and I have suffered losses and seen triumphs. We have grown, professionally and personally. We have striven, each of us and each in our own ways, to grow better at what we do, to learn and continue to hone ourselves as artists. We have pushed ourselves, professionally and personally. We have changed.

Through all of that, we have orbited *Whiteout,* not so much bound by its gravity as impelled by it. It's been our Jovian accelerator, and we have sling-shotted from its mass at incredible speed and reached undiscovered, even uncharted, territories—we have reaped successes, both together and apart, that we never dared imagine.

No matter where we've gone—and forgive me, because this is beating the analogy bloody at this point—we've been able to look back and see *Whiteout,* this fixed point, the place where we each, in our own way, began.

That is a hell of a thing. That is a remarkable and precious thing.

To everyone who joined us in this journey, who helped us get here, thank you. To everyone at Oni Press—and in particular to James Lucas Jones especially—unending and everlasting gratitude.

And to everyone who has shivered alongside Carrie, my sincerest wishes that you always find a place warm and dry, safe and sound.

GREG RUCKA / AUGUST 2017
PORTLAND, OR